Critical Approaches to American Working-Class Literature

Routledge Studies in Twentieth-Century Literature

1. Testimony from the Nazi Camps
French Women's Voices
Margaret-Anne Hutton

2. Modern Confessional Writing
New Critical Essays
Edited by Jo Gill

3. Cold War Literature
Writing the Global Conflict
Andrew Hammond

4. Modernism and the Crisis of Sovereignty
Andrew John Miller

5. Cartographic Strategies of Postmodernity
The Figure of the Map in Contemporary Theory and Fiction
Peta Mitchell

6. Food, Poetry, and the Aesthetics of Consumption
Eating the Avant-Garde
Michel Delville

7. Latin American Writers and the Rise of Hollywood Cinema
Jason Borge

8. Gay Male Fiction Since Stonewall
Ideology, Conflict, and Aesthetics
Les Brookes

9. Anglophone Jewish Literature
Axel Stähler

10. Before Auschwitz
Irène Némirovsky and the Cultural Landscape of Inter-war France
Angela Kershaw

11. Travel and Drugs in Twentieth-Century Literature
Lindsey Michael Banco

12. Diary Poetics
Form and Style in Writers' Diaries, 1915-1962
Anna Jackson

13. Gender, Ireland and Cultural Change
Race, Sex and Nation
Gerardine Meaney

14. Jewishness and Masculinity from the Modern to the Postmodern
Neil R. Davison

15. Travel and Modernist Literature
Sacred and Ethical Journeys
Alexandra Peat

16. Primo Levi's Narratives of Embodiment
Containing the Human
Charlotte Ross

17. Italo Calvino's Architecture of Lightness
The Utopian Imagination in an Age of Urban Crisis
Letizia Modena

18. Aesthetic Pleasure in Twentieth-Century Women's Food Writing
The Innovative Appetites of
M.F.K. Fisher, Alice B. Toklas,
and Elizabeth David
By Alice Lee McLean

19. Making Space in the Works of James Joyce
Edited by Valérie Bénéjam
and John Bishop

20. Critical Approaches to American Working-Class Literature
Edited by Michelle M. Tokarczyk

Critical Approaches to American Working-Class Literature

Edited by
Michelle M. Tokarczyk

Routledge
Taylor & Francis Group
NEW YORK AND LONDON

First published 2011
by Routledge
711 Third Avenue, New York, NY 10017

Simultaneously published in the UK
by Routledge
2 Park Square, Milton Park, Abingdon, Oxfordshire OX14 4RN

First issued in paperback 2014

Routledge is an imprint of the Taylor & Francis Group, an informa business

© 2011 Taylor & Francis

The right of the Michelle M. Tokarczyk to be identified as the author of the editorial material, and of the authors for their individual chapters, has been asserted in accordance with sections 77 and 78 of the Copyright, Designs and Patents Act 1988.

Typeset in Sabon by IBT Global.

All rights reserved. No part of this book may be reprinted or reproduced or utilised in any form or by any electronic, mechanical, or other means, now known or hereafter invented, including photocopying and recording, or in any information storage or retrieval system, without permission in writing from the publishers.

Trademark Notice: Product or corporate names may be trademarks or registered trademarks, and are used only for identification and explanation without intent to infringe.

Library of Congress Cataloging-in-Publication Data

Critical approaches to American working-class literature / edited by Michelle M. Tokarczyk.
  p. cm. — (Routledge studies in twentieth-century literature ; 20)
  Includes bibliographical references and index.
  1. Working class writings, American—History and criticism. 2. American literature—20th century—History and criticism. 3. Working class in literature. 4. Social classes in literature. 5. Working class—United States—Intellectual life. I. Tokarczyk, Michelle M., 1953–
  PS228.L33C65 2011
  810.9'920624—dc22
                          2010052682

ISBN 13: 978-0-415-88546-1 (hbk)
ISBN 13: 978-1-138-84970-9 (pbk)

For my husband, Paul J. Groncki

Contents

List of Figures	xi
Publication Acknowledgments	xiii
Acknowledgments	xv
Introduction MICHELLE M. TOKARCZYK	1

PART I
The Realities of Working-Class Life — 15

1 "between the outhouse and the garbage dump":
   Locating Collapse in Depression Literature — 17
   PAULA RABINOWITZ

2 Work is a War, or All Their Lives They Dug Their Graves — 35
   RENNY CHRISTOPHER

3 Respectability, Refinement, and the Underclass:
   Uncle Tom's Cabin and *Incidents in the Life of a Slave Girl* — 52
   SYLVIA J. COOK

PART II
Pedagogy and Promises — 69

4 Bridges, Not Ladders: Working-Class Women Poets on
   Education, Class Consciousness, and the Promise of
   Upward Mobility — 71
   KAREN KOVACIK

5 Charlotte Simmons as Working-Class Heroine in Tom Wolfe's
   I Am Charlotte Simmons — 87
   DAVID McCRACKEN

6   (Un)teaching the Anthology: Pedagogy versus Canon in
    Working-Class Literature   103
    NICHOLAS COLES

PART III
The Experience of Poverty   123

7   Agency, Not Alligators: Poor Women and Outside Assistance
    in Three Short Stories   125
    MICHELLE M. TOKARCZYK

8   Homeless in Seattle: Class Violence in Sherman Alexie's
    Indian Killer   141
    MICHELE FAZIO

9   Cultural Geography and Local Economies: The Lesson from
    Egypt, Maine   159
    PHOEBE S. JACKSON

PART IV
Reconsidering Class, Gender, and Nation   175

10 A Body of Work: Imperial Labor and the Writing of American
    Manhood in London's *The Sea-Wolf*   177
    MATTHEW BROPHY

11 "The Man in the Family": Staging Gender in *Waiting for Lefty*
    and American Social Protest Theatre   204
    MARIA F. BRANDT

12 Henry Roth's Reimagination of Class Consciousness
    from *Call it Sleep* to the *Mercy of a Rude Stream* Novels:
    Class Consciousness, Nationalist Politics, and Working-Class
    Studies in the Age of Cosmopolitanism   219
    TIM LIBRETTI

Notes on Contributors   237
Index   241

Figures

1.1	Dorothea Lange, "Slums of San Francisco, California."	18
1.2	Arthur Rothstein, "Squatters' shacks along the Willamette River in Portland, Oregon."	20

Publication Acknowledgments

PAULA RABINOWITZ

Chapter 1, A longer version of "'Between the Outhouse and the Garbage Dump': Locating Collapse in Depression Literature" originally appeared in *American Literary History* 23.1 (Spring 2011).
Figure 1.1 "Slums of San Francisco, California." June 1935. Library of Congress, Prints and Photographs Division, FSA/OWI Collection, LC-USF 34-002331-C.
Figure 1.2 "Squatters' shacks along the Willamette River in Portland, Oregon. Many of the men living here during the winter work in the nearby orchards of the Williamette and Yakima Valley in the summer." July 1936. Library of Congress, Prints and Photographs Division, FSA-OWI Collection, LC USF 34-004831-E.

RENNY CHRISTOPHER

Excerpt from "Digger Gets a Checkup" from *Digger's Blues*. Copyright © 2002 by Jim Daniels. Reprinted by permission of Adastra Press.
Excerpt from "Our Fathers" from *Blind Horse*. Copyright © 1999 by Jean Bryner. Reprinted by permission of Bottom Dog Press.
Excerpts from "Furnace Greens" and "Number 6 and 7 Furnaces" from *Last Heat*. Copyright © 1999 by Peter Blair. Reprinted by permission of the author.
Excerpt from "Now It Is Broccoli" from *October Light*. Copyright © 1987 by Jeff Tagami. Reprinted by permission of Kearney Street Workshop.
Excerpt from "Disabled List" from *Working Hard for the Money*. Copyright © 2002 by Will Watson. Reprinted by permission of Bottom Dog Press.

KAREN KOVACIK

Excerpt from "Red Wagons" from *My Father Was a Toltec*. Copyright © 1995 by Ana Castillo. Reprinted by permission of Anne Edelstein Agency.
Patricia Dobler, *Talking to Strangers*. Copyright © 1986 by the Board of Regents of the University of Wisconsin System. Reprinted by permission of the University of Wisconsin Press.
Dorianne Laux, "What My Father Told Me" from *Awake*. Copyright © 1990 by Dorianne Laux. Reprinted by permission of BOA Editions.

Excerpt from "An Academic Fantasy" from *The House I'm Running From.* Copyright © 1989 by Michelle M. Tokarczyk. Reprinted by permission of West End Press.

Excerpt from "Acknowledgments" from *Calling Home: An Anthology of Working-Class Women's Writing.* Copyright © 1990 by Michelle M. Tokarczyk. Reprinted by permission of the author.

Patricia Smith, "Building Nicole's Mama" from *Teahouse of the Almighty.* Copyright © 2006 by Patricia Smith. Reprinted with the permission of the Coffee House Press.

DAVID McCRACKEN

Excerpts from *I Am Charlotte Simmons* by Tom Wolfe. Copyright © 2004 by Tom Wolfe. Reprinted by permission of Farrar, Straus and Giroux.

PHOEBE S. JACKSON

Excerpts from *The Beans of Egypt*, Maine by Carolyn Chute. Copyright © 1985 by Carolyn Chute. Reprinted by permission of Houghton Mifflin.

Acknowledgments

An edited anthology is a community endeavor, and there are many people who helped to bring this text to fruition. First, I thank Goucher College for a sabbatical during the spring of 2009. I am also grateful to those who offered advice and encouragement along the way, especially Sherry Lee Linkon and Janet Zandy. For constructive feedback on the introduction to this text, I thank Michele Fazio and Christie Launius. I am grateful to the two anonymous reviewers who made constructive comments on the proposal. I received invaluable assistance in formatting the manuscript from Donna Lummis and Fran White at Goucher's Center for Teaching and Learning Technology. Reference librarian Randy Smith helped me track down sources, saving me much time and frustration. Finally, I thank my spouse, Paul Groncki, for his unfailing love and support throughout the years.

Introduction
Michelle M. Tokarczyk

My purpose in compiling this anthology can be compared to Nicholas Coles and Janet Zandy's purpose in compiling an anthology of working-class American literature, which is described by Coles as "gather[ing] into one material space a range of writings many of which were scattered, ephemeral or obscure" (105). An MLA search of the words "working-class [and] American [and] literature" will yield about four hundred entries. Yet the search engine's criteria for "most relevant" is undefined, its ideology obscure, and its arrangement of articles random. As a scholar of working-class literature and culture, I've benefitted enormously from anthologies in the field that have been compiled by scholars with a clear focus and training in working-class studies, works such as such as Janet Zandy's *Calling Home: An Anthology of Working-Class Women's Writing* or John Russo and Sherry Lee Linkon's *New Working-Class Studies*, an interdisciplinary collection of articles.[1] However, I can't go to an anthology and find the current work of literary scholars in the field. Nor can I turn to a journal in the field, as multiethnic scholars can look to *MELUS*.[2] So the impetus behind this collection was to bring together articles on American working-class literature, especially articles that represent a variety of approaches to the field so that scholars—professors, graduate students, and undergraduates—would have a hard copy resource they could locate in their libraries or on their bookshelves.

Although there is a scarcity of anthologized criticism in working-class studies, there is exciting work being done in the field; more graduate students are writing dissertations in working-class literature. The canon of working-class writing is being defined even as it is continually being revised. We are at a point in the field where we can ask not so much what working-class literature is but how it works, how it affects the reader and reflects its community. We are also at a point where we can reflect on the critic's role and consider what approaches in the rich field of literary criticism are most applicable for understanding particular working-class texts. To begin addressing such issues, in this introduction, I will first trace the arc of working-class studies in general and the study of working-class literature in particular. As is the case with many forms of contemporary criticism (postcolonialism, feminism, eco-criticism) the literary criticism and movement of which it is part, in this case working-class studies, are intertwined and regularly inform one another. Moreover, it would be extremely difficult to understand the development of working-class studies without understanding the study of working-class literature because, as I will later discuss, the pioneers in working-class studies were scholars of literature and American studies. Hence, some of my discussion will refer to scholarship in working-class studies.

THE DEVELOPMENT OF WORKING-CLASS STUDIES

The ground for working-class studies was paved in the 1970s with a reconsideration of the (white, male, middle-class) American literary canon. Numerous scholars have been involved in this endeavor; Paul Lauter's compilation of *The Heath Anthology of American Literature*, which added previously excluded voices and forms of literature, opened the door to considerations of what literature is and who writes it. His 1980 article in *Radical Teacher*, "Working-Class Women's Literature: An Introduction to Study," was a pioneer work on class, gender, and literature. Lillian S. Robinson's *Sex, Class and Culture* (1979), although not focused on American literature, helped to ignite class considerations. In the following decade, more literary scholars began investigating class, and by the 1990s their efforts yielded publications. Janet Zandy, the foremost literary scholar in the field of working-class literature, edited *Calling Home: An Anthology of Working-Class Women's Writings* (1990); I and Elizabeth A. Fay coedited *Working-Class Women in the Academy: Laborers in the Knowledge Factory* (1993), a collection of articles and essays by women from the working-class who had become academics. Literary scholars drew upon Marxist critics such as Raymond Williams and Terry Eagleton as well as working-class writers such as Tillie Olsen, Sue Doro, and Jim Daniels. Critics turned back to the proletarian literature that had been discredited in the era when the new criticism dominated. Texts such as Paula Rabinowitz's *Labor and Desire* (1991), Barbara Foley's *Radical Representations* (1993), Constance Coiner's *Better Red: The Writing and Resistance of Tillie Olsen and Meridel Le Sueur* (1995), and Bill Mullen and Sherry Lee Linkon's edited collection *Radical Revisions: Rereading 1930s Culture* (1996) followed.[3] As was the case in feminist criticism, much of the early scholarship in working-class literature also consisted of recovering texts that had been forgotten or unrecognized by the dominant paradigm: Pietro di Donato's *Christ in Concrete* (1939), Meridel Le Sueur's *The Girl* (1929), Grace Lumpkin's *To Make My Bread* (1932), and Agnes Smedley's *Daughter of Earth* (1929).

Across the field of working-class studies, scholars were establishing programs of study and talking to one another. In 1995 John Russo and Sherry

Lee Linkon formed the Center for Working-Class Studies at Youngstown State University, and the first Working-Class Studies Conference was held in Youngstown that year, providing a venue for scholars across the disciplines, but with a focus on the cultural manifestations of working-class life, such as literature. Literature written by working-class people about their lives had been given a name, and scholars were developing ways to study this literature.

EXPANDING THE FIELD

Although critics of working-class literature applaud the rediscovery of proletarian literature, they have become aware of the pitfalls of a very heavy emphasis on this writing. This emphasis can have the dual impact of making working-class literature seem synonymous with literature of the 1930s and with white male literature because many of the recognized writers during this period were white and male. Working-class literature is far broader than the literature produced by politically minded whites writing during the 1930s. Hence, critics began to investigate literature of other periods and, as important, literature by various ethnic and racial groups. We first see such an examination in Janet Zandy's *Calling Home*, which included contemporary and multiethnic writing and later in the exhaustive anthology she and Nicholas Coles edited, *American Working-Class Literature*, which included not only literature from the 1600s to the present but also materials such as songs, petitions, and letters. In *Class Definitions* (2008) I examined the interconnected lives and writings of Maxine Hong Kingston, Sandra Cisneros, and Dorothy Allison as writers who are working-class and ethnic, as well as writers who represent different regions and sexual orientations. It is not only the fact that writers of different backgrounds are included, but the way they are included that is crucial for the study of working-class literature. Marxist scholars see class as a defining status that supersedes identities such as gender and race. Working-class scholars, in contrast, practice intersectional analysis. According to literary critic Karen Gaffney, such an analysis "resists the divisions that separate categories like race and gender and instead allow for analysis of how individuals are positioned in multiple categories simultaneously" (1).The roots of this approach are in *Black Feminist Thought*, in which Patricia Hill Collins comments upon the many resemblances she found in feminist and black ideologies and concluded that "[t]he similarity suggests that the material conditions of race, class, and gender oppression can vary dramatically yet generate some similarities in the epistemologies of subordinate groups" (207). To understand the experience of subordination and the strategies of coping and resistance, we should look at the contact point between the two groups rather than add one status to another. Working-class literary critics look at numerous contact points—sexual orientation, region, ethnicity—as well as class to see how the experience of class is inflected by other statuses. The intersectionality of identities and the refusal to use "working class" as code for "white" are firmly entrenched in the field, which necessitates our examining texts that are not commonly thought of as working class but may, for example, be classified as ethnic literature.

Early working-class studies also drew upon Marxist theory and was often influenced by feminist theory. Janet Zandy has repeatedly cited the work of Raymond Williams, particularly his *Marxism and Literature* (1977) and *Resources of Hope* (1989). Paul Lauter draws upon Williams's *Culture and Society* (1958). Elizabeth A. Fay and I drew upon Fredric Jameson's *The Political Unconscious* (1981) and Henry A. Giroux's *Theory and Resistance in Education* (1983). For those of us in the forefront of working-class studies, Marxist analysis provided the most obvious and useful set of analytic tools. Similarly, feminism provided a model of a literary criticism that could critique hegemony. Lillian S. Robinson's rereading of Virginia Woolf's "A Room of One's Own" in "Who's Afraid of Virginia Woolf?" is often credited with founding the field of Marxist feminism. Janet Zandy looked to Tillie Olsen's critical and creative work for a model of how a working-class woman might read and write. Janet Zandy's career as a working-class critic was launched with *Calling Home* and with her three-year editorship of *Women's Studies Quarterly*. As the study of working-class literature expanded and new scholars entered it, critics of working-class literature began to apply a variety of critical approaches to the study of working-class literature: ethnic studies, postcolonial studies, and media studies are among the approaches represented in this anthology. Class is no longer a topic of concern only for Marxists and Marxist feminists; rather, class issues are being mainstreamed into criticism. Working-class critics are asking new questions about the representation of class and its intersection with region, gender, race, and nation.

THE CRITIC'S TASK

The critic of American working-class literature writes out of a particular context that demands conscious choices. Working-class literature has been marginalized in American literary publications and in the academy itself. To even mention working-class status is seen as either an act of naïveté (there are no classes in the United States) or of subversion (class warfare among nonexistent classes). Given this environment, the working-class critic is charged with maintaining respect for working-class writers and writing—even if she/he is criticizing the writing's shortcomings.

In the introduction to *Calling Home*, Janet Zandy stated that a theory and criticism of working-class literature, which had yet to be developed, should not alienate workers from the texts about their lives and should not privilege the critics over the writers (10). In her later work, *Hands*

(2004), she delineates the characteristics of working-class texts. Notably, these texts represent the lived experiences of working-class people so that working-class people can recognize themselves in these literary works. Zandy's discussion focuses on writing primarily by working-class people writing for a working-class audience. The working-class critic has the task of illuminating the writing for an academic audience of mixed class backgrounds. Working-class writer Sandra Cisneros described bicultural writers as "amphibians" and bridges to communities (U of Minn); they are able to live in two cultures and enable the cultures to understand one another. The working-class critic is in a similar situation. Through upbringing and/or study, the working-class critic has become attuned to the stylistic and thematic features of working-class writing and can make these visible for students and scholars in the academic community. The critic can thus act as a bridge between working-class and academic sensibilities.

In order to do so, the working-class critic must apply a critical methodology that is appropriate for his/her task as well as ask the right questions about the texts. Audre Lorde in her landmark essay "The Master's Tools Will Never Dismantle the Master's House" warned feminists about the dangers of applying critical methodologies developed by dominant groups to the texts of women and people of color. Janet Zandy has voiced the need for a working-class criticism that does not buy into middle-class paradigms (*Hands* 84–87). Renny Christopher and Carolyn Whitson in "Toward a Theory of Working Class Literature" find notable differences between bourgeois and working-class literature, such as working-class literature's implicit demand for action from the reader. Yet there are a number of critical approaches that are amenable to seeing working-class literature as an artistic expression of working-class people's lives with its own aesthetics and themes.[4] Postcolonialism, feminism, cultural geography, and other contemporary critical schools attempt to honor the subjectivity of the writers they study and the specific circumstance out of which the literature they study was written.

Any academic text will necessarily be removed from the commonplace reader, be the reader middle, upper, or lower class. However, literary theory or criticism of working-class texts that is filled with jargon is, I argue, incompatible with representation of working-class lives. In my calls for papers and conversations with prospective authors, I stated that all critical approaches were welcome and added only one caveat: jargon should be kept at a minimum to keep the language accessible. Although many people outside the academy are unlikely to read critical articles, jargon-laden prose in articles about working-class literature creates an unhealthy incongruity and distance between the critic and the literature. Moreover, jargon alienates academics from the working class, especially those who are still struggling to establish themselves in the academy. When I had recently received my doctorate in the theory-laden 1980s, I realized I would have to be more conversant in literary theory in order to attain an academic position. I subscribed to journals such as *Critical Inquiry* and *New Literary History* and read them during my only available time: my hour-long commute from New York City to Rutgers, New Jersey. A couple of months into this process I attended a talk and heard a young literary critic rattle off theories and terminologies. I wondered how many train rides it would take me to absorb this content. Since that realization, I have worked to apply theory to literary criticism in a way that is accessible and enlightening, in a way that illuminates rather than obscures the literature.

Because working-class literature is grounded in the experiences of working-class people, it is appropriate to begin the anthology with articles that focus on the representations of working-class experiences. Representation is particularly important because many aspects of working-class lives—family, jobs, economic struggle—are either left out of mainstream commentary or caricatured. In comparing working-class writing to documentary photography, Zandy suggests the writer is like the photographer capturing "what is" with his/her artist's eye, capturing the subject from the right angle and composing it through his/her vision. Contemporary critics are conscious enough to understand that "what is" is the artist's vision which, in working-class writing, reflects not so much individual experiences as the experiences of a people. The critic takes another lens—a particular critical approach coupled with his/her understanding of the unique characteristics of working-class literature—and emphasizes features or themes of literary works.

Paula Rabinowitz examines representations of both the Great Depression and the Great Recession by focusing on the actual spaces of economic collapse—the shuttered storefronts, vacant buildings, and empty lots. Her wide range of novels, poetry, videos, and photographs suggest how economic collapse alters not only the once-familiar places around one but also one's concept of space—a concept that has been interlocked with American notions of possibility. The discussion of Mazie in *Yonnondio* focuses on how the Great Depression made childhood poverty—which never disappeared from the American landscape—not a stage to be passed through but a condition to be endured.

That factory workers or miners are part of the working class has never been contested. However, there have perhaps been less-visible members of the proletariat, notably, slaves. Labor historians are divided as to whether American slaves should be categorized as working class because they did not work for wages or possess even the limited autonomy that wage workers did. Furthermore, animosity between whites and blacks undercut the possibility of working-class solidarity between slaves and white workers. Sylvia Cook argues that, in effect, literary forms can tease out the nuances of class and race relationships. In her critiques of Harriet Beecher Stowe's *Uncle Tom's Cabin* and Harriet Jacobs's *Incidents in the Life of a Slave Girl*, she finds that the authors apply "paradigms of class to a group of people conventionally characterized by race" (65). Stowe and Jacobs create characters who see poor whites, of whom they may disapprove, as degraded by the South's race and class hierarchies. The slaves depicted value gentility and respectability, which are favorable attributes of nineteenth-century citizens. A classed reading of these texts suggests the possibility that slaves might become part of an angry proletariat that recognized the source of its hardships.

Michele Fazio makes a similar argument for including class in the examination of Native American texts. She focuses on a particularly controversial work by the nation's preeminent Native American author, Sherman Alexie. *Indian Killer* was criticized as sensational and was even disavowed by the author himself. Fazio argues that the disturbing features of this novel might be contextualized and looks at the economic tensions in 1990s Seattle. Such tensions are represented in the novel by the juxtaposition of the relatively affluent white Smith family that adopted the Native American protagonist and the city's homeless. For the diverse population groups in this novel, the "Indian killer's" murders function as a Rorschach test for attitudes toward race, class, and capitalism.

As Elizabeth A. Fay and I noted in the introduction to *Working-Class Women in the Academy*, one of the characteristics of the working class is that their jobs are physically demanding or dangerous. And perhaps these jobs are more dangerous in the United States. Renny Christopher notes this country has a higher accident rate on jobs than many other industrial nations. This troubling fact may partially explain why so many working-class texts—*Christ in Concrete*, The Book of the Dead, and *China Men* among many others—depict death or injury on jobs. Christopher's discussion of several novels and poems depicting workplace accidents grapples with the artistic tensions working-class writers face: how does one effectively render the horrors of a workplace accident in an aesthetic manner that does not descend into sensationalism but that does capture the violence of these often-preventable accidents? Her article, one of the first to tackle this subject, examines several strategies.

In reading about the extreme struggle that some families faced during the Depression or of the subsistence living that characters in Carolyn Chute's *The Beans of Egypt, Maine* eke out, the question arises as to whether such people are part of the working class or part of a separate poverty class. This issue has been particularly thorny in working-class studies. In *The Working-Class Majority* (2000) Michael Zweig argues that the poor are part of the working class because poverty is something that happens to working-class people who either don't make very much money or because they can't find jobs (78). In contrast, scholars such as Vivyan C. Adair, who grew up in and spent much of her adult life in poverty, argues that treating poverty class women as a "synecdoche" to the working class denies the experiences of those who have lived in poverty ("Absences" 596). Moreover, poverty-class scholars argue that including the poor and working class together ignores the gender dynamics of poverty: many of those in poverty are women with children.

My article takes up Adair's criticism and makes a slight detour with the question of why many working-class people are resentful of those in poverty.

Through an examination of short stories written by working-class women from different ethnic backgrounds, I demonstrate that the protagonists who accept social services or charity have deeply ambivalent views toward this assistance. On the one hand they fear—and to some extent experience—a loss of agency; on the other hand, they decide accepting assistance is preferable to struggling without it and find ways to maintain their dignity. In emphasizing the protagonists' independence, self-reliance, and capacity for hard work, the stories also represent how much these women have in common with more comfortable members of the working class.

Working-class studies scholars have indeed stressed the need to examine class with race and other identities. As my discussion of Fazio's article suggests, they have also argued for the importance of place in the formation and expression of class identity. Don Mitchell in his article on the development and importance of working-class geographies argues, "Understanding the intersection of location, place, and mobility in relation to the logic of capital circulation allows us to understand how both social and political contradictions and social and political power are rooted in place and space" ("Working Class" 85). Phoebe S. Jackson examines the characters in Carolyn Chute's *The Beans of Egypt, Maine* through the lens of location, arguing that they suffer from the diminution of their rural spaces that are lost to exurban and often affluent settlements. This geographical shift turns working-class people who made their livings in lumber, fishing, and the like into impoverished people.

Given the increasingly precarious nature of working-class employment, the imperative for working-class youth to get a college education is ever stronger. Yet a plethora of personal essays collected in the anthologies *This Fine Place So Far From Home*, *Teaching Working Class*, *Working-Class Women in the Academy*, and *Liberating Memory* show that working-class students often feel alienated in higher education. David McCracken and Karen Kovacik turn to creative work to tease out the nature of such students' feelings of isolation.

Surprisingly, McCracken turns to a text by Tom Wolfe, *I Am Charlotte Simmons*, recognizing that Wolfe is not a proletarian writer and arguing for a more inclusive definition of the working-class novel that focuses on the nature of crises working-class protagonists face. McCracken's categorization of this novel may be disputed. However, he does demonstrate similarities between the fictional Charlotte Simmons and fictional working-class protagonists, such as Sara Smolinsky, as well as working-class essayists such as bell hooks. It is also necessary to continually reconsider given definitions of working-class literature against work that is actually being written, for working definitions must shift as literature does.

Karen Kovacik focuses on contemporary poets who entered college during what she calls the "narrow window of opportunity" in higher education that opened in the 1950s, when enrollment policies became friendlier to working-class students and the cost of higher education was less prohibitive than it is today, and began to close in the 1980s. Drawing upon material in sociology and education, Kovacik interrogates the marked ambivalence of several women poets who successfully completed higher education and often found good careers. What troubles these poets, she argues, is an understanding of the ways that institutions such as colleges and universities, which are essentially middle class, serve to reproduce class. Moreover, they fear that the "price of the ticket" for their education and admission to the middle class will be a renunciation of their families and backgrounds. Their poetry reflecting personal experiences and anxieties reflects those of a generation of working-class students; the poems are not individual lyrics, but collective reflections.

Although the shock of middle-class culture on campus, reflected in student discussions of family vacations, parents' financial support, and the like, can be unsettling for working-class students, the actual material being taught is crucial in communicating to students what their relationship is to their society. Earlier generations of scholars in feminist studies and African American studies questioned the literary canon as white and male. Working-class scholars likewise bemoan the lack of attention to working-class texts and celebrate the arrival of Janet Zandy and Nicholas Coles's exhaustive anthology *American Working-Class Literature*. Reflecting both on the process of making the anthology and of teaching it, Coles takes up the position of "amphibian" and asks how a teacher could make visible the labor of making an anthology and the labor of those represented in the various texts included in the collection.

His question is a crucial one, for in working-class studies the relationship between teaching and research has always been dialectical; pedagogy is a form of praxis. Yet teaching working-class texts has always had particular challenges. For one, working-class students are not as likely as students in some other groups (women, African Americans, gays) to embrace their status. Many working-class students have pursued higher education with the express purpose of leaving the working class; they are embarrassed by their class origins.[5] Studying working-class texts and enabling dialogue about the literary representations of class might help students to reconcile their aspirations with their origins, and it might help middle-class students to understand working-class people whom, given the economic segregation in American society, they likely have never met. Through a discussion of innovative teaching practices that enable students to talk to one another and to see working-class lives from inside, Coles shows how the body of working-class literature can be appreciated by student bodies.

As was previously mentioned, working-class literary criticism has a strong feminist component. Yet while essays, poems, and short stories have been examined by working-class scholars, drama has been neglected.[6] Maria F. Brandt takes an important step in correcting this omission by critiquing gender disruption in several Depression-era plays. She begins with Clifford Odets's well known *Waiting for Lefty*, then examines newspaper plays of the day to see how they reflect and represent to viewers gender anxiety about what seemed a "topsy-turvy" society in which men could no longer support their families and women stepped into traditional male roles.

Gender disruption, of course, had impacts outside the family; hence the Holfield family in *Yonnondio* becomes representative of the crisis in American society in which families cannot maintain themselves. Indeed, intersections between the performance of gender and the performance of nationality have long been the subject of feminist studies such as Annette Kolodny's *The Lay of the Land Before Her*. Within the last several years, the field of masculinity studies has grown. This field is not in opposition to feminist or gender studies and often works in tandem with these fields. Masculinity studies looks at our construction of what it means to be a man and how masculinity is enacted. In his chapter, Matthew Brophy takes on the question, first raised by Mike Gold, of how a writer could be masculine.[7] The twentieth-century fear of a man losing his masculinity in "soft" jobs is represented in *The Sea-Wolf* when the citified Humphrey van Wyden is forced to work under Wolf Larsen in grueling sea conditions. The representation of this forced tutelage is, Brophy argues, a response to a heroic vision of masculinity on the frontier. In effect, Jack London constructs an imperialist vision of rejuvenating American manhood by reintroducing it to the labor of American empire. In addition to masculinity studies, Brophy draws upon postcolonial studies and working-class studies to examine the contradictions within this text, contradictions that reflect the paradoxes of an emergent culture of U.S. global power.

Although scholars on the Left have usually played down the importance of nationhood in relation to class, national identity and origin are crucial, if only because different countries have different conceptions of the value of class identifications. In the United States and Great Britain, for example, people have very different perceptions of what being working class means. Tim Libretti examines Henry Roth's *Call It Sleep*, the case of a writer acclaimed for his first novel about a working-class Jewish boy who goes on to embrace an Israeli identity and Zionism after the Six-Day War in 1967, saying he was unable to find the affiliation he needed in the United States. Tim Libretti reads Henry Roth's reimagination of class consciousness and national politics in the *Mercy of a Rude Stream* novels, seeing in them an assertion of progressive Zionist possibilities not only against postcolonial theory but also against simplistic Marxist internationalist narratives. The classed implications of Roth's belief are that the individual disintegrates unless he/she affiliates with an institution, and the institution of nation, especially if this nation is in crisis, which may related to the institution of class.

As my discussion of the articles has suggested, all of them do not fit neatly into the categories in which they are placed. This slipperiness is inevitable with any anthology of articles. However, I hope it will also be noted that many of the articles "talk" to one another. Fazio and Cook both address working-class populations that are racial minorities and are often excluded from constructions of the labor force. Jackson, McCracken, and Rabinowitz in various ways take up the questions of spaces, places, and mobility. The question Brophy takes up as to whether writing is a suitable profession for a male surely informs a number of works in Zandy and Coles's anthology.

It is my intention that *Critical Approaches to American Working-Class Literature* will facilitate considerable "talking" and "talking back." This collection, hopefully, will be useful to individual scholars who reflect on the articles and base other research on them. In classrooms and at conferences, these articles will be discussed and used as a springboard for work we have not yet imagined. The articles collected here represent the best scholarship being done in working-class American literature and point the way for new areas to be investigated.

NOTES

1. There is some literary criticism in *New Working-Class Studies* and Sherry Lee Linkon's *Teaching Working Class*, and in Janet Zandy's *What We Hold in Common*, but none of these collections is dedicated to literary criticism. *A Class of Its Own:Re-Envisioning American Labor*, edited by Laura Hapke and Lisa Kirby, contains a number of critical articles, but also considerable pedagogical material such as articles on teaching particular authors and course syllabi.
2. The Working-Class Studies Association has for years discussed establishing a journal, but it does not yet have the resources to do so. *Women's Studies Quarterly*, *PMLA*, and *Western American Literature* featured special issues on class and literature. These special issues were edited respectively by Janet Zandy and Lisa Orr, Cora Kaplan, and Renny Christopher.
3. Other pioneers in the study of working-class literature include Renny Christopher and Laura Hapke.
4. In *Hands* Zandy notes the particular aesthetic features of working-class texts, notably that they "question and challenge dominant assumptions about aesthetics. They contextualize aesthetics, insisting on the contingent nature of aesthetic form and practice, and the complexities of local knowledge, and other circumstances" (92). Christopher and Whitson find that "the working-class aesthetic usually involves a distrust of authority and an aversion to paternalism" (75). Paul Lauter's "Under Construction: Working-Class Writing" notes working-class writing's focus on external threats rather than internal strife and the motif of usefulness in working-class texts. See Shevin, Smith, and Zandy's *Writing Work* for more reflections on working-class aesthetics.
5. See Constance Coiner's "U.S. Working-Class Women's Fiction" for a discussion of this topic.
6. One notable article is Christie Launius "*Real Women Have Curves*: A Feminist Narrative of Upward Mobility."
7. See Michael Gold's "Go Left."

WORKS CITED

Adair, Vivyan C. "Class Absences: Cutting Class in Feminist Studies." *Feminist Studies* 31.3 (Fall 2005): 575–603. Print.

Alexie, Sherman. *Indian Killer.* New York: Grove, 1996. Print.
Chute, Carolyn. *The Beans of Egypt, Maine.* San Diego: Harcourt Brace, 1995. Print (1985).
Christopher, Renny, ed. *Western Working-Class Literature.* Spec. issue of *Western American Literature* 40.4 (Winter 2006). Print.
Christopher, Renny, and Carolyn Whitson. "Toward a Theory of Working Class Literature." *The NEA Higher Education Journal* 15.1 (1999): 71–81. Print.
Coiner, Constance. *Better Red: The Writing and Resistance of Tillie Olsen and Meridel Le Sueur.* Oxford: Oxford UP, 1995. Print.
———. "U. S. Working-Class Women's Fiction: Notes Toward an Overview." *Women's Studies Quarterly* 23.1-2 (Spring/Summer 1995): 248-67. Print.
Collins, Patricia Hill. *Black Feminist Thought.* New York: Routledge, 1990. Print.
Dews, C. L., and Carolyn Leste Laws, eds. *This Fine Place So Far from Home: Voices of Academics from the Working Class.* Philadelphia: Temple UP, 1995. Print.
Di Donato, Pieto. *Christ in Concrete.* 1939. New York: New American Library, 1993. Print.
Foley, Barbara. *Radical Representations: Politics and Form in U.S. Proletarian Fiction, 1929–1941.* Durham: Duke UP, 1993. Print.
Gaffney, Karen. "Excavated from the Inside: White Trash and Dorothy Allison's *Cavedweller.*" *MLS* 32.1 (Spring 2002): 43–57. Print.
Giroux, Henry. *Theory and Resistance in Education: A Pedagogy for Opposition.* New York: Bergin and Garvey, 1983. Print.
Gold, Michael. "Go Left, Young Writers!" In Zandy and Coles 380–83. Print.
Hapke, Laura. Daughters of the *Great Depression: Women, Work, and Fiction in the American 1930s.* Athens: U of Georgia P, 1997. Print.
Jameson, Fredric. *The Political Unconscious: Narrative as Socially Symbolic Act.* Ithaca: Cornell UP, 1981. Print.
Kaplan, Cora, ed. *Rereading Class.* Spec. issue of *PMLA* 115.1 (Jan. 2000). Print.
Kingston, Maxine Hong. *China Men.* 1980. New York: Knopf; New York: Vintage, 1985. Print.
Kolodny, Annette. *The Lay of the Land.* Chapel Hill: U of North Carolina P, 1984. Print.
Launius, Christie. "*Real Women Have Curves*: A Feminist Narrative of Upward Mobility." *American Drama* 16.2 (June 2007): 15–27. Print.
Lauter, Paul., ed. *The Heath Anthology of American Literature.* 1989. Print.
———. "Under Construction: Working-Class Literature." In Russo and Linkon 63–77. Print.
———. "Working-Class Women's Literature: An Introduction to Study." *Radical Teacher* 15 (Mar. 1980): 16–26. Print.
Le Sueur, Meridel. *The Girl.* 1929. Albuquerque: West End, 1978. Print.
Linkon, Sherry Lee. *Teaching Working Class.* Amherst: U of Massachusetts P, 1999. Print.
London, Jack. *The Sea-Wolf.* 1904. Oxford: Oxford UP, 2000. Print.
Lorde, Audre. "The Master's Tools Will Never Dismantle the Master's House." *Sister Outsider: Essays and Speeches.* Trumansburg: Crossing P, 1984: 110–13. Print.
Lumpkin, Grace. *To Make My Bread.* 1932. Champlain: U of Illinois P, 1996. Print.
Mitchell, Don. "Working-Class Geographies: Capital, Space, and Place." In Russo and Linkon 78–97. Print.
Mullen, Bill, and Sherry Lee Linkon, eds. *Radical Revisions: Rereading 1930s Culture.* Urbana: U of Illinois P, 1996. Print.

Odets, Clifford. *Waiting for Lefty.* Waiting for Left and Other Plays. (1935). New York: Grove, 1979. Print.
Olsen, Tillie. *Yonnondio: From the Thirties.* New York: Delacorte P, 1974. Print.
Rabinowitz, Paula. *Labor and Desire: Women's Revolutionary Fiction in Depression America.* Chapel Hill: U of North Carolina P, 1991. Print.
Robinson, Lillian S. *Sex, Class and Culture.* Bloomington: Indiana UP, 1979. Print.
Roth, Henry. *Call It Sleep.* New York: Avon, 1964. Print.
Rukeyser, Muriel. The Book of the Dead. *US1.* New York: Covici Friede P., 1938. Print.
Russo, John, and Sherry Lee Linkon, eds. *New Working-Class Studies.* Ithaca: Cornell UP, 2005. Print.
Shevin, David, Larry Smith, and Janet Zandy, eds. *Writing Work: Writers on Working-Class Writing.* Huron: Bottom Dog, 1999. Print.
Smedley, Agnes. *Daughter of Earth.* 1929. New York: Feminist, 1993. Print.
Tokarczyk, Michelle M. *Class Definitions: On the Lives and Writings of Maxine Hong Kingston, Sandra Cisneros, and Dorothy Allison.* Selinsgrove: Susquehanna UP, 2008. Print.
Tokarczyk, Michelle M., and Elizabeth A. Fay, eds. *Working-Class Women in the Academy: Laborers in the Knowledge Factory.* Amherst: U of Massachusetts P, 1993. Print.
University of Minnesota. *Sandra Cisneros: Voices from the Gap.* 7 Oct. 2004. Web. 17 Sept. 2010.
Williams, Raymond. *Marxism and Literature.* Oxford: Oxford UP, 1977. Print.
———. *Resources of Hope: Culture, Democracy, Socialism.* London: Verso, 1989.
Wolfe, Tom. *I Am Charlotte Simmons.* New York: Picador, 2004. Print.
Woolf, Virginia. "A Room of One's Own.: (1929) New York: Harcourt Brace, 1989. Print.
Zandy, Janet, ed. *Calling Home: An Anthology of Working-Class Women's Writing.* New Brunswick: Rutgers UP, 1990. Print.
———. *Hands: Physical Labor, Class, and Cultural Work.* New Brunswick: Rutgers UP, 2004. Print.
———, ed. *Liberating Memory: Our Work and Working Class Consciousness.* New Brunswick: Rutgers UP, 1994. Print.
Zandy, Janet, and Lisa Orr, eds. *Working-Class Literature.* Spec. issue of *Women's Studies Quarterly* 23.1-2 (Spring/Summer 1995). Print.
Zandy, Janet, and Nicholas Coles, eds. *American Working-Class Literature: An Anthology.* Oxford UP, 2006. Print.
Zweig, Michael. *The Working-Class Majority: America's Best Kept Secret.* Ithaca: Cornell UP, 2000. Print.

Part I
The Realities of Working-Class Life

Because working-class life is frequently either ignored or caricatured in the United States, critics of working-class literature often focus on unearthing working-class writers' representations of the lived experience of class. These imaginative reconstructions of working-class lives reaffirm suppressed histories for working-class audiences and challenge middle- and upper-class readers to recognize the tangible effects of class inequity.

Paula Rabinowitz, in a move signaling our increased awareness of the importance of visual culture, examines both literary and photographic landscapes of economic depression. In writing about literary and visual texts about the Great Depression, she examines the physical places of poverty, such as the Hoovervilles that were built along roads, as well as the displacement of families who were uprooted from their homes or jobs or both. Rabinowitz also examines contemporary work on the Great Recession, which is characterized by abandoned homes and industrial buildings left shuttered and crumbling. Such places are repositories of memory: memory of community and a time when middle-class comfort was within reach.

Whereas Rabinowitz examines representations of how economic crises alter people's physical and psychic landscapes, Renny Christopher's article underscores the danger inherent in working-class jobs. I use the word "inherent" with some hesitation, for while much blue-collar work may be more risky than white-collar desk jobs, Christopher notes that the United States has a high rate of work-related injury relative to other industrialized nations. The numerous industrial, agricultural, and other accidents that occur in literature are violent and, as readers of texts such as Pietro di Donato's *Christ in Concrete* can attest, difficult to read. Christopher, in her study of numerous novels and poems, thus compares the challenges of writing about work-related accidents to the challenges of writing about combat casualties: she asks how a writer can render the realities of horrific accidents and deaths without being sensational or "pornographic."

Sylvia J. Cook also takes up a work-related question that has horrific dimensions: slavery. Cook, however, begins with the question hotly debated by literary critics and labor historians as to whether slaves should be considered part of the working class. In her examination of Harriet Beecher Stowe's *Uncle Tom's Cabin* and Harriet Jacobs' *Incidents in the Life of a Slave Girl*, Cook argues that each author put class at the center of her narrative. The centrality of class does not suggest that class is more important than race, which would certainly be a peculiar formulation in an abolitionist novel, but rather suggests how class and race may be interlocked and how this intersection is understood by the protagonists. In showing how slaves in both texts adapted nineteenth-century codes of respectability and refinement, as well as instances of both identification and tension with poor whites, Cook emphasizes the complexity of the questions and advocates for reading these texts as "resources" that help us to understand rather than as "symptoms" that point to problems with ready diagnoses.

1 "between the outhouse and the garbage dump"
Locating Collapse in Depression Literature

Paula Rabinowitz

KENNETH FEARING, DEAD RECKONING

Flying by the seat of one's pants, guesswork because the instruments have failed, the stars cannot be sighted, one's location unfixed. It was the title of Kenneth Fearing's mid-Depression volume of poems—a navigational term of unknown origin describing the method of plotting a course based on past positions. Because space and velocity are relative—because the rug's been pulled from beneath one's feet, with each reckoning, the possibility for error increases exponentially. As such pathbreaking works by Caren Irr (*The Suburb of Dissent*) and Jani Scandura (*Down in the Dumps*) have shown, Depression-era literature was rife with tropes of positioning, of location, of place; or rather of displacement, derailment, missing locations, and missed connections. Spatial order—central to demarking borders between industrial and residential zones, between men and women, between workers and their bosses, between races, between parents and their children—although sharply visible, still tangibly in effect, could no longer be counted on to signify as they once had. Kenneth Fearing outlines this vanishing urban space "[b]etween the haberdasher's and the pinball arcade," a "heelpocked pavement" distinguished only by a cigarette butt in "Memo" (77).

In our current "Great Recession," these "heelpocked" locations of collapse have become even harder to discern as they have extended beyond the cheesy cityscapes "between the haberdasher's [if there any left in America] and the pinball arcade" across landscapes of subdivisions and big-box stores. The space of the "doubly occupied," as anthropologist Kathleen Stewart calls it, "a space on the side of the road" (marginal areas where dispossessed people congregate and exchange hardship, survival, and other stories), at once controlled by forces beyond the locales in which people reside—military occupiers, industrial and financial giants—yet still remaining repositories of local forms of memory, desire, and imaginative rumination—and possibly even organization. In short, what were once "places," suffering but iconic, during this current episode of depression known as recession, are now *displaced*, dispersed across an invisible terrain, "up in the air" where, as Frank Rich points out, the movie based on Walter Kirn's 2001 novel dematerializes this site.

It was not until 1928, according to the *Oxford English Dictionary*, that the term "depressed areas" came into use to describe zones of economic devastation.[1] Not that these locations of collapse were not obvious, and obviously cordoned off, before then. In the 1880s, following the English graphic artists (Samuel Luke Fildes, Hubert von Herkomer, Francis Montague Holl) he admired, Vincent van Gogh knew to sit before the poor houses and churchyards and potato fields to find the "orphan men," those destitute old homeless men, he was drawing.[2] In America, Dutch émigré Jacob Riis knew where to find "the other half" who lived crammed together in the Lower East Side of New York—the place where Michael Gold would later find "Jews without Money" living amid dumps and among bedbugs (a literary form that Michael Denning dubbed "the ghetto pastoral" [230]). Spatial metaphors limn class divisions—the topos is the trope.

Figure 1.1 Dorothea Lange, "Slums of San Francisco, California." June 1935. Library of Congress, Prints and Photographs Division, FSA/OWI Collection, LC-USF 34–002331-C.

Depression—a word dating at least to 1391 when Geoffrey Chaucer used it to describe the astronomical phenomenon of the lowering of a polestar or planet beneath the horizon—is literally a condition of being lowered in position. Pressed down, sinking, it refers to elevation or rather its opposite—structurally or figuratively—tracking horizons, fortunes, powers, affects: these more metaphorical and psychological senses emerge in the mid-seventeenth century and explode into the nineteenth century as surgery, gunnery, algebra, pathology and medicine, geology, musicology, philosophy, meteorology, finance, all begin to use the term to denote a lessening or lowering of or within.[3] Codified as a psychiatric disorder only in 1905, it finally settles as the term for the Great Depression following the 1929 stock market crash and its aftermath, settles in part as a gentler antidote to the harsher nineteenth-century terms panic or crisis (Bird 89, qtd. in Dickstein 6). Thus the slippery usage of this word—a term of mobility itself—veers from the cosmic across an array of fields of specialization to eventually land in the interiority of the psyche and then extend outward again into the realm of economics. Contemporary usage toggles between the psychological and economic, though as our current euphemism of recession suggests, it's now a term to be avoided—through infusions of Prozac or TARP.[4] Yet the two modern meanings are so embedded within middle-class life they resist troping, or rather, they have become the trope—the "turn," "manner," "way" according to *Webster's Universal Encyclopedic Dictionary*—in which we live, the figuration of this doomed location.

The Great Depression was figured as a collapse—literalized in Pietro di Donato's 1939 novel, *Christ in Concrete*, as a collapsing building that smothers its workers alive under tons of debris—or as a massive flow of drowning workers migrating across regional borders to connect those passing along the edges of John Dos Passos' *49th Parallel*. Either trope—vertical instability and collapse or horizontally emptied spaces—made visible this ruin, a vision of diminishment, seen through predictable icons of men lined up along streets for bread or work (seen, for instance, in Dorothea Lange's 1931 photograph *White Angel Bread Line*) or uprooted families strewn along dust-filled landscapes (found in Paul Taylor and Dorothea Lange's *American Exodus: A Record of Human Erosion,* or Erskine Caldwell and Margaret Bourke-White's *You Have Seen Their Faces*, or James Agee and Walker Evans's *Let Us Now Praise Famous Men*) or squatting in substandard housing zoned to contain impoverished immigrants and migrants, ethnically and racially marked as unfit or undeserving (seen in Richard Wright's *12 Million Black Voices*). Its inhabitants, despite being found everywhere, were nevertheless sent to the corners and margins of visibility. As Miles Orvell has pointed out, this extended to bastions of capitalism: in "the first year of the depression . . . *Fortune* . . . devoted to stories about gold and wine, Macy's and the Vanderbilts, the *New York Times* and the International Paper Company . . . [printed] an article called 'Vanishing Backyards', an article on junk. . . . America is likened to a child that recklessly 'hurls its refuse out the window, and doesn't care how high are piled

20 *Paula Rabinowitz*

Figure 1.2 Arthur Rothstein, "Squatters' shacks along the Willamette River in Portland, Oregon. Many of the men living here during the winter work in the nearby orchards of the Willamette and Yakima Valley in the summer." July 1936. Library of Congress, Prints and Photographs Division, FSA-OWI Collection, LC USF 34–004831-E.

the tin cans in the backyard'" (287). The connection between marginal spaces (backyards) and marginalized people (children) was firmly in place immediately after the crash.

TILLIE OLSEN: YONNONDIO

The "one patch of green"—"there was no other place for Mazie"—is found "between the outhouse and the garbage dump," a zone suffused with "a nauseating smell," but affording the child enough privacy to indulge daydreams (4–5). Throughout the rest of Olsen's fragment of a novel, these two eccentric monuments (to shit, to trash)—especially the garbage dump at the river's edge—sites of refuse, debris, waste, "places piled high with collections of used-up things still in use"—become refuges for the imagination of the "doubly occupied." (Stewart 41, 61). This elision, from refuse to refuge, that sibilant *s* easing into a soft *g*, is a common thread of locating "a space of alterity," according to anthropologist Kathleen Stewart as an entire ethos and aesthetics of "making do"—of dead reckoning—maintained daily life in these edge zones (Stewart 91, 68). As Mazie sinks deeper into lethargy and lassitude with each move across the destroyed landscape of midcontinental United States, the dump becomes a tangible location of her collapse—and a refuge from it.

What begins for her when she peers into the mouth of the pit mine and its fiery backdrop as a vision of hell—the depression below the horizon—extends briefly from her cramped and violent childhood in a Western mining camp out across a huge prairie landscape to encompass the stars lowering to its flat expanse. It quickly contracts again when her family's financial disaster as sharecroppers leaves them mired in debt. But the city dump, down by the river bank, finally opens an exciting new space of exploration: "On the inexhaustible dump strange structures rise: lookout towers, sets, ships, tents, forts, lean-tos, clubhouses, cities and stores and train tracks, cabooses, pretend palaces—singularly fitted with once furnishings, never furnishings, or nothing at all" (150). Ultimately, this refuse refuge, this stagnant "space on the side of the road" congeals into a tomb for her listlessness: "Where you going?" "No place" (169). "And there was nothing really new on the dump. It smelled sewer, smelled garbage, smelled crap 'cept right at the river-bluff edge" (168).

"I don't *have* no place...." "*Why don't I have no place?*" (178). Mazie finally confronts her mother who has tossed out—dumped—her homemade "perfume," a stinking brew concocted for her dump girlfriend Ginella from scavenged flower petals rotting in a discarded and corked bottle. The entirety of Omaha becomes no place, a kind of refuse pile, circulating the smells of the slaughterhouse and pork processing plants, the dead riverbanks, at once empty and overripe. Susan Edmunds, commenting on the perfume scene, notes its debt to what she outlines in *Grotesque Relations* as "the domain of the domestic exterior" (125), especially as it was promulgated during the early 1930s by the Hoover administration, which she finds stressed through its publication *The Home and the Child* the importance of "proper disposal of garbage . . . the harmfulness of residences located 'unduly near railroad . . . dumps, marshes, or obnoxious industries'" (137–38). And, this pamphlet goes on to insist, a la Virginia Woolf's call for *A Room of One's Own* a few years earlier, upon "'privacy . . . each child should have a place'" (qtd. on 139).

In *Yonnondio*, Olsen delineates the space between outhouse and garbage dump as one of simultaneous confinement and imagination in which the borders—differentiating childhood from adulthood, men from women, rich from poor—stand in relief, become outlined, only to be derailed. This is a boundary at once below and above—the dump is piled high with junk but lies beneath the horizon of the city along its sunken railroad tracks and river banks. It is isolated and confined—"my momma don't let me go down by the river" because "bad people's there that hurts girls"—yet wide open and mobile—as "the gondola of a sluggish freight train" passes by (168–69). The scene of exploration and escape—"All the way to California"—only to be called back by a mother's hollering "Gertrude Skolnick" destroying the fantasies of reenacting *Human Wreckage* (184). If Mazie and her friends get lost in dump fantasies (though ones superintended by the potential of sexual violence, "bad people . . . that hurts girls"), Paul, the child protagonist of Pietro di Donato's *Christ in Concrete*, which owes much to Michael Gold's *Jews without Money* (1930) and Henry Roth's *Call It Sleep* (1934), is trapped between the "cliff with sightless windows and crumbling fire escapes" of the tenement which, like a dump, houses "its distinctive powerful odor": "the winding staired passage of Tenement hallway gaseous in its internationality of latrines, dank with walls that never knew day, acrid in the corners where vermin, dogs, cats and children relieved themselves." Finding respite from his family and job and illness, "He lay down on his back looking up through the bars of the fire escape, up past the rusty tin cornices of the tenement parapet, up at a distant sky . . . then wander about the building going up on the roof . . . sit on the stoop or on the curb. . . . He became spectator . . ." (98). Seeking escape, "Paul wandered the waterfront. . . . But he knew he was afraid of the river" where even good swimmers who dived off the wharf might get their head "stuck in the top of an old milk can down on the bottom of the river" (114). Wharf, river's edge, fire escape, rooftop, stoop—the locations of urban escape, like those between the Wyoming mining camp's outhouse and garbage dump, repeat the spatial arrangements of depressions—beneath and beyond the horizon: edging buildings and cities, the most dangerous lie out of sight but within the range of smell. They are treacherous but alluring places for children of both sexes; they are the space where drifters gather, an unsanctioned zone collecting lone men.

Many of the great 1930s coming-of-age novels—*Yonnondio, Christ in Concrete, Young Lonigan, Their Eyes Were Watching God, Call It Sleep, Jews without Money*—are actually set in the teens and twenties.[5] It is not that novels of poverty were not being published before or after—one need only think of Anzia Yezierska's *The Bread Givers* (1925) and Betty Smith's *A Tree Grows in Brooklyn* (1943)—but the Depression provided a narrative and lyric purchase, a surround, that allowed these works a "space on the side of the [literary] road" and offered a clearer legibility; it made childhood poverty in America decipherable—not merely as a stage, but as a condition. The Great Depression thus consolidated both a topic and a tropic—a metaphorical and spatial convention—that of a lowering. From the trolley tracks cutting the Eastside streets in *Call It Sleep* to the pears hanging from the tree in *Eyes* to the bedbugs crawling under the mattresses in *Jews*, depression in its ramifying meanings provided a contour so that the toll of *Human Wreckage* might finally be reckoned. That 1923 film about drug abuse which so captivated Ginella, made by the widow of Hollywood actor Wallace Reid who died of morphine overdose, stands in as a popular cultural reference to the sensations behind the dump girls' reenactments of movie melodrama and true romance.[6] These girls are a far cry from the child stars who would captivate 1930s movie audiences through "the unspoiled but cloying innocence of Shirley Temple and Deanna Durbin" (Dickstein 402).

Olsen's novel—written during the Depression but set in the 1920s—expresses something any poor person already knew: the edges of poverty were sharply defined and visible before the crash.[7] What had changed after October 1929 was the scale of this devastation, its collective fall, which I am calling a collapse in contrast to its definition by Jared Diamond in his 2005 book entitled *Collapse*: "a dramatic decrease in human population size and/or political/economic/social complexity, over a considerable area, for an extended time" (3). And this scale, its repetition across regions and its literary depictions, made the Great Depression (which according to Diamond should actually be seen as a "milder type of decline . . . normal rises and falls of fortune . . .") an emblem marked by collapse: wreckage, waste, anxiety, languor. Mazie and Paul and Mikey and Davey and Janey and Studs may have spent their impoverished childhoods in the 1910s and 1920s, but their narratives required the Depression to be written. There was no chart for the locations of collapse earlier.[8]

Lauren Gilfillan's 1934 novel *I Went to Pit College* was among the first by and about radical intellectuals to grasp this depressive logistic. Her novel, a *Bildungsroman* about a vaguely left-wing middle-class student, Lauren, who descends literally into the coal mines of Western Pennsylvania as she enters its labor struggles only to find herself sinking into madness, encapsulates the variety of economic, spatial, and psychological senses of depression already captured by working-class writers. Dressing as a boy—with freshly cropped hair and a miner's "costume"—her Slavic grandma host thinks she's "crazy" (86); but Lauren's childlike epistemophilia, her need to know this place mired in poverty and labor violence to which she has come seeking to become "a sort of writer" (6), leads her not to enlightenment but into Avelonia's sulfurous hell: as her cabbie reminds her, it's not "the Isles of the Blest," just another place (3). Her description of descending into the mine anticipates her eventual fall into a depressive madness (and note how the physical details mirror those used to convey the psychic):

> Blackness. A tiny bluish-white light glimmering far, far away. . . . Grind, roar, grind, down a long black tunnel. Darkness, night. Walls of dust hanging about us, floating, suspended, always the same. Flashing patches of light glistening luridly on eternal black wall. We were sliding down a huge black coffin. A red light coming closer. . . . Perpendicular white streaks in the distance, growing into pallid posts, ghosts of branchless trees under the black roof. We are moving swiftly; they flash by so fast. Blue flames about our heads. Crackling blue flashes beneath the wheels.

Coal, coal. We are living coal. We are incarcerated in coal. Velvet black smears in gliding glittering walls—manholes. Great pallid timbers, bearing up the hillside. Another red light flying above us. Now gone. Grind, roar, grind, swiftly sliding deeper, deeper, into the earth. (89)

JOHN DOS PASSOS, U.S.A.

What brought Mazie's no place and Laurie's deep slide into relief, so to speak, was precisely its magnitude—a national one tramped by adults as well as dreamy children; "all right we are two nations," declares a speaker responding to the executions of Sacco and Vanzetti in *U.S.A.* The scale of devastation and its ubiquity paradoxically hides a sense of the liminality and possibility—for new kinds of coming-of-age narratives. The alternative, third "space on the side of the road," the "doubly occupied space," the "patch of green" "between outhouse and garbage dump," "a huge black coffin," beneath the horizon, on the edge, underground, was diminished; children themselves are a sort of "space on the side of the road" to adulthood, the time of life that matters and thus operate as a figure for what Alan Wald has called the "populist version of romanticism" (*Exiles* 33).[9] As Carolyn Steedman notes, there is a "long established association between littleness and interiority and between history and childhood" so that children stand metaphorically for these depression sites: they literally are below the eye line of adults, out of sight (*Strange* 77).[10] These 1930s child-centered novels deflected the external locations of collapse inside, or rather alongside, the contours of social and economic space; Michael Gold describes this great ambivalent zone, the open lots in the Lower East Side, as "the ruins of Pompeii, except that seven million animals full of earth-love must dwell in the dead lava streets" (40). This "[s]habby old ground, ripped like a battlefield by workers' picks and shovels, little garbage dump lying forgotten in the midst of tall tenements, O home of all the twisted junk, rusty baby carriages, lumber, bottle, boxes, moldy pants and dead cats of the neighborhood. . . . No place will ever seem as wonderful again" (46).[11] Forgotten yet wonderful, wonderful because forgotten, a home of rust, mold, and dead cats; this space nourished childhood reverie and adult literature.

Instead, with the collapse and within the narratives tracking adults, the landscape was rezoned into a starkly divided space: Dos Passos's two nations. As James Scott notes, the high modernist state is a progressive project of large-scale mapping designed to remake populations and their spaces. In its productive workings things get built—dams, bridges, skyscrapers, and so on[12]—but in its "depressive" mode, as Jani Scandura calls it, the same principles of scale work to unmake society, rezoning it in similar if more ad hoc ways. John Lowney notes this oscillation: "Whether as a sordid site of childhood poverty or a spectacular site of mass cultural junk, the dump signifies the social contradictions of the 1930" (24). Ultimately, then, as adults reckon with these locations in and of collapse, they become differentially scaled within Depression narratives—from Mazie's "no place" to Josephine Johnson's *Jordanstown* (1937) to John Dos Passos's *49th Parallel* (1930)—extending from a patch of green to a small city to the entire nation.

Johnson's novel charts the collapse of a small-sized Missouri city as the Depression forces the inhabitants of Fox Basin, the poor, working-class, and African-American section of town, to interact in new ways, as beggars or as strikers, for instance, with those living on the Bluffs. Johnson had won the Pulitzer Prize for her 1934 novel *Now in November*, a lyrical study of coming-of-age in the rural Midwest; and like many of her contemporaries, she moved her gaze outward from the psychological inspection of a singular consciousness to rescale this figuring of depression onto an economic system contained within a small American city marked by class and racial divisions suffering through extreme conflicts—but also newfound solidarities—during the economic crisis. Mapping the Depression onto a town figured the coming-of-age story across a broad field and shifted the psychological onto the social. Johnson's novel—a year in the life of city instead of a character—narrates its distress through a radicalized young man come home to deal with his father's foreclosed house; his initial intake of the town sweeps across a familiar graded landscape of distinct sectors. "The stores, and beyond them the factory, were fog-colored, and the windows grayish gold, square, and more dull than ominous in the new year's light; behind the small factory a huddle of houses. . . . Around the abandoned packing house, enormous and gray, with its empty yards full of the dry, cold dust, were the Negro shacks . . . small boxes hard set in the winter mud. . . . the land was flat and naked as a ball field. In the low part of Jordanstown near the river the houses of Fox Basin were still in the shadow of the Bluff . . ." (5). The town is thus like a consciousness: familiar yet uncanny, gray, flat, dull, dusty, shrouded in fog yet etched with distinct outlines that recall the past, once seen in sharper relief.

There are other examples of spatialized depressive narratives: *Waste Heritage*, Irene Baird's 1939 novel of the unemployed movement in Vancouver, British Columbia, follows two lone teenagers through the rail depots and back alleys and flophouses of the Western Canadian city as they search for work and join the mass movement of unemployed workers. Based on the occupation of the Vancouver post office by an army of unemployed men in 1937, reported on by Baird, it graphs the city's divisions by tracking each character's movements from the streets to the rail yard to the port to the open field where the men have gathered after eviction. Ruth McKinney's 1939 *Industrial Valley* also maps the story of the Akron rubber workers' sit-down strike onto the geography of the city; Meyer Levin's *Citizens* (1940) does the same for Chicago and the Little Steel Massacre. Each place, each strike, serves as allegory for the larger story of union. In fact, Caren

Irr argues that "U.S. proletarian fiction is premised on projection of long-standing local conflicts onto a national screen" (147). American regionalism, always the derided stepsister of "the great American novel," takes on new heft (akin to the ways in which the children I have been describing enabled a new look at what was beneath view) as the Depression and its effects spreads across the continent.[13]

The logic and logistics are microcosmic—delineating the precise boundaries of local zones of collapse then mapping them across the nation so that each iteration reprises a well-known vision of lone men standing around transient camps and Hoovervilles where anxious yet defiant women worry over food and potential violence. The city, or its makeshift version along water's edge or highway shoulder or railroad track, is figured as a space between, a generalized collapsing in on itself of the classed and racial divides zoned into American capitalism once detailed through precise tracking of who moves and lives where. Charting this space is the work of narrative: "Matt sat there a long time hunched against the piled junk. He watched the broken squads drift back, the side door open and shut, the thin shaft of yellow light that struck the step each time a man went in or out. Those that came outside to bed down looked like grave-robbers, stepping, stumbling among the sleepers. Those that lay beneath the billboard drew their blankets up or used their arms to shield their faces from the light. . . . He listened to the far-off howl of the train, began to count the number of times the police patrol went around the block" (Baird 70).

Thus, locations of collapse during the Great Depression move both inward and outward, below and beneath, in these narratives. Pressed down, brought low, belittled, looked down upon, men are beaten down and "sick," "invalid," "distressed," say many of the letters written to the First Lady and President Roosevelt (McElvaine 97–112). Latching on to the forgotten men theme as well as that of FDR's crippled body as an identity, these victims of depression become children—or worse.[14] They sink below the surface, appear as "grave-robbers . . . with the burning eyes of the sleepless" (Baird 70). Giving up, exhausted, "facing poor house or suicide" (McElvaine 103), women scrape together food and clothing for their children, make do, and plead with Eleanor Roosevelt for hand-me-downs. In John Ford's rendering of John Steinbeck's *Grapes of Wrath*, Jane Darwell as Ma explains why women can bear suffering better than men, who live in "jerks" while women's lives extend pain from childhood on. The two nations get figured in a number of ways: the haves and have-nots, of course; but also those who are able to "make do" (Ma) and those who cannot (Pa); those who fight (like Preacher) and those who give up, go crazy (like Mulie); those with a plan, a racket, (like the 1930s movie gangsters in *Little Ceasar, The Public Enemy*, or *Scarface*) and the mugs who get worked over by the system (like their siblings). Or in Johnson's rendering "the dark living, and the pink living dead" who can be seen in the nation's courtrooms divided between "two kinds of people" (202). "Pink zombies [the judges, notaries, attorneys and clerks serving capital].... And on the other side, the living, the tramp arrested for vagrancy, with his gray torn beard, his pouched eyes and tough yellow skin; the battered boy auto thief; the three Negroes murmuring to each other, their black, grinning faces silver with sweat; the relatives and friends, the idly curious; the jobless, their dark faces gullied with knowledge not realized; suffering, hate, amusement, anxiety—faces, hair, hands, clothes, eyes all bearing witness to their lives—these are the living. These are the Used" (Johnson 203). For Johnson, death and life, darkness and light, reverse their allegorical trajectories; the "pink zombies" are deader than the dark living, who may be used but who have history on their side.

In short, the dump has spread from the doubly occupied childhoods on the margins, along the riverfront or across the tenement airshaft, to the back door of a bakery where "[t]heir feet done up in enormous bundles of sacking, and ragged mufflers tied around their ears, the two old tramps sit patiently together on the steps" (Johnson 11), and beyond, into the seats of power. In the process, its middle range—that green patch—seems diminished, flattened from a "monument" to merely its parts, "piled up boxes / outlined with shoddy fret-work, half-fallen off, / cracked and unpainted" (Bishop 24). Johnson's vision of the "Used," who are subject to the law, as alive, in contrast to the dead "zombies" who superintend American justice, suggests that the space between dump and outhouse is no longer the ambiguous realm of childhood poverty and play but an aspect of the total American social fabric sunk down, used and confused.

MARK NOWAK, SHUT UP SHUT DOWN

Mark Nowak's 2004 collage volume of photographs and poems made almost entirely from found language, *Shut Up Shut Down*, redirects depression outward and "documents the debris, the detritus" of plant closures, what happens when work goes missing through what he calls "geographic hemorrhaging" ("Public"); an updated *U.S.A.*, indebted to the defiant insertion of people's voices in Muriel Rukeyser's "Book of the Dead," as much as it owes to the hip-hop sampling of Jay-Z. It picks up on Dos Passos's chorale through three-voiced poems, adding a fourth visual dimension—the photograph and the concrete form of the poem itself. For instance, "$00 / Line / Steel / Train," the first section in *Shut Up Shut Down*, references Bernd and Hilla Becher's photographs catalogued in *Industrial Facades*. Because of intense copyright restrictions on the republication of the Bechers' images—they control all images and insist on ordering them for publication or exhibition—Nowak's poems about the disappearance of the steel industry from Buffalo, New York, intensify this absence. The Bechers' formal vision of brick, concrete, and steel regularized into a monumental tribute to industrial capital also records its disarray, an orderly process of disarray. These (unseen) photos—and the visible ones by Nowak himself—indicate that industrial facades are just that: false fronts inevitably crumbling before our eyes, to be replaced by For Sale signs in boarded-up windows. One has access to the images of loss and emptiness only through the words inscribed beneath a number—which refers to the Bechers' ordering; to see them the reader must become doubly occupied herself: in the poems and in a trip to a library or bookstore for the images. Twice removed from the visual source, the reader hears only fragments of collected speech, excerpts of printed text amid the few spare descriptions of the images and Nowak's occasional references to his own labor as poet, which he describes as indebted to the Japanese form *haibun* and to *exteriorismo*, Ernesto Cardenal's method of inscribing interiority through objects and documents, to capture base and superstructure on the page. The heavy square of text in "$00" rests precariously above a thin scaffold of five open lines of a few words: base and superstructure are reversed now that accumulation occurs by dispossession.

Take "92," which refers to a seemingly abandoned Detroit factory from 1974. Among the earliest in the Bechers' collection, this image points to the transitional moment when modern industrial strength in the United States began to give way to the pressures of global capital flight; the "rust belt" was born from the wreckage of smokestacks. The pall of loss covering the Bechers' images means that even when a building is obviously still in use—fresh tire tracks lace the mud in front of a façade whose doors are open (rather than bricked over or boarded up or simply broken apart)—it still appears evacuated, frozen, as if waiting for its moment of disuse to come. Eliding the bodies of workers, these beautiful black-and-white renderings of emptiness are implacable. Modernism was premised on this very precarious certainty; Benjamin's civilization/barbarism dialectic; Rukeyser's channeling of the Egyptian *Book of the Dead* to convey an episode of government and industry conspiring against workers, of decay (silicosis) embedded into the "natural resources" necessary to its construction (or extraction).However, Nowak wants to hear voices. Reading is voiced—reading aloud as a child might—in renderings of found speech and cut-up techniques. In sections 89 and 92 from "$00 / Line / Steel / Train," straightforward narration by the poet—"After lunch at Lucky's Texas Red Hots I took my grandfather to the steel/plant. . ." or "Doors torn away in Detroit, 1974"—is intercut with direct but unsourced quotations gleaned from some seemingly official outlet, which in turn are sampled with boldface comments by anonymous displaced workers. These multiplying sets of voices provide for a markedly ironic take on power differentials, most clearly observed in the poem "Capitalization," which stages a dramatic confrontation among a 1980s English grammar textbook, news reports of the PATCO strike of air-traffic controllers and Ronald Reagan's successful efforts to bust the union, and an oral history of 1930s union organizing of Westinghouse (for which Reagan later became, in the 1950s, a spokesman).

Nowak's recent book, *Coal Mountain Elementary*, is even more connected to Rukeyser's documentary exposé of extraction industries and government neglect; it continues his project to draw attention to a key "ideological state apparatus," according to Louis Althusser—schools—and the unequal education system maintaining class differences, but extends it transnationally, linking the international catastrophes of coal mining.[15] This attention to the corrosive language of "social studies" echoes Olsen's singsong incantation of pedagogical condescension she and her brother encountered upon entering Omaha's public school: "'MazieandWillHolbrookhavecomefromthecountrywheretheygrowthecornandwheatandallourmilkcomesfromsayhellotoMazieandWillchildren'" (70–71). In *Shut Up Shut Down*, "Capitalization" splices a 1980s grammar book's ideologically inflected lessons, exhorting "Capitalize the Republican Administration/Capitalize the Administration/Capitalize the Reagan Administration," with a mournful memorial to an earlier era of union organizing set in boldface and the defiant strikers' accounts relayed through a skeptical media (43). *Coal Mountain Elementary* uses the same ironic technique, this time echoing James Agee and, later, Elizabeth Bishop (who both reproduce verbatim pages of geography textbooks);[16] it layers a coal-friendly grade school curriculum—say for a lesson in "Cookie Mining," ["Overview: Students participate in a simulation of the mining process using chocolate chip cookies and toothpicks. The simulation helps to illustrate the costs associated with the mining of coal" (65)], designed for use in West Virginia, with accounts of mining disasters in the United States and China. Relying on English-language translations of Chinese survivors' stories and location photographs taken by himself and China-based British photojournalist Ian Teh, the book builds a sense of the international dimensions of extraction industries' destruction, both physical and psychical, on people and their environments.

The volume returns us to the coal pits that beckoned Mazie and Laurie in the 1920s and 1930s—gaping holes into which, when there is work, the vulnerable (female) body is lowered—and which form empty depressions in the landscape when they shut down, as Stewart reminds us: "[I]n mining country, the evidence of mining activity [headframes, mine buildings, and ore dumps] pervades every scene, reinforcing the dominance of a single industry in the life of the settlement and its residents" (Francaviglia, *Hard* 85). The girls descend into madness in the face of the implacable depths opened by these multivalent depressions—physical, geological, financial, ideological, and metaphysical. Miners all over China and West Virginia are buried under the weight of collapsing earth and the collapsing economies of scale. Unlike Frank Rich's assertion that this, our Great Recession, has left people "up in the air," Nowak's poetic documentary of mining disasters make clear that we are still in the pits, as Lauren Gilfillan learned in the 1930s. We already know the end: structures turn to junk, decaying long before expected. Indeed, we are the effects of planned obsolescence. Nowak's visual rendering of our contemporary cyclings through recession/depression locate collapse on the bottom of the page, within the poem's text, within everyday speech. Depressed under the stanza's horizon, however, lies another space of reverie, of pain and play, visible to the page reader but otherwise inaudible. This is the poem's edge—another kind of outhouse, another dumping ground, with the potential for free play, crossing borders, and mocking through reappropriation—and like the dump of Mazie's Omaha or Mikey's New York childhood, it offers materials for instruction, not yet collapsed.

NOTES

1. "Already the local rates in depressed areas have to shoulder too large a part of the burden of relieving unemployment" Quote from the *OED* taken from *Britain's Industrial Future* 20: 276. By 1958, the *OED* noted this sentence "There are no depressed areas now" from *Listener* (11 Sept.) 371–72.
2. Letter from Vincent to Theo 8–9 January 1882:
    I got a great bargain on some splendid woodcuts from The Graphic. . . . The drawings by Herkomer, Frank Holl, Walker, and others. . . . Some of them are superb, including the Houseless and homeless by Fildes (poor people waiting outside a night shelter) and two large Herkomers and many small ones, and the Irish emigrants by Frank Holl and the 'Old gate' by Walker. And especially a girls' school by Frank Holl and also that large Herkomer, the invalids. . . .
    I'm struggling and striving to make something myself that is realistic and yet done with sentiment. I have around 12 figures of diggers and people working in the potato field, and I'm wondering if I couldn't make something of them, you also have a couple of them, including a man putting potatoes in a sack . . .
    Letter to Anthon van Rappard, The Hague, 28 May 1882:
    . . .sites being levelled or raised, sheds, planks, huts, fences &c. &c., everything you can imagine.
    Another pleasing sight here is the soup kitchens, and always, always the 3rd-class waiting room. If I didn't have to earn a living, that's to say by drawing those townscapes, I would do only figures in times like these, but as yet I have no one who will buy them, and I still have the costs of a model, although I can often get someone.
3. For a literal instance that slides into the metaphoric, see Whibley, 161.
    "If Poe's life was a tangle of contradiction, his posthumous fame has been a very conflict of opposites. He has been elevated to heaven, he has been depressed to hell; he has been pictured angel and devil, drunkard and puritan. His poetry has seemed to this one the empty tinkling of a cymbal, to that the last expression of verbal beauty. But despite the warfare of opinions, he has been read and imitated throughout the world, and he still is, after half a century, the dominant influence of three literatures. An inventor in many fields, he deserves whatever homage may be paid him; and if his genius has been somewhat obscured by the monument, in ten volumes, of late erected to his honour, the zealot will discover many a block of pure marble, half hidden in the heap of shot rubble . . ." Thanks to Lauren Curtright for this.
4. For an analysis of how the diagnosis of depression, especially in women, actually is productive within contemporary postindustrial affective work zones, see Swenson.

5. Le Sueur's novel, written at the end of the 1930s, is set entirely during the 1930s; however, the eponymous heroine has already left home, for work in the city, when the tale begins.
6. See Heard, ch. 3, "Consuming Melodrama in Black and White" in which she shows how Depression-era black girls also devoured these stories and Kunzel for more on the ways popular narratives allowed working-class and poor women a frame to describe themselves.
7. "There seems to be quite a furor in the country over a big stock market crash that wiped a lot of people out. We are ahead of them. The hailstorm in July of 1928 and bank failure that fall wiped out a lot of people locally. As far as that goes, most of North Dakota was hard hit last year," records Low in her diary entry of 9 November 1929 (33).
8. Obviously, the great childhood tales of privation from Charles Dickens and George Eliot codified brutalized youth and the lack of family fortune in nineteenth-century Britain, whereas Horatio Alger's stories redirected the terrors of the orphan boy in the city into stories of upward mobility for Americans; but the many childhood narrators during the Depression suggests a modernist retelling. These novels are to be distinguished from the many children's books written by left-wing authors during, but mostly after, the Depression in response to both post–World War II anxieties about raising fascist youth and cold war blacklists of one-time communist authors who moved into the underscrutinized area of children's books, according to Mickenberg.
9. This book has received scant critical attention despite its popularity during the 1930s. For details on the actual descent into madness of its diminutive author, Harriet Woodbridge Gilfillan, see the remarkable detective work of Wald (*Trinity*, ch. 5, "Disappearing Acts"). For more on the place of this novel within 1930s literary radicalism, see Rabinowitz (*Labor*, ch. 4, "Grotesque Creatures").
10. The connection between children and littleness is cemented in Johann Paul Wich, "Hobbyhorse and Doll," (1843):
    Before the little town there sits a little dwarf,
    Behind the little dwarf there stands a little hill
    From the little hill there flows a little hill
    Upon the little stream there swims a little roof,
    Beneath the little roof there is a little room,
    In the little room there sits a little boy,
    Behind the little boy there stands a little bench,
    Upon the little bench there stands a little chest,
    In the little chest there lies a little box,
    In the little box there sits a little nest,
    Before the little nest there sits a little cat,
    For certain I'll remember to note the little spot (qtd. in Benjamin 252).
11. For an evocative analysis of the spaces of dumps and detritus within Depression-era poetry, see Lowney, ch. 1, "The Janitor's Poems of Everyday: American Poetry and the 1930s."
12. Scott argues the "high modernist ideology" of the state dovetails with large-scale construction projects that both remake the landscape and the people living upon it, so that both land and people become at once mapped nation and numbered citizenry. "High Modernism was about 'interests' as well as faith [in scientific and technical progress]. Its carriers, even when they were capitalist entrepreneurs, required state action to realize their plans. In most cases they were powerful officials and heads of state. They tended

to prefer certain forms of planning and social organization (such as *huge dams, centralized communication and transportation hubs, large factories and farms, and grid cities*), because these forms fit snugly into a high-modernist view and also answered their political interests as state officials" (4–5 [emphasis added]).
13. For insights into the remappings of America's Main Streets over time and across space, especially how the automobile ushered in neon and streamlining despite the Depression, see Francaviglia, *Main*.
14. Speaking of nineteenth-century London, Steedman notes: "'Street children', in all their contemporary divisions and subdivisions, were deeply unattractive, very poor, children, who were consistently represented as such. The greater burden of distaste fell on the girls, to be sure, probably because they wore the length of 'foul matted hair, which looks as if it would defy sponge, comb or brush to purify it. Though the broken and filthy boots and stockings which they seem never to button or garter' belonged to both sexes" (*Strange* 115). Steedman's title shows how important it is to think about location and childhood together. A more contemporary view of girls as trash can be found in Damon. Thanks to Pat Crain for reminding me of Steedman's book.
15. As I was completing this essay, major mining disasters killing dozens of workers in China (Wangjialing) and the United States (Upper Big Branch) dominated headlines. As I was editing it, the ongoing BP Deepwater Horizon oil rig spill in the Gulf of Mexico, the result of an explosion killing eleven rig workers, continued unabated.
16. Agee quotes from *Around the World With the Children* by F.B . Carpenter (published by The American Book Company): "*1. The Great Ball on Which We Live. . . . 2. Food, Shelter, and Clothing. . . .* Let us imagine that we are far out in the fields. The air is bitter cold and the wind is blowing. Snow is falling, and by and by it will turn into sleet and rain. We are almost naked. We have had nothing to eat and are suffering from hunger as well as cold. Suddenly the Queen of the Fairies floats down and offers us three wishes . . ." (xviii). In *Geography III*, Bishop begins with quotations from *First Lessons in Geography: Monteith's Geographical Series, A.S, Barnes & Co., 1884.* "Lesson VI . . . *What is the shape of the Earth?/* Round, like a ball" (157).
  On the impoverishment of school texts, see Benjamin, Steedman, and the magisterial study of American primers by Crain.

BIBLIOGRAPHY

Agee, James, and Walker Evans. *Let Us Now Praise Famous Men*. 1941. New York: Ballantine, 1966. Print.
Althusser, Louis. "Ideology and Ideological State Apparatuses (Notes towards an Investigation) (January-April 1969)." Trans. Ben Brewster. *Lenin and Philosophy, and Other Essays*. New York: Monthly Review: 1971, pp. 127–86. Print.
Becher, Bernd and Hilla. *Industrial Facades*. Cambridge, Ma.: MIT Press, 1995.
Benjamin, Walter. "Children's Literature." In *Selected Writings: Volume 2, 1927–1934*. Ed. Michael W. Jennings, Howard Eiland, and Gary Smith. Trans. Rodney Livingstone and others. Cambridge, Ma.: Belknap P, 1999. 50–256. Print.
Baird, Irene. *Waste Heritage*. Toronto: Macmillan, 1939. Print.
Bird, Caroline. *The Invisible Scar*. New York: McKay, 1966. Print.
Bishop, Elizabeth. *The Complete Poems: 1927–1979*. New York: Farrar, Strauss and Giroux, 1983. Print.

Caldwell, Erskine and Margaret Bourke-White. *You Have Seen Their Faces*. New York: Viking, 1937. Print.
Crain, Patricia. *The Story of A: The Alphabetization of America from* The New England Primer *to* The Scarlett Letter. Stanford: Stanford UP, 2000. Print.
Damon, Maria. "Tell Them about Us." *Cultural Critique* 14 (1989–90): 231–57. Print.
Denning, Michael. *The Cultural Front: The Laboring of American Culture in the Twentieth Century*. London: Verso, 1996. Print.
Diamond, Jared. *Collapse: How Societies Choose to Fail or Succeed*. New York: Penguin, 2006. Print.
Dickstein, Morris. *Dancing in the Dark: A Cultural History of the Great Depression*. New York: Norton, 2009. Print.
Di Donato, Pietro. *Christ in Concrete*. 1939. New York: New American Library, 2004. Print.
Dos Passos, John. *The Big Money*. 1936. *U.S.A.* New York: Signet/New American Library, 1969. Print.
Edmunds, Susan. *Grotesque Relations: Modernist Domestic Fiction and the U.S. Welfare State*. New York: Oxford UP, 2008. Print.
Francaviglia, Richard V. *Hard Places: Reading the Landscape of America's Historic Mining Districts*. Iowa City: U Iowa P, 1991. Print.
———. *Main Street Revisited: Time, Space, and Image Building in Small-Town America*. Iowa City: U Iowa P, 1996. Print.
Fearing, Kenneh. *Dead Reckoning. Collected Poems of Kenneth Fearing*. 1940. New York: AMS Press, 1977: 73–114. Print.
———. "Memo," *Collected Poerms of Kenneth Fearing*. 1940. New York: AMS Press, 1977: 77. Print.
Gilfillan, Lauren. *I Went to Pit College*. New York: Literary Guild, 1934. Print.
Gold, Michael. *Jews without Money*. 1930. New York: Carroll and Graf, 1996. Print.
Heard, Sandra R. "The 'Bad' Black Consumer." PhD diss. George Washington U, 2010. Print.
Hurston, Zora Neale. *Their Eyes Were Watching God*. 1937. Champaign: University of Illinois Press, 1978. Print.
Irr, Caren. *The Suburb of Dissent: Cultural Politics in the United States and Canada during the 1930s*. Durham: Duke UP, 1998. Print.
Johnson, Josephine. *Jordanstown*. New York: Simon and Schuster, 1937. Print.
Kim, Walter. *Up in the Air*. New York: Doubleday, 2001. Print.
Kunzel, Regina. "Pulp Fictions and Problem Girls: Reading and Rewriting Single Pregnancy in the Postwar United States." *American Historical Review* 100 (Dec. 1995): 1465–87. Print.
Lange, Dorothea and Paul Shuster Taylor. *An American Exodus: A Record of Human Erosion*. New York: Reynal and Hitchcock, 1939. Print.
Levin, Meyer. *Citizens*. New York: Viking, 1940. Print.
Le Sueur, Meridel. *The Girl*. Albuquerque: West End, 1978. Print.
Low, Ann Marie. *Dust Bowl Diary*. Lincoln: U of Nebraska P, 1984. Print.
Lowney, John. *History, Memory, and the Literary Left: Modern American Poetry, 1935–1968*. Iowa City: U Iowa P, 2006. Print.
McElvaine, Robert S., ed. *Down and Out in the Great Depression: Letters from the Forgotten Man*. Chapel Hill: U of North Carolina P, 1983. Print.
McKinney, Ruth. *Industrial Valley*. New York: Harcourt, Brace and Co.: 1939. Print.
Mickenberg, Julia. *Learning from the Left: Children's Literature, the Cold War, and Radical Politics in the United States*. New York: Oxford UP, 2006. Print.
Mickenberg, Julia, and Philip Nel, eds. *Tales for Little Rebels: A Collection of Radical Children's Literature*. New York: New York UP, 2008. Print.

Nowak, Mark. *Coal Mountain Elementary*. Minneapolis: Coffee House, 2009. Print.

———. "Public Poetics in the Era of Accumulation by Dispossession." U of Minnesota, Minneapolis. 28 Sept. 2006. Speech.

———. *Shut Up Shut Down*. Minneapolis: Coffee House, 2004. Print.

Olsen, Tillie. *Yonnondio: From the Thirties*. New York: Delacorte, 1974. Print.

Orvell, Miles. *The Real Thing: Imitation and Authenticity in American Culture, 1880–1940*. Chapel Hill: U of North Carolina P, 1989. Print.

Oxford English Dictionary Online www.oed.com. Web.

Rabinowitz, Paula. *Labor and Desire: Women's Revolutionary Fiction in Depression America*. Chapel Hill: U of North Carolina P, 1991. Print.

Rich, Frank. "Hollywood's Brilliant Coda to America's Dark Year." *New York Times* 13 Dec. 2009: WK 9. Print.

Roth, Henry. *Call It Sleep*. 1934. New York: Avon, 1964. Print.

Rukeyser, Muriel. "The Book of the Dead." *U.S. 1*. New York: Cocivi, Friede, 1938. Print.

Scandura, Jani. *Down in the Dumps: Place, Modernity, American Depression*. Durham: Duke UP, 2008. Print.

Scott, James. *Seeing Like a State: How Certain Schemes to Improve the Human Condition Have Failed*. New Haven: Yale UP, 1998. Print.

Smith, Betty. *A Tree Grows in Brooklyn*. New York: Harper & Brothers, 1943. Print.

Steedman, Carolyn. *Childhood, Culture and Class in Britain: Margaret McMillan, 1860–1931*. New Brunswick: Rutgers UP, 1990. Print.

———. *Strange Dislocations: Childhood and the Idea of Human Interiority*. Cambridge: Harvard UP, 1995. Print.

———. *The Tidy House*. New York: Random House, 1987. Print.

Stewart, Kathleen. *A Space on the Side of the Road: Cultural Poetics in an "Other" America*. Princeton: Princeton UP, 1996. Print.

Swenson, Kristin A. "Productive Bodies: Women, Work, and Depression." *Governing the Female Body: Gender, Health, and Networks of Power*. Ed. Lori Reed and Paula Saukko. Albany: SUNY P, 2010. 134–55. Print.

van Gogh, Vincent. "Letter to Anthon Van Rappard." The Hague, on or about 20 Jan. 1883. 2009. Vincent van Gogh, the Letters: Van Gogh Museum, Amsterdam. Accessed 24 Dec. 2009. Web.

———. "Letter to Theo van Gogh." 8 or 9 Jan. 1882. 2009. Vincent van Gogh, the Letters: Van Gogh Museum, Amsterdam. Accessed 20 Apr. 2010. Web.

Wald, Alan M. *Exiles from a Future Time: The Forging of the Mid-Twentieth-Century Literary Left*. Chapel Hill: U of North Carolina P, 2002. Print.

———. *Trinity of Passion: The Literary Left and the Antifascist Crusade*. Chapel Hill: U of North Carolina P, 2007. Print.

Whibley, Charles. "Edgar Allan Poe." *Studies in Frankness*. London: William Heinemann, 1898, 161–185. Print.

Wright, Richard and Edwin Rosskam. *12 Million Black Voices*. New York: Viking, 1941. Print.

Yezierska, Anzia. *The Bread Givers*. 1925. New York: Persea Books, 1999. Print.

2 Work is a War, or All Their Lives They Dug Their Graves

Renny Christopher

> Army vets would fit right in. They knew the slang,
> the smoldered deference to authority,
> the snicker and snort as the foreman left
> the room. They knew it was war.
>
> Peter Blair, "Furnace Greens," *Last Heat*

Working-class writing contains incidents of death and mutilation through industrial accidents, agricultural processing plant accidents, and long-term exposure to debilitating conditions. This level of violence makes working-class literature in some respects similar to the genre of the war novel, yet the toll of working-class labor and the challenge of representing that toll in literary terms have never been adequately addressed in criticism. The United States has the highest rate of industrial deaths in the developed world, thirty-six times higher than Sweden's and nine times higher than Great Britain (Chasin 106–7). During the World War II, more Americans died on the job than in battle ("Industry Deaths"). Both the reality of death and mutilation on the job and the attempts of working-class writers to portray these incidents need to be foregrounded.

Traumatic workplace accidents present a particular challenge to the writer: we don't see this level of violence and gore in any genre other than the war novel. As with all depictions of violence, the challenge to the writer is to depict horrific events and their physical consequences in such a way as to make an impact on a reader and yet not to create a sensationalized or pornographic portrait through the writing. Readers are aware of the toll of war in terms of deaths and injuries; the toll of working-class labor is not at the forefront of the national consciousness the way war is. However, it should be.

THE HIDDEN INJURIES OF WORK

Because there is not a public consciousness of the conditions of working-class labor that result in a high toll of injury and death, some background information is invaluable as a context for reading the literary works that depict these conditions.

The history of ruin wreaked upon workers runs across the twentieth century. "In the year 1904, 27,000 workers were killed on the job in manufacturing, transport, and agriculture" (Zinn 319); "in 1914, 35,000 workers were killed in industrial accidents and 700,000 injured" (320). To understand the scale of this, it's necessary to remember that in 1910 the total population of the United States was 92 million. The National Safety Council figures date from 1933, when 14,500 workers died, to 2007, when 5,657 workers died. The "death rate" is also listed, that is, the number of deaths per 100,000 workers. The worst year was 1937, with a death rate of 43 per 100,000; the best year was 2007, with a death rate of 3.8.[1] The most dramatic comparisons, though, come through worker casualties and war casualties during World War II and the war in Viet Nam.

According to a *New York Times* article of 1944, "[i]ndustrial casualties between Pearl Harbor and Jan. 1 of this year [1944] aggregated 37,600 killed, or 7,500 more than the military dead, and 210,000 permanently disabled, and 4,500,000 temporarily disabled, or sixty times the number of military wounded and missing" ("Industry Deaths" A34). If we take the World War II period as a whole, about 262,000 Americans were killed in the war and 651,911 wounded, whereas about 62,000 were killed in industrial accidents during the whole war period ("Front Toll" A4, National Safety Council). But work injuries continued to exceed war injuries: in the year 1944, 2,230,400 workers were disabled. In 1945, 2 million workers were disabled ("Fewer Workers Injured" A33), 84,500 of them permanently, including 1,800 "so seriously hurt as to be unfit for any future employment in industry" ("2,000,000 Disabled in 1945" A25). Thus the total of disabling work injuries for the war period totaled 8,730,400, whereas the total wounded, missing, and killed in the war was 1,070,524.

Some of those wartime injuries resulted from the conflicts over speed-up and safety generated by the wartime demand for more and more production. A Chrysler worker, Edward Osbert, remembers:

> We were making airplane engines.... They had to go, go go. Whenever engineers and general superintendents devised a new process to make something faster or better, they went ahead and did it. They didn't care if it killed someone or if the fumes and dust were dangerous.... One of the worst accidents I remember involved one of our maintenance men. He was oiling the gears of the hundred-ton sand mixer in the aluminum foundry, and he got his fingers in too far. Little by little the machine pulled in his fingers and hand until finally his arm was jerked off at the shoulder girdle. (American Social History Project 460–61)

This description is certainly as gruesome as descriptions of traumatic amputations suffered in warfare.

Astonishing as the comparison of work injuries and war casualties figures for World War II is, even more astonishing, perhaps, are the figures for the period of the U.S. war in Viet Nam. The Vietnam Veterans Memorial lists the 58,220 names of Americans who died in that war during the period between July 1959 and April 1975. The national safety council records the deaths of 210,900 workers in "unintentional work-injury deaths" for that same period (National Safety Council 45).[2] The nation has mourned long and hard for those 58,000 dead in Viet Nam[3] while not knowing about, acknowledging, or publicly mourning the 210,000 dead on the battlefield of the job.

As Barbara Chasin points out in *Inequality and Violence in the United States*, harm to workers "results from decisions made by corporate executives, not because they are malicious, but because they are doing their jobs and looking after their own interests" (104). She notes that it is in the economic interest of employers to keep production costs low. She writes:

> The weaker workers are in relation to their employer and the more probusiness government is, the more dangerous workplaces are likely to be. It should not be surprising then that, according to the National Safety Workplace Institute, the United States holds the developed world's worst job safety record. United States workers are thirty-six times more likely to be killed on the job than workers in Sweden and nine times more likely to be killed than British laborers. (106–07).

Workers die not just in dramatic accidents, but also from occupationally induced illnesses. However, it is difficult to get statistics on these deaths because the United States is the only industrial country that doesn't have a national system for reporting occupational illness (Chasin 107). Estimates of how many workers die every year from occupational illnesses vary from 50,000 to 100,000.[4] When these figures are added to the numbers killed on the job, the death toll of work rises spectacularly. As Chasin notes, even using the most conservative estimates, in 1992, indirectly and directly, a minimum of 58,500 people died because of the work they had been doing. The number of people who were murdered that year is 24,500. Put another way, there were more than twice as many deaths among workers as a result of their employment than as a result of actions by those most likely to be called criminals (107).

Yet although there is a great public consciousness of violent crime and its consequences, there is very little public consciousness of the toll that work takes.[5]

LANGUAGE AND THE REPRESENTATION OF WORKPLACE CASUALTIES

How have class-conscious working-class writers written these realities into literature? Paul Fussell writes, in *The Great War and Modern Memory*:

> One of the cruxes of the war, of course, is the collision between events and the language available—or thought appropriate—to describe them. To put it more accurately, the collision was one between events and the public language used for over a century to celebrate the idea of progress. Logically there is no reason why the English language could not perfectly well render the actuality of trench warfare: it is rich in terms like *blood, terror, agony, madness, shit, cruelty, murder, sell-out, pain* and *hoax*, as well as phrases like *legs blown off, intestines gushing out over his hands, screaming all night, bleeding to death from the rectum*, and the like. Logically, one supposes, there's no reason why a language devised by man [sic] should be inadequate to describe any of man's [sic] works. The difficulty was in admitting that the war had been made by men and was being continued *ad infinitum* by them. (169–70)

Fussell's discussion fits working-class literature representing workplace casualties as well as it fits the literature of the World War I. In the United States, not only the language of progress, but also the language/ideology of the American Dream, of "hard work will pay off," makes the description of the deadly realities of labor unspeakable.

One of the strategies working-class writers have taken to confront this ideological silencing is the direct approach, in which work injuries are described in brutal detail. The master of this strategy is Pietro di Donato, whose *Christ in Concrete* contains one of the most harrowing scenes of death by industrial accident in literature. The mason Geremio falls and is impaled on reinforcing rods, then wet concrete pours over him. He tries to cry out to be saved:

> He paused exhausted. His genitals convulsed. The cold steel rod upon which they were impaled froze his spine. He shouted louder and louder. 'Save me! I am hurt badly! I can be saved I can—save me before it's too late!' But the cries went no farther than his own ears. The icy wet concrete reached his chin. . . . Savagely he bit into the wooden form pressed upon his mouth. An eighth of an inch of its surface splintered off. Oh, if he could only hold out long enough to bite even the smallest hole through to air!. . . . He had bitten halfway through when his teeth snapped off to the gums in the uneven conflict. The pressure of the concrete was such, and its effectiveness so thorough that the wooden splinters, stumps of teeth, and blood never left the choking mouth. (17)

As with steelworkers who fall into vats of molten steel, Geremio becomes incorporated into the material of his work. Nicholas Coles notes the symbolism of Geremio being skewered through the groin by the steel bar, and points out that Geremio's death shows that "whatever his ideal vision of himself, in the face of his work a man is finally a matter of so much blood, muscle and bone" (25).

Working-class novels that represent industrial accidents, like war novels, are faced with a dilemma of representation: how to record scenes of such horror that there is no ordinary vocabulary with which to deal with them? Coles rightly notes that Di Donato himself introduces the comparison of work to warfare: "[I]n one strand of the novel's imagery, Job is a form of warfare: 'It was war for living, and Paul was a soldier . . . . it was man's siege against a hunger that traveled swiftly, against an enemy inherited'" (109) (26).

When Geremio's son Paul takes over the support of his family, the work provides him with a source of pride, but it also takes a terrible toll on his young body. "The thin fingers of Paul's left hand were abrased right through the skin and pinpoints of raw flesh and blood showed, his thumb nail was swollen dark red and black, his right hand was angry-sore with mortar and his wrist inflamed" (Di Donato 79). Nazone, his patron, shows him how to pee on his hands so that his hands will toughen to the work. The work thus mutilates Paul even as he grows more capable of doing it.

Di Donato shows how men's work is simultaneously a celebration of strength and a subsuming of humanity into machinery: Paul "sweated, and human water commingled with lime-mortar and brick. This is the fresh stink of Job, this is the eight-houred daily duel, this is the sense of red and gray, and our bodies are no longer meat and bone of our parents, but substance of Job" (142). Thus are the workers transformed from human beings into tools, machines working in service of Job and subject to its whims and power. So even while they take pride in their skill, their skill is the efficiency of machines and their humanity is leached away.

Through his experiences Paul comes to understand the life of labor: work to live, yet in that work, every day to risk death because of the exploitation of the capitalist system. Paul understands the workers to be very much like soldiers at war, at constant risk of violent death on the job:

> The scaffolds are not safe, for the rich must ever profit more.
> The men are driven. And they prefer death or injury to loss of work. Work and die. Today I did not die. I have been let to live today and must be thankful that tomorrow I may return to work—to die. (228)

Napolitano writes that what "shocks in di Donato's work is the horrible detailed images of the suffering victim. What is even more shocking in *Christ in Concrete* is that the cause of the victim's demise is not a demented individual but so-called normal individuals whose greed society sanctions—those who make up the corporation" (81–82). As Fussell points out, the grotesqueries of war injuries are "unspeakable" not because the words don't exist to describe the horrors, but because to describe them is to admit that war is created by humankind and perpetuated by humankind; just so, Di Donato, by speaking the unspeakable, describes the violence done to workers through a capitalist system that puts profit ahead of humanity.

THE STEEL MILL AS MEAT GRINDER

The steel industry is one that has invited literary depictions of industrial accidents. Steel mill accidents, like battlefield casualties, have been depicted as particularly gruesome and devastating to the human body. Will Watson's "Disabled List" chronicles the paradoxical pride, the insouciance, with which a group of steelworkers carry the marks of their injuries. Each of its four stanzas details an accident experienced by a coworker of the poem's speaker. "Ever the smart ass, Red Husiar sports / a polaroid of his stump squirting blood." His coworkers "rigged a tourniquet / from a crescent wrench and some rags / and tried not to act as sick as we felt." Equipped with a hook where his arm used to be, Red still works at the same job and jokes about how the accident "played hell with my piano lessons."

Terry D. cuts the tendons of his fingers with a buck knife and ends up with a hand that looks "like a claw" as a result of his accident: "they took our knives away / the only tools we owned ourselves." In the next stanza, "Henry Ciezahn found five tons / would drive a steel toe boot / clean through his foot / and weld the whole mess to the floor / licketysplit." All of the accidents are described in a language of detached observation, and this one is described almost as if Henry Ciezahn had been performing a laboratory experiment on himself. But the speaker directly challenges the reader at the end of the third stanza, after describing how another worker made fun of Henry Ciezahn's limp: "the crew figured even a mean joke / was better than acting like nothing / had happened. What do you think?" The speaker and his coworkers are displaying a symptom of post-traumatic stress disorder: emotional numbing or distancing, and their laughter in the face of grave injury is reminiscent of war novels in which soldiers take a callous, detached, and sardonic attitude toward dismemberment and death as a survival tactic.

The speaker concludes with the most spectacular accident, one that he does not describe at length, leaving it to the reader to fill in the gruesome details.

> Worst I ever saw though
> was Hi Highlands cut in two
> by a seven-foot twenty-ton batch anneal
> just hot enough to cauterize
> everything it didn't squash
> so he didn't bleed to death.

The cause of the accident is described with precision—the size and weight of the batch anneal that injured Hi Highlands—but the nature of Hi Highlands's injury is almost mythical in proportion: how can someone survive being cut in two? Is the speaker exaggerating? Is Hi Highlands left with one arm, one leg, one side of his face? We're left uneasily trying to picture the extent of this legendary injury, while the speaker tells us that his survival of it, his refusal to die, his insistence on continuing to work "like the rest of us," gives him "real class." It is not the mill owners or managers who have "real class," it is Hi Highlands, half a man, and more man than anyone.

In another of Watson's poems, "Wire, Wireman, Stripper, Splice," an old man, Nick, a maker of hook-blade wiring knives that the steelworkers carry as status symbols, tells a story of Little Mike:

> "well, the day he fell all on fire
> into the submarine car was first time
> we tapped old #7 and we didn't even try
> to find the body. Why? Cause it just didn't exist
> no more and that fucking heat, the very first?
> Well, it ended up in the Empire State Building
> Little Mike and all may he rest in peace."

Little Mike becomes part of the steel, absorbed into it, becoming part of an iconic building of the nation, thus metaphorically showing that the workers' bodies are just part of the building materials,[6] similar to the way Geremio is buried in and incorporated into the concrete of the building he is working on. Joe E. Gutierrez's story "Missing at Work," from *The Heat: Steelworker Lives and Legends* also paints a portrait of someone who falls into the steel:

> Two feet from the edge of the fire, he felt the wheel slip off the board. He pushed the handles to the right, but to no avail. And just like in his dream, as if in slow motion, he began to fall. Stubbornly, he refused to let go of the wheelbarrow. He had worked too hard, and after all, it was a matter of pride. There was no time to scream as he fell into the molten steel. Jose could see his wife and children as he followed his nemesis into the fire. He suddenly released his hold, but it was too late—his hands pushed into and parted the flaming liquid, making way for the rest of his body. The molten steel closed quietly over Jose Rubio, leaving only the stench of his burned flesh, which immediately mingled with the captured breath of this wretched building. Jose Rubio became one with it all, and to look for a trace of him on the molten surface would have been futile. (Institute for Career Development 153)

In this version of the motif of incorporation, the body of the worker becomes one not only with the building material, the steel, but with the steel mill itself. Like a soldier who takes a direct hit from high explosive, these steelworkers are utterly obliterated.

The Heat: Steelworker Lives and Legends is a collection of writings by steelworkers that came out of a workshop led by Jimmy Santiago Baca. In his introduction to the volume, he writes that the purpose of the book is "so the public could read [the stories and poems] and know their fellow Americans, the men and women who supplied the steel to build American cities" (Institute for Career Development 13). The writing exemplifies a working-class aesthetic: it is simple and straightforward and makes use of blunt, graphic language aimed at the heart of the reader. Jerry Ernest's "Scottie" is a memoir of a friend he had worked with and who had an accident working an overtime shift that Ernest himself had turned down.

> Scott knew the dangers. Taking the lead, he walked over the tank and started stripping off the top boards when one of them snapped. Scott fell backwards, disappearing into the hole. The tank had been cooling down. It was 160 degrees and only knee-deep. His fellow crew members rushed to him and held out their arms to pull him out.
> His head was down and when he looked up he had tears in his eyes and said, 'I'm a dead man. I swallowed this shit'. . . .
> They finally pulled him out and stripped his clothes off. Someone called for help while others started hosing him down with water. His skin fell off like jelly. . . .
> They kept Scott doped up and comfortable. He died two days later. (Institute for Career Development 61–62)

Ernest narrates the story in a straightforward, calm manner that contains the (irrational) guilt he feels because, first, it was his initiative that got them both the jobs on which Scott died, and second, because he had turned down the extra shift that Scott took. The details of the story—Scott's skin sloughing off, the leather of his boots turning white overnight—paint a clear enough picture for any reader to understand the horror of this particular danger of steel mills.

Jeanne Bryner's poem "Our Fathers," from her collection *Blind Horse*, emphasizes the legendary and yet everyday nature of a mill death similar to the one described by Jerry Ernest in "Scottie."

> The day Joe Brodie fell into the acid pit
> they say he screamed bigger than Texas
> When they pulled him out, his legs slid
> off his waist like melted red candles (69).

The horror of this image takes Joe Brodie's accident into the realm of legend, but the everydayness of this horror is underlined in the remainder of the poem:

> Joe Brodie died on the way to the hospital.
> Our fathers finished their shift.
> That night, my Dad and his best friend, Ted,

went to Tony's Bar and got slop-the-hogs-
falling-down drunk (69).

In their drunkenness, the two men talk about their youth, working on farms. The nostalgia of that memory serves as a balance to the current reality of the mill where they work, but those memories, too, are of labor—of tossing hay bales. Above all, they are workers: "And our fathers never missed a shift" (69). They go on in the face of the prejudice from the people in the mill town directed against them because they are "hicks," in the face of the acid pit, and for this the poem lifts them to legendary status as "Our Fathers," an almost biblical naming.

Peter Blair's award-winning poetry collection *Last Heat* chronicles the mills and the deindustrialization that has consigned them to rust. These poems emphasize the paradoxical nature of the mills: they had both the power to kill and to provide a way of life and pride in one's work, and now they themselves are dead. In "Number 6 and 7 Furnaces," he chronicles the murderousness of the now-dead mills in a flat, reportorial tone:

> One night when these furnaces still burned
> two men lay on the tracks,
> heads against the rail under a coal car.
> They were fixing the brakes,
> and forgot to clamp the red metal warning flags
> to the rails. A diesel engine heading
> through darkness didn't stop.
> When it hit the coal car,
> the wheels rolled over their necks,
> clean and vicious as a guillotine's blade. (10)

The poem goes on to describe the decay and destruction of the shut-down mills, then concludes,

> Maybe they'll make a museum here.
> We can approach the furnaces
> from the river. We can touch
> their cold iron skin.
> We can leave flowers. (11)

The mill is turned, at poem's end, into a cemetery more than a museum, where flowers might be left for the dead workers and the dead mill itself. This trope is reminiscent of Pete Seeger's "Where Have All the Flowers Gone," in which battlefields turn to graveyards—and then to battlefields again.

Blair also blurs the distinction between men and machines with the line "their cold iron skin." This same transmuting of animate and inanimate takes place in "Furnace Greens":

> I learned the pick and shovel, the sledge,
> the post-hole digger, and the jack hammer.
> I kept company with cranes,
> backhoes, sheers, presses, and vats of acid.
> My hands became steel hooks; my arms,
> #10 cables; my joints, chain links.
> My eyes turned into glass, plastic,
> and wire mesh. I saw a man lose fingers
> when a lift-chain crushed them against steel plates.
> I saw a hot strip of sheet metal jump the rolls
> and sidewind across the floor
> like a red snake. I saw the full moon rippled
> into rags of light above a furnace stack. (12–13)

While man becomes machine, the machine becomes animate, but what the watcher's "glass, plastic, and wire mesh" eyes witness reminds us that it is still flesh that is vulnerable, that the distinction between men and machines is that it is the men who bleed.

Jim Daniels's "Small Catch" from his collection *Punching Out* similarly takes subjectivity away from humans and animates machinery. A man, never referred to by name, is the victim of an accident in which he loses a finger, but the man is not the subject of the poem: he is devoid of subjectivity in the mechanized environment. Daniels's poems are set in an auto factory, not a steel mill, but the collection has a focus on industrial accidents and injuries markedly similar to the works set in steel mills. Daniels also makes an explicit connection to war literature in that the first section of the book is called "Basic Training."

Returning to Fussell's point that to speak the unspeakable is to acknowledge that it is people who make and perpetuate war, and people who make and feed the industrial machine, that insight is underlined by Jeanne Bryner's "Another Abraham: for my Father-in-Law, John, Who Worked in the Mill," in which the father sacrifices his sons:

> Oh breath, oh labor of the father and the sons.
> Did you stand there fearing the knife in your pocket
> and the table which consecrates bread and wine?
> Even then did you believe what your life's angel
> whispered? You'd take these boys, your fine sons
> to learn the mill's language of *graveyard* and *slitter*. (87)

In this version, no Jehovah stops Abraham from the sacrifice, and the pagan god to which this "Abraham" sacrifices these sons is the Mill itself. This poem is reminiscent of Wilfred Owen's war poem, "The Parable of the Old Man and the Young," in which Abram builds "parapets and trenches" in preparation for the sacrifice, and when an angel calls to him to "Offer the

Ram of Pride instead," Owen's Abram, like Bryner's Abraham, does not follow Genesis. "But the old man would not so, but slew his son, / And half the seed of Europe, one by one" (Owen 151). For Owen, the war is a mass-sacrifice of the young. For Bryner, the mill is the same. Peter Blair, too, uses this formulation in "Furnace Greens":

> Army vets would fit right in. They knew the slang,
> the smoldered deference to authority,
> the snicker and snort as the foreman left
> the room. They knew it was war. (13)

Work is a war when it ends in the deaths of workers; the steel mill is clearly a battlefield. But steel mills are not the only battlefields.

KILLING FIELDS

It is not only industrial work that destroys laborers, but agricultural work as well, and agricultural work is one that employs many minority workers.[7] According to a recent study by the Bureau of Labor Statistics, the "rate of on-the-job deaths for all Hispanics has been 20 percent higher than for whites or blacks" (Greenhouse A11). The two main occupational areas in which Hispanic workers have died, according to the study, are construction and agriculture: "Hispanic construction workers have died when they have slipped off wet roofs and when the trenches they have been digging have collapsed and buried them. These reports also detail numerous incidents in which migrant farm workers died when crowded vans crashed while their foremen were driving them to the fields" (Greenhouse A11). Further, in a time when rates of workplace accidents have generally been declining, the rates for Hispanics grew by 68 percent between 1999 and 2001. In 1999, Hispanic workers had a fatality rate of 5.2 per 100,000 compared to 4.4 for white workers and 4.1 for black workers. The study suggests a number of reasons for this, including lack of safety instructions supplied in Spanish and lack of proper training in safety procedures, and cites one startling statistic: "12 percent of serious injuries occurred during a worker's first day at a job site" (Greenhouse A11). This is reminiscent of a number of Viet Nam war novels and memoirs that indicate "new guys" were more likely to die on their first few days in the war.

In Milton Murayama's *All I Asking for Is My Body*, the sugarcane plantation workers struggle for survival in brutal working conditions and with low wages. The ethnic hierarchy is used against the workers. When eleven hundred Filipino workers strike, Nisei seventh and eighth graders are recruited to do some of the work the Filipinos had been doing. So all the workers continue in appalling conditions for terrible wages. The narrator's family, the Oyamas, struggle under a $6,000 debt incurred during the depression when the father of the family was trying to be a fisherman. As he says, "fishing is gambling. You could put in twelve hours a day and lose money" (89). The father gives up on fishing, and moves the family back to the plantation, where the nature of the work is brutal:

> The dust hangs in reddish clouds all around us. We are drenched, our denim pants cling to our wet legs, sweat trickles down faces and necks and moistens palms and backs of hands. We wipe continually, hands on pants, shirt sleeves over eyebrows, blue handkerchief around neck. You wear a brown straw hat against the sun, you hold your breath and try to breathe the less dusty air in gasps, you tie the bottom of your pants legs to keep the dust and centipedes out, you stop and clean your nostrils of chocolate dust with the blue handkerchief wet from wiping your neck. Life is fifteen minutes for breakfast, thirty minutes for lunch, *pau hana* at 2:30. (39)

The last sentence of this passage makes clear that work itself is not "life," but a kind of living death.[8]

In Tomás Rivera's *Y no se lo tragó la tierra/And the Earth Did Not Devour Him*, migrant farm workers labor under excruciating conditions. In a section titled "The Children Couldn't Wait":

> It was so hot that the bucket of water the boss brought them was not enough. He would come only two times for the midday and sometimes they couldn't hold out. That was why they took to drinking water from a tank at the edge of the furrow. The boss had it there for cattle and when he caught them drinking water there he got angry. He didn't much like the idea of their losing time going to drink water because they weren't on contract, but by the hour. He told them that if he caught them there again he was going to fire them and not pay them. The children were the ones who couldn't wait. (86)

Although the reason given for the boss's anger is that they're "losing time" and they're getting paid by the hour, it's also clear that he has more regard for his cattle than his workers, echoing a common theme of working-class literature, that animals and machines are often treated better than people.

This boss also doesn't allow them to take their own water with them, so the children and adults suffer greatly in the heat. The children begin going down to the tank, pretending they're going to pee, in order to get a drink. The boss decides to give the kids a scare. He brings his rifle. "What he set out to do and what he did were two different things. He shot at him once to scare him but when he pulled the trigger he saw the boy with a hole in his head. And the child didn't even jump like a deer does. He just stayed in the water like a dirty rag and the water began to turn bloody[. . . .]" (87 [ellipses in original]). The metaphoric relationship between boss and worker is literalized when the boss kills the worker as a hunter kills a deer. Although a chorus of voices discusses the fact that the boss nearly went crazy afterwards and loses his fortune, noting that he may have tried to kill himself, one voice sardonically says, "But he didn't kill himself, did he?" (87). He has killed his workers, little by little, through the conditions under which he has employed them just as surely as he has killed the one boy outright.

Images of fire and burning permeate the text: children die in a house fire while their parents are out working, a spurned lover kills himself by throwing himself onto an electrical transformer, a truck carrying workers is hit by a car and burns. The boy who's the novel's unnamed protagonist first begins to lose his religious faith and turn toward anger when his father gets sunstroke. The boy and his siblings go on working; later, his mother asks him why they didn't come home right away when their father got sick. "I don't know," the boy replies:

> Us being so soaked with sweat, we didn't feel so hot, but I guess that when you're sunstruck it's different. But I did tell him to sit down under the tree that's at the edge of the rows, but he didn't want to. And that was when he started throwing up. Then we saw he couldn't hoe anymore and we dragged him and put him under a tree. (108)

The boy "became even angrier when he heard his father moan outside the chicken coop. He wouldn't stay inside because he said it made him feel very anxious. Outside where he could feel the fresh air was where he got some relief. And also when the cramps came he could roll over on the grass. Then he thought about whether his father might die from the sunstroke" (108). The rest of the family, however, has to keep working.

The boy takes his younger siblings back to the field the next day, and while they try to work, the conditions overwhelm them:

> During the morning, at least for the first few hours, they endured the heat but by ten-thirty the sun had suddenly cleared the skies and pressed down against the world. They began working more slowly because of the weakness, dizziness and suffocation they felt when they worked too fast. . . . At four o'clock the youngest became ill. He was only nine years old, but since he was paid the same as a grown up he tried to keep up with the rest. He began vomiting. He sat down, then he laid down. Terrified, the other children ran to where he lay and looked at him. It appeared that he had fainted and when they opened his eyelids they saw his eyes were rolled back. The next youngest child started crying but right away he told him to stop and help him carry his brother home. It seemed he was having cramps all over his little body. (111)

The father and the child both survive, but only to go on to a life of more of the same. The boy curses God, and when the earth does not swallow him, he ceases to believe or to be comforted by his mother's religious vision of a better life in the hereafter. In this, Rivera's protagonist is very similar to Paul in *Christ in Concrete*; for both, witnessing the toll that labor takes on workers arouses a new, politicized conscience.

Jeff Tagami, in "Now It Is Broccoli," writes of his mother working in a food processing plant. She literally and figuratively has pieces of herself cut off in her job:

> My mother who loses a piece
> of herself each day
> is bowing before the conveyor belt
> as a river of broccoli
> rolls by under the fluorescent. . . .
> She remembers, once, in another shed
> slicing off part of her index finger.
> It wasn't the pain
> or horror she remembered
> but how the day was hot. . . .
> It wasn't the kindness
> of the floor lady turning off the machine
> that she wanted to remember. . . .
> No, it was the face
> she longed for, that serene
> face she lost years ago. (17–18)

The worker here literally cuts off her finger, but the working conditions, that endless river of broccoli or cabbage or whatever the season brings, has caused her also to lose her face, to lose her self. The cut-off finger serves as a metonym for the whole life that she has lost in the packing sheds, the forty years she has "given up . . . . / to the passing of vegetables" (19).

> Now she keeps the finger in the freezer
> in an envelope with a plastic window.
> Because it is still a part of her
> she cannot let go. . . . (18)

The nail of that finger in the freezer "slowly turns black," metaphorizing the darkness and loss of this life of labor that not only dehumanizes through alienation of labor, but that can kill and maim (19).

These lines are reminiscent of lines from Jim Daniels's "Digger Gets a Checkup," from *Digger's Blues*:

> Your hand missing one finger,
> the day the press surprised you.
> You remember that finger,

how it used to point. How it knew
where to place the blame. (np)

Daniels displaces the political knowledge of "where to place the blame" from Digger himself, a very average, "ordinary joe," to the missing finger. The case with Digger is the same as with Tagami's mother: the toll of the numbing routine of the work itself, of marching along like a good soldier, as well as the danger of death and injury, have numbed and paralyzed them.

WHERE TO PLACE THE BLAME

In all the works examined here, the work ethic and the pride that workers try to take in their work keep them working in conditions that bring injuries, death, and psychological wounds to the survivors who witness these injuries and deaths. Just as our culture continues to see war as an opportunity for individual heroism and meaningful communal sacrifice even in the face of numerous narratives that show war to be a meaningless experience of suffering injuries both physical and psychological, so too does our culture continue to believe in the value of hard work. Even if working-class literary depictions of workplace suffering, injuries, and death were to reach a wider audience, the weight of the Protestant work ethic, as it is linked to the American Dream of economic prosperity and upward mobility, is so great that this literature will displace it no more than endless war novels and memoirs have changed our collective minds about warfare.

NOTES

1. The figures before 1992 are National Safety Council estimates; they define workers as "persons ages 16 and older gainfully employed"; from 1992 onward, figures come from the Bureau of Labor Statistics, Census of Fatal Occupational Injuries.
2. The deaths are listed year by year; I took half the totals for the years 1959 and 1975 because the VVM goes from July 1959 to April 1975.
3. While not caring at all, it seems, for the more than two million Vietnamese who died in that war.
4. An effective depiction of death by cancer caused by workplace exposure is in Ana Castillo's *So Far From God*, which I discuss in "A State of Courage and Wisdom."
5. We're concerned here with violence on the job done to workers, but Chasin also cites unemployment as a form of structural violence done to workers; she cites evidence that a 1.3 percent increase in unemployment correlates with an additional 21,000 deaths a year, a 1.8 percent increase in admissions to mental hospitals, and a 1.3 percent increase in the suicide rate (118).
6. In William Attaway's *Blood on the Forge*, one character's coworkers make watch fobs out of the batch of steel he has fallen into, and they wear the

watch fobs made out of the steel of which his body has become part as a memorial to him. See Coles, "Mantraps" 28 for a comment on this.
7. Barbara Chasin notes that agricultural work is "among the most dangerous in the United States. Thirty-eight percent of farm workers are Latino, although this group is only about 9 percent of the labor force. Agricultural workers are frequently exposed to high levels of pesticides which leads to severe nerve damage, cancer, sterility, birth defects. . . . Dangerous pesticides are used in the fields, and often there are no places for workers to wash. According to the . . . . EPA, there are three hundred thousand illnesses each year among farm workers from pesticides" (112–13). Directly relevant to Rivera's novel, which is set in the 1950s, is the fact that it was "not until 1987 that agricultural enterprises were required to provide toilets and fresh drinking water for agricultural workers, and the rules are frequently ignored" (113).
8. One of the reasons the family has moved back down into these conditions is that Mrs. Oyama has worked herself sick. There is another reason besides overwork that Mrs. Oyama is ill; she has borne seven children. Mrs. Oyama's burden is that of all working-class women of the early twentieth century: part of her role is to reproduce the workforce through childbearing, which is nonetheless not counted as work, is not paid labor; and yet it takes a physical toll on women who, like her, have many children, just as certainly as the other forms of work they and their working-class men do. This subject is also worth further study.

BIBLIOGRAPHY

"2,000,000 Disabled in 1945." *New York Times* 1 Feb 1946: A25. Web.
American Social History Project. *Who Built America?* New York: Pantheon, 1992. Print.
Attaway, William. *Blood on the Forge*. (1941) New York: Random House, 2005. Print.
Blair, Peter. *Last Heat*. Washington DC: Word Works, 1999. Print.
Bryner, Jeanne. *Blind Horse*. Huron: Bottom Dog, 1999. Print.
Bureau of Labor Statistics. *Census of Fatal Occupational Injuries*. 10 April 2010. Web. 13
May 2010.
Chasin, Barbara. *Inequality and Violence in the United States*. New Jersey: Humanities, 1997. Print.
Christopher, Renny. "'A State of Courage and Wisdom. . . . Not an Uncontrollable Participation in Society': Ana Castillo's Novel of Feminist and Working-Class Resistance." *A Class of Its Own: Re-Envisioning American Labor Fiction*. Ed. Laura Hapke and Lisa A. Kirby. Newcastle: Cambridge Scholars, 2008. Print.
Coles, Nicholas. "Mantraps: Men at Work in Pietro di Donato's *Christ in Concrete* and Thomas Bell's *Out of This Furnace*." MELUS 14.3–4 (1987). Print.
Daniels, Jim. *Digger's Blues*. Easthampton: Adastra, 2002. Print.
———. *Punching Out*. Detroit: Wayne State UP, 1990. Print.
Di Donato, Pietro. *Christ in Concrete*. c. 1937. New York: Signet, 1993. Print.
"Fewer Workers Injured." *New York Times*. 11 Feb. 1945: A33. Web.
"Front Toll 1,070,524." *New York Times*. 13 Oct. 1945: A4. Web.
Fussell, Paul. *The Great War and Modern Memory*. New York: Oxford UP, 1975. Print.

Greenhouse, Steven. "Hispanic Workers Die at Higher Rate." *New York Times* 16 July 2001: A11. Web. 13 May 2010.
"Industry Deaths Since Pearl Harbor 37, 600." *New York Times,* 21 Jan 1944: A34. Web.
Institute for Career Development. *The Heat: Steelworker Lives and Legends.* Mena: Cedar Hill, 2001. Print.
Murayama, Milton. *All I Asking for Is My Body.* Honolulu: U of Hawaii P, 1975. Print.
Napolitano, Louise. *An American Story: Pietro di Donato's* Christ in Concrete. New York: Peter Lang, 1995. Print.
National Safety Council. *Injury Facts 2000 Edition.* Itasca: National Safety Council, 2000. Print.
Owen, Wilfred. *The Poems of Wilfred Owen.* Ed. Jon Stallworthy. New York: Norton, 1986. Print.
Rivera, Tomás. *Y no se lo tragó la tierra/And the Earth Did Not Devour Him.* Trans. Evangelina Vigil-Piñón. Houston: Arte Publico, 1992. Print.
Tagami, Jeff. *October Light.* San Francisco: Kearny Street Workshop, 1987. Print.
Watson, Will. "Disabled List." *Working Hard for the Money.* Ed. Mary Weems and Larry Smith. Huron: Bottom Dog, 2002. 165–66. Print.
———. "Wire, Wireman, Stripper, Splice." Unpublished poems. c. 1999. Print.
Zinn, Howard. *A People's History of the United States.* New York: Harper and Row, 1980. Print.

3 Respectability, Refinement, and the Underclass
Uncle Tom's Cabin and *Incidents in the Life of a Slave Girl*

Sylvia J. Cook

Harriet Beecher Stowe and Harriet Jacobs produced their two great abolitionist works, *Uncle Tom's Cabin* (1852) and *Incidents in the Life of a Slave Girl* (1861), in the context of fervent national controversies about the relationship of chattel slavery to wage slavery, and the possible emergence of a new American working class. Stowe, as a novelist, and Jacobs, as a literary autobiographer, had no obligation to enter historical disputes about whether slaves were proletarians, or if free laborers were worse or better off than or properly analogous to laborers in bondage. Both, however, chose in their books to juxtapose and explore the situation of slaves and wage workers in the United States and internationally. At the same time a linked, but not exactly consonant, pattern of class development was occurring in American life, a pattern that established a code of putatively middle-class social and cultural values as desirable traits for respectable citizens of a democratic republic. This American "bourgeois revolution," and its preoccupation with comportment, sensibility, and fine furnishings, is also not self-evidently a concern for an abolitionist author.[1] Nonetheless Stowe and Jacobs made the potentially class-based association between civic worthiness and cultural refinement central to their stories of race relations. They scrutinized rituals of public display and private practice at all levels of American life and measured them against evolving national definitions of full human development. They also created multiple and unpredictable permutations of caste, character, and condition, transcending their own inherent didacticism through the imaginative scope of their narratives.

That the two authors elected to put the operations of class at the heart of their accounts of racial enslavement argues neither for the primacy of class over race nor for its subordination as a perspective for literary analysis. When Eric Schocket explored early American class narratives through the lens of race, he found that despite the power of slavery as a trope for critiquing injustice, "blackness" retained profoundly deterministic associations whereas "whiteness" suggested greater freedom of opportunity (xiii). By performing the obverse of this approach and examining the ways Stowe and Jacobs applied various paradigms of class to both enslaved and free people, I hope to show how they complicated and challenged such racial fatalism, rethinking the durability and the anticipated alliances of caste and color and reapportioning to the "lowly" many characteristics that were being appropriated by the elite.

I

The question of whether enslaved people in the United States might validly be considered members of the working class has troubled and divided labor historians. Against the obvious advantages of envisioning solidarity between a black proletariat and a white proletariat lie the undeniable problems of competing racial loyalties as well as the fundamental logical challenge of assuming an equivalency between free and slave labor. In the associated debate about whether Southern slaveholders were conventional capitalists or American exceptionalists, the authoritative voices of Karl Marx, W. E. B. Du Bois, and C. L. R. James are commonly invoked.[2] Their diverse conclusions led one historian to remark skeptically that "[t]he real world is infinitely more complex than can be presented in an analysis, no matter how fundamental" (Glaberman 214). Although the real world is also infinitely more complex than a work of fiction or a fictionalized memoir, these literary forms permit mediating narrators, an array of diverse characters, richly detailed settings, and dramatic incidents to shape compelling and often clashing responses without having to promulgate a triumphant explanatory theory. In *Uncle Tom's Cabin* and *Incidents in the Life of a Slave Girl*, Stowe and Jacobs both engage in comparisons and contrasts of the conditions of slaves and industrial wage workers, initially assuming opposite sides in the argument about the identification of people in bondage with proletarians. By the end of their respective books (which in no sense mark the culmination of their thinking on the subject), both have encompassed elements of the contrary position into their narratives and demonstrated the provocations as well as the intellectual pleasures of imposing paradigms of class on constructions of blackness and whiteness.

When the serial publication of *Uncle Tom's Cabin* began in *The National Era* in June 1851, the recent revolutions of 1848 in Europe were a more immediate warning of social upheaval than the future prospect of civil war in America. Consequently, Stowe's account of the "peculiar institution" in the United States is filled with allusions to insurrections of oppressed peoples in Europe and in slaveholding societies in other parts of the New World. Her alternate title, *Life Among the Lowly*, contains not only Christian but class-conscious implications, both of which are reiterated in the apocalyptic conclusion, when demands for "freedom and equality" are "surging and heaving the world, as with an earthquake," and every nation "that carries in its bosom great and unredressed injustice has in it the elements of this last convulsion" (629). As a general rule, however, almost all such class-based revolutionary analogies for slavery come not in this way, from the narrator, but from Stowe's incongruously "red republican" aristocrat, Augustine St. Clare (392). Thus they are presented with all the eloquence and duplicity of a tortured intellectual who brings the particular contingencies of his own personality and circumstance to his vivid analysis of dominant ideology.

It is St. Clare, whose "'forte lies in talking'" rather than doing, who makes the connections between the exploitive framework of European and American society; who describes as a universal phenomenon the "'lower class used up, body, soul and spirit, for the good of the upper'"; who endorses the view that "the American planter is 'only doing, in another form, what the English aristocracy and capitalists are doing'"; and who argues that the laborer in England "'is as much at the will of his employer as if he were sold to him'" (274, 319, 340). It is St. Clare who draws the parallel between the slave revolt in Santo Domingo and the French Revolution, who insists that inevitably "the masses are to rise, and the underclass become the upper one," who explains the brutal operation of base and superstructure in the universally exploited generic slave "Quashy," and who detects the more subtle currents of hegemony in his manservant Adolph's gentlemanly affectations of elegance (392, 331). Even in his final, futile determination to "do something for a whole class" by emancipating his own slaves, St. Clare mixes the lexicon of labor with that of black and white bondage, arguing that he will emulate the "Hungarian nobles [who] set free millions of serfs" (451–52). There is both grandeur and grandiosity in his comparisons because they envision and justify a cosmic radicalism while also vindicating his own procrastination in so cataclysmic a process. Whether his theories on the universality of class warfare are shared by Stowe is a question raised not merely by St. Clare's sardonic self-reflexivity but also by her fictional narrator's tendency at times to echo his rhetoric. At others, however, the narrator offers very different options for how freedom may be attained and equality practiced in the United States.

St. Clare's prophesy of "a mustering among the masses" that will occur in "Europe, in England, and in this country" is matched by the narrator's ultimate anticipation of the world's nations "trembling and convulsed" by the forces of justified retribution (344, 629). However, at exactly this point the narrator asks a not entirely rhetorical question that would be inconceivable from the gloomy pessimist, St. Clare: "is America safe?" (629). Are his ominous predictions a conviction that the future lies with a revolutionary international underclass, or a warning of America's last chance to preserve itself from destruction by the emancipation, education, and perhaps reexport of its slave population?[3] Although the advocacy of colonization as a first step toward a white republic has often been treated as Stowe's unhappy final choice over future domestic turmoil, she charted almost the opposite likelihood in her second abolitionist novel, *Dred: A Tale of the Great Dismal Swamp* (1856). In *Uncle Tom's Cabin*, too, she proffered many other possibilities for the future of free black labor. George Shelby expects that many of his freed slaves will remain on the plantation where they will work for wages "'such as we shall agree on,'" and he adds that he will expect them "'to be good, and willing to learn'" (616). Such paternalism (but not anticipated colonization) is also suggested by St. Clare's speculation that he might wish Adolph to train, after emancipation, as a "clerk" or "mechanic"—surely as unsuitable occupations for the "distingué" valet as for his lordly owner (452, 254). Stowe also provides quite different evidence of independent entrepreneurship among freedmen, listing anecdotes of former slaves who have succeeded not in the working class but as members of a property-holding bourgeoisie. Their "worth" is reckoned by longstanding membership in church and community, by the amount of land they own, and by the thousands of dollars in their bank accounts (627–28). Such stories are at odds not just with repatriation schemes but with St. Clare's assumption of the inevitably proletarian nature of a free black population, and with some of the utopian fantasies of collaboration between former American slaves and European radicals that *Uncle Tom's Cabin* famously spawned (see Fisch 108–09).

Stowe has frequently been blamed and credited for the imposition and dismantling of sets of binary oppositions—male/female, black/white, North/South, public/private (see Buell 193). In depicting the complex interplay of bond and free labor, she considers epistemologies of race and class that are not, however, directly oppositional and thus not easily resolvable into the satisfyingly simple paradoxes of her reputed typology—the tender man, the aristocratic slave, the atheist believer, or the murderous mother. Instead the paradigms overlap, often undermining any certainty of what kind of new social relations may lie beyond the admonitions and rallying calls of Stowe's immediate abolitionist goal. Although her slave characters are drawn with a confident hand, their liberated future in a new hierarchy makes them much more fluid and indefinable in terms of their rank and status. George Harris will spend five years in a mechanic's shop in Montreal followed by four years at a French university, from which he will be curiously driven by "political troubles in France" before moving to Liberia and to the establishment there of a "mighty republic" (608, 609). The timid and proper Emmeline will marry a sailor encountered on shipboard; the feisty Topsy will become first a dutiful New Englander and then a missionary schoolteacher (a somewhat grotesque outlook for the mischievous and creative child, though perhaps no more so than that of Dolph as a journeyman). Stowe's fertile imagination envisions many diverse futures, including colonization and amalgamation abroad and education, reparation, and upward mobility at home. These varied prospects, alongside St. Clare's apocalyptic forecasts of violence, are equally results of the dynamic synergy of race and class that promotes productive uncertainty rather than doctrinaire optimism or pessimism about the future.

As a memoirist, rather than a fiction writer, Harriet Jacobs did not have the onus of representing the typical or the possible, only the personal and the actual. Nonetheless she chose, in *Incidents in the Life of a Slave Girl*, to consider the same intersections of race and class in both national and international contexts as did Stowe. Jacobs, who had fled north in 1842 and found a position in the household of Nathan Parker Willis, began to write her story in 1853 and completed it in 1858, in the same context of labor and antislavery ferment as Stowe's abolitionist books (*Incidents* 224). In 1845, as nursemaid to Willis's baby daughter, she made a trip to England where she encountered the appalling oppression of poor people who were legally free. However, speaking as Linda in *Incidents*, she asserted that even the poorest of English workers "was a thousand fold better off than the most pampered American slave" (184). She belittled the advantages of material comfort without legal freedom and also noted that, in England, she was for the first time "in a place where [she] was treated according to [her] deportment, without reference to [her] complexion" (183). Interestingly, her employer Willis had precisely the opposite response to Britain's poor, commenting on "'the *utter want of hope* in the countenances of the working classes—the look of dogged submission and animal endurance of their condition in life'" (qtd. in Yellin 86). Of national colorblindness he observed, disapprovingly, "'I see, daily, blacks, walking with white women, and occupying seats in the dress-circle of theatres, quite unnoticed by the English'" (qtd. in Yellin 85). Although Willis and Jacobs are reacting to the same essential facts, they each drive toward even more extreme rhetorical poles. Willis asserts: "'I would prefer being an English horse to being an English working-man,'" whereas Jacobs deems it "'far better to have been one of the starving poor of Ireland whose bones had to bleach on the highways than to have been a slave with the curse of slavery stamped upon yourself and Children'" (qtd. in Yellin 86; qtd. in Tricomi, "Dialect" 632n23). Despite Jacobs's recognition that illiteracy, ignorance, and religious manipulation are the common instruments of the powerful everywhere against the powerless, she shows virtually no inclination to identify slaves with an English, Irish, or American working class so long as the condition of bondage separates them.

Even when Jacobs receives her long-awaited freedom, her response is curiously ambivalent, and she finds little occasion for solidarity with members of a white American working class that she has encountered personally as persecutors of her apprentice son and as enforcers of racist codes of segregation. She calls the fact that she and her children are now as free as Northern whites an "inestimable boon" but also remarks, with some disillusion, that this is "not saying a great deal" (201). Her many experiences of racial prejudice after she leaves the South, together with her close allegiances and affinities with white middle-class abolitionists, provide few inducements for her to identify with a white proletariat and more opportunities to develop the set of cultural values now coming increasingly to be considered "genteel."[4] However, the grounds for Jacobs's pessimism about alliances between former slaves and lower-class whites were apparently established much earlier, in North Carolina, in her experiences there with poor Southern whites, a group whom Harriet Beecher Stowe also described with unqualified negativity.

II

Jacobs's first detailed account of lower-class whites comes when Linda, her barely fictionalized alter ego, describes a muster in Edenton, North Carolina, in the immediate aftermath of Nat Turner's insurrection. Linda recounts in meticulous detail the clash of the complex hierarchies of race and class in the small Southern community of slaveholding and nonslaveholding whites, and free and enslaved blacks. She immediately notes the class divisions within each of the racial groups: "the so-called country gentlemen wore military uniforms" whereas the "poor whites took their places in the ranks in every-day dress, some without shoes, some without hats." The slaves too are distinguished by their status and their gullibility: the confident Linda imparts information "to the few [she] could trust" and comments on the others, "Poor creatures! They thought it was going to be a holiday." Distinctions between superior and inferior develop an additional tension when Linda, knowing that nothing bothers poor whites more than seeing "colored people living in comfort and respectability," puts fresh white quilts on the beds of her grandmother's house and engages in some provocative flower arranging in order to taunt the white underclass with her elegant ways (63).

What follows is a scathing description of the encounter of white vulgarity, idiocy, illiteracy, and petty malice with black refinement, literacy, style, and hauteur, ironically all performed under the protective surveillance of one of the local "gentlemen." Linda graphically reports and intervenes to help us understand the crude dialect and ignorance of the ruffians who are pillaging her grandmother's well-stocked pantry: "One of them, who was helping himself freely, tapped his neighbor on the shoulder, and said, 'Wal done! Don't wonder de niggers wants to kill all de white folks, when dey live on ''sarves' [meaning preserves].'" Their response to the discovery of Linda's correspondence is equally envious and racialized: "'Dis 'ere yaller gal's got letters!'" And of the household's linen supply they exclaim in astonishment, "'Where'd the damned niggers git all dis sheet an' table clarf?'" The grandmother's contemptuous response, "'You may be sure we didn't pilfer'em from *your* houses,'" and Linda's high-handed reprimand, "'You were not sent here to search for sweetmeats,'" are artistically effective though perhaps historically improbable (66, 65). Linda explains them, however, with yet another turn of the screw of class and caste: she and her grandmother are "emboldened by the presence of our white protector," a "gentleman who was friendly to us," whom they had asked to be present during the search (65). Like other members of the "better class" of the white community, he protects the better class of the black from the "drunken mob" who are prepared to shoot even "a respectable old colored minister" (66). This chapter of Edenton life, which began with the threat to slaveholders posed by Nat Turner's revolt, concludes with quite a different set of alignments: the community's white "citizens" are now driving out "the lawless rabble they had summoned to protect them" (67).

Jacobs, through Linda, articulates both a personal revulsion from a brutish white underclass and a more impersonal political analysis of poor whites as unaware that "the power which trampled on the colored people also kept themselves in poverty, ignorance, and moral degradation" (64). Present-day historians of race and class in the antebellum South have noted the ever-present fear of planters that poor whites and enslaved and free blacks, "if united in opposition to the South's ruling class, could have posed a formidable danger to the institution of slavery," though such fears "always exceeded actual subversive behavior" (Bolton 43; Forret 131). Frederick Douglass put the threat in prophetic tones when, in 1855, he wrote that consciousness of the damaging contest between slave and free white labor would "one day, array the non-slaveholding white people of the slave states, against the slave system, and make them the most effective workers against the great evil" (226). Harriet Beecher Stowe, too, in her *Key to Uncle Tom's Cabin* (1853) noted this feared alliance and the consequent careful nurture by the master class of antagonisms between poor whites and slaves. However Stowe, like Jacobs, also applies the terminology of extreme debasement to the class of "white trash" (*Key* 365). Whereas Jacobs envisions them as rude beasts, hungry wolves, and wild demons, for Stowe they are "heathenish, degraded, and miserable" (*Key* 365). The conceptualization of the Southern white underclass was in some ways an issue of even more immediate significance for these two abolitionist writers than anticipations of potential future coalitions or antagonisms among different segments of lower-class people. If the deterministic power of environment and the hegemony of a plantation culture produced such debasement in poor whites, what might the effects of this hideous dominance be on its most direct victims, the slaves themselves?

Both Stowe and Jacobs chose to focus on poor whites not merely as the manipulated products of a slaveholding oligarchy but as an ominously damaged human population. For Stowe they are "a luckless race of beings," "material for the most horrible and ferocious of mobs," "ignorant, and inconceivably brutal, ... like some blind, savage monster, which, when aroused, tramples heedlessly over everything in its way" (*Key* 367–68). Although she has few poor white characters in *Uncle Tom's Cabin*, she devotes an entire chapter of *Key* to "Poor White Trash," arguing in it that "the institution of slavery has accomplished the double feat, in America, not only of degrading and brutalising her black working classes, but of producing. . . . a white population as degraded and brutal as ever existed in any of the most crowded districts of Europe" (365). Jacobs also applies virtually identical vocabulary to poor white and slave debasement: the former are kept in "poverty, ignorance and moral degradation"; the latter are "inferior," "poor creatures," "brutalized" by "ignorance" and "degraded by the system" (64, 63, 44, 16). The careful alignment in the two writers of impairments to black and white alike makes important moral and political arguments about the pervasive wrongs wrought by the Southern system and the terror that may be unleashed when, as St. Clare puts it, *"the boilers burst"* (391).

These parallels, however, are not without caveats, especially when the sense of horror and revulsion created by the poor whites suggests that their condition may be incorrigible and they themselves irredeemable. They challenge abolitionist writers to show why the determinism of white peonage is more enduring than that of black bondage, or how poor whites can be so hopelessly damned and slaves nonetheless be saved. Both Stowe and Jacobs present poor whites in terms that might well seem to anticipate, in Patrick Moynihan's controversial terminology a "tangle of pathology."[5] In doing so, and in connecting them closely to the deterministic circumstances of enslaved people, they invite an implication ominous for the politics of abolition—the possibility of emancipated people at risk of becoming a permanent underclass. The two writers counter this threat of an intractable, unpredictable, and unthinking lower order not by economic or sociological analyses[6] or massive accumulations of evidence, but in a wholly imaginative way. They create what has been described as a near "improbability"— slaves who are fully literary characters and thus more familiar than the disturbingly alien poor whites, who appear as an indistinguishable mob.[7] These slave characters meditate and debate the extent of their responsibility and powerlessness, and they manifest a range of virtues, vices, abilities and eccentricities that neither subordinate individuality to type, nor neglect the shaping effect of the environment on the choices they make.

III

In light of their broad thematic focus on the sinister and destructive elements of slavery, both Stowe and Jacobs place what seems like an extraordinarily heavy emphasis on the responsibility and culpability of slaves for their moral conduct. In *Uncle Tom's Cabin*, Stowe devotes the chapter "The Quadroon's Story" almost in its entirety to a debate between Tom and Cassy on whether they have been placed in a situation where they "'can't help but sin'" (515). Tom's statement, "'I think we *can* help it,'" would seem to be logically undermined by virtually every detail of existence on the Legree plantation, from the presence of slaves who have sunk as nearly to the level of brutes "as it was possible for human beings to do" to Cassy's account of her murder of her beloved child (495). Of this ultimate unnatural act she avers that it is "'one of the few things that I'm glad of'" (521). By the end of her story, Tom has tactfully silenced his simple assertions of Christian conscience in the face of the mounting crescendo of Cassy's tragedy. The logic of the situation gives her despair the victory in both intellectual and emotional terms, but it is Tom who gains the ultimate moral ascendancy in this debate about human agency by choosing, as he does, to die rather than sin. Like Starbuck in Melville's *Moby-Dick* (published just one year earlier) who makes the determination that "'faith' can 'oust fact,'" Stowe insists on Tom's will to refuse despair even against the common sense of its triumph (qtd. in Railton 107). She virtually acknowledged as much when she later wrote to her husband, "I did not actually know when I wrote 'Uncle Tom' of a living example in which Christianity had reached its fullest development under the crushing wrongs of slavery" (qtd. in Fields 138). Tom's insistence that, even at his most vulnerable, he still retains authority and blame for his good deeds and transgressions, makes him a model (later much ridiculed and rejected) of virtuous self-sacrifice. However, in doing so, Stowe resists the potentially greater danger of pathologizing slaves into people demeaned into complete irresponsibility by their near intolerable circumstances.

Jacobs, like Stowe, devotes a central chapter of *Incidents* to the paradox of slave agency, intensified and complicated by the fact that she herself is the responsible slave and that her innocence or guilt is further exacerbated because she is a woman and the offense is sexual. The chapter "A Perilous Passage in a Slave Girl's Life" is Jacobs's extended and agonized quarrel with herself (through her pseudonymous Linda) on the question, "What *could* I do?" (53). It oscillates between anguished guilt and angry self-exoneration, between shame and embittered vindication for her sexual intimacy with a prominent white slaveholder who is, nevertheless, not *the* prominent white slaveholder who exercised the power of possession over her. Linda lists many rationalizations, as a free agent, for her "plunge into the abyss," then retracts them as "sophistry"; then insists, "I know I did wrong," but counters this confession with the ironic apostrophe, "O virtuous reader! You never knew what it is to be a slave.... entirely subject to the will of another" (53, 55). Virtually every paragraph alternates between the defense that "the slave woman ought not to be judged by the same standard as others" and the need to believe that, although she was a slave, virtue and respect were valid aspirations (56). Linda's accusations and justifications reveal the struggle between a highly refined conscience resisting her calculations and an intelligent analytical consciousness pleading her necessity. Her grandmother's reaction to her "fall" further exposes both the integrity and the almost unbearable absurdity of Linda's scruples: "'I had rather see you dead than to see you as you now are,'" she says. "'You are a disgrace to your dead mother'" (56). As in *Uncle Tom's Cabin*, claims of self-control by subservient people are both preposterous in their idealism and necessary to their respect—not just as dying saints on their way to heaven, but also as potentially autonomous members of a new democratic republic.

Harriet Jacobs's biographer, Jean Fagan Yellin, notes that Jacobs extends her personal assumption of responsibility for her actions and makes the same demand of others. In her account of wartime slave refugees, written in 1862 for the *Liberator* at William Lloyd Garrison's request, Jacobs presents them "as active agents capable of learning to build lives in freedom for themselves and their children." In doing so, "she writes without explanations or apologies, addressing her audience as equals, an audience with whom she shares the values of hard work, literacy, cleanliness, and Christianity" (161). When the *Liberator* published her report, it referred to the writer as "Mrs. Jacobs"; in Yellin's words, this was "a significant honorific" and one that measured the degree of "respectability" that the unmarried mother had now obtained (161). Yellin's implicit argument is that Jacobs's respect derives not only from her willingness to take responsibility for her actions but also from her confident assumption that she shares common standards of civilized behavior with the majority of Americans.[8] Precisely what those standards were, and whether they were a reflection of a desirable national ethos or merely the imperial strivings of a single class or race, were fundamental concerns of both *Incidents* and *Uncle Tom's Cabin*.[9] Remarkably, Jacobs and Stowe succeeded in fusing the grand existential questions of dominance, determinism, and human responsibility with precisely these concerns—with civility, individuality, and personal distinction—and their often surprising modes of expression in everyday life. Their abolitionist manifestoes are thus simultaneously two of the most acute studies of manners as well as morals in all of antebellum literature.

IV

If the question of whether a slave might be a member of the proletariat (or more ominously, the *lumpenproletariat*) was controversial, the notion that a slave might be genteel or well bred seems, almost by definition, grotesque. Richard Bushman argues that in nineteenth-century America, gentility served to stabilize identity, to show that people "had cast off their rude and simple pasts," and enabled them to assert their power (404–05). Its codes required decorum, literacy, verbal fluency, hospitality, discrimination, diligence, and fastidiousness—all part of the "cultural capital" of respectability (Vogel 9). Yet these are exactly the qualities attributed by Jacobs to her "slave girl" Linda Brent and dramatically denied not only to the poor white rabble but frequently also to the most elite class of slaveholders. Her opening chapter, "Childhood," sets the tone with a history of Linda's intelligent, hard-working, and generally superior family, betrayed at every turn by their dishonorable owners. Linda's contempt for the moral hypocrisies of the Flint family is closely entwined with her sense of their uncouthness, boorish manners, and lack of social savoir faire. Dr. Flint purports to be an "epicure," but Mrs. Flint spits crudely in the cook pots to prevent the slaves from sharing her food (12). Her jealously of Linda causes her to engage in the unseemly behavior of rising at night to whisper suggestively in her servant's ear, although Linda acknowledges disdainfully that indeed "the hoary-headed miscreant was enough to try the patience of a wiser and better woman" (34). The doctor's undignified efforts to communicate crudely in signs provoke Linda to remark in contempt, "He invented more than were ever thought of in a deaf and dumb asylum" (31). Flint's son, "a chip of the old block," speaks coarsely of having Linda "broke in," a grammatical error she immediately and repeatedly parodies (86, 87, 94). Of her mistress Linda comments, "She was not a very refined woman, and had not much control over her passions"; of a neighboring planter, he was "uneducated" and "ill-bred" (34, 46).

By contrast, Linda Brent's family exhibits exemplary restraint and decorum, knows how to properly host a tea party, exercise tact, interpret subtleties of demeanor, and speak formal and correct English. Unlike Flint, who "storms and swears," Benjamin exercises "self-control"; rather than using a dinner party to display venom, as the Flints do, Linda's grandmother entertains graciously, her "snow-white cloth, and . . . . china cups and silver spoons" offered for the delight of her guest (77, 21, 88). Whereas the Flints' language is intemperate and vulgar, Linda is embarrassed at the mention of "impure things," and her daughter's diplomatic delicacy prevents her from alluding to her mother's sexual "troubles" (29, 188). Whereas the Flint family is shameless, Linda's son is too "spirited" a boy to brook insults, and her Uncle Phillip merits a rare obituary for a black man in Edenton, with the proudly sardonic comment from Linda, "So they called a colored man a *citizen*!" (186, 201). Linda's family displays every quality associated with refinement and respectability in nineteenth-century America, a literary "fact" corroborated by the historical evidence of many witnesses of Harriet Jacobs and her family, both in terms of their social finesse and their moral integrity.[10] Although abolitionist irony directed at the loutish behavior of the supposed Southern aristocracy was not unusual, it is Jacobs's positive emphasis on the slave's inviolable dignity that produces the shocking disjunctions in *Incidents*, such as when the fastidious and cultivated Linda, who longs for "intelligent conversation" and "opportunities for reading," is trapped in a vermin-infested attic, or ejected from a public dining-room (169).

Although Jacobs does not suggest that the remarkable combination of manners and virtue in her narrator's family is representative of a larger class, she certainly implies that the qualities they display constitute the civic values appropriate for a democratic republic. She also believes these qualities can and must be taught. Thus, after acquiring her own freedom she devoted herself at once to the education and improvement of "contraband" slaves who had left their owners at the onset of the Civil War and were often living in utter destitution (Yellin 158, 176–79). Jacobs's belief that such desperate refugees could become "exemplary Americans" was challenged by the fears of more-affluent free black people that the "influx of degraded contrabands would drag them all down to the same level in social estimation" (Yellin 184, 178). Well versed in the false pretensions of white elitism, based on property and appearances, Jacobs resisted such standards of superiority in an aspiring African American gentry. Instead, she continued to embrace the values of industriousness, propriety, restraint, self-improvement, and public spiritedness as ideals of citizenship—values that were, ironically, in the process of being appropriated as essentially white and middle class.

For Harriet Beecher Stowe, the refined and respectable slave was, as with all her myriad literary characters, never simply a type; and gentility itself—even of the most authentic kind—was only one among many sets of admirable human qualities that might manifest themselves in unexpected places. The opening chapters of *Uncle Tom's Cabin* satirize two ungentlemanly men, the vulgar but candid slave dealer Haley and the cultured but disingenuous slaveholder Shelby, before introducing the true man of honor and gentle man, Tom. Tom's refinement, like Linda Brent's, is equally of morals and manners. Like her, he has authority, tact, and competence; his home is a center of decency and hospitality; his family is loving and loyal; and he will be subjected to extremes of mental and physical deprivation without becoming depraved. Like Jacobs, Stowe argues for both the determining influence of environment and for the mysterious agency of individual characters. The evidence of the people and events in her novel always exceeds the boundaries of the theories that are voiced in it and the paradigms and critiques that have been applied to it—of romantic racialism and sentimental domesticity, elitism and populism, essentialism and antiessentialism, social realism and Christian idealism. In everything except its abolitionist commitment the novel is speculative, assertively contradictory, and subversive of readers' expectations. We never know where Stowe will discover not just uprightness but also intriguing human potential; although we might anticipate admirable worthiness from the militant George Harris, the devoted Eliza, or the saintly Tom, it is sometimes among the minor ranks that the most remarkable abilities and incisive intellects reside—in Tom's comic partner, Chloe; in St. Clare's extravagantly slovenly cook, Dinah; and most unlikely of all, in the breeder's imp, Topsy.

Chloe and Dinah, as cooks for the large Shelby and St. Clare households in *Uncle Tom's Cabin*, are both, like Linda Brent's grandmother, artists in the kitchen. They are women of superior talent who produce masterpieces with the material to which they have access. That Chloe is an orderly perfectionist while Dinah is a chaotic genius may derive partially from the shaping family standards of the Shelbys and St. Clares (or artfully reflect on the different sisterly methods of Catherine Ward Beecher and Stowe herself), but it explains neither their notable skill nor their perspicacity.[11] Chloe far outshines her mistress in culinary art, planning, and foresight; not only does she outrank all others in the neighborhood in her handling of pies and "poetry," she excels in her understanding of the ways of her world and in her effective operations within her limited sphere of power (374). Dinah calls upon "inspiration" and the "Muses" to produce her "sublime" kitchen creations, but she also displays her shrewd intelligence in her analysis of the operations of hegemony among St. Clare's house slaves (311, 317). Compared to her master's wordy and overwrought parables of Quashy and Scipio, Dinah is devastatingly succinct and incisive (331, 345). When Adolph and Rosa flaunt their light skin and silky hair and boast of their elegant entertainments, she responds, "'Don't want none o' your light-colored balls, ... cuttin' round, makin' b'lieve you's white folks. Arter all, you's niggers, much as I am'" (322). It is a remark we are not likely to forget later when Rosa is sent out to be whipped and Adolph put on the auction block.

Topsy, the most enigmatic of these three characters (though the one, ironically, most quickly assimilated as a minstrel favorite)[12] has not only an acute and calculating intelligence but also an artistry less utilitarian than the two cooks, in that it is wholly devoted to inventive play and beauty. Topsy, like Dinah, is a "conjuror" who can create "a perfect carnival of confusion," and her imagination and irrepressible high spirits fascinate the ailing Eva, who is slowly losing all her childlike vitality and resourcefulness (364, 366). Topsy exhibits "surprising quickness" in all that she is taught, learns her letters "as if by magic," has a talent for drollery that is "inexhaustible," and asks questions about language and meaning (is Kentucky a state or a condition?) that are unthinkable by the doomed Evangeline (366, 364, 368). Her desire to unite beauty, meaning, and form is exhibited in her imaginative games, her admiring eye for all the artifacts and embellishments that she cannot possess and, most symbolically, in the "singular" bouquet of a "brilliant scarlet geranium" and "one single white japonica" that she makes for Eva: "it was tied up with an evident eye to the contrast of color, and the arrangement of every leaf had carefully been studied" (414).

The fact that Topsy, like the other two portraits of the artist in *Uncle Tom's Cabin*, is a lowly black female and that all are handled more or less in the comic mode is a matter ripe for theoretical speculation. What is certain is that all three are juxtaposed to more conventionally refined characters who do not profit by the comparison. Topsy, with her unique bouquet, is chased from Eva's bedroom by Marie St. Clare, but it is St. Clare himself, who has gratified his exquisite taste in the furnishing of his beloved daughter's room, who comes under Stowe's critical lens. The fond father has surrounded Eva with all the finest artifacts of his cultural heritage—paintings, sculpture, books, an elegant writing-stand, a Parian vase, a carpet imported from France, an alabaster bracket and angel, and "a beautifully wrought statuette of Jesus" (413). Nevertheless, it is the everyday environment of horror that sinks into the child's heart and symbolically destroys her. Whatever cultural capital or class prerogative is witnessed by such good taste, it is for Stowe no barrier to the devastation of the adored child by the corruption at the heart of her father's culture. Stowe's objection to St. Clare's fine household effects does not reside in their worldly display or even in their lavish materialism. Indeed Tom and Chloe too appreciate beautiful things and relish the comforts and decorations of their cabin, whereas Simon Legree's neglect of his domestic furnishings is one of the most prominent signs of his degeneracy. Her concern is the fear that aesthetic refinement may be displacing ethical responsibility in American society and thus the danger of its internal self-destruction may be as ominous as any threat from an external "mustering among the masses."

Neither Stowe nor Jacobs suggests that the love of beauty and elegance is an inappropriate indulgence for Americans, whether their station is high or low. Nor do they imply that civility is a bourgeois virtue. At the same time they note how such refinements may be tainted, distorted, and appropriated in the shifting processes of class and race definition, and even how they may become the ammunition in a bitter cultural and economic war. Both explore the many permutations of refinement and respectability that could become the hallmarks of authentic and fully developed citizens—or the signs of ever increasing envy, affectation, and decadence. Both take seriously the likelihood of slaves assuming full and valuable membership in society, as well as the possibility of their becoming an angry proletariat or an erratic and disaffected underclass. In applying such paradigms of class to a group of people conventionally characterized by race, they approach their subjects not as sociologists, psychologists, historians, or political theorists but as imaginative writers, whose methods consist of novel perspectives and singular insights rather than the vindication of hypotheses and assured prognostications. Their books reaffirm what Joel Pfister has described as the power of literature to act as an ongoing "critical and theoretical *resource*" rather than "as an historical and ideological *symptom*" (579). In *Uncle Tom's Cabin* and *Incidents in the Life of a Slave Girl*, Stowe and Jacobs certainly do not provide resolutions for the dynamic conflicts and intricate convolutions of race and class, but they furnish provocative ways of thinking and talking about them that have not diminished, either in fascination or in relevance.

NOTES

1. See Martin Glaberman on the bourgeois revolution and the advantages and disadvantages of viewing slaves as proletarians (210–12). For a valuable overview of respectability and the standards it entailed, see Richard Bushman's chap. 12, "Culture and Power."
2. See David Roediger, *Wages* 6–8 and 188–89; and *Colored* 190–91; see also the debate between Glaberman and Ignatiev in *Labour/Le Travail*.
3. See Larry Reynolds's important study of American writers' responses to European revolutions in 1848. He argues that Stowe creates a "Red Scare" (53) to enhance her abolitionist argument with the threat of a fearful alternative.
4. These values include an emphasis on mental culture, religion, civility, aesthetic sensibility, moral restraint, public service and industry. See Bushman 434–40; and Vogel 1–17.

5. The highly controversial phrase is in Moynihan's report, *The Negro Family: The Case for National Action*, chap. 4, produced for the U.S. Department of Labor in 1965. His precise application of the term was to African-American family structure, but his larger context was the question of the enduring legacy of centuries of mistreatment.
6. However, in *The Key to Uncle Tom's Cabin*, Stowe added these approaches when her fiction's truthfulness was challenged.
7. Myra Jehlen, who asserts in general the difficulties of creating slave characters, names *Uncle Tom's Cabin* as "the extraordinary exception" (70).
8. Albert Tricomi in "Harriet Jacob's" argues forcefully for a greater editorial role on the part of Lydia Maria Child than Child concedes, especially in downplaying Jacobs's militancy. At no point, however, does he suggest that the endorsement of propriety in *Incidents* is anything other than Jacobs's own.
9. Both Amy Schrager Lang and John Ernest make the case for connections between the codes of race and class. Lang argues that, for Stowe, "slavery is the testing ground of middle-class culture" (84); John Ernest asserts that "arguably *all* American novels are novels of racial manners" (763).
10. Jacobs and Stowe came to their abolitionist writings from seemingly very different backgrounds: a former slave and a free white woman from an elite family. However, each had considerable experience in the realm of the other, in addition to her own distinctive characteristics. Jacobs regularly impressed people with her dignity and high moral tone. By the time she wrote *Incidents* she had moved widely among the Northern white and black bourgeoisie (see Yellin 104, 118, 177, 264, 75–79). Stowe, despite her privileged upbringing, was "perfectly unpretending" and daily familiar with the exigencies of a working woman's life (see Hedrick 91, 199–221).
11. See Joan Hedrick's biography (124–25, 321) for accounts of Stowe's disorderliness.
12. See Sarah Meer's exploration of Topsy's relationship to minstrelsy, 36–40, 59, 63–64, 68.

BIBLIOGRAPHY

Bolton, Charles C. *Poor Whites of the Antebellum South: Tenants and Laborers in Central North Carolina and Northeast Mississippi*. Durham: Duke UP, 1994. Print.

Buell, Lawrence. "Harriet Beecher Stowe and the Dream of the Great American Novel." *The Cambridge Companion to Harriet Beecher Stowe*. Ed. Cindy Weinstein. Cambridge: Cambridge UP, 2004. Print.

Bushman, Richard L. *The Refinement of America: Persons, Houses, Cities*. New York: Knopf, 1992. Print.

Douglass, Frederick. *My Bondage and My Freedom*. 1855. Introd. John David Smith. New York: Penguin, 2003. Print.

Ernest, John. "Still Life, with Bones: A Response to Samuel Otter." *American Literary History* 20 (2008): 753–65. Print.

Fields, Annie, ed. *Life and Letters of Harriet Beecher Stowe*. Boston: Houghton Mifflin, 1898. Print.

Fisch, Audrey. "Uncle Tom and Harriet Beecher Stowe in England." *The Cambridge Companion to Harriet Beecher Stowe*. Ed. Cindy Weinstein. Cambridge: Cambridge UP, 2004. Print.

Forret, Jeff. *Race Relations at the Margins: Slaves and Poor Whites in the Antebellum Southern Countryside*. Baton Rouge: Louisiana State UP, 2006. Print.

Glaberman, Martin. "Slaves and Proletarians: The Debate Continues." *Labour/Le Travail* 36 (Fall 1995): 209–14. Print.
Hendrick, Joan D. *Harriet Beecher Stowe: A Life*. New York: Oxford UP, 1994. Print.
Ignatiev, Noel. "Reply to Martin Glaberman." *Labour/Le Travail* 36 (Fall 1995): 215–16. Print.
Jacobs, Harriet A. *Incidents in the Life of a Slave Girl, Written by Herself*. 1861. Ed. Jean Fagan Yellin. Cambridge: Harvard UP, 1987. Print.
Jehlen, Myra. *Readings at the Edge of Literature*. Chicago: U of Chicago P, 2002. Print.
Lang, Amy Schrager. *The Syntax of Class: Writing Inequality in Nineteenth-Century America*. Princeton: Princeton UP, 2003. Print.
Meer, Sarah. *Uncle Tom Mania: Slavery, Minstrelsy and Transatlantic Culture in the 1850s*. Athens: U of Georgia P, 2005. Print.
Moynihan, Daniel Patrick. *The Negro Family: The Case for National Action*. U.S. Dept. of Labor, March 1965. Office of Policy Planning and Research. Web. 8 July 2010.
Pfister, Joel. "A Usable American Past." *American Literary History* 20 (2008): 579–88. Print.
Railton, Stephen. "Black Slaves and White Readers." *Approaches to Teaching Stowe's* Uncle Tom's Cabin. Ed. Elizabeth Ammons and Susan Belasco. New York: MLA, 2000. Print.
Reynolds, Larry J. *European Revolutions and the American Literary Renaissance*. New Haven: Yale UP, 1988. Print.
Roediger, David R. *Colored White: Transcending the Racial Past*. Berkeley: U of California P, 2002. Print.
———. *The Wages of Whiteness: Race and the Making of the American Working Class*. Rev. ed. London: Verso, 1999. Print.
Schocket, Eric. *Vanishing Moments: Class and American Literature*. Ann Arbor: U of Michigan P, 2006. Print.
Stowe, Harriet Beecher. *Dred: A Tale of the Great Dismal Swamp*. 1856. Ed. Robert S. Levine. New York: Penguin, 2000. Print.
———. *The Key to Uncle Tom's Cabin*. 1853. Preface by William Loren Katz. New York: Arno, 1968. Print.
———. *Uncle Tom's Cabin, or Life Among the Lowly*. 1852. Ed. Ann Douglas. New York: Penguin, 1981. Print.
Tricomi, Albert. "Dialect and Identity in Harriet Jacobs's Autobiography and Other Slave Narratives." *Callaloo* 29 (2006): 619–33. Print.
———. "Harriet Jacob's Autobiography and the Voice of Lydia Maria Child." *ESQ* 53 (2007): 216–52. Print.
Vogel, Todd. *ReWriting White: Race, Class, and Cultural Capital in Nineteenth-Century America*. New Brunswick: Rutgers UP, 2004. Print.
Yellin, Jean Fagan. *Harriet Jacobs: A Life*. New York: Basic, 2004. Print.

Part II
Pedagogy and Promises

Although many blue-collar jobs are dangerous or monotonous or both, after World War II unions negotiated good working conditions and excellent benefits, making it possible for working-class people to earn a relatively comfortable living. As these jobs have been lost to deindustrialization and replaced with nonunion service jobs that offer low salaries, no security, and minimal (if any) benefits, white-collar employment has become the possibility (just a possibility) for earning a living wage. Higher education has thus become the ticket to a chance for economic security. Working-class students increasingly feel the imperative to go to college, yet many students never receive even an associate's degree.

Although academic preparedness is certainly an issue, given the quality of schools in many working-class and poor neighborhoods, there are other barriers. Working-class students have often found the college experience to be alienating and humiliating, to a great extent because institutions of higher education are middle class. Professors often have little understanding of working-class life, and more-affluent peers may not grasp the extent to which working-class students are pressed for money and, because they often work in addition to carrying full course loads, time. As the numerous sessions on pedagogy at Working-Class Studies Association conferences indicate, critics and scholars of working-class literature are keenly interested in voicing the issues that working-class students face and in interrogating the academy's norms. They ask questions such as: who are our working-class students? What and how should we teach them?

Karen Kovacik is interested in the poetry of five contemporary women who have completed undergraduate and, in some cases, graduate degrees and have become recognized writers. Although some might expect such writers to laud their educations, Kovacik finds deep ambivalence in their work, largely because they fear their degrees will alienate them from their working-class communities.

David McCracken examines a recent text that has not been recognized as working class, *I Am Charlotte Simmons*, and argues that the novel represents the same struggles as those narrated by former working-class students, such as bell hooks. Although Tom Wolfe has stated that Charlotte had betrayed her values for status among her peers, McCracken argues that she has successfully navigated her first-year experience and emerged as a wiser student still negotiating the values of home versus college and of the working class versus middle class.

Undergraduate culture can be an issue, but values are reproduced by the curriculum itself, by the choice of what is taught and how it is taught. Nicholas Coles, coeditor of a comprehensive anthology of American working-class literature, addresses the problem of coverage in teaching a canon of working-class texts. More important, he discusses the challenges of representing working-class lives to middle-class students unfamiliar with them and working-class students who may want to distance themselves from their pasts.

In their careful examinations of representations of working-class students' experiences in education and of teaching literature about the working class, these articles underscore problems and possibilities in education.

4 Bridges, Not Ladders
Working-Class Women Poets on Education, Class Consciousness, and the Promise of Upward Mobility

Karen Kovacik

Even as the United States has become the most unequal industrialized nation in the West, with 1 percent of its citizens holding 40 percent of its wealth, it's possible to watch American television and read mainstream newspapers for weeks at a time without once encountering the phrase "working class" (Lang and Tichi 9). The power of the American working class has been eroded, as well, because of globalization, union-busting tactics, and tax laws that favor the rich. Yet scholars and writers in the growing field of working-class studies have sought to remedy this cultural amnesia and to strive for social and economic justice for working people. Recent collections such as *What's Class Got to Do With It?*, edited by Michael Zweig, and *New Working-Class Studies,* edited by John Russo and Sherry Lee Linkon, have emphasized the centrality of class to our lives and offered nuanced new ways of defining "working class," taking into account race, gender, ethnicity, geographical location, and access to political power. In this chapter, I make use of such an intersectional approach to class by examining how representations of American class identity and conflict persist even in the literary genre often perceived as the least revolutionary: the contemporary lyric poem.

A little over ten years ago, I began studying how a diverse group of twenty-one women poets from working-class backgrounds created rhetorics of class solidarity in their writing. Born between 1940 and 1960, these poets slipped through the narrow window of opportunity in higher education that opened after World War II until the mid-1970s.[1] All came from families supported by blue-collar, pink-collar, or low-level service sector work, and all were the first in their families to attend college. Unlike some poems that can be read purely as works of the imagination, these are often rooted in the biographical and socioeconomic realities of the poets. In analyzing their work, I consider their contextualizing comments on the poems as well as relevant historical and sociological materials. This intertextual literary-critical practice builds on working-class studies and feminist research methods to redress the power differential in traditional modes of research and to minimize the distance between the researcher and the object of her research.

According to sociologist David Karen, between 1960 and 1975, total enrollment in American universities and colleges more than tripled because of greater prosperity, increased opportunities for financial aid, and mobilizations by the civil rights and women's movements (212). Considerable public investment in public education during that period kept tuition costs affordable for families of modest means (Newfield). The majority of the poets I studied earned both undergraduate and graduate degrees, and a number have published several books of poetry. Higher education provided them with leisure time for reflection, the chance to develop their craft, contacts with publishers, and in some cases, incomes sufficient to comfortably support them. It also pushed them to depict worlds remote from privilege and comfort.

Given their individual achievements in publishing and higher education, these poets might be expected to celebrate upward mobility and to downplay their class origins. However, their work reminds me of Janet Zandy's observation that "the foregrounded working-class 'I' is never isolated, but crowded from within with other voices" (*Liberating Memory* 6). Instead of climbing up the social ladder, these poets have produced multivoiced, socially engaged poems that build bridges with working-class communities.[2] Refusing to assimilate quietly into the middle class, they challenge American ideologies of the "melting pot," individualism, and equality of opportunity, particularly in poems about schooling or higher education. They defy what Tillie Olsen called the "coercians to 'pass': to write with the attitude of . . . or in the manner of the dominant" (287). Refusing to adopt the attitudes of condescension or obliviousness toward the working classes that such "passing" would entail, they seem to answer in their poems about schooling and mobility Olsen's call for a literature that "validate[s] our different sense of reality, [that raises our] own truths . . . against the prevalent" (288). Indeed, whereas some would see their educational and literary attainments as legitimating the notion of America as a classless society—one in which the daughter of a steelworker and the daughter of a stockbroker are equally likely to succeed—these writers, in their poems about education, call attention to inequalities, both structural and symbolic.

The five poets who are the focus of this chapter—Patricia Dobler, Ana Castillo, Dorianne Laux, Patricia Smith, and Michelle Tokarczyk—write from oblique perspectives, often contrasting the worlds of home and school, sometimes drawing on the devices of pastiche and parody, to offer a portrait of American life as they knew it: urban, industrial, marked by hunger and, often, violence. Their poems, largely in free verse, often mimic other genres: reportage, a children's book, an acknowledgments page in a dissertation or scholarly edition. At times, their ambivalence about education recalls that of the working-class men interviewed in Richard Sennett and Jonathan Cobb's *The Hidden Injuries of Class*, many of whom had "risen" to white-collar occupations. Yet their poems about schooling and mobility speak against the erasure of working-class consciousness so prevalent in our culture and call attention to ways in which race, ethnicity, and gender complicate class identity.

BACKTALK: CLASSROOM POEMS ABOUT CLASS

In early twentieth-century America, a rigid program of tracking and "Americanization" was first implemented by urban public school systems to immerse large groups of immigrants from southern and eastern Europe in the values of white, Anglo-Saxon Protestant culture and to equip them for the increasingly mechanized routine of the factory. Students in the lowest tracks were subjected to more authoritarian discipline and rote learning. Class differences, notes Canadian sociologist Jane Gaskell, were often marked in schools as "achievement and ability differences. Those who [were] less bright [took] vocational courses and [got] working-class jobs. Such is the IQ ideology... or the masking of cultural privilege through an ideology of unequal giftedness" (52). In his history of the American urban working-class, Paul C. Violas argues that not only the implementation of vocational tracks in high schools, including part-time co-op education programs that actually took place in factories, but also the structuring of students' leisure activities—playgrounds, school sports, and student governments—were conceived by both progressive reformers and corporate elites as means of controlling a heterogeneous school population. Since World War II, the system of funding public schools through property taxes has, of course, further reproduced social stratification, and discriminatory tracking of African American, Latino, and Asian American students has been widespread.[3]

In their poems representing elementary schools from the 1950s and '60s—an era before multicultural education—Patricia Dobler, Ana Castillo, and Dorianne Laux challenge the WASP, middle-class values implicit in curricula and leisure activities by writing about class in terms of religion, ethnicity, and gender, respectively. Through what Adrienne Rich would call the "eye[s] of the outsider," these poems critique the dominant cultural norms of whiteness, middle-class status, and patriarchal privilege, which are often transmitted unquestioningly in school readers and history texts.

Patricia Dobler (d. 2004), a poet originally from the Armco Steel city of Middletown, Ohio, who lived and taught most of her life in Pittsburgh, depicts a nun shepherding her class of fourth-graders in "Field Trip to the Mill." Sister Monica frames her opposition to the mill directors' practice of inviting schoolchildren to the factory in terms of religious difference:

> She passes out
> sourballs for bribes, not liking
> the smile on the foreman's face,

the way he pulls at his cap,
he's not Catholic. Protestant madness,
these field trips, this hanging from catwalks
suspended over an open hearth. (3)

Instead of removing his cap, the foreman merely tips it in a gesture of courtliness that the nun considers inappropriate. Sister Monica's observations about Protestant difference are rooted in a working-class politics because so many of the southern and eastern European workers in the mill, in contrast to native-born management, subscribed to the Catholic faith. Sister views the mill as a Protestant "Hell," in which "cranes clawing / their way through layers of dark air / grew leathery wings and flew screeching," and the molten steel poured out "liquid fire like Devil's soup." This "field trip," which disturbs Sister Monica, is meant to excite the children, to initiate them into the mysteries of the place that, ten years later, will employ them. Such trips were part of working-class experience in America. In addition to funneling working-class children into vocational courses, schools often collaborated with industry to bring students into worksites under the auspices of co-op programs and class trips (Violas 124ff.). Sister Monica wants to distance herself from such a collusion—"Industry and Capital and Labor, / the Protestant trinity"—and therefore, "she trembles . . . , the children clinging / to her as she watches them learn their future." That final image movingly conveys the unequal opportunities these working-class children will have in life; instead of visiting a park or zoo, they tour a steel mill on their class trip. The perspective of Sister Monica, mistrustful of management, allows Dobler to present a moral counterweight to this dubious collaboration between industry and schools.

In her book *My Father Was a Toltec*, Ana Castillo (b. 1953) satirizes the white middle-class bias in Eisenhower-era textbooks by contrasting the suburban version of reality presented in a school primer with her experience growing up Chicana and working-class in Chicago:

Red Wagons

c. 1958

In grammar school primers
the red wagon
was for children
pulled along
past lawns on a sunny day.
Father drove into
the driveway. "Look,
Father, look!"

> Silly Sally pulled Tim
> on the red wagon.
>
> Out of school,
> the red wagons carried
> kerosene cans
> to heat the flat.
> Father pulled it to the gas
> station
> when he was home
> and if there was money.
>
> If not, children went to bed
> in silly coats
> silly socks; in the morning
> were already dressed
> for school. (5)

Norma Alcarón has noted that Castillo favors a sardonic approach when her "experience is viewed ... in opposition to another's subjectivity" (94). Castillo mimics the primer's stilted syntax to unmask the class privilege and suburban bias implied in the landscape of driveway, lawn, and car. In the reader, the wagon is used for child's play because the white middle-class father has a car, but in the narrator's life, it is her father's only means for transporting fuel to their apartment. A lack of heat and a shortage of money never get mentioned in the Dick and Jane books, on which Castillo is modeling her poem. For the narrator, learning to read means more than sounding out words and acquiring vocabulary: it means contrasting school and home, parsing differences of class and race that the primer passes over in silence.[4]

Dorianne Laux (b. 1952), who grew up in a white working-class family in San Diego, compares the world of home, dominated by a sexually abusive father, with the stock lessons about U.S. presidents and white settlers that she encounters in school. Her poem "What My Father Told Me" illustrates the destructive ways in which class and gender can intersect. The speaker, a dutiful working-class child who has always done "what was asked," begins by listing her chores. Though containing such ordinary tasks as laundry, dishwashing, and yard work, the list bears connotations of violence and death: "The slack of a vacuum cleaner cord / wound around my hand. Laundry / hung on a line. . . . / I do the chores, pull weeds out back, / finger stink-bug husks, snail carcasses, / pile dead grass in black bags." The speaker seems to be moving through these tasks in a trance. As matter-of-factly as she mentions the chores, she reveals her experience of incest: "I do as I am told, hold his penis / like the garden hose, over the toilet / or my bare stomach. . . . / His voice, the hiss of lawn sprinklers, / the wet hush of sweat in his hollows."

The second stanza features the child-speaker at school, trying to integrate this experience of sexual violence into a standardized lesson about (white male) American presidents and the "settlers" conquering the West:

> Summer ends. Schoolwork doesn't suit me.
> My fingers unaccustomed to the slimness
> of a pen, the delicate touch it takes
> to uncoil the mind.
> History. A dateline pinned to the wall.
> Beneath each president's face, a quotation.
> Pictures of buffalo and wheatfields,
> a wagon train circled for the night,
> my hand raised to ask the question,
> Where did the children sleep? (20–21)

The terse list of what counts as knowledge at school—a collection of stock images that have little relevance to the child's life—resembles the numbing sequence of chores. But the poem's final question, which indicates the speaker's hunger for making sense, for bringing together the two parts of her life, is a hopeful omen, the possibility of transforming rote knowledge into something the child can use.

Through ironic shifts in perspective—from school to work, or school to home—Dobler, Castillo, and Laux place class at the center in their poems about 1960s elementary schools. These dynamic shifts illuminate what is often hidden in mainstream American discussions of class: unequal life opportunities, the material conditions of poverty, and the ability to see class oppression in the contexts of race and gender identity.

BENEDICTION AT THE EDGE OF THE GRAVE: PATRICIA SMITH'S "BUILDING NICOLE'S MAMA"

Since the decades of the '50s and '60s depicted in the classroom poems of Dobler, Castillo, and Laux, American schools have been resegregated, as Marian Wright Edelman of the Children's Defense Fund, Beverly Daniel Tatum, Jonathan Kozol, and others have demonstrated.[5] It is a Miami school rather like the ones in Kozol's *Shame of the Nation* that Patricia Smith depicts in her passionate ars poetica "Building Nicole's Mama." Smith (b. 1955 in Chicago), four-time National Poetry Slam champion, author of five volumes of poetry, and 2009 National Book Award finalist for *Blood Dazzler*, her collection of poems about Hurricane Katrina, has dedicated her poem to the sixth-grade class of Lillie C. Evans School in Liberty City, Miami (*Teahouse* 1–3), and in readings, she always begins with it, letting audiences know that the poem grew out of a workshop she gave at the school. Liberty City, a Miami neighborhood that's predominantly black and poor, is named for the Liberty Square Housing Project, built by the Public Works Administration during the 1930s (Mohl 10). Miami's elites sought to expand the business district by removing the city's black residents from a shantytown near the city center to this housing project north of downtown (11). As a statement from one such elite, attorney John C. Gramling, attests, segregationist and paternalistic whites had ulterior motives for supporting the housing project: "It [Liberty Square] will not only eliminate the possibility of fatal epidemics here, but fix it so that we can get a servant freed from disease" (qtd. in Mohl 11). Nonetheless, a 1942 edition of the NAACP journal *Crisis* praised the "lovely" courts of the housing complex, noting that its community building contained a social and recreational hall, a doctor's office, a federal credit union, a nursery school, and study classes for the adult tenants (Scott 87). But by 2008—two years after Smith's poem was published and twenty years after the area was hit hard by the crack cocaine epidemic—47.5 percent of the Liberty City population lived below the poverty level ("Liberty City Neighborhood").

Smith's poem, though dedicated to the children at the Evans School, uses an activist rhetoric to persuade other American poets to help children scarred by violence and poverty to come to voice. Early in the poem, she explicitly urges "[a]ngry, jubilant, weeping poets," who "are all / saviors, reluctant hosannas in the limelight" to "bless" this large sixth-grade class of forty students, all of whom have known someone who has died, most frequently by murder or drug use.

In an earlier poem, "Blonde White Women," Smith had presented an uncomfortable early encounter with a white teacher, who wanted physical distance between herself and the black speaker:

> In first grade, my blonde teacher
> hugged me to her because I was the first
> in my class to read, and I thought the rush
> would kill me. I wanted her to swallow
> me, to be my mother, to be the first fire
> moving in my breast. But when she pried
> me away, her cool blue eyes shining with
> righteousness and too much touch,
> I saw how much she wanted to wash. (21)

But in "Building Nicole's Mama," the speaker shows a much warmer and livelier interaction with the children at Lillie C. Evans School. Smith describes how they "shout me raw, bruise my wrists with pulling, / and brashly claim me as mama as they / cradle my head in their little laps, / waiting for new words to grow in my mouth" (1). In a public lecture, she spoke of teaching these children who had felt silenced by excessive emphasis on grammar and spelling to learn to use their "second throat"—to write about the most pressing experiences of their lives in intimate vernacular.[6]

The children, in Smith's presence, testify to the death they've seen—"pushing the button for the dead project elevator, / begging for a break at the corner pawn shop, cackling wildly in the back pew of the Baptist church"—and Smith compiles a litany of their suffering:

> O'Neal,
> matchstick crack child, watched his mother's
> body become a claw, and 9-year-old Tiko Jefferson,
> barely big enough to lift the gun, fired a bullet
> into his own throat after Mama bended his back
> with a lead pipe. Tamika cried into a soft pillow
> when Daddy blasted Mama into the north wall
> of their cluttered one-room apartment,
> Donya's cousin gone in a drive-by. Dark window,
> *click, click, gone,* says Donya, her tiny finger
> a barrel, the thumb a hammer. (2)

The litany or list occurs frequently in poetry of witness or activism.[7] It pushes the lyric poem beyond an individual speaking subject to bring attention to a problem shared by an entire community, whether that be violence, poverty, racism, or inequality. In the above list, what's striking is the contrast between the children's small size and the magnitude of the violence they've experienced in one of Miami's poorest, most segregated neighborhoods.

Smith, whose own father had been murdered, depicts herself as a muse and a mentor to this class of children, especially Nicole, mentioned in the poem's title, who asks, "*Can you teach me to write a poem about my mother? / I mean you write about your daddy and he dead, / can you teach me to remember my mama?*" (3). It's the first time the girl has admitted her mother has been "murdered by slim silver needles and a stranger / rifling through her blood, the virus pushing / her skeleton through for Nicole to see" (3). Smith helps this child "with rusty knees and mismatched shoes" to find the "words to build her mother again. / Replacing the voice. / Stitching on the lost flesh." Although some might find this faith in poetry to be too absolute, too easy a resolution, Smith invites her readers both to empathize with the individual case of Nicole (and with the litany of other children who lost loved ones to violence or drug use), but also to stand in solidarity by building coalitions to protect children and seeing our poetry as a vehicle for activism.[8]

The final part of the poem urges American poets, often known for our triviality and solipsism, to dwell on the example of Nicole:

> So poets,
> as we pick up our pens,
> as we flirt and sin and rejoice behind microphones—

remember Nicole.
She knows that we are here now . . . (3)

Like Gwendolyn Brooks in her 1975 poem "The Boy Died in My Alley," who admits culpability when a young man is killed in her alley because she saw herself as a mere bystander ("I joined the Wild and killed him [the boy] with knowledgeable unknowing"), Smith makes use of a rhetoric of interrelation, inviting poets to become bridges where others can "[cross] over, on" in the words of another Chicago working-class poet, Carolyn M. Rodgers (11).

Important to this idea of becoming a "bridge" is that the poet explicitly claim allegiances: Smith with the children at Lillie C. Evans School, Brooks with the boy killed in her alley and with the surrounding Bronzeville community. To claim allegiances is to "defy the coercians to pass," as Tillie Olsen urged. In the next section, we'll see two more examples of this defiance in Michelle M. Tokarczyk's poems that lay claim to her working-class background as she completes her doctoral degree.

COMING OUT AS WORKING-CLASS IN THE MIDDLE-CLASS ACADEMY

Michelle M. Tokarczyk (b. 1953) grew up in the Bronx and Queens in New York City. A professor of English at Goucher College, she has written monographs on working-class writers Maxine Hong Kingston, Sandra Cisneros, and Dorothy Allison and on E. L. Doctorow, in addition to editing *Working Class Women in the Academy: Laborers in the Knowledge Factory*, a collection of autobiographical essays by women academics from working-class backgrounds. Striking in that collection was the women's expression of ambivalence, of feeling "torn" between their communities of origin and university culture:

> We found that women academics from the working class . . . wanted to maintain their ties to their families, but wanted to fit into the academy as well. Often, they feared they fit into neither world. They were frequently uncomfortable with the language they used. . . . And they were angry at being ignored or at being expected to be middle-class professionals, socially and economically. (Tokarczyk and Fay 1)

Tokarczyk's poem "Acknowledgments" is remarkable in that it challenges the assumption that all graduate students are from the middle or upper classes by revealing the speaker's working-class background. Written after the poet's PhD defense, the poem borrows from the generic expressions of indebtedness with which writers introduce books or dissertations. Instead of the customary roster of colleagues, mentors, and family members,

Tokarczyk dedicates the different sections of her poem "to the services and people who helped me to become a woman who could get a Ph.D" and expresses gratitude "[t]o free therapy for college students"; "[t]o AA and others who helped me stop drinking"; "[t]o legalized abortion"; and "[t]o social services."

First published in 1990, in an era of bipartisan backlash against the working poor and people on welfare, Tokarczyk's poem offers an eloquent appeal for more, not fewer services. In the "social services" section, for example, Tokarczyk writes:

> There's nothing good
> about aluminum chairs
> near a park where
> the homeless no longer
> hear of revolution.
>
> Hours of waiting,
> hours of forms,
> tired tobacco breath:
> "Why'd ya lose
> that job, sweetie?"
>
> Except
> without that room
> without those coupons
> you could not clutch
> milk, bread, eggs.
> You could not place
> cereal, rice
> in the cupboard.
>
> You could not eat. (330–31)

Unlike writers who express gratitude for generous grant funding or editorial support, Tokarczyk emphasizes more fundamental needs. The word "clutch" suggests a hunger so powerful that it would override the fear of humiliation associated with receiving public assistance. When she wrote this poem, Tokarczyk was an untenured faculty member at Goucher College in Baltimore, Maryland. By publishing it, she chose to "come out" as a food stamps recipient, to stand in solidarity with people who endure daily indignities and red tape to put food on the table.

As an academic and PhD recipient, Tokarczyk is implicitly debunking common myths about people who receive government assistance: they're lazy, they don't want to work, they stay on welfare all their lives, they live extravagantly. She also expresses solidarity with poor women who find themselves pregnant when she dedicates a section of her poem "[t]o legalized abortion":

> In a white room
> in a white paper gown
> they bled me red.
> At twenty, I sat
> recovering, turning
> my eyes toward the horizon
> I could not see. (330)

In these short, stark lines, Tokarczyk points out the bodily trauma of choosing abortion, just as in the social services section she emphasized the indignities that welfare recipients face. Yet her purpose in both sections is to argue for the legitimacy of those services as choices for poor and working-class women.

In a second poem, "An Academic Fantasy," Tokarczyk imagines holding a tenured professor's position. Initially, the poem seems to offer yet another vision of moving out of and away from the working class:

> I still have hope
> that one day after,
> please, not too many more
> years of teaching all day
> writing all night
> I'll get that job. . . .
>
> After all these years
> I'll get tenure,
> I'll never drink another
> cup of coffee. Never eat
> dried cheese while running
> down the street.
> My body will sway
> in the freedom of daily
> jazz classes. I'll lie
> in a chair, feel the sun's
> rays warm my eyelids. . .
>
> I'll have my own money,
> my own health insured,
> my own title will inscribe
> my own office door.
> I'll fill my shelves
> with dusted books. (24)

From the poem's title, a reader might expect a scholarly fantasy—the anticipation of a well-received book, the discovery of a manuscript. Yet the fantasy focuses almost exclusively on the body at leisure and on the acquisition of certain academic privileges: the possessive pronoun "my" appears seven times in ten lines. However, Tokarczyk calls into question this individualist fantasy of assimilation in the poem's final stanza:

> That childhood crying unheated
> under an old winter coat of a blanket,
> closing my eyes to the muffled
> sounds of my mother's cries,
> that childhood, those years expiated.
> They'll see it, point to me,
> dream of me, the American Dream.
> And I will tell them no, no.
> I will tell them dreams require sleep.

Tokarczyk is questioning several elements of the American Dream logic that one will succeed if one works hard enough. Can a childhood of cold and hunger ever be "expiated"? What about those who work hard and don't succeed? What if an individual prospers and her community falls away? Whose interests does the American work ethic ultimately serve? And can one pay too great a price for success? In the epilogue to the volume of essays by working-class women academics, which she edited with Elizabeth Fay, Tokarczyk told a related anecdote about a conference she attended in Hungary:

> Many participants queried me about my obviously Slavic last name and wondered if I had any knowledge of Ukrainian. When I explained that it was difficult for my grandparents to pass down the language because they were illiterate, people at the conference were astounded. I was, one of them responded, an example of American upward mobility. Yes, in a way, I answered. But I never want to be viewed . . . as a symbol of American success. I know the price of that success. And I don't trust it. (315)

In her poems about women from working-class backgrounds in the academy, Tokarczyk challenges the expectation that all academics are "middle-class professionals, socially and economically" (Tokarczyk and Fay 1). Pointing out disparities between middle-class and working-class ethical and epistemological systems, calling attention to material markers of class difference, she writes an explicitly politicized poetry that defies "coercians to pass" and rejects visions of individual attainment, emphasizing instead relationships of solidarity and sustaining social structures.

CHOOSING CLASS CONSCIOUSNESS

In an often-cited passage, the British historian E. P Thompson remarked on the "making" of the working classes: "We cannot have love without lovers, nor deference without squires or labourers. And class happens when some [people], as a result of common experiences (inherited or shared), feel and articulate the identity of their interests as between themselves, and as against other [people] whose interests are different from (and usually opposed to) theirs" (9). Significantly, Thompson defines class in terms of relationship—the identification of shared interests and "common experiences," as well as a sense of those "whose interests are different." Class, by this definition, is somewhat fluid and can include gendered, racial, and ethnic commitments as well as relationships with others in the same socioeconomic category. Such a notion of class implies a choice: whether or not to identify or affiliate with others. American labor historians have often observed that given the individualist work ethic, the promise of upward mobility, the myth of the classless society, and government and corporate collusion to limit workers' rights, American working-class culture has traditionally been fragmented. David Hogan, for example, asserts that "[c]ompared to English working class culture, American working class culture is not as cohesive, thickly textured, or self conscious; it is more diffuse, fractured internally, divided along regional, racial and ethnic lines; its repudiation of bourgeois ideology less deep and incisive; its institutional infrastructure—trade unions, political organizations, voluntary associations—less extensive and weaker" (32).[9]

Given the "diffuse" quality of American working-class culture and given the significant educational attainments of these women poets of the working classes, it would not be surprising if they chose to write a very different kind of poetry, one suppressing mention of poverty or hunger, one that attempts to pass as upper-middle class. Yet poet Dorianne Laux has responded angrily to the sort of poetry that attempts "to rise above . . . ordinary lives": "To be published in the *New Yorker*, for instance, seems to be an achievement of a high order which gains a poet entrance to a higher class. Many of the poems published there are interchangeable in terms of language, tone, and subject matter. No nasturtiums in a jam jar, no battered women poems, no sexual abuse poems, no poems of working class lives, fewer poems by women, few poems by blacks, Hispanics, Native Americans, Asians, lesbians and gays, bisexual, poems of sexuality in general, few political poems . . . I have nothing against a life of gentility and grace, but few of us . . . possess them" (letter to Karen Kovacik).

Instead of writing a poetry of assimilation, these women, in their poems about schooling, have explicitly identified with working-class issues, working-class lives. In the face of great hostility toward poor and working-class people in recent legislative agendas, their poems challenge us to become activists in our neighborhoods, schools, and cities, to insist on the tax policies, school funding, financial aid, and social services that open opportunities for more than a privileged few. These poets demand that instead of working our way up the narrow ladder of upward mobility, we become bridges on which others can "cross over, on."[10]

NOTES

1. The poets I included in this study are Gloria Anzaldúa, Lenore Balliro, Jan Beatty, Karen Brodine, Ana Castillo, Lorna Dee Cervantes, Nancy Vieira Couto, Kate Daniels, Patricia Dobler, Mary Fell, Tess Gallagher, Dorianne Laux, Chris Llewellyn, Linda McCarriston, Donna Masini, Thylias Moss, Carolyn M. Rodgers, Patricia Smith, Carol Tarlen, Michelle M. Tokarczyk, and Janet Zandy. Dobler, in fact, was born in 1939. See also other articles of mine that have grown out of this research, such as "Between L=A=N=G=U=A=G=E and Lyric. The Poetry of Pink-Collar Resistance," *NWSA Journal* 13.1 (2001): 22–39, and "Words of Fire for Our Generation: Contemporary Working-Class Poets on the Triangle Fire," *Women's Studies Quarterly* 26.1 & 2 (1998): 137–58.
2. Janet Zandy used the "ladders and bridges" metaphor in her keynote address at the Youngstown University's Center for Working-Class Studies' fourth biennial conference in June, 1999.
3. See, for example, Rosenbloom and Way; and Oaks.
4. Admittedly, the Dick and Jane books are easy marks that have often been satirized. See also, for example, Agueros.
5. See, for example, Tatum; Kozol; and Edelman.
6. At Indiana University-Purdue University Indianapolis, 26 February 2010.
7. See, for example, Martín Espada's poem "Imagine the Angels of Bread" in his book of the same title or Tillie Olsen's "I Want You Women Up North to Know," which quotes from workers' letters to call attention to sweatshop labor, reprinted in Nelson 105.
8. A faith in the power of books is something that working-class women writers often express. Suzanne Sowinska, a specialist in proletarian literature, has observed that "a deep passion for reading . . . is part of the reality of almost all the poor and working-class women in academia I know" (Tokarczyk and Fay 152).
9. This "intersectional" approach, initially promoted by bell hooks and Patricia Hill Collins, is now an essential element of working-class studies' methodology. See, for example, hooks; Collins; but also Russo and Linkon.
10. I'd like to thank Michelle M. Tokarczyk for her generous and very helpful comments on an earlier draft of this essay.

BIBLIOGRAPHY

Agueros, Jack. "Halfway to Dick and Jane: A Puerto Rican Pilgrimage." In *Crossing Cultures*. Ed. Henry and Myrna Knepler. 3rd ed. New York: Macmillan, 1991. 25–38. Print.

Alcarón, Norma. "The Sardonic Power of the Erotic in the Work of Ana Castillo." *Breaking Boundaries: Latina Writings and Critical Readings*. Ed. Asunción Horno-Delgado et al. Amherst: U of Massachusetts P, 1989. 94–107. Print.

Brooks, Gwendolyn. "The Boy Died in My Alley." *Anthology of Modern American Poetry*. Ed. Cary Nelson. Oxford: Oxford UP, 2000. 777–78. Print.

Castillo, Ana. *My Father Was a Toltec*. New York: Norton, 1995. Print.
Collins, Patricia Hill. *Black Feminist Thought*. London: Routledge, 1991. Print.
Dobler, Patricia. *Talking to Strangers*. Madison: U of Wisconsin P, 1986. Print.
Edelman, Marian Wright. "The Dangerous Drift Back Toward Segregated Schools." Children's Defense Fund. 2 Apr. 2010. Web. 20 July 2010.
Espada, Martín. *Imagine the Angels of Bread*. New York: Norton, 1997. Print.
Gaskell, Jane. "Course Enrollment in the High School: The Perspective of Working-Class Females." *Sociology of Education* 58 (Jan. 1985): 48–59. Print.
Hogan, David. "Education and Class Formation: The Peculiarities of Americans." *Cultural and Economic Reproduction in America*. Ed. Michael Apple. London: Routledge, 1982. 32–78. Print.
hooks, bell. *Yearning: Race, Gender, and Cultural Politics*. Boston: South End, 1990. Print.
Karen, David. "The Politics of Class, Race, and Gender: Access to Higher Education in the United States, 1960–1986." *American Journal of Education* 99.2 (1991): 208–37. Print.
Kovacik, Karen. "Between L=A=N=G=U=A=G=E and Lyric: The Poetry of Pink-Collar Resistance." *NWSA Journal* 13.1 (2001): 22–39. Print.
———. "Words of Fire for Our Generation: Contemporary Working-Class Poets on the Triangle Fire." *Women's Studies Quarterly* 26.1–2 (1998): 137–58. Print.
Kozol, Jonathan. *The Shame of the Nation: The Restoration of Apartheid Schooling in America*. New York: Crown, 2005. Print.
Lang, Amy Schrager, and Cecelia Tichi. "A New Critical Realism: Introduction." *What Democracy Looks Like: A New Critical Realism for a Post-Seattle World*. Ed. Amy Schrager Lang and Cecelia Tichi. New Brunswick: Rutgers UP, 2006. 32–34. Print.
Laux, Dorianne. *Awake*. Brockport: BOA, 1990. Print.
———. Letter to Karen Kovacik, 1 Jan. 1996.
"Liberty City Neighborhood in Miami, Florida: Detailed Profile." *City-Data.com*. Web. 24 July 2010.
Mohl, Raymond A. "Of Miami's Liberty City." *Florida Environmental and Urban Issues* 12 (July 1985): 9–12. Print.
Nelson, Cary. *Repression and Recovery in Modern American Poetry and the Politics of Cultural Memory, 1910–1945*. Madison: U of Wisconsin P, 1989. Print.
Newfield, Christopher. "Avoiding the Coming Higher Ed Wars." *AAUP Academe Online*. May-June 2010. Web. 25 June 2010.
Oaks, Jeannie. *Keeping Track: How Schools Structure Inequality*. New Haven: Yale UP, 2005. Print.
Olsen, Tillie. *Silences*. New York: Dell, 1978. Print.
Rich, Adrienne. "Eye of the Outsider: The Poetry of Elizabeth Bishop. *Boston Review* June 1984. Web. Acc. 5 Feb. 2011.
Rodgers, Carolyn M. *How I Got Ovah*. New York: Anchor; Doubleday, 1978. Print.
Rosenbloom, Susan Rakosi, and Niobe Way. "Experiences of Discrimination Among African American, Asian America, and Latino Adolescents in an Urban High School." *Youth Society* (June 2004) 35.4: 420–51. Print.
Russo, John, and Sherry Lee Linkon, eds. *New Working-Class Studies*. Ithaca: Cornell UP, 2005. Print.
Scott, James E. "Miami's Liberty Square Project." *Crisis* (Mar. 1942): 87–89. Print.
Sennett, Richard, and Jonathan Cobb. *The Hidden Injuries of Class*. New York: Vintage, 1972. Print.
Smith, Patricia. "Blonde White Women." *Big Towns, Big Talk*. Cambridge: Zoland, 1992. Print.

———. Joseph Taylor Symposium. Indiana University-Purdue University Indianapolis. 26 Feb. 2010. Lecture.
———. *Teahouse of the Almighty*. Minneapolis: Coffee House, 2006. Print.
Sowinska, Suzanne. "'Yer Own Motha Wouldna Recognized Ya': Surviving an Apprenticeship in the Knowledge Factory." In Tokarczyk and Fay. 148–61. Print.
Tatum, Beverly Daniel. *Can We Talk About Race? And Other Issues in the Era of School Resegregation*. Boston: Beacon, 2007. Print.
Thompson, E. P. *The Making of the English Working Class*. New York: Pantheon, 1964. Print.
Tokarczyk, Michelle M. "Acknowledgments." *Calling Home: Working-Class Women's Writings*. Ed. Janet Zandy. New Brunswick: Rutgers UP, 1990. 330–31. Print.
———. *This House I'm Running From*. Albuquerque: West End, 1989. Print.
Tokarczyk, Michelle M., and Elizabeth A. Fay. *Working-Class Women in the Academy: Laborers in the Knowledge Factory*. Amherst: U of Massachusetts P, 1993. Print.
Violas, Paul C. *The Training of the Urban Working Class: A History of Twentieth-Century American Education*. Chicago: Rand McNally, 1978. Print.
Zandy, Janet. "The Complexities and Contradictions of Working-Class Women's Writings." *Radical Teacher* 46 (1995): 5–8. Print.
———. *Liberating Memory: Our Work and Our Working-Class Consciousness*. New Brunswick: Rutgers UP, 1995. Print.
Zweig, Michael, ed. *What's Class Got to Do With It? American Society in the Twenty-First Century*. Ithaca: Cornell UP, 2004. Print.

5 Charlotte Simmons as Working-Class Heroine in Tom Wolfe's *I Am Charlotte Simmons*

David McCracken

In late August of 2008, just before fall classes began, Glenn Beck devoted one of his CNN programs to "Life on Campus: Problems and Solutions." After initial introductions, Beck prepared viewers to be shocked: "Tonight, it's going to be an hour of frank questions, frank answers. Honest, possibly a little uncomfortable. But it's something that everybody, every parent should see.... [One of his guests, a professor] gave me ... *I Am Charlotte Simmons*. Read that. If you're sending your kids, especially your daughter, to college, you'll lock her in the basement." Most viewers probably saw through Beck's rhetorical strategy of evoking fear about the current state of higher education in general and campus life in particular to draw an audience, but there were undoubtedly some who took what Beck presented at face value, subsequently buying into his position (emphasized throughout the program) that students on American campuses typically participate in sexually licentious behaviors on a scale rivaling that of Sodom and Gomorrah. In his zealousness to sensationalize Tom Wolfe's *I Am Charlotte Simmons*, Beck exaggerated his description of the college experience and perpetuated a stereotype promoted throughout popular culture. This stereotype might provide provocative entertainment, but it sends exactly the wrong message to those unfamiliar with the collegiate experience, especially blue-collar or working-class parents who are preparing to send their sons and daughters, perhaps the first in their families to attempt a college education, to academic campuses across the country.

Beck selected an appropriate novel to serve his purpose; but amid all the hyperbole, Wolfe provides a representative sampling of issues affecting major facets of American higher education, including campus diversity, collegiate athletics, administrative politics, and Greek life. Critics have addressed how Wolfe treats these controversial issues, as well as how effectively he has captured the essence of the collegiate experience, but they have generally neglected what is perhaps at the center of the novel: the obvious issue of class conflict within the academy, and more specifically, how a first-generation college student makes the transition from a working-class home community to the middle-class culture traditionally associated with higher education.[1] Over the course of a few months, Charlotte must not only adapt to but excel in a middle-class dominated environment. At the beginning of *I Am Charlotte Simmons*, Charlotte's only expectation is that her college-level courses should be challenging. Her primary resource concerning the college experience is Martha Pennington, and her mentor mostly offers advice about academics instead of the more treacherous social aspects. Charlotte adjusts her working-class values throughout her various experiences, and by the end of the novel, she possesses a self-confidence, a self-trust, a self-reliance rooted in her working-class background. Charlotte must constantly negotiate within a collegiate environment, ideally constructed on altruistic liberal arts and humanist principles, but which actually operates through those of solipsistic individualism and capitalistic egocentrism. During this process, Charlotte learns to synthesize what she learns from her experiences with the fundamental ideology she has internalized from her family. The last pages might suggest Charlotte has sacrificed her character and her integrity for superficial status and campus popularity, but the opposite is more likely the case. As a working-class heroine, Charlotte eventually learns how to maintain her own sense of cultural identity—to transcend class and social limitations—within the often morally ambiguous atmosphere of higher education, an environment that fosters the hedonism Beck graphically described for his viewers.

On the surface, *I Am Charlotte Simmons* might not seem to fall into the category of working-class fiction, and Tom Wolfe (noted for his trademark white linen suit, high-collar shirt, and faux spats) may not fit the typical persona of a working-class author, but the novel meets a fairly elastic definition of the genre. In "Toward a Theory of Working Class Literature," Renny Christopher and Carolyn Whitson point out the working-class novel "will focus on crisis, and that crisis is usually, one way or another, about loss: loss of persons through death, loss of job or means of survival, loss of values through a quest for upward mobility, or a loss of some element that made someone's life meaningful—religion, perhaps, or an immigrant's high hopes" (76). Charlotte's crisis is unquestionably affiliated with the loss of her working-class values in favor of ones that will promote her social status at Dupont. She does not, however, lose her values as much as redefine their meaning. Charlotte appears ready to sacrifice her indigenous beliefs in favor of ones that will secure her upward social mobility, but when soon after Christmas break she is at her lowest, Charlotte maintains an allegiance to the values with which she was raised. As Charlotte attempts to climb the social ladder at Dupont, she internalizes the significance of her indigenous values, and although she loses their perfunctory relevance, she gains a deeper understanding of their core significance. In "Working-Class Women's Literature: An Introduction to Study," Paul Lauter is more inclusive in his definition: "It seems best to use relatively loose definitions and broad categories, but we must remain sharply aware of the difficulties involved, [. . .] I discuss [working-class literature] by *and* about working people. [. . .] I refer to people who, to improve their lot, must either move in *solidarity* with their class or leave it [. . .]" (111). Idealistic Charlotte leaves her working-class community to achieve something better. Whether she returns to her community after this is attained is beyond the scope of the novel, but in all likelihood, Charlotte will probably return to Sparta during the summer after her frosh year a different person in the same way she is different when she returned home for the Christmas vacation. Charlotte obviously cares for the people in Sparta and tightly embraces her sense of home, but her journey is unmistakably one initiated by the dream of a more prosperous life through a higher education. Wolfe's novel addresses the difficulties connected with such a journey, one in which a person appears to give up relative security, support, and safety for the possibility of economic opportunity and social advancement, a trade-off traditionally associated with moving from the working class to the middle class.

Wolfe's treatment of Charlotte is similar to portrayals of working-class women making the transition from home to academy in Anzia Yezierska's *Bread Givers* (1925) and Joyce Carol Oates's *Marya, A Life* (1986). In a sense, Wolfe provides an updated version of the working-class heroine type of bildungsroman. Charlotte's family is certainly not as impoverished as the Smolinskys, and Yezierska devotes most of her novel describing the events that precipitate Sara's desire to become a teacher, but Charlotte and Sara share the same insecurities attached to moving from one class to another. Both women feel out of place because of their clothes, their speech, and their mannerisms. They follow a rigorous work ethic but have difficulty deciding what to prioritize. They have trouble fitting in with other students and then make impulsive decisions about whom to befriend. When their academic work is evaluated, they have difficulty accepting the assessment. Charlotte's suspicion her C- in Modern Drama is the subjective whim of her teaching assistant is not as naïve as Sara's request for tuition reimbursement because she failed Geometry, but both suggest Charlotte and Sara are frustrated with the seemingly nebulous system by which they are judged. Oates's account moves well beyond Marya's frosh semester, but there are several similarities between how Charlotte and Marya perceive their homes, families, and acquaintances. Marya and Charlotte feel intellectually superior to their peers (both are valedictorians) yet want desperately to be accepted inside the popular social circles, although Oates's depiction of this is much darker than Wolfe's. The attempted gang rape of Marya before she leaves Port Oriskany is quite different from the incident at the Simmons graduation party, but both demonstrate how Marya and Charlotte share a deep desire to fit into the peer groups they are leaving. This sense of social ridicule only exacerbates their feelings of disconnectedness while they are at college, making them feel as if they are exiles in both places. Each novel ultimately provides a type of reconciliation between home and academy primarily through the reunion of parent and child. Sara decides to let her father, who had renounced her as a selfish daughter, move in with her and

Hugo, bridging the gap between her past and her present. Marya pulls a letter from her mother out of an envelope and thinks to herself "this is going to cut your life in two" (Oates 310); but glancing at the included photo, Marya identifies with her mother's physicality, which in turn reinforces her self-identity. When Charlotte considers her mother's suggestion to search her soul, she also thinks about Dr. Starling's comment that the soul does not exist. Charlotte redefines her concept of self as she contemplates the nature of her soul, providing an ideological bridge between Sparta and Dupont.

The apparent differences between home and academy are immediately established in the novel. In the first few pages devoted to Charlotte's family, Wolfe describes them as possibly poverty class rather than working class. Allegheny County is a beautiful, picturesque region, and its primary industry is Christmas trees, but a large part of the economy depends upon the seemingly affluent "summer people" (14) from Charlotte and Raleigh to fish, golf, hunt, or shop at the local craft stores. Charlotte is the shining star in Sparta, and most of its inhabitants know she has had the unprecedented fortune to be awarded a scholarship to Dupont. Emphasizing the Simmons's financial troubles and stoic simplicity, Wolfe describes Charlotte's upbringing as difficult but not unbearable. Charlotte's father is laid off from the Thom McAn shoe factory (outsourced to Mexico) but works part time at a summer resort; Charlotte's mother supports the family through her job at the sheriff's office, and the family home was once just a dug-out in the mountainside:

> The house was a tiny one-story wooden box with a door and two windows facing the road. The only halfway ornamental touch was the immovable awnings over the windows, made of wooden slats nailed in place. The door opened directly into the front room, which, although only twelve by fifteen feet, had to serve as the living room, workroom, TV room, playroom, and dining room. That was where the picnic table stood ordinarily. The ceilings were right down on top of your head, and the whole place was soaked with a countrified odor that came from using coal stoves and kerosene space heaters. Until Charlotte was six, they had lived belowground in what was now the foundation. Charlotte had thought nothing of it at the time, since they were far from being the only ones. (21)

After her graduation speech, Charlotte senses the incredible responsibility she has assumed to take advantage of her academic acumen for what is essentially a higher economic level. In "Promises to Keep: Working Class Students and Higher Education," Michelle M. Tokarczyk comments that working-class young people typically understand a college degree will provide them—and by extension, their families—entrance into the middle class. Moreover, Tokarczyk notes these students also understand there will be a range of obstacles between them and the college diploma (161). As with most working-class students, Charlotte's obstacles are less academic than cultural. For her to succeed at Dupont, Charlotte must learn how to apply the strong working-class values cultivated during her upbringing in Sparta to a totally different cultural paradigm. Charlotte's role as a working-class heroine depends finally upon how well she accomplishes this goal.

Unfortunately, Charlotte consistently undermines any progress she makes by questioning her own self-identity, and this is complicated by her social expectations of how others perceive her. She is relatively secure in Sparta because her personas are concretely defined by her family (Momma views her as daughter), her English teacher (Miss Pennington perceives her as student), and her best friend (Laurie McDowell sees her as confidante), and this social network enables her to solve typical teenage problems. When Charlotte is forced to apply the values she has relied upon for self-worth and communal stability to situations at Dupont, she has difficulty reacting to the various challenges of contemporary college life, an atmosphere in which she discovers most eighteen- to twenty-two-year-olds routinely push the moral boundaries of decorum. In short, Charlotte discovers there is a different cultural system operating at Dupont. During the first third of the novel, she proclaims her mantra, "I am Charlotte Simmons," to reaffirm her academic stardom at Alleghany High School, but in the middle sections, these words are often posed in more of a question than a declaration. Several months into her frosh year, after she experiences almost every self-destructive event a freshman can, Charlotte announces "I am Charlotte Simmons" to assert she is not simply a caricature of someone attached to a particular clique, sorority, team, or group. Charlotte discovers she can be popular without giving up all her fundamental values, and she is finally able to maintain this stance among many of the other Dupont students who wholeheartedly, desperately attach themselves to the various collegiate stereotypes. Even though others might perceive Charlotte as a type (e.g., Jojo sees her as intellectual, Beverly sees her as hillbilly, and Adam sees her as victim), she conversely tries to contradict those perceptions when she notices they are applied. At home, Charlotte passively accepts how people define her, but at Dupont, even though she experiments with various roles, she nonetheless casts them aside as she reaffirms her identity. In fact, she is the only character in the novel who rejects assimilation into a campus subculture; Charlotte remains independent while she interacts with people from the broad spectrum of campus affiliations.

These stereotypical subcultures are obvious enough through the three alpha males in the novel: Hoyt Thorpe is the ultramasculine, opportunistic frat guy; Jojo Johannsen is the academically challenged, morally naïve basketball star; and Adam Gellin is the nerdish, resentful, self-deceived intellectual. If the novel's development depended entirely upon their motivations, the critics who ridicule Wolfe for writing a vacuous novel would be correct.[2] On the contrary, Charlotte's motivation is not so linear or shallow. In the first section of the novel, Wolfe describes the experiment that ultimately led to Professor Starling's Nobel Prize. Elaine Showalter sarcastically explains the passage's significance: "control cats developed uncontrollable sexual arousal when they lived near cats surgically altered to become sexually insatiable. Or, to put it in undergraduate terms, even a sweet and intellectually gifted country girl like Charlotte Simmons will be rutting around like an old pro once she had been exposed to the coed bathroom and the fraternity formal" (B14). Charlotte, however, moves beyond just an instinctive or visceral response to the collegiate environment. As a typical freshman, Charlotte wants to find her place in the collegiate community and avoid being the outsider, but her inclusion is ultimately dependent upon her own definition of self-identity, not the stereotypical labels differentiating all the other characters. Even though she is classified as "Jojo's girlfriend" in the last sentence of the novel, Charlotte does not see herself in this way. She is simply Charlotte Simmons. Granted, Charlotte identifies herself most of the time with whom she socializes, but unlike the group-driven cats, Charlotte is motivated by a conscience that prohibits her from crossing the threshold into anything antithetical to her working-class values. Even when Charlotte tries, for instance, to act like the others at the Saint Ray dance, her conscience will not allow her to ignore her culturally inculcated definitions of appropriate social behavior. In other words, Charlotte cannot go against how Momma taught her to act.

The Simmons family clearly influences Charlotte's early self-identity and initial expectations about college. Charlotte scored a perfect sixteen hundred on the SAT, and she exempted four out of five introductory college courses through the advanced placement exam. To her father and mother, Charlotte represents a way for a Simmons to advance several steps on the socioeconomic ladder, and Charlotte wants desperately not to let them down. Physically, she looks a little too adolescent for an eighteen-year-old, and she feels self-conscious about how males view her virginity. Her mother and Miss Pennington have been the defenders of her virtue, although both have led Charlotte to hold inaccurate expectations about the college experience. The English teacher tells Charlotte, "if you're so fortunate as to find a student, one student, a *single* student—like Charlotte Simmons—and you spend four years working with that student and seeing that student become what you are today—Charlotte, that justifies all the struggle and frustration of forty years of teaching" (30). This only adds to the pressure Charlotte feels about leaving the relatively safe haven of Sparta for the unknown territory of Dupont.

When Charlotte arrives on campus, she feels ashamed of her family's apparent working-class position, and she fears what other students think about her parents' appearance and worries about the sparsity of her belongings. Obviously, Wolfe uses the incident at the Sizzlin' Skillet to show how diverse the two roommates are. The Amorys clearly represent everything despicable associated with the middle class. Charlotte's family fills up on the oversized plates of country cooking full of meats and gravies, but the Amory family prefers to nibble on small pieces of chicken and lettuce. Beverly's trip to the restroom clearly suggests bulimic behavior. Wolfe emphasizes the disparity between the wealthy, prep-schooled Beverly and the poor, public-schooled Charlotte, and this reinforces the class differences Charlotte faces from the onset at Dupont. Charlotte is embarrassed by the "nice ink" (63) comment because she relates her father's mermaid tattoo with the working class, which illustrates how Charlotte wants to distance herself from her cultural heritage.

After her family leaves Dupont, Charlotte situates herself in a socially ambiguous place. She envies Beverly's adroitness to make friends and have fun. She says to herself, "*I'm Charlotte Simmons. . . . You are unique. You . . . are Charlotte Simmons*" (78), but this confidence quickly deteriorates after she has listened to the scatological sounds of two other freshmen in the community bathroom and has seen Beverly leave to go to dinner with friends she made after only knowing them for two hours. Charlotte is literally thrown out when Beverly "sexiles" her to the common room. Charlotte thinks, "Self-discipline was one of the things that had always made Charlotte Simmons . . . Charlotte Simmons . . . that, and her power of concentration" (131). Afterward, she writes a make-believe letter to her mother that reveals her apparent frustration at Dupont. Directing most of her anger toward Beverly, Charlotte describes wanton girls with fifteen hundred SATs who "rut-rut-rut" (150) and cry out that they must have sex. Charlotte ends her letter asking her mother what she should do. Worth noting is that Charlotte has this soul-searching dialogue with herself rather than with her mother, and the result is Charlotte's decision to model her own identity after several of the Dupont stereotypes: uncomfortable in her own skin, Charlotte explores trying on the social personas of others. The descriptors smart, athletic, and cute—ones she believes carry with them connotations of working-class Sparta—do not have the social currency necessary for her to be popular, so she experiments with other labels, ones she believes have more value at middle-class Dupont. After Charlotte is finished alternating as Hoyt's, Jojo's, and Adam's love interest (essentially moving between the different subcultures on campus), she is perhaps the most confused and frustrated about her self-identity.

The incident at the Saint Ray formal offers a strong example of Charlotte's internal conflict concerning self-identity. After Charlotte lets down her moral defenses and is basically date raped, she questions the event in terms of how other students will perceive her, not how she was sexually violated. Charlotte realizes the gamble of placing status ahead of academics has failed, and this unsuccessful attempt at raising what she perceived as the "clueless public school hillbilly girl hidden up-hollow in the Blue Ridge Mountains of North Carolina to the summit of female competition at the great Dupont" (496) has shaken her self-confidence. During the next few days, Charlotte tries to avoid anyone related to the event. At Mr. Rayon, Charlotte realizes the rumors have already begun through the social game of telephone from Gloria to Lucy Page to Erica to Beverly. When she slips into Edgerton House, trying to sneak into her room, Charlotte overhears Mimi and Bettina talking about the bloodstain left on the hotel sheet. Charlotte became the topic of the day, acquiring the opposite kind of popularity she had desired. At this point in the novel, Charlotte is forced to recognize she cannot try to become something quite foreign to her moral upbringing, and she faces the fact she cannot assume values contradictory to those she acquired in Sparta. She finds out the consequences are socially (as well as emotionally) devastating.

When Charlotte returns home for Christmas vacation, she is able to put what has happened at Dupont into a working-class perspective, giving her a chance to process her experience with Hoyt within the security of community. Not surprising, Charlotte automatically feels guilty for letting her family and Miss Pennington down. Her mother and father want to know everything about the college experience, and Charlotte senses her mother recognizes why she is so obstinate. She worries her mother, and probably Miss Pennington, will notice immediately that she had "committed moral suicide" (525). After a night of insomnia and introspection, Charlotte has a heart-to-heart with her mother, and this is the moment she realizes she has strayed from her family's values: "'one thing I learned, and I had to go all the way to Pennsylvania to learn it.' Pennsylvania. For some reason she didn't want to utter the name Dupont. 'I don't care about everyone else. I just don't want to let *you* down'" (532). Charlotte is also saying she does not want to let herself down. Her mother represents all of the values associated with working-class females in her community, and Charlotte does not want to lose her connection with that bloodline. In contrast, Laurie McDowell seems to be adjusting quite well at North Carolina State University, but this is because Laurie has not maintained her connection to her roots. Losing her virginity is not a major event for Laurie. In fact, it is a collegiate rite of passage that she is willing to experience early in the fall semester. Laurie looks "absolutely glorious" (541) from Charlotte's perspective, but Laurie seems to be a lot like Beverly. Charlotte thinks that Laurie "had gotten *fucked*, same way she had" (worth noting is the profane way Charlotte defines the sexual act) and notices how Laurie uses affective, Beverly-like language full of "like totallys," "cools," "awesome," and "ohmygods" (543). Laurie has sacrificed working-class values for middle-class ones, and Charlotte seems willing to let the friendship atrophy. Charlotte's reluctance to call Laurie or Miss Pennington after the turkey dinner indicates she is also grappling with which ideology to identify. Charlotte's fear that Lucy Page has told people in Sparta about the Saint Ray formal forces her to acknowledge that she cannot keep Dupont completely separate from Sparta, a realization that also precipitates Charlotte's decision to stick more closely to her indigenous ideology.

This trip, her reconnection with her home soil, is the catalyst toward Charlotte's transformation. After returning to Dupont, Charlotte goes into a deep depression, skips classes, and shacks up with Adam. As time passes, Charlotte finds out she has not done well in her fall courses, and this increases her anxiety concerning where she actually is—socially, academically, and psychologically—after Christmas break. At this point, Charlotte has an epiphany about the real purpose for attending Dupont, to achieve a higher cultural education as well as an academic one. This is evident in her realization that trying to join Hoyt's social group has been disastrous, and she understands there is no reason why she should not maintain her working-class values because they are actually empowering instead of debilitating: "she envies them for being economically comfortable, for having money and all the clothes they wanted, for their natural assumption of social superiority and their actual attainment and enjoyment of it. She admitted this to herself, and it seemed like little more than an observation" (658). At this crucial moment, Charlotte realizes Hoyt and his crowd are not better than she is socially, culturally, or most important, morally, and she refuses to continue giving these people emotional power over her. When Charlotte exclaims "*I am Charlotte Simmons*" (658), she is essentially declaring her decision to no longer consider herself inferior to people like Hoyt Thorpe. This is literally Charlotte's defining moment when she recognizes, without remorse or shame, all of her experiences have shaped who she is, a crucial self-discovery. Charlotte comprehends she has held on to misconceptions about higher education and the college experience, and she now depends upon her own moral code. This transformation, or perhaps apotheosis, is what establishes Charlotte as a working-class heroine in the novel.

In a 2008 interview with Carol Iannone, Wolfe offers a quite different interpretation of Charlotte. Wolfe claims Charlotte was motivated by a desire for social status that ultimately led to her moral demise, and this ending was more appropriate than having Charlotte give in wholeheartedly to sex and drugs, an example of complete degeneration, or the opposite, depicting her as an advocate for complete "moral rearmament" (158) on the Dupont campus. Wolfe points out Charlotte's forfeit of her moral integrity for social popularity makes the chosen ending particularly tragic: "But when it came right down to it, her concern was status. And she had blown her career the first semester in college by failing courses, practically failing—she got a couple of Ds for the most slovenly of reasons" (159). Wolfe argues his characterization of Charlotte is realistic, without melodramatic embellishment or political correctness. As he comments, "I didn't write the book in moral terms [. . .]. I just tried to give a completely accurate picture of what really goes on. And I have a feeling I did" (161). Wolfe evidently believes the conclusion illustrates Charlotte's fall rather than her rise, her fate as pathetic instead of uplifting. He does not take into account that Charlotte can both rise in status *and* remain loyal to her working-class values, and he fails to concede the relationship between Jojo and Charlotte is not based on status but on circumstance. Wolfe's novel is not so much about Charlotte's academic matriculation as it is her social maturation. In the final chapter, Charlotte appears to have control over her destiny, she is seemingly empowered, and this can only be interpreted as positive compared to her initial position during her arrival at Dupont. Wolfe admits sympathy for his character, going so far as to call her "[p]oor Charlotte" (161). Actually, there is nothing "poor" about Charlotte in the end, and to give up to debauchery or to start a campus-wide support group would be completely uncharacteristic of her personality. If either of these occurred, it would have been totally illogical, if not ludicrous. In many ways, Charlotte rises above the others not "because of" but "in spite of" what has happened to her. If Charlotte had conceded or surrendered, she would not have become the unquestionably stable person at the end of the novel.

This stability is the result of the conversation Charlotte has with her mother about her fall semester grades. Elizabeth Simmons is known for having two "releases": her "fervent religious faith" and her daughter (Wolfe 24). Charlotte often feels guilty for not possessing her mother's strong religious conviction and "absolute moral certainty" (24), but she understands the reason is generational. Charlotte consistently plays with the idea of telling her mother about her sexual problems, but she realizes her mother was raised in conservative western North Carolina culture in which discussing sex is socially taboo, so Charlotte can only try to figure out what to do on her own. She can no longer identify with Laurie, and she cannot talk about such matters with Miss Pennington. After Christmas vacation, Charlotte has the epiphany that "home" is conceptual rather than geographical: "Sparta, Alleghany County, and County Road 1709 were no longer a retreat she could return to. There existed on this earth no home, no peaceful place where she could lay her head" (564). The importance here is that Charlotte feels as if she is totally cut off, completely culturally isolated, and because of this, she could have become the despondent, puerile, or defeated character Wolfe described in his interview; but she instead became the opposite. After her breakdown and stay with Adam, Charlotte learns to rely on herself. This is evident when she tells Beverly what happened with Hoyt and becomes the "resurrected Charlotte Simmons" (615). Before her conversation, Charlotte expects to receive "Momma's mercy" (657), but she gets instead reverent spiritual instruction: "sounds to me like what you need right now is a talk with your own soul, an honest talk" (661). For Charlotte to be honest with herself, she must filter through all the experiences she has undergone while at Dupont and at Sparta during the past several months and make a decision about which values constitute the nature of her soul. This stance determines Charlotte's ultimate moral position.

Charlotte's situation of being in almost two distinct worlds is emblematic of what many working-class students undergo when they make the move into academia. In C. L. Barney Dews and Carolyn Leste Law's *This Fine Place So Far From Home: Voices of Academics from the Working Class*, academics describe the cultural no-man's-land between where they came from and the seemingly unwelcoming, unreceptive, and exclusionary domain of higher education. The shift from a world in which one's worth is dependent upon hourly wages, physical prowess, and overt materialism to everything stereotypically associated with the life of the mind demands a cultural flexibility and social eclecticism most are unwilling to assume. When Charlotte states she no longer has a home, she is asserting a sentiment expressed in one way or another by every contributor to Dews and Law's anthology. In her introduction, Law mentions a common quality is "the uncomfortably ambiguous stance of the border crosser. Crossing from one world to another is never fully achieved for the working-class academic; the transformation is never complete. [. . .] While one can appear to be a native in an adopted land, one is always haunted by voices from the other side of the border. These are narratives of the profound conflict, of persons feeling out of place in both worlds [. . .] of an ongoing search for community, a sense of being pushed and pulled between fear of alienation and the desire for camaraderie" (6–7). In an essay from Dews and Law's anthology called "A Real Class Act," Julie A. Charlip poignantly describes her difficulty making the class transition into higher education. In a section entitled "Where Do I Belong?" Charlip writes, "To what class do I belong now, as I head from grad-school poverty to the rather ill-paid life of the mind? [. . .] I can never escape from my class background, and there's nothing quite like the hallowed, upper-class halls of academe to remind me of it" (39–40). In "Work and Class in the Box Store University: Autobiographies of Working-Class Academics," Raymond Mazurek surveys various anthologies addressing the kind of dilemma people like Charlip experienced, and although Charlotte is only a freshman possessing the potential to become an academic, she experiences the same limbo between home and academy articulately expressed in various professors' testimonies and illustrated fictionally through Sara in *Bread Givers* and Marya in *Marya, A Life*.[3]

In *Where We Stand: Class Matters*, many of bell hooks's descriptions correspond to Charlotte's collegiate experiences. Hooks grew up in a rural Kentucky community much like Charlotte's Sparta, and although she faced racial as well as economic challenges, she tackled the same academic adversity as Charlotte. A gifted student, hooks had to attend a college near her hometown before transferring to Stanford University, an academic opportunity only possible because of scholarships, paralleling Charlotte's opportunity to attend Dupont only with the help of academic awards. At Stanford, hooks felt the same social exclusion as Charlotte based upon her working-class background; and just like Charlotte, when hooks did socialize, there was still disconnectedness based upon class differences. Hooks felt the same economic pressures as Charlotte, and she describes one roommate, a scholarship student like herself, who succumbed to status pressure:

> Like my friend during freshman year she shared the understanding of what it was like to be a have-not in a world of haves. But unlike me she was determined to become one of them. If it meant she had to steal nice clothes to look the same as they did, she had no problem taking these risks. If it meant having a privileged boyfriend who left bruises on her body now and then, it was worth the risk. Cheating was worth it. She believed the world the privileged had created was all unfair—all one big cheat; to get ahead one had to play the game. To her I was truly an innocent, a lamb being led to the slaughter. It did not surprise her one bit when I began to crack under the pressure of contradictory values and longings. (34)

Mimi and Bettina are clearly motivated by different values and longings from Charlotte. They are members of Charlotte's first Dupont social community, but Charlotte does not feel a true connection with them. When Charlotte realizes the only glue that keeps the three of them together is sexile, gossip, and boredom, the others have no moral value to her, and she eventually stops hanging out with them. The same is true for Hoyt, who seems to be one of the "haves" in Dupont social culture. After Charlotte realizes he has no moral worth, she no longer maintains an alliance with him; granted, he also no longer desires her as a sexual commodity. Charlotte's relationship with Adam has potential because of his academic intelligence, but his emotional collapse in the face of cheating charges exposes his moral vacuity. Jojo has yet to demonstrate completely that he "has" the moral core with which Charlotte wants to associate. The plagiarism case and his social conformity have lessened his moral worth to Charlotte, but she has not totally given up on him, especially since he is now academically engaged. If Charlotte had been like hooks's roommate, she would have taken something of social or cultural value gratuitously and possibly ruthlessly, but from her Dupont peers she has really only taken experience, nothing more.

Instead of exploiting others, Charlotte grows from her interactions with them. Conversely, the others commodify Charlotte. After they realize Charlotte has garnered Hoyt's attention, Mimi and Bettina want to increase their social status via association. Even Beverly displays jealousy toward Charlotte after she finds out Charlotte is interacting in the same social circle as Hoyt. All three males sexually objectify Charlotte, but Adam begins to interpret his relationship with Charlotte as something less superficial when he begins helping her after her emotional meltdown. Hoyt loses interest in Charlotte after the sexual conquest. Jojo seems to view Charlotte as an academic savior, someone who (comparable to an assistant coach) will keep him focused on his courses and not just on the court. Hooks provides a way to interpret the significance of these relationships to Charlotte by differentiating the materialism of a "have" from the asceticism of a "have-not": "In part, youth culture's worship of wealth stems from the fact that it is easier to acquire money and goods than it is to find meaningful values and ethics, to know who you are and what you want to become, to make and sustain friends, to know love" (85). As she sits in the Buster Bowl, Charlotte understands who she is, and unlike the other characters, she no longer assumes a social persona or a cultural mask. Adam is still the intellectual nerd, although his intellectual integrity has been questioned; Hoyt is still the arrogant frat boy, albeit he has been exposed as unscrupulous; and Jojo is still the athletic jock, yet he has aspirations to succeed scholastically. In the end, Charlotte is the only character who is just herself, exclusively "Charlotte Simmons." Through her experiences, the "I am Charlotte Simmons" at the end of the novel is not the same as she was in the beginning. She has learned to bridge the values of Sparta with those of Dupont, and she has decided to maintain a loyalty to the only ideology that truly matters, the one with which she can identify and apply to live a morally satisfying life for herself, nobody else.

Charlotte's transition from working-class Sparta to middle-class Dupont provides her the opportunity to differentiate the positive from the negative, the good from the bad, the self-fulfilling from the self-destructive. She thinks about a hypothetical conversation she would have with her mother, "All right, I'll say, 'I am Charlotte Simmons'" (674), and then thinks to herself, "You can't *define* a person who is unique" (675), but she might be really defining "unique" as someone beyond cultural representation. Charlotte has a certain status at home, one at Dupont, and probably a host of others in various contexts, but *she is fundamentally working class*. No matter how hard Charlotte attempts to distance herself from where she comes from, she remains tethered morally, ethically, and spiritually to her home, instinctively tied to the ideology cultivated by her family and her community. Even though Charlotte is apparently frustrated by the changes in herself and her family during her first trip back to Sparta, she still seems to intuitively understand that she will always be connected with her working-class roots. Charlotte's position at the end of the novel is dependent upon her realization that she must not imitate to succeed, and in a few months during her freshman year, she learns more about herself and her environment than most students figure out in four or five years. Charlotte is only nineteen years old at this point, and even though she is in the spotlight—as the narrator comments, "[o]f all the female freshmen at Dupont, how many were truly better known than Charlotte Simmons?" (671–72)—there are clues that her relationship with Jojo will not last. Charlotte might be taking advantage of Jojo's campus worth to increase her social status, but more likely she is a normal college student who is exploring her romantic options. Charlotte was gaining social stardom in the middle of the novel with Hoyt, so she did not really achieve sudden campus fame by attaching herself to Jojo. Realistically, she should be with Jojo at the end of the novel. After all, unlike everyone else whom she has befriended at Dupont, Jojo has not been eliminated from Charlotte's life. Jojo is Charlotte's only remaining friend at Dupont when readers last see her.

Charlotte has not given up her values for popularity, although reading the final section in isolation might suggest such an interpretation. She is instead having an introspection to reinforce her choice at the moment. Wolfe makes Socrates a constant literary reference for an important reason: Charlotte knows herself better than during any point in her life. Charlotte will continue to redefine who she is based upon her own belief system, but when she declares for the final time "I am Charlotte Simmons," she is referring to the core working-class ideology instilled in her before attending Dupont precisely because her moral center has its foundation in Sparta. Although she wavers by complacently saying "All right," as if she will make the statement even if it may be condescending, sarcastic, or false, she says the four key words that constantly keep her focused and consistently reveal her inner strength. Wolfe confessed to Tavis Smiley that the inspiration for his novel was Theodore Dreiser's turn-of-the-century bildungsroman *Sister Carrie*. Comparing Charlotte to Dreiser's heroine, Wolfe commented,

> [Charlotte] seemed to me like the perfect person because through her, the reader would be introduced to each one of the unusual things about college life, kind of like Sister Carrie in Dreiser's great novel. Sister Carrie, she's this little girl, Carrie Meeber, [Dreiser] gave her the most weak name he possibly could, who introduces you to the city of Chicago as the first great American metropolitan novel. So at first, [Charlotte] was for me, a device, but then I became more and more interested in her as a person.

Like Carrie, who left rural Wisconsin for a better life in bustling Chicago, Charlotte fled the Blue Ridge Mountains for prestigious Dupont University to achieve something higher, in her case to pursue the "life of the mind" (525). Most significant similarity ends there. At the end of *Sister Carrie*, Carrie sits laconically in a rocking chair as the narrator comments, "by your window, shall you dream such happiness as you may never feel" (Dreiser 369). At the end of *I Am Charlotte Simmons*, however, Charlotte is certainly no weakling, and her conversion is still in the process of evolving. Charlotte has the potential to experience much happiness as she moves forward as a self-confident, experience-wise, second-semester Dupont coed, one still formulating exactly what kinds of dreams she wants to fulfill.

NOTES

1. Most treat the novel as social fable or cultural parable and argue Wolfe never goes beyond the obvious about the college experience. Critics point out college students have always abused alcohol, had sex, missed class, and generally taken advantage of newly bestowed freedom. On the other hand, some praise Wolfe's realism, detail, and candor. For instance, Daniel Kennelly asserts that "[i]f Wolfe's novels could be said to make on overarching epic tale of

America, then *Charlotte Simmons* is the chapter on the decadence of modern American college life" (55). Peter Berkowitz writes, "In early twenty-first century America, with the eyes and ears of a master journalist and employing the art of the popular novelist, Tom Wolfe has added another chapter to this large and long-running story. In its dramatization of how our universities miseducate the finest fed, the finest clothed, and freest generation the world has ever seen, *I Am Charlotte Simmons* captures an alarming dimension of our times" (85).
2. Elaine Showalter's criticism is particularly derisive. After she calls Wolfe "essentially voyeuristic," Showalter asserts, "it takes a writer as snobbish, superficial, and insecure as Tom Wolfe [...] to write such puerile rubbish" (B14). She argues Wolfe, for all intents and purposes, writes a novel about male-dominated culture devoid of any feminist power: "Wolfe totally misses the feminist revolution that has given us so many more women students, faculty members, deans, and presidents. Neither producing a professorroman nor a bildungsroman, he tells us little about the nature of the academy or anything about student life and thought that transcends the grossest of stereotypes" (B14).
3. Mazurek's discussion includes Janet Zandy's *Liberating Memory*; Sherry Lee Linkon's *Teaching Working Class*; Jake Ryan and Charles Sackrey's *Strangers in Paradise*; Stephen L. Muzzatti and C. Vincent Samarco's *Reflections for the Wrong Side of the Tracks*; and Alan Sheppard, John McMillan, and Gary Tate's *Coming to Class*, each describing experiences similar to Charlotte's. Mazurek provides an excellent summary of sources addressing this subject.

BIBLIOGRAPHY

Berkowitz, Peter. "He Is Charlotte Simmons." *Policy Review* 129 (2005): 78–86. Print.
Charlip, Julie A. "A Real Class Act." *This Fine Place So Far From Home: Voices of Academics From the Working Class*. Ed. C. L. Barney Dews and Carolyn Leste Law. Philadelphia: Temple UP, 1995. 26–40. Print.
Christopher, Renny, and Carolyn Whitson. "Toward a Theory of Working Class Literature." *Thought and Action* 15 (1999): 71–81. Print.
Coles, Nicholas, and Janet Zandy, eds. *American Working-Class Literature: An Anthology*. New York: Oxford UP, 2007. Print.
Dews, C. L. Barney, and Carolyn Leste Law, eds. *This Fine Place So Far From Home: Voices of Academics From the Working Class*. Philadelphia: Temple UP, 1995. Print.
Dreiser, Theodore. *Sister Carrie*. 1900. Ed. Donald Pizer. 2nd ed. New York: Norton, 1991. Print.
hooks, bell. *Where We Stand: Class Matters*. New York: Routledge, 2000. Print.
Iannone, Carol. "A Critic in Full: A Conversation with Tom Wolfe." *Academic Questions* 21.2 (2008): 138–63. Print.
Kennelly, Daniel. "Sex and Drink Make a Dull Girl." *American Enterprise* 16.3 (2005): 55–56. Print.
Lauter, Paul. "Working-Class Women's Literature: An Introduction to Study." *Women in Print I*. Ed. Joan E. Harman and Ellen Messer-Davidow. New York: MLA, 1982. Rpt. in *Politics of Education: Essays from Radical Teacher*. Ed. Susan Gushee O'Mallery, Robert C. Rosen, and Leonard Vogt. Albany: SUNY UP, 1990. 110–39. Print.

"Life on Campus: Problems and Solutions." Narr. Glenn Beck. *Glenn Beck*. CNN. New York, 22 Aug. 2008. Television.

Linkon, Sherry Lee, ed. *Teaching Working Class*. Amherst: U of Massachusetts P, 1999. Print.

Mazurek, Raymond. "Work and Class in the Box Store University: Autobiographies of Working-Class Academics." *College Literature* 36.4 (2009): 147–78. Print.

Muzzatti, Stephen L., and C. Vincent Samarco, eds. *Reflections for the Wrong Side of the Tracks*. New York: Rowan and Littlefield, 2006. Print.

Oates, Joyce Carol. *Marya, A Life*. Ontario: Ontario Review, 1986. Print.

Ryan, Jake, and Charles Sackrey. *Strangers in Paradise: Academics from the Working Class*. Boston: South End, 1984. Print.

Sheppard, Alan, John McMillan, and Gary Tate, eds. *Coming to Class: Pedagogy and the Social Class of Teachers*. Portsmouth: Boynton/Cook, 1998. Print.

Showalter, Elaine. "Peeping Tom's Juvenile Jaunt." *Chronicle of Higher Education* 12 Nov. 2004: B14. Print.

The Tavis Smiley Show. Narr. Tavis Smiley. PBS. WNET, New York, 16 Nov. 2004. Television.

Tokarczyk, Michelle M. "Promise to Keep: Working Class Students and Higher Education." *What's Class Got To Do With It: American Society in the Twenty-First Century*. Ed. Michael Zweig. Ithaca: Cornell UP, 2004. 161–67. Print.

Tokarczyk, Michelle M., and Elizabeth Fay, eds. *Working-Class Women in the Academy: Laborers in the Knowledge Factory*. Amherst: U of Massachusetts P, 1993. Print.

Wolfe, Tom. *I Am Charlotte Simmons*. New York: Picador, 2004. Print.

Yezierska, Anzia. *Bread Givers*. New York: Doubleday, 1925. Print.

Zandy, Janet, ed. *Liberating Memory: Our Work and Our Working-Class Consciousness*. New Brunswick: Rutgers UP, 1995. Print.

6 (Un)teaching the Anthology
Pedagogy versus Canon in Working-Class Literature

Nicholas Coles

> I feel like I found a subject that not only interested me, but told the story of my life and those I know. The idea and concepts of working-class literature combine my two worlds of working society and academia. I have struggled to find a balance, and will continue to do so until I finally pick a side or manage to fuse the two. (Abbi)

> These particular people and stories were chosen for a reason; they are the ideal members of their group (it may be due to their successes or their failures). And although the situation may not have been the same for every member of the working class, those stories were chosen for a reason. (Meredith)

> And these pieces were not individual; they were class writing through and through. Indeed, working-class literature is a woven textile of thousands of pieces, authors, groups, and views on working life. Together these pieces are a class of writing, and embody group authorship and a form of socialized art. (Sean)

> What am I going to do with my life? The spirit of the rallies, protests, and revolutions that focused on our lives alongside one another, and wrote our nation's history, feel lost or distant to me today. Where is that spirit of togetherness now? (Deanna)

These students' responses to an undergraduate literature course in which they studied an anthology of American working-class writing frame the project of this chapter. I will examine pedagogy for working-class literature through a focus on the problematics of the anthology form: that is, in my students' words, "a class of writing" "chosen for a reason," that both tells "the story of my life" and, on the contrary, feels "lost and distant." My central concern as a teacher of this literature is to explore what I have come to see as the productive difficulties of working with and against the anthology-textbook as a canonizing institution of literary pedagogy.

THE ANTHOLOGY

In "The Making of American Working-Class Literature," Janet Zandy writes, "Embedded in the machinery of literary anthologies is the relationship of power to cultural formation. Generally, this is called canon-formation" (2). In 2007, Zandy and I published the anthology *American Working-Class Literature* (*AWCL*) we had been working on for many years. Oxford University Press produced the book through its textbook division, intended primarily for use in college classrooms. The book's scope is ambitious, gathering more than three hundred texts from colonial times to the year 2002, and framing them with a full apparatus of historical introductions, author headnotes, bibliographies, and illustrations. Our goal as editors was to make visible and available for teaching and study a body of work that had largely been either obscured or devalued by the canon-making processes of "Literature." Without making definitive claims, we aimed to represent the range of writing produced over time by the men and women of all races and ethnicities who make up the extraordinarily diverse American working class: from ballads of indentured servants and sorrow songs of African slaves to contemporary poetry, fiction, and memoir; with speeches, manifestoes, letters, oral history, reportage, and other noncanonical genres included along the way. We wanted in particular to foster recognition of the double character of American working-class literature as, in Zandy's words, "a literary line, a body of work, and a labor line, the work of bodies."[1] For this is a textual tradition that emerges from contexts of labor—in fields, factories, kitchens, offices, and neighborhoods—that mark the text as much as they mark the minds and bodies of workers and writers.

Since *AWCL* has been in use in classrooms for several years now, we are in a position to look into the pedagogical implications of producing an anthology to represent this "literary and labor legacy," including the contradictions implicit in contributing to the formation of a "noncanonical" canon. In teaching the anthology, I have been led to question how the gathering of a selection of working-class writings into a textbook affects their status and function as items of "Literature," especially in the classroom, the primary site where canons play out their effects; how we can make legible and significant for students the histories of struggle and labor, including rhetorical and literary labor, out of which many of these texts are produced; and how we might take advantage of the double (literary and labor) character of these texts to promote forms of response, dialogue, and inquiry that extend or even subvert canonical practices of literary reading.

For this inquiry, I am drawing in part on my experience teaching Working-Class Literature at the University of Pittsburgh (Pitt), where, as a course meeting general humanities requirements, it is always fully enrolled with students drawn from a range of majors, including history, economics, urban studies, English writing, and literature. My research process also entailed corresponding with and interviewing several instructors who have taught the anthology both at Pitt and other schools, in order to learn about their approaches and to get their responses to the questions I am posing here.[2] I have also studied final reflections written by students in my own classes—as well as comments posted to online discussion boards—to assess what, in their own terms, they have been learning through the course and its readings.

Let me note at the outset that the testimony of teachers using the book suggests that *AWCL* meets a need in the field of working-class studies and provides a valued resource for classroom use.[3] The anthology gathers into one material space a range of writings many of which were scattered, ephemeral or obscure, and it presents these writings in a framework that supports the linking of a text and its context, the circumstances of its production and reception. Beyond the classroom, the anthology has been useful for some faculty in making the curricular case to their departments for developing a course in working-class literature. *AWCL* has been deployed within the academy, in other words, as evidence of the currency of the field and the feasibility of teaching it. Each of these apparent benefits, however, has a problematic shadow side: the contradictory countereffects of this process of anthology making. In valorizing certain works by collecting them between the covers of a textbook, we run the risk of submitting this living tradition to the institutional procedures that have formerly devalued it.

CANON FORMATION

The production of any anthology is necessarily an imperfect and compromised process. The attempt to delineate a field and define its key terms, to set boundaries of time and space, and to establish criteria for selection is inevitably slippery and contested. Even if the field the anthology attempts to represent were relatively stable in definition and scope—which working-class literature is not—the editors' knowledge of the field and all the texts that might possibly comprise it will always be partial.[4] And even with stable definitions, wide reading, and a supportive cast of advisors, the editors must make thousands of decisions as to what to include and what to leave out, and these will sometimes be based as much on the economic constraints of page limits and permissions costs as on agreed criteria. The resulting compilation, appearing on course syllabi as required reading, encased between the covers of a volume bearing the imprint of a university press, and costing upwards of $50, has an authority—a material and academic heft—that belies these imperfections.

In routine practice, of course, students are accustomed to buying hefty textbooks for classes, and faculty understand that any anthology is by definition incomplete, a more or less informed choice of swatches from an unfinished fabric. Instructors will choose for their students the anthology whose contents and organization best meet their purposes.[5] The larger problem that concerns me here lies beyond these practical considerations, in the institutional conditions they point to: the function of the anthology-textbook as a regulatory mechanism for producing "Literature" as students are to understand it. Simply put, the trouble with textbooks is that they claim, implicitly or explicitly, to contain what a student needs to know about a subject. As an assemblage of texts sanctioned by the curricular and publishing conventions of the academy as representative of a field and worthy to be taught, the anthology-textbook serves the project of canon formation.

In *Cultural Capital: The Problem of Literary Canon Formation*, John Guillory argues that a literary canon is not formed by a set of discrete judgments, whether by contemporary editors or by their historical ancestors, made with conscious intent to include or exclude certain social groups; rather, canons arise as a consequence of histories of unequal access to literacy and to what Pierre Bourdieu calls "cultural capital." Guillory explains, "The theory of cultural capital implies that the proper social context for analyzing the school and its literary curriculum is *class* . . . [T]he fact of class determines whether and how individuals gain access to the means of literary production, and the system regulating such access is a much more efficient mechanism of exclusion than acts of judgment" (viii-ix). "In the present regime of capital distribution," he continues, "the school will remain both the agency for the reproduction of unequal social relations and a necessary site for the critique of that system" (55). If the school, or university, is the institution in which canons achieve their most consequential enactment, it is also then potentially the site of their undoing and remaking. Although, as Guillory points out, "[c]hanging the syllabus [or creating an anthology] cannot mean in any historical context overthrowing the canon," it is also the case that "every construction of a syllabus institutes once again the process of canon formation" (31).

There are particular problems, then, in forming a canon of works composed by noncanonical writers—problems that, I will suggest, can be seen to offer productive questions for pedagogy. As well as separating certain voices out from the multiplicity of working-class cultural production, an anthology threatens to elevate literature above the flow of historical time. And this is so, ironically, even when the anthology is insistently historical in its method and organization: it deploys works from the past for study in the contemporary classroom, where it will require conscious acts of imagination by teachers and students to disembed them from the historical present. On the other hand, the fixing in print of any canon can obscure the currency of literature as an ongoing social process in which new work is constantly emerging and receding, challenging received notions of what literature can be and do. Unless we work consciously against this tendency, the texts chosen for the reformed canon can become static objects, "verbal icons" to be admired or explicated. In "Rethinking Working-Class Literature," Sonali Perera asks, "[h]ow do we write about the necessarily disappearing objects of working-class literature . . . without freezing them into emblematic objects?" (8). And in the classroom, how might we rescue this literature from the fate of the verbal icon?

A further problem, carefully worked out by Guillory, is that the establishment of a countercanon is tied in problematic ways to the multicultural projects of identity politics. Selected texts and authors may be treated as representative of the "experiences" or "values" of a dominated social group, as if these experiences or values were somehow unique or consistent within the group, and as if they could be transmitted to students simply by reading the right texts. The works included in the anthology may be read as confirming a particular representation of the American working class, valorizing its "culture," including an ethic of hard work and solidarity. Such a notion of class identity, intended to be inclusive for working-class students, may in practice make it easier for those and other students to distance themselves from the literature. How do we affirm the salience of class analysis without homogenizing the diversity of working-class identity, including the ways it intersects with students' and writers' self-identification by race, gender, and sexuality?

If, then, there is a countercanon being constructed by means of the anthology and its classroom use, it will need to be questioned, critiqued, constantly revised by students and teachers. In the best case, these critiques will be launched from a perspective enriched by the resources of the anthology itself, which is designed to promote inquiry into the complex relations of class and literature, anchored in an understanding of histories of labor, struggle, and cultural production. The work of the teacher would then include historicizing the individual literary text, working back and forth between text and context, undoing the distancing effect of seeing working-class realities as either "back then" in the past or belonging to "others"—or both. It would involve helping students get inside texts that seem removed from them in time and social position—asking how they might speak to us now—and also outside of them, understanding where these texts came from and what cultural work they performed in their time. And if a key question in a course is, "What counts as literature, and how do certain texts come to be counted?" then the problems of canon formation can also be foregrounded with students: how and why these texts were chosen, what these choices imply, what other texts can be seen to represent working-class cultural production.

In what follows I explore the use of the anthology-textbook as a terrain for staging these questions pedagogically. I hope to demonstrate how it can be treated not only as a sourcebook for a revised canon but also, contrarily, as a means of pointing to what is beyond the scope of the book, in daily life, in culture and history, in students' backgrounds—to draw out and examine what the textbook cannot know.

CLASSROOM STRATEGIES

I want to look now at a set of classroom strategies designed by teachers of the anthology: 1) an online discussion project, 2) a family work history project, 3) a group theater project, and 4) an anthology-building project.[6] Each of these strategies has particular purposes connected to the focus of the course being taught, which I will describe in introducing the vignettes that follow. They also suggest, in differing ways, how far pedagogy might go in addressing the problematics of canonization outlined above.

1   Online Discussion

In my course, I use online discussion to promote interaction between readers and texts, as well as reciprocal response among students.[7] At the start of term we read texts about familiar contemporary workplaces and working conditions, setting them alongside corresponding writings from earlier periods. Jan Beatty's "A Waitress's Instructions on Tipping" (1995) is one of a sequence of poems grounded in her work waiting tables, including relations with customers, coworkers, food, and life outside of work. Beatty had worked her way through college in restaurants and diners, and students readily connect to her outspoken diatribe. Like her, many are laboring to pay their way in school, and everyone in the class has had experience eating out and tipping. We discussed Beatty's work alongside I. G. Blanchard's 1866 poem "Eight Hours," in order to set up a dialogue between texts—two poems of protest and exhortation addressing central conditions of labor: money and time, respectively—from the current service economy and the nineteenth-century industrial revolution. Set to music by the Reverend Jesse Jones in 1878, "Eight Hours" became an anthem of the movement for an eight-hour work day, with its compelling chorus: "Eight hours for work, eight hours for rest, / Eight hours for what we will" (138). Beatty's poem takes the form of a list of demands:

> Twenty percent minimum as long as the waitress doesn't inflict
>   bodily harm.
> If you're two people at a four top, tip extra.
> If you sit a long time, pay rent. (854)

At this early stage in the semester, I pose the questions for online discussion; in later weeks, groups of students write and post them. My prompt for this discussion forum included these questions:

(Un)teaching the Anthology 109

- What makes Jan Beatty's list of instructions on tipping a "poem"? What do you notice about its language, structure, and movement? How does it differ in form and purpose from Blanchard's "Eight Hours"? What do they have in common?
- When you read Beatty's other poems on waitressing, how do they change the perspective you get from her tough-talking "Instructions"? What do these poems suggest about "service" work, beyond the economic exchange of tipping?
- Trace the argument of "Eight Hours." How does Blanchard make the claim that workers deserve an eight-hour day? What poetic or rhetorical devices does he use? For instance, why are there so many references to God, or to the human/animal distinction?
- We've listened to Anne Feeney's song, "Whatever Happened to the Eight-Hour Day?" Do some research into this question. How did it come about? Is it still federal law? What's the deal with Walmart and unpaid overtime?

Students' responses, which I do not have space to quote in detail, show them sharing experiences of service work ("I will tell you everything Beatty says is true!"), comparing emotional effects of literary language ("While Beatty made me feel obligated to tip higher, Blanchard made me both sympathetic and proud of the workers"), considering audience relations ("Blanchard seems to be writing to inspire the movement but also as a warning to those who live in 'plenty'"), contrasting disparate time periods ("Labor workers of the nineteenth century were part of the manufacturing machine. . . . For the career-oriented person today, is the eight-hour day relevant?"), and making general assertions about purpose and value ("It seems to me that it is more important to analyze these poems in terms of their historical importance than their aesthetic value") that we will debate in class. One student posted a detailed summary of Walmart's labor practices and lawsuits against the corporation. Another student issued this spirited call to her classmates:

> The voices crying out to us in Blanchard's poem feel soulless, slaves to staying alive, yet in the end they are shouting "hurrah, hurrah for labor." They believe in each other. That "the world were wise to listen to the monetary hum" still applies to us today. What do you find the challenge in "Eight Hours" to be? Who can unite their experiences with Jan Beatty's poems?

A primary goal of this online discussion was to foster students' interaction with these texts, based on careful reading and bringing their own knowledge and experience to bear on what they read, and to jump-start their conversation with each other over meaning and values. Their responses demonstrate that they are also beginning to reflect on the social function of literature, to make connections between periods and workplaces, and to look into historical and economic conditions reflected in the chosen texts.

2 Family Work History

A related strategy, from the classroom of Kathleen Welsch at Clarion University, invites a more sustained exploration of connections between anthologized texts and lived realities, including students' work experience and their family histories. Welsch, editor of the anthology *Those Winter Sundays: Female Academics and Their Working-Class Parents*, has a personal as well as academic investment in the course she designed in American working-class literature. She grew up in Pittsburgh and was educated at Pitt, where her father worked as a telephone technician. She sees a reflection of herself in many of the students who come to Clarion from rural working-class families in northwestern Pennsylvania. A high proportion of her students, like mine, are working either full or part time while in college. Offered for the first time in 2009, Welsch's course reached full enrollment quickly, and she attributes its appeal to students' expectation that the course would connect literature with what they know from experience.

This connection is a major focus of Welsch's teaching. In a two-part essay project, students examine their own family work histories, to articulate for themselves and each other, in Welsch's words, "what kind of people they come from," what work older family members did and how they view their class position. (She draws on Michael Zweig's definitions of the U.S. class structure for this project.)[8] As she tells her students in the assignment directions, "[t]his project is an opportunity to talk with family members, gather stories about working, look at family photo albums in new ways, identify artifacts representing work in your family, and tell the story of your heritage from a new perspective." In a second phase of the project, students go on to connect their family work-histories with pieces of literature they've been reading, in order to explore "how the workers in your family are part of a larger, historical picture":

> The connection can be through an historical event, or in the form of work represented, working conditions, the lifestyle created by work, the impact of work on an individual's life or body, the influence of work beyond the individual (political/economic); it can even be to a particular character or setting.

The pieces students choose in order to make these connections include contemporary works like Beatty's "Instructions on Tipping" discussed above, Peter Oresick's "My Father," or Kate Rushin's "The Black Back-Ups," as well as historical texts such as Hamlin Garland's "Under the Lion's Paw" (1881, about Midwestern farm-work and debt) or Edith Summers Kelley's

"Billy's Birth" (1923, the deleted childbirth chapter from her novel *Weeds*), among many other texts.

Through this kind of literary-personal-historical project, Welsch suggests, some students recovered a sense of pride in family members' work and what it made possible for them. Others, including students identifying as members of the professional middle class, reflected on their own social position, how they came into their class legacies, and the nature of their relationships to students of other class backgrounds. For many students, building on those recognitions, the course encouraged reflection on the choices they are making about what they study, about their future careers, and about meanings of "success": what will you do with your qualifications, your background and education? What kind of person do you want to be? The anthology supports this project because, Welsch says, "Collecting works like these exposes students to parts of themselves they haven't named or looked at before. It can create a kind of cohesion in their understanding of what has happened in their lives, expanding their sense of identity and location, socially and historically."

3 Group Theatre Project

A creative strategy for setting literature into an active relation to the past and to students' current social position entails rewriting and updating texts by transforming their genre. In the process, students rearticulate key ideas in historical texts to contemporary conditions. William Scott's course at Pitt, in the language of the course description, "explores writing produced by working-class men and women. It traces its textual traditions and explores questions of the status of the 'working class,' its relation to self-understandings in ethnic, racial, or gender terms, as well as the effect of class on social experience, social vision, and cultural production." As the title of his forthcoming book—*Troublemakers: Power, Representation, and the Fiction of the Mass Worker*—suggests, Scott is concerned in his course with the ways in which texts in successive historical periods represent workers and workplaces differently, particularly with regard to modes of workers' power and/or powerlessness. To engage students in thinking actively about how work is organized and disciplined, and about the ways workers have resisted bossing and exploitation, he has devised "group theater projects."[9] The class is divided into groups of four or five, each of which will be responsible for writing, rehearsing, and performing their own original fifteen- to twenty-minute play. According to Scott's assignment, "Group Theater Projects should: 1) be directly or indirectly inspired by one of the texts we are reading for the course, and 2) take the form of a narrative and tell a story" using "scenes that connect to one another and advance the basic story-line," "recognizable protagonists and antagonists—as well as dramatic conflicts and reversals," and "standard theatrical devices to enhance the impact of the drama," such as costumes, props, and music. Groups are free to script as little or as much of their play as they wish, and Scott recommends some combination of scripted and improvised material. Class members discuss and debate each play for a further twenty minutes after the performance.

The resulting plays (which I have watched on video) are remarkable for the quality of the writing, the energy of the performances, and the ways—by turns comic and melodramatic—they connect labor issues arising in the literature with students' workplace experiences and their sense of their prospects as college graduates in the Great Recession. Titles and topics in the 2009 course included:

Let's Just Chalk About It—a local teachers' strike
Daily Bread—the work lives of Pitt's cafeteria staff
1–800-Snuggies—a worker's heart attack at telemarketing company provokes strike talk
Writer's Block—creative writing majors' career prospects in light of the Writers Guild strike
Technological Canyon—student workers organize when denied holiday pay

Scott notes that in creating their own dramatizations, students transposed issues and problems from the assigned texts onto new, contemporary scenarios—in the process shifting the locus of power in the classroom, at least temporarily, from teacher and text to their own collective activity. In the response sessions that followed each performance, students used threads from the plays to discuss their present situations, their expectations of their college experiences, and what their work-lives after college might look like. When the class went back to discussing literary texts, students looked for echoes of issues that had been dramatized in the plays and debated afterwards. A group agenda had been set, directing renewed attention to texts along the lines Constance Coiner lays out in her key article on working-class women's literature: "We want readers to decipher the cultural work done by working-class texts and the ways in which readers are invited to participate in that cultural work" (230).

4 Anthology Project

To address questions of canon formation in my own classroom, I have engaged students in the kinds of editorial decision making that go into creating an anthology, in two ways: 1) by forming "clusters" of readings from *AWCL* around themes of their choosing, and 2) by composing a mini anthology drawing on their own reading, viewing, and listening beyond the scope of the textbook.

Throughout the earlier historical sections of *AWCL*, Zandy and I assembled "clusters" of readings focused on significant events, such as the Triangle Factory Fire of 1911, or on cultural formations like the Harlem Renaissance. The two-hundred-page-long section of contemporary works ("The New World Order and Its Consequences: 1980s to 2005"), on the other hand, was arranged chronologically by author's date of birth, rather than thematically. To open up this ample collection of contemporary writings, students working in groups selected texts to form clusters on topics of mutual interest, such as: "Rust Belt Blues" (with works by Phil Levine, Jeanne Bryner, Jim Daniels, Sue Doro, Larry Smith), "Border Crossings" (Gloria Anzaldúa, Helena Viramontes, Nellie Wong, Martín Espada, Melida Rodas), and "Women Doing 'Men's Work'" (Sue Doro, Susan Eisenberg, Leslie Feinberg, Carolyn Chute).

This practice in selecting and clustering individual texts prepared students for editing a mini anthology, one of the options for a final project that would constitute their own "contribution to working-class studies." The assignment calls for a compilation of texts designed to illuminate an aspect of working-class culture that had not been well represented in the course, often one with which they feel a special identification. They select and assemble a dozen or more works, with illustrations and attached CDs if they choose, into some form of binding. They then write an introduction explaining the editorial rationale for their choices. Individual texts are sometimes accompanied by the equivalent of the headnotes in *AWCL* or liner notes on a music album. Many of these projects are presented or performed for the class in the final weeks. A sample of titles may give a sense of their scope, which ranges widely across periods, locations, subcultures, workplaces, and social movements:

> "The Revolution Will Not Be Televised":[10] a Call to Action Through Music
> Workplace Comedy: Cultural Text for the New Working Class
> When Coal Was King [in the eastern Pennsylvania anthracite region]
> Kitchen Table Journey: "Perhaps the World Ends Here"[11]
> Out of the Mud [the Johnstown flood of 1889]
> Class, Race, and Gender: A Poetic Triad
> I Wear Work Boots in the Library to Remind Me

In producing and introducing their own anthologies, some students articulate an intention to broaden the canon of working-class cultural production, as the titles of some musical compilations make clear: "Born in America's Cities: The Voices of Hip Hop" or "Loud Labor: Working-Class Punk." Whether or not they are conscious of canon reform, students are involved in reshaping the curriculum, at least of this classroom, with their interventions. In doing so I believe they demonstrate, like Scott's and Welsch's students, an expanded understanding of what constitutes literature and of the work it can perform in the world.

STUDENT REFLECTIONS

I want to look now at students' written reflections on their course in working-class literature in relation to the goals articulated through these pedagogical strategies: how do they connect to the labor heritage reflected in the anthologized texts; how do they perceive literature's cultural work and their role in it; how does the course address their understanding of class and the ways it shapes social experience and action? More broadly, what do they stand to gain from studying this literature in this institutional context, and what problems and resistances are encountered?

I'll begin with an exchange between two students from a middle-class and a working-class background, respectively. This is excerpted from an online discussion in the second week of the semester, after students have read the introduction to *AWCL*.

> The introduction states, "Many of the writings, songs, and speeches come from these other labor contexts and were not originally designed for the interpretive and defining frameworks of the academy" (xxiii). This class challenges us to interpret the development of working-class culture and the experiences of working-class people, while we ourselves sit in our Scottish-style classroom far from the factory assembly line, or the waiter's maze of tables. Given the predicament of our distance both physical, mental, and in some ways periodic from the working-class environment, how shall we rise to the challenge of wearing the coal-miner's work boots or the waitress's uniform in order to better understand a culture so important to our present existence, and yet so overlooked by historic and literary examination? Will you relate your own experiences of work to better uncover and comprehend this buried culture? Or must you rely on the work experiences of your parents or relatives? Will you allow your perception of present-day working-class culture to change by looking at literature of the past? Finally, how will you justify your new understanding of working-class culture when your experience of it has been informed by the academic study of its literature; all the while knowing that your educational pursuits mirror the culture of the "educated class" that has for so long overlooked expressions of working-class culture? (Monica)

As we have seen, Monica's list of "will you" questions here predicts quite accurately some of the strategies students will be using to engage this literature from within the "frameworks of the academy": connecting the literature of the past to their work experience, to family work histories, and to present-day cultural production. Her initial conception of working-class culture, though, takes it to be "buried," remote from her/our present situation. Monica's post prompted this response from her classmate Sam:

> I think that what needs to be understood is that as struggling college students many, but not all, of us are in the working class. . . . I've always had a job. Prior to coming to college, I had assumed everyone worked their way through high school; I was wrong. I had also assumed everyone worked their way through college; I was dead wrong.

During freshman year, I couldn't find five friends who did have jobs. I had never met more nice, but spoiled, people in my entire life. I was baffled. So, yes, we may all be striving to be a part of that "educated class," but many of us are not there yet.

In turn, I think that those of us who can relate to these authors . . . will share many stories throughout this semester to better illustrate our work experiences. I have plenty to tell.

Because my aim is to allow students' testimony largely to "speak for itself," I'll resist the temptation to analyze the differences in class register between these two students' discourses and the knowledge-claims they enact. Suffice it to say that the stories told in class and online by students like Sam formed a major part of the learning afforded to this mixed-class group of students.

One of the most telling stories, however, was not heard by the group, for reasons Kayla explains in her closing reflections on the course:

In one week, I will be leaving Pittsburgh indefinitely. Financial strain in my family and Pitt's pricey tuition is the reason why. For months I have kept it a secret. . . . I didn't want to make a fuss about it and bring attention to the fact that my family is not as economically stable as other families. It was a bit embarrassing to me.

It is difficult to suddenly change the class you are in. I was born into the working class—my mom used to drive a forklift before taking an office job and my dad is a construction worker and involved in an ironworker union. . . .

Spending a semester reading selections from the *Working Class Literature* anthology, in some sections, was like reading a story similar to my family's. It was both refreshing and comforting. . . . With working-class literature, there was a connection I haven't found in a lot of other literature. The theme "just getting by," which I am very familiar with. Self-sacrifice for your family, which I worked with in my paper on "class." The importance of unity, "solidarity," and the strength that comes with it. Upward mobility, which I'm trying my best to represent even with the stress of leaving the school I love.

Kayla concluded her reflection by stating, "I am from a working-class family—these days, I say it with pride."

In an article on "Diversity, Discourse and the Working-Class Student," Janet Galligani Casey suggests that "working-class pride would seem to have no place in academia, which by its very existence encodes class superiority, and where students are being prepared explicitly for white-collar jobs" (35). And yet, the assertion of pride was echoed by a number of Kayla's classmates, even as they recognize the painful "in-between" position they occupy as students in an institution designed to change their class affiliation.

The most common response of self-identified working-class students to the anthologized literature was this sense of recognition of common experiences and affirmation of class identity. For many, this identification led to finding a new value in reading literature. As Eric wrote, "I wish I could have read and heard working-class works in high school. I think I could have had a better connection with the working roots of my parents, grandparents, and community." And this response by Marybeth certainly gladdened the heart of the anthology's editor: "Instead of selling this textbook back to the bookstore, I plan to bring it home and share it with my family so that they too can be introduced to the literature that they can relate to so well."

For some, though, a strong and unambiguous class identification, while it might be, as Kayla wrote, "refreshing and comforting," could lead to uncritical reading or complacent thinking. It is hard to fully credit Dave's claim that "[c]oming from a working-class family, [he] really understood all the messages that each piece was trying to convey." Similarly, for Greg, who has "always considered [his] family to be working class . . . , these writers have vindicated a lot of [his] beliefs that were already pretty rock solid at the foundation of [his] character at the beginning of the course." Neither student had spoken much during sometimes heated and digressive interpretive discussions, perhaps regarding them as "academic" in the conventional sense. Ironically, it seems the texts they identified with had remained "verbal icons" for them.

Resisting the academy's designs on one's thinking may be a necessary survival strategy for some working-class students, especially if one's thinking, in the case of Bill, a sophomore economics major also from a labor-class family and working his way through school, runs in opposition to what he sees as the dominant motif:

> One thing in the class I did not like was the fact that all of the readings we had gone over seemed to glorify the working class. The working class was always viewed as abused and beaten by the upper class and capitalists. When not in this context the working class was viewed as always right and their actions were always just.

Another student's resistance to what she sees as a form of political groupthink in the class leads to a productive line of questioning about the class-based effects, and the ambiguous value, of a college education:

> Many of my classmates have commented with deep resentment toward our system. Considering that each of us is obtaining a college education, why are we so hostile toward the system? Perhaps part of the problem is that 1) our working-class roots breed feelings of guilt because we have what previous generations did not, and 2) education, which was once seen as the solution and an escape from the labor classes, does not guarantee a comfortable lifestyle. In fact, many students are beginning their adult lives with an immense amount of debt; in essence, we are further behind than our predecessors were. (Anne)

For Anne, as for Kayla, economic insecurity haunts higher education's promise of upward mobility—no matter how one feels about the ideologies of working-class literature.

Finally, beyond these effects of identification and resistance, what are students claiming to have learned about the "cultural work" performed by this literature? A senior history major writes:

> While I knew a great deal about the working class and labor movements, what the members of those groups themselves had said I was, for the most part, entirely unfamiliar with. . . . This is what I will have taken with me when the course is a distant memory—the ability to relate to the working class in a new manner. (Brandon)

Siobhan puts it this way:

> Coupled with my recognition of human experience and feeling in the pieces of literature we have read, my views of the medium have expanded to include the realization that literature has the ability to act as a unifying force, as well as to inspire change in social situations. I believe this is the point I have leaned the most about, by studying the works we have read within their historical contexts, and assessing their aims.

For some, the "aims" of this work are directly political:

> The topics we discussed throughout the semester, capitalism, class mobility, race politics, literature as a tool for social change (just to name a few), are issues that are of the utmost importance in understanding our specific historical moment. (Evan)

For others, the political and the literary are interwoven:

> And these pieces were not individual; they were class writing through and through. Indeed, working-class literature is a woven textile of thousands of pieces, authors, groups, and views on working life. Together these pieces are a class of writing, and embody group authorship and a form of socialized art. . . . People thrive mutually, and so does art. (Sean)

CONCLUSIONS

This essay has been motivated by a set of questions about pedagogy for working-class literature, arising from the classroom deployment of the anthology *American Working-Class Literature*. I was concerned that, for all the rich resources and careful contextual framing of *AWCL*, the book's status as a required textbook, a canonizing institution of "Literature," could compromise its effectiveness in opening working-class writing up to students' thinking and use in productive ways. I wanted to explore what our students stand to gain from studying this literature and paying attention to the contexts in which it is produced; what problems and resistances are encountered; and what new or revised directions might be suggested by their responses.

Although my method of looking at multiple instructors' strategies and students' reflections does not lend itself to definitive conclusions, it seems clear that many of the goals I and others have articulated for the teaching of working-class literature are being met: making the study of literature (a centerpiece of a liberal education) engaging for working-class students; developing an appreciation of a shared legacy of labor and struggle; generating empathy across class lines; promoting concern for social and economic justice; affirming the labor that underlies all cultural production; challenging the classism of the academy.[12] It is also clear that some students resist some of these goals, whatever their class positions.

What I also learn from examining students' assessments of their work in the course, and from the reflections of colleagues who teach working-class literature, is the necessity of pushing beyond the categories of identity and ideology upon which canons and countercanons are assumed to be constructed. I conclude with some examples of what this conceptual shift implies for my own future teaching:

1. Without undermining the pleasures of recognition many working-class students encounter, I need to encourage them to read beyond the comfort of identification, into the terrain of "people and stories" that do not fit readily with their "experience" or that challenge their notion of what it means to be working class, sometimes from a "lost or distant" historical location or from a shifted ethnic or gendered point of view.
2. Without blunting the "unifying force" and the political thrust of much of this writing—its indictment of exploitation, its demonstration of resistance through collective action or authorship—I need to unsettle the notion that this is a class that speaks with one voice, expressing a single ideology or set of class values. This will require questioning the tendency, built into the "machinery" of even the most inclusive anthology, to thematize what are in fact very diverse articulations of working-class experience.
3. Along these lines, I plan to bring forward as a more explicit focus of collective inquiry the question of how class interacts with race and ethnicity, gender and sexuality, in the literature, in our educations, and in our work, including both the work of upward mobility and the struggle against unjust power. As I've often found in teaching, a student's comment points a way forward. Monica, quoted earlier on the complications of our location as readers of working-class literature within the "frameworks of the academy," wrote in her final reflection:

In addition to searching for a bridge between the educated middle class and the working class by examining literature, I became interested in the role of gender and ethnicity. These two factors challenge the notion of working-class solidarity, because they show that working-class unity can be easily divided along these lines. Many of my thoughts in this class have been directed towards the plight of the immigrant worker, ethnic minority worker, and the woman worker and how they add to the multidimensionality of the working-class identity, while retaining unique and significant characteristics of their own.

This is a perspective made possible both by the resources of the anthology itself and by the impulse to question and read beyond its boundaries. It suggests that the work of pedagogy would include opening for students the multiplicity of forms of classed identity and consciousness expressed in the book and in the world—both the local cultures they inhabit and the global spaces of contemporary history-in-the-making.

The literature classroom, it turns out, can be a productive site for doing this cultural work. Literature draws on and illuminates lived histories; it is composed of language(s), and language structures consciousness; and it functions most commonly through narratives of one kind or another, our oldest and most popular form of verbal communication. In working-class literature we encounter alternative narratives that challenge the dominant national stories of individual striving in the context of American exceptionalism. Engaging working-class literature demonstrates that the new narratives we need in the United States will in some ways be old ones; or rather, they will graft older narratives of struggle, resilience, and caring onto current concerns, using emerging modes of representation (digital media and popular music, for instance) as well as the forms gathered in the required anthology-textbook.

NOTES

1. In her article, Zandy provides an historical account of this "literary and labor legacy," as represented in the anthology. My focus here is less on the contents of *AWCL* than on the possibilities for pedagogy, especially in relation to the problematics of canon formation.
2. Courses in which *AWCL* has been assigned, with whose teachers I have talked and corresponded, include: Working-Class Literature and Film (humanities); The Working-Class Experience in America (American studies); Class and Gender in the "Post-Industrial" U.S. (English composition/gender studies); Narratives of the American Workplace (sociology); Images of Working-Class Life (English/sociology).
3. Larry Smith, editor of Bottom Dog Press, who teaches at Firelands College in Huron, Ohio, writes, "As someone who seeks to recognize and establish working-class literature in the minds and hearts of America, I am constantly refreshed and heartened by [*AWCL*'s] weight and vision. There is a wealth of American history here . . . the untold story of labor . . . and I try to cover it,

while also keeping a focus on the literary aspects: how did they write, how does this come down to us today?" (personal e-mail).
4. Zandy and I compensated for this limitation by consulting broadly with colleagues and a group of editorial advisors—Cary Nelson, Florence Howe, Barbara Smith, John Crawford, and Larry Smith—in setting our criteria and making our selections. Crawford and Smith are two of the instructors with whom I corresponded for the present article.
5. Ken Boas, who teaches both at Pitt and at Point Park University in Pittsburgh, comments "We all know no textbook can be definitive. But it's a valuable tool for teaching, providing ease in moving into these texts and beyond them. It's a welcoming door into working-class lit, and there are lots of rooms in the house to be explored" (interview transcript).
6. I will not address here some of the more common strategies instructors I interviewed employed to bring the anthology's contents to life for students and to set them in productive contexts. These include: using film, photography, and other images to connect texts to visual representations of lived history; using music and group performance to engage students in the oral/aural dimensions of collective forms of expression; inviting guest speakers to the classroom as witnesses and storytellers, or guest writers to give voice to words on the page; extending the reading beyond the anthology, for example, to full-length novels or texts of historical or economic analysis; encouraging identification with characters and situations from earlier historical periods, for instance, by writing letters to fictional ancestors; conducting research motivated by the literary example of working-class authors, for example, oral history interviews; taking advantage of what is happening in the world, around town, or on campus during the course, as an occasion for learning about how class operates.
7. See my article "Integrating Online Discussion into a Literature Course" for a fuller account of this strategy.
8. See the introduction to *What's Class Got to Do with It?* (Zweig 4–8) for a more succinct statement of the class definitions laid out in chap. 1, "The Class Structure of the United States" in Zweig, *The Working-class Majority*, 9–37.
9. Scott's group theater projects are based indirectly on "theater of the oppressed" as this has been repurposed for classroom use by Denver University History professor James Walsh, director of the Romero Theater Troupe (http://romerotroupe.org).
10. Title of a song/poem by Gil Scott Herron (1971).
11. Title of a poem by Joy Harjo, in Coles and Zandy 795.
12. See cited works by Renny Christopher, Constance Coiner, Nicholas Coles, Laura Hapke, Sherry Lee Linkon, Michelle Tokarczyk, and Janet Zandy for full articulations of the goals summarized here.

BIBLIOGRAPHY

Bealty, Jan. "A Waitress's Instructions on Tipping." In Coles and Zandy, *American Working-Class Literature*. 854–5. Print.

Blanchard, I. G. "Eight Hours." In Coles and Zandy, *American Working-Class Literature*. 139–9. Print.

Casey, Janet Galligani. "Diversity, Discourse and the W-C Student" *Academe* 91:4 (2005): 33–36. Print.

Christopher, Renny. "Teaching Working-Class Literature to Mixed Audiences." In Linkon, *Teaching Working Class*. 203–22. Print.

Coiner, Constance. "US Working-Class Women's Fiction: Notes Toward an Overview," *What We Hold in Common: An Introduction to Working-Class Studies*. Ed. Janet Zandy. New York: Feminist P., 2001. 223–38. Print.
Coles, Nicholas. "Democratizing Literature: Issues in Teaching Working-Class Literature" *College English* 48.7 (Nov.1986): 664–80. Print.
———. "Integrating Online Discussions into a Literature Course" *Teaching Times* (CIDDE, University of Pittsburgh), Mar. 2007. Print.
Coles, Nicholas, and Janet Zandy, eds. *American Working-Class Literature: An Anthology*. New York: Oxford UP, 2007. Print.
Guillory, John. *Cultural Capital: The Problem of Literary Canon Formation*. Chicago: UP of Chicago, 1993. Print.
Hapke, Laura. "Telling Toil: Issues in Teaching Labor Literature." In Linkon, *Teaching Working Class*. 179–90. Print.
Linkon, Sherry Lee, ed. *Teaching Working Class*. Amherst: U of Massachusetts P, 1999. Print.
———. "Why Working-Class Literature Matters." *Working-Class Perspectives*. Blog. 14 Feb. 2010. Web.
Perera, Sonali. "Rethinking Working-Class Literature: Feminism, Globalization, and Socialist Ethics." *Journal of Feminist Cultural Studies* 19:1 (2008): 1–31. Print.
Scott, William. *Troublemakers: Power, Representation, and the Fiction of the Mass Worker*. New Brunswick, NJ: Rutgers UP, 2011. Print
Tokarczyk, Michelle M. "Promises to Keep: Working-Class Students and Higher Education." In Zweig, *What's Class Got to Do with It?* 161–67. Print.
Welsch, Kathleen, ed. *Those Winter Sundays: Female Academics and Their Working-Class Parents*. Lanham: UP of America, 2004. Print.
Zandy, Janet. *Hands: Physical Labor, Class, and Cultural Work*. New Brunswick: Rutgers UP, 2004. Print.
———. "The Making of American Working-Class Literature" *Literature Compass* 4 10.1111 (2007). Web. 15 Jan. 2008.
Zweig, Michael. *The Working Class Majority: America's Best Kept Secret*. Ithaca: Cornell UP, 2000. Print.
———, ed. *What's Class Got to Do with It? American Society in the Twenty-First Century*. Ithaca: Cornell UP, 2004. Print.

Part III
The Experience of Poverty

For several years, scholars of working-class studies have debated whether the poor should be considered as a separate class or whether they should be seen as part of the working class. Some scholars who have experienced long periods of poverty argue that incorporating the poor into the working class erases the specific and extremely harsh experience of poverty. Because many self-identified poverty-class scholars are women and because a high proportion of those below the poverty level are women, there are gender implications to a possible erasure. On the other hand, scholars who see the poor as part of the working class argue that poverty is experienced by many working-class people at some point during their lives; to place those in poverty in a separate class is to further isolate them and to ignore the economic and social conditions that produce poverty.

Critics of working-class literature examine the representations of lives that, for the most part, slide in and out of poverty. These critics reveal how literary works interrogate the fear that working-class people have of not being able to provide for themselves. They further examine the representation of late capitalism and its effects on working people.

Michelle Tokarczyk is interested in the tensions between more comfortable members of the working class (such as those who belong to unions and have steady jobs) and those who live on the edge of or in poverty. She argues that the public assistance or charity that "the poor" sometimes accept are particularly loathed by more comfortable working-class people because taking aid is, to them, tantamount to surrendering agency. In her study of three ethnic short stories, she examines the ambivalent attitudes the protagonists have toward accepting assistance and demonstrates that their temporary reliance on this aid does not diminish their independence or self-reliance.

Michele Fazio takes up Sherman Alexie's *Indian Killer*, a highly controversial text even described as "racist" by the author himself. She argues for reading beyond the apparent sensationalism of the novel's brutal unsolved murders and viewing this Native American text as a working-class text. As a working-class text, it underscores the growing inequality of Seattle in the

1990s when the homeless, whom Fazio sees as casualties of globalization, increasingly populated the streets.

Phoebe Jackson likewise interrogates the forces that produce poverty rather than questioning the actions of poor people themselves. Through the lens of cultural geography, she sees the Bean family in Carolyn Chute's *The Beans of Egypt, Maine* as people who were once able to support themselves through occupations such as logging, but who see their livelihood disappear as forests are lost to gentrification.

Working-class people, it is sometimes said, are but one or two paychecks away from the street. The texts examined in this section emphasize how fearful working-class people are that they will be pushed into poverty and shame.

7   Agency, Not Alligators
Poor Women and Outside Assistance in Three Short Stories

Michelle M. Tokarczyk

One of the thorniest controversies in working-class studies is the question of whether the poor constitute a class by themselves or are part of the working class.[1] The question is not merely one of classification or rhetoric. Rather, scholars who argue that the poor are part of the working class view poverty as a result of structural conditions (job losses, housing prices, medical crises, and the like) that impact on working-class people. As Michael Zweig says, the poor are working-class people "who don't make very much money either because they aren't working or they make low wages" (78). He furthers his argument by stating that most of the poor are not from generations of poverty; rather, people cycle in and out of poverty, depending on fluctuations in employment, family makeup, health, and the like; and that in a ten-year period more than half of working-class people will experience poverty. Finally, he argues that placing the poor in a class by themselves ignores the economic causes of poverty and encourages the too-common problem of blaming the poor for their poverty.

In grouping the poor and the working class together, Zweig hopes to both shed light on the actual, often precarious, conditions of working-class people's lives and to advance a rhetoric that reflects the systemic causes of poverty. His persuasive arguments are further developed by Jack Metzgar, who warns that isolating the poor from other classes and then stigmatizing them or publicly blaming them for their condition, as is routinely done in the United States, is politically debilitating. One might expect that impoverished people would welcome working-class studies' reconceptualization of the poor.

However, some self-identified poverty-class scholars have vigorously argued that working-class studies cannot represent the lived experience of those, especially women, whose lives have been marked by persistent and extreme economic deprivation. Poverty-class scholar Vivyan C. Adair recalls an incident in which a working-class student disdained the poor as busily breeding and eating junk food ("Class Absences" 595) and understands this disdain as typical of society's different views of the poor and the working class: "Whereas the poor are imagined—and then as a result punished and disciplined—as single mothers who are marked by race, lack male authority and values, make bad choices, and are a threat to our nation and indeed their own children, the working class is often imagined as unmarked in terms of race and consisting of families with male heads of households, who, although 'rough,' work diligently and embody and enjoy independence, legal heterosexuality, autonomy, logic, and order" (590). Given the differences between the two groups—especially the imagined gender differences—it is not surprising that Adair would argue against including the poor in the working class, as she forcefully does: "to represent the poverty class as a synecdoche for the working class is to co-opt, repress, misrepresent, and dismiss the lives of poor women in and out of academe" ("Class Absences" 596).

Adair's critique goes to the heart of what working-class studies is and, as important, who working-class people are. Working-class studies is a field in which praxis is important, so issues of exclusion must be addressed. Partially in response to critiques by poverty-class scholars, working-class scholars are coming to terms with the fact that the working class is, as Jack Metzgar notes, more diverse than we have acknowledged. It contains factions and tensions (as other classes do) including rifts between more settled members of the working class (such as unionized workers) and struggling members (such as minimum-wage employees). Working-class scholars must reckon with this divide, as scholars of women's studies, queer studies, and the like have had to wrestle with differences within the ranks of their members and strategize as to how to meet members' diverse needs.

Scholars must also continue to investigate why many working-class people often resent being placed in the same category as the poor—especially if the poor accept charity or are on public assistance. Zweig traces the resentment to deteriorating economic conditions that prompt the working class to use the poor as scapegoats. Metzgar examines attitudes toward the segment of the poor who are particularly resented by the working class (and other classes as well): those on public assistance.[2] His explanation rests with an analysis of the cultural repertoire of the working class, which values hard work and persistence in the face of adversity.

As Adair's critique of working-class studies indicates, and indeed as the very collection she coedited reinforces, gender is a significant factor in both the imagination and the representation of poverty. Much of the stigmatization of those in poverty is gender-based, which originates, Adair claims, in "a deep-seated fear of poor women outside of male authority and a need to regulate their bodies through patriarchal institutions and imposition and reification of inviolate male authority." ("Class Absences" 599). Poor women, Adair argues, have been "branded," physically as well as socially, as deviant and in need of institutional regulation because they do not have male partners to regulate their lives.

Although Adair is certainly correct in this assessment, she does not address the fear that impoverished women generate among more "settled" working-class people—men and women.[3] Richard Sennett and Jonathan Cobb in their landmark *The Hidden Injuries of Class* underscore that two key concepts are critical in class dynamics: freedom and dignity. Class is a system for limiting freedom; the lower classes have fewer options available to them. Class threatens the dignity of working people because it is challenging to maintain personal dignity in the face of societal devaluation. The freedom and dignity that working-class people have is highly prized. With little power in society and over their lives, working-class people are loathe to give up agency and equate accepting institutional support with doing so, with entering a state of dependence and relinquishing control of their own actions.

Furthermore, evocations of working-class culture have often been suffused with masculine appeals. Mike Gold in his "Go Left, Young Writers!" juxtaposes the working-class writer with the temperamental bohemian and compares the Left with the frontier; the working-class writer is a "wild youth, the son of working class parents" who works in places such as mines, steel mills, and other workplaces associated with heightened masculinity. The combination of muscular caricatures of the working class and a struggle to maintain dignity creates a sensibility that values independence and self-sufficiency among both working-class men and women. Working-class men and women who are gainfully employed are self-sufficient, proud, and part of a community. Impoverished women, in contrast, are isolated and represented as immobile, having surrendered agency, and perhaps even subjectivity.

These fears play out in political battles. During the 1995 hearings on welfare reform, one congressman from Florida compared welfare recipients to alligators and alluded to public signs that read "Don't feed the alligators." These powerful animals, the congressman argued, could easily fend for themselves unless they became used to being fed, at which point they would become dependent and "otherwise able-bodied alligators [can] no longer survive on their own" (*Cong. Rec.*). Critics of welfare reform, notably Adair, have justly condemned the equation of poor people (women) with alligators. However, if the comparison is given any weight, it is worthwhile to consider to whom the comparison is addressed. If the wealthy were to consider powerful beings rendered helpless through repeated assistance, that might actually be reassuring, as no revolution would be in the offing. Middle-class audiences might reevaluate how to assist the lower classes, and those in the working class would likely not only be resentful of those in this dependent position, but also be fearful of ending up in it. An overfed, domesticated alligator becomes a metaphor for an emasculated working class.

However, the fact that many struggling women use social services or charities for a short period of time underscores the dynamism of the working class/poverty class: one does not become permanently enmeshed in social service networks but moves in and out of them as working-class people drift in and out of poverty. These periods of poverty, vividly remembered by many working-class people, evoke fear of permanent downward mobility and degradation.[4] This fear is somewhat ironic because women's decision to use these services often reflects a calculated choice that doing so, despite its drawbacks, offers the best chance for improving life, if only for a short period of time.[5]

Literary texts can represent the complex feelings and experiences of women accepting social services, and my purpose is to unpack some of these texts. Using an analysis informed by Metzgar's work on poverty and the working class, as well as by scholarship by poverty-class women who have used social services, I will first examine "Source," a short story by Alice Walker that represents a woman who works in a government-funded program as well as a woman who receives public assistance. This text demonstrates biases against public assistance, and it raises questions about alternatives to government programs.

I will then examine two texts that underscore the problems of women using social-service networks: Tillie Olsen's "I Stand Here Ironing" and Anzia Yezierska's "The Free Vacation House." Each of these texts expresses anger at social-service providers who don't understand the protagonists' lives; each protagonist regrets surrendering some control. Each also reflects some of the attitudes surrounding assistance for the impoverished during the periods in which it was written. Each text also, however, represents women deliberately choosing to accept these services despite the pitfalls associated with doing so. Most important, in each text the woman maintains agency in her dealings with institutions. The contradictory feelings about accepting social services and negotiating with them, despite the humiliation that women suffer, act both as a lens into the experience of impoverished women and as a cautionary tale to the working class.

"SOURCE"

"Source" depicts the different life choices made by two longtime friends, Irene and Anastasia. It first focuses on their early postcollege years when one woman, Anastasia, is living in a communal household and her lifelong friend, Irene, is working in a literacy program for adult women in a Southern town. Ultimately, the story is about African American identity and self-sufficiency, and as such its representation of social programs is telling.

The two women reunite in San Francisco in the 1960s when Irene visits Anastasia in her communal home. The mercurial Anastasia is a direct contrast to the politically active and committed Irene; Anastasia adapts the latest fashions and attaches herself to the identities of the men with whom she is involved. In many respects, she is also a caricature of the welfare recipient reviled by many Americans. With food stamps and relief, she stocks a full pantry in a spacious, airy house. When Anastasia mentions her public assistance, Irene notes her attitude: "There was . . . dissatisfaction in it; there was also acceptance. Missing—and, suddenly, it seemed to Irene—was defiance" (Walker 141). "Defiance" here is shorthand for anger at one's condition and determination to change it, both qualities that the complacent Anastasia lacks. She is not tough as members of the idealized working class are. The woman further grates on key values in the cultural repertoire of working class—responsibility and hard work.[6] In response to Irene's comment that in parts of the country public assistance provides insufficient income, she replies that in affluent areas the wealthy are pleased to support the poor. Anastasia's lifestyle and attitude are emblematic of those that were pilloried by welfare reform advocates with slogans such as "Don't feed the alligators." Indeed, in the 1980s, when this story was published, the image of the "welfare queen" was that of a black woman.[7]

At the time of their meeting, Irene is discouraged because she has lost funding for her literacy program. The women in Irene's education program represent another ramification of government funding. Before they had received government assistance, these women had persuaded younger black women to teach them. The experience of government funding, Irene explains, had a paradoxical effect: "At first, it lifted our spirits, made us believe someone up there in D.C. cared about the lives of these women. . . . As amazingly as the funding began, though, it ended. We had just enough time to get used to more than we had before when suddenly there was none at all. We had 'progressed' to a new level only to find ourselves stranded. To go back to the old way would feel like defeat" (145). Government funding, it seems, undercut people's self-reliance and community building. However, it is important to note that, unlike in the next two stories to be discussed, in "Source" we get the evaluation of the effectiveness of government assistance from someone who is giving rather than receiving it; the voices of the women who participated in this literacy program are absent.

For Irene, community building or involvement in movements is a positive action to improve people's lives, especially those who have suffered discrimination. Anastasia, in contrast, has adopted an apolitical stance and embraced the beliefs of a charismatic man named Source. He negates collective forms of identity—the family and race in particular. He faults Africans as backward and stupid, partially because they claim a black identity, and he insists "nobody's anything" (151). Most important, he teaches that it is impossible to change the world and that those who suffer choose to do so. Because she follows his teaching, Anastasia blames Irene for her own unhappiness because Irene chooses to teach people who are miserable "in this incarnation" (154). It is not surprising that Irene is asked to end her visit because of her perceived (and real) disapproval of Source.

When the two meet again years later in Alaska, they mend their friendship and ponder the different choices they have made. Irene is teaching Native Americans; Anastasia, tired of Source, had as a means of escape married a man who had secured work on the pipeline. After divorcing him, she began a relationship with a Native American man and redefined herself as white. Significantly, Irene voices that Anastasia has served as her "objective correlative"; as a young, gifted black woman, Irene feared a mediocre bourgeois life and took refuge in Anastasia's confusion. Yet she failed to acknowledge her own conflicts. She summarizes, "I was looking toward 'government' for help; you were looking to Source. In both cases, it was the wrong direction—any direction that is away from ourselves is the wrong direction" (166).[8] Irene echoes the script of self-reliance and antigovernment intervention, even equating an advocacy of government programs for the poor with allegiance to a cultlike figure.

The question raised by Irene's comment is who "we" are. Given the context of Walker's work and her commitment to womanism, we might surmise that the "we" are African American women. One might thus ask if African American women, in addition to the many burdens they already carry, should be expected to shoulder the responsibility for teaching those whom the public schools have failed. One might ask more fundamentally why looking to a government that is ostensibly by and for the people is looking away from oneself. Irene's summary statements about the government do not answer the question of what is to be done for people such as her former students who did not choose to be poor or illiterate and indeed would choose to improve their lives, if given the opportunity. Despite the challenges of teaching these poor women, the worst aspect of the government program is that it ended. To conclude, as Irene does, that its existence bred dependency is to erase the benefits of a structured program in which teachers are (minimally) compensated for educating others.

We are told that Irene is contemptuous of the black middle-class of which, objectively, she is "now" a member, indicating that she was formerly a member of the working class. Her inability to understand many of her students' attitudes—their reluctance to understand oppression as she did, their seemingly passive approach to learning, their reluctance to read depressing material—suggests that she has moved away from this class's sensibility. She is what Alfred Lubrano calls a "straddler," someone with working-class roots in a middle-class profession who is caught between two worlds. Irene fears being part of a disempowered lower class as much as she fears being part of a complacent middle class.

The text does not resolve the issues of government assistance and collective action as neatly as Irene herself does. The story ends with an image of smiling tourists who believe they are looking at Mt. McKinley in the distance. In reality, "[i]t was yet another, nearer, mountain's very large feet, its massive ankles wreathed in clouds, that they took such pleasure in" (Walker 167). This erroneous viewing of the mountain symbolizes the many false visions that the women have had throughout the story; for example, Irene thinking she understood blackness better than Anastasia and Anastasia's enthrallment with Source. Irene's current understanding of the role of government programs is also likely flawed.

"Source" contains several examples of individuals who are unable to "see" or "read." Irene's student Fania Evans could not read anything that was depressing; a Native American woman claimed that her people never needed glasses before they began reading. With their eyestrain, they now likely resisted reading because of "a basic distrust . . . about acquiring knowledge in a way that can make you blind" (156). It is very possible that Irene resists reading her life and her experiences in teaching others in a way that would challenge her class-based assumptions. Ultimately, though written by a progressive woman, "Source" reinscribes the equation of government assistance with helplessness; the story is unable to reconcile accepting assistance with acting on one's own behalf.

Although this woman-centered story is in keeping with Walker's ideology, it might irk those who see value in poor women being connected to strong men. "Source" is named for a male figure, and indeed he plays a more prominent role in this story than do the males in "I Stand Here Ironing" or "The Free Vacation House." Despite his charisma, however, he does not function as a strong male figure, but rather as another kind of welfare stereotype. His followers support him with their public assistance. He will not provide for himself or his family or have any meaningful participation in the world outside his cult. Hence, he represents a failed male authority, one whom Anastasia does in fact leave.

"I STAND HERE IRONING"

As is often the case with poverty-class narratives, all the characters in this story are women. Although we are told that the mother has remarried, the second husband is absent from the story, save for mention of children by him for whom the mother must care, sometimes with her daughter Emily's help. This absence may reflect a 1950s emphasis on the mother as the one responsible for children, but it may just as likely represent society's inability to visualize a household with a father who could not earn enough to support his family. Such a man is erased. Without ever having had a strong male hand to guide her, the mother has seemingly made poor choices about the care of her oldest daughter. The protagonist in Tillie Olsen's "I Stand Here Ironing" narrates the story of her efforts to use social services to enhance her daughter's life during the "pre-relief, pre-WPA world of the depression" (629) after her first husband had abandoned the family. A social worker from daughter Emily's school has visited the mother in the hopes of getting her to come in for an extensive talk about her daughter. The mother briefly relates and reflects on her daughter's experiences growing up, all the while ironing. Finally the mother, in what could seem like an act of callousness, refuses to come to the school and acknowledges that her daughter will not reach her potential. In this refusal, the mother exercises her independence and shows that she has learned to question the advice professionals give to her.

The mother's interaction with the social worker is indicative of the two different, likely classed, views of agency these two women hold. Whereas the social worker sees the mother as being in control of her daughter's environment, the mother, as Joanne S. Frye has argued, recognizes that Emily's personality has been shaped by forces beyond the mother's control: the father's desertion because he could not support them, the mother's struggle to balance nurturing with work and inadequate childcare arrangements, and her unfortunate decision to put her daughter in institutional care. The mother's ostensible monologue becomes a meditation on the interplay among external contingencies, individual needs, and individual responsibilities (Frye 133). "I Stand Here Ironing" was published in 1961 when the glorification of the stay-at-home mother was still strong. Thus the mother's refusal to accept total responsibility for her daughter's emotional difficulties is a kind of oppositional discourse.[9]

Whereas the text acknowledges that the environment is beyond the mother's control, it writes against the idea that those who use social services are passive subjects. Rather, the story represents the woman attempting to use the resources at her disposal to cope with being a single, poor parent.

The text depicts Emily as a young woman "branded" by her family's poverty in ways similar to those described by Adair ("Disciplined and Punished"). She is pockmarked from chicken pox and suffers from having been in a nursery school and endured "the lacerations of group life," that is, the strict codes imposed upon those receiving public assistance. Regulations are more stringently enforced in the convalescent home to which Emily is sent, her mother having been persuaded that the girl would get better care there. With parental visits tightly scheduled and personal possessions kept to a minimum, the institution implicitly espouses an ideology Adair describes, one that associates poor women with chaos as opposed to the order and progress associated with "deserving" (middle-class) citizens ("Disciplined and Punished," 29). Hence, Emily's stay in the group home, which strained the mother-child bond, is emblematic of the control people may surrender if they accept social services. The girl's own response to both her difficult economic circumstances and the state's corrective is signaled by her asthma, which is in fact disproportionately common among the lower classes. Symbolically, the girl's "harsh and labored" breathing signifies Emily's struggle for air in such a cramped environment. (Her success as a stand-up comic, in contrast, represents her attempts to reclaim her life and her "branded" body.)

Throughout the story her institutionalized care is juxtaposed with the care that her mother, despite her limited resources, tried to give her. The child was nursed, and her mother rushed home from work every day to see her. Moreover, the sheer amount of information that the mother is able to give the social worker about the Emily's history, her talents, and her inadequacies suggests the mother's attentiveness.

These signals of attentiveness must be kept in mind when considering Laura Hapke's argument that the story requires readers to balance scrutinizing the flawed mother with locating her within her classed circumstances. The mother's final response to the social worker is indeed jarring: "Why did you want me to come in at all? Why were you so concerned?

She will find her way" (633), as she seems to suggest that Emily needs no guidance. The mother immediately, however, implores the social worker to assist Emily, probably in a way different than the social worker expected: to help the girl to realize that she has agency. At this point the metaphorical possibilities of the act of ironing are realized. Emily must know, the mother emphasizes, "that she is more than this dress on the ironing board, helpless before the iron" (633). The mother realizes that there is a vast gap between the middle-class dream of reaching one's full potential and the lower-class nightmare of wasting one's life because one is powerless. She is not, I argue, as lacking in maternal care as her earlier words might indicate.

In expressing the hope that Emily will realize that she is not helpless before the forces in her life, the mother is asserting that she, too, was not helpless in hers. She may have made mistakes or she may have made the best of poor choices, but she did not at any point surrender agency. Moreover, she turns to the social worker to do the work that she herself feels she cannot do, and thus continues to try to make the best choices for her daughter.

Whereas the mother's final words are direct, much of her story is, as Constance Coiner notes, circuitous and reflexive as, for example, when she states that she nursed her children and then rhetorically asks "Why do I put that first?" (629). Coiner identifies the mother's discourse with what Bakhtin calls "heteroglossia," or many-voiced discourse. Such a discourse seems particularly appropriate for a mother who has been the conduit of her family and its experiences. She speaks not only for herself, but for young ones who cannot speak for themselves. It is also a discursive style that admits contradictions and gaps, and thus reveals the complexities of the choices impoverished women make.

"THE FREE VACATION HOUSE"

Significantly, although the narrator in "The Free Vacation House" refers to her husband, he is absent from the narrative, presumably working and not in need of the respite this family ostensibly receives in the vacation home. In "The Free Vacation House" as in "I Stand Here Ironing," the management of the poor household is in the hands of a woman. Women are, in fact, disproportionately impoverished. However, the absence of males in "The Free Vacation House" and in "I Stand Here Ironing" reflects the feminization of poverty in the imaginary as well as the actual realm. Working-class people who fall into poverty or who accept the social services that poor people accept have lost the "muscularity" and "toughness" of the working class. Published in 1920, this story reflects the charity offered to poor immigrants before government social services were developed.

The pitfalls of enmeshment within social services are more extensively described in this story. Moreover, whereas Olsen's narrator captures the experience of poverty in Emily's physical ailments, Yezierska's mother focuses on their cramped urban environment. Her narration is linear, and her story is told in her immigrant dialect, which gives readers a sense of how she might have been perceived by middle-class Americans. As Joann Pavletich has argued, racism is a subtext in much of Yezierska's work; Jews were barely considered white in the early twentieth century and were consequently perceived as inferior beings.[10] Ethnicity and racial categorization thus compound the stigma of poverty.

In this short story, set in the early twentieth century, a young mother of six children is approached by a teacher who is concerned that the children are often late for school. Seeing that the young mother is exhausted and overwhelmed, the woman suggests that the mother and her children go for a rest at a free country home. The mother soon regrets agreeing to this arrangement because the Social Betterment Society, in ways similar to those described by Adair in her work on welfare mothers, pathologizes its clients. The representative from this society appears in a white starched gown as though she were a nurse, yet the questions she asks are about work and finances. Upon hearing that the society can extend *charity* to only a limited few, the mother reacts in a way typical of working-class people who are proud of their labor: "Charities! . . . Ain't the charities those who help the beggars out? I ain't no beggar. I'm not asking for no charity. My husband, he works" (Yezierska 329).

Reluctant as she is to accept this charity, the mother desperately needs an escape from her circumstances, even if the escape is only short lived. In moving words, she says, "I felt if I didn't get away from here for a little while, I would land in a crazy house, or from the window jump down. Which is worser, to land in a crazy house, jump from the window down, or go to the country from the charities?" (330). The dilemma this mother describes has been articulated by welfare mothers, such as those in Adair and Dahlberg's collection, who struggle to support their children. Essentially, women decide the humiliation of public assistance is better than the constant stress and fear of unmitigated struggle.

The family's stay at the vacation house replicates the humiliation and regulation that the mother initially felt. She is repeatedly asked the same questions about her income and living arrangements and is thus forced to continually reenact her humiliation, first in her own home, then publicly in the charity's office. The doctor who examines the family does so warily, as though afraid of being contaminated. In addition to being perceived as diseased, family members are treated as mentally deficient: the mother is admonished not to lose appointment cards and is walked from one office to another as though she could not find her way around a building.

The vacation home itself is, similar to the convalescent home in which Emily resided, strictly regulated. As soon as the mother relaxes at the table and starts to feel "like a somebody" the nurse reads an extensive set of regulations, reminding the charity clients of how much they are distrusted. The place is run in military fashion, with designated bells for waking up, getting food, and bathing. If the bells are missed, food or other items are withheld. The children's play, the mother hears from her son, is likewise strictly regimented, with very few activities allowed. Such extensive regulation reflects the Other category into which the poor and immigrants are placed.[11] Wealthy women who visit describe its charity clients as "creatures," again suggesting subhumans in need of supervision.

Thus it is not surprising that when the mother leaves her vacation house, she describes it as a "prison," and when she returns to her cramped apartment it is transformed in her eyes: "How good it was feeling for me to be able to move around my own house, like I pleased" (333). In going to the vacation house and adhering to its strict regimen, the mother had given up all semblance of mobility, a key value that is tied to upward mobility. On her ride home she explicitly questioned why the families in the home are treated as they are, and finally concludes that the worn-out mothers are "part of the show" for rich women. Rather than being a show of how their donations are being used, the mothers may be viewed as a spectacle of failure and pity, in much the same way as the punished body is displayed in Foucault's work. Those who might be reluctant to travel to see poor people can thus see them in safe, comfortable environs. The experience represented in this text might be viewed as a cautionary tale to poor or working-class people. However, it is important to note that the mother is never passive in her interactions with the charities; she repeatedly protests her treatment and critiques the charity. Her dialect suggests the distinctiveness of her immigrant voice and vision as well as her resistance to adopting the middle-class vision of her life-style.

The stay in the vacation home has the ironic effect of making the mother appreciate her ghetto apartment. Similarly, I argue that the spectacle of demonized welfare mothers makes working-class people grateful for the lives, for the small amounts of power they can exercise and dignity they experience in independently providing for themselves. Their struggle may be inherently unfair, but it still affords them a modicum of mobility and choice in their own lives.

The difficulty that working-class people have placing themselves in this discourse around agency and assistance is reflected in the writing of one former welfare mother. In her article "To Be Young, Pregnant, and Black" in Adair and Dahlberg's collection of writings by poor women, Joycelyn Moody takes issue with the feminist dismissal of the term "victim" and claims the status. If there is no victim, there is no perpetrator; such a construction perpetuates the belief that people are poor because of the choices they have made, not because of what was done to or happened to them. This formulation makes the working class particularly resentful and fearful of the poor in their ranks. Yet Moody's discourse itself displays the tension in reconciling victimhood and agency. She chastises those who refer to welfare mothers as "survivors": "We are nobody's exceptions, not casualties of the latest 'war on poverty' but sufferers of it—and valiant soldiers against it" (96). "Survivors" are not defined. It is difficult to parse "sufferers," "victims," "survivors," and "soldiers," and this difficulty reflects the problem of reconciling acceptance of social services with agency.

DEBUNKING THE MYTH OF PUBLIC ASSISTANCE

"Source" indeed represents the source of the nation's deep distrust of public assistance, as well as the way use of government assistance is conflated with questions of ambition and self-worth. While her own government program is ending, Irene witnesses her friend receiving public assistance and using part of it to support a cult figure. Resignation to government aid and dependence on a controlling and politically backward man are twin facets of Anastasia's lack of faith in her own agency. Ultimately, Irene voices suspicion of looking to the government for answers. However, she can articulate no better alternative for those who are not as fortunate as she. Indeed, in stating that *she* was looking to the government for answers, she erases the situation of those illiterate black women who might be better off looking to a government program than to the generosity of upwardly mobile young black women. Ultimately, Irene is unable to sort out her feelings as an upwardly mobile black woman afraid of being entrenched in the middle class and unsure of how to connect with the lower class from which she comes.

Anastasia's claim that nothing can be done to aid those in need reflects fatalism as well as a deep-seated belief that the poor are somehow to blame for their poverty. The decision of this light-skinned African American to pass (although she will not use this word) as white brings to mind an American belief that people can, Gatsby-like, constantly reinvent themselves and erase attributes that give them difficulty. The combination of a belief in the possibility of reinvention and a belief that those who have failed to reinvent themselves and escape from poverty are responsible for their condition would make one distrustful of the poor and of any organized attempt to eradicate or at least ameliorate poverty.

"Source" reveals the too-common discourse around government programs by those who are not recipients of them. Discouraged that her program lost funding, Irene comes to the conclusion that she should not have expected the government to solve problems rather than conclude that she should have expected the government to do more for people in need. Uncomfortable with perceptions of herself as a light-skinned African American, Anastasia links herself to men who, in different ways, negate her racial identity. She further dismisses the women who attend a government-funded reading program while she herself relies on public assistance to support herself and her life with Source. Her contradictory attitudes are reflective of the middle class and more settled members of the working class who may use benefits such as unemployment insurance, yet scorn those who turn to welfare.

The short stories by Tillie Olsen and Anzia Yezierska demonstrate the contradictory impulses women who accept social services feel. Rather than adhering to an underclass ideology, they share values common among working-class people. They disdain charity, value time with their children, and are suspicious of social services even though they may accept them because these services offer the most viable options for taking care of themselves and their families. In this respect, the protagonists in these stories exhibit traits identified with what Dorothy Allison calls "the noble poor" as opposed to those who are considered "trash."[12] Their supposed virtue, however, does not save them from public scorn. Partially for this reason, in each story the theme of regret is strong; Emily should not have been sent to the convalescent home; the stay at the vacation house was an exercise in humiliation. From a working-class perspective, it may be easy to see the women in these stories as surrendering agency and dignity. That no men are represented in these stories suggests both the reality of poor women's lives and the difficulty of imagining wage earners who cannot support their families. The helplessness the mothers feel in the face of difficult decisions could suggest an erasure of agency. The humiliation they feel under the constant surveillance could dissuade proud working-class people from seeking aid. These stories thus represent working-class fears about becoming dependent on outside assistance and the consequent revulsion toward those who would use these services.

Olsen and Yezierska struggle to reconcile agency and acceptance of aid. The mother in Olsen's story argues with the social worker from the school; the one in Yezierska's story constantly critiques the demeaning treatment she receives and makes it clear that her husband works. These protagonists' efforts, however, are complicated by the cultural script that sees any social service as a disabling handout rather than as a resource to which working-class people, who lack power over their economic conditions, might have to turn. And they turn to these resources for short periods of time. Rather than being stuck in poverty, the mothers in these stories, similar to many people who have relied on public assistance, move in and out of acute need. There may not be upward mobility; that possibility is not available to many working-class people, but for struggling members of the working class there is movement from less to more security, as there is for the protagonist in "I Stand Here Ironing."

In his discussion of working-class attitudes toward those unable to support themselves, Metzgar draws upon the example of his Uncle Georgie, the poster child of the undeserving poor, to whom family members will give financial assistance but not respect or dignity. The refusal to dignify recipients of aid is most glaring in "The Free Vacation House," but it also permeates "I Stand Here Ironing": the convalescent home's numerous regulations signal a clientele that cannot be trusted or respected. However, the protagonists themselves never surrender their dignity.[13] Olsen's mother not only voices her opinions to the social worker, but also works continually during the visit, refusing to subordinate her tasks. Yezierska's mother declares her pride in her husband's employment and criticizes officials for their treatment of the poor.

"I Stand Here Ironing" and "The Free Vacation House" represent the fortitude and spirit of working-class women as well as their agency. With Olsen's protagonist constantly ironing and Yezierska's mother voicing how difficult it is to care for several children, these characters also demonstrate that women who turn to outside assistance share in the cultural repertoire of the working class. They work hard and value respectability. These traits are not often enough recognized, and thus the experiences of women in poverty are erased from some working-class narratives. Rather than demonstrating the accuracy of the saying "Don't feed the alligators," "I Stand Here Ironing" and "The Free Vacation Home" represent the continued independence of women while they accept social services. These stories also represent the amount of responsibility poor women must take for their families, even if they are married. The texts thus undercut the cultural script that offers marriage as the solution to poor women's problem. Simultaneously, they evoke fears of women living without the control of *strong* men who would support their families and guide their wives' actions.

Taken together, these three stories give a fleshed-out representation of the perceptions of outside assistance by those who do not use it and the experience of accepting charity or public assistance by those who do. In realizing the truthfulness of this depiction of working-class women, we are taking a step toward what Adair calls "a more complex, more inclusive, and even more contradictory conceptualization and decoding of what it means to be working class" ("U.S. Working Class/Poverty Class Divides" 830). "I Stand Here Ironing" and "The Free Vacation House" represent the ambivalent attitudes of struggling working-class women toward outside assistance. The texts articulate many reasons why working-class people would hesitate to turn to outside services. They also, however, demonstrate that women who choose these services are acting to better their lives and those of their families. The women are agents, not passive recipients. They are working-class people with dignity who are struggling more than some more fortunate—often male—members of the working class are. Far from being a synecdoche to the working class, as Adair fears these women are seen to be, they are a core part of it.[14]

NOTES

1. Many of us in working-class studies utilize a division of class developed by economist Michael Zweig. Rather than divide classes into the upper, middle, and lower, as is commonly done, Zweig divides the American classes into the capitalist or ruling class, the middle class, and the working class. There are other more elaborate class division systems in use. For a quick overview of them, see Metzgar.
2. Welfare, especially before it was reformed in the 1990s, evoked anger from the middle class as well, but as scholars such as Metzgar have noted, working-class people who have strenuous or monotonous jobs are likely to more vehemently resent those perceived to be avoiding work.

3. Metzgar draws upon Lillian Rubin's distinction between "settled" and "hard-living" members of the working class. The former have steady jobs and stable families, are churchgoing and respectable. The latter are employed sporadically, have shifting family structures, and generally more chaotic lives. Metzgar argues that there is a relationship between economic insecurity and life stability; hence, he believes that "hard-living" people are more likely in the lower rungs of the working class.
4. For narratives of working-class people experiencing periods of poverty, see these collections: Tokarczyk and Fay, eds., *Working-Class Women in the Academy: Laborers in the Knowledge Factory*; Dews and Law, eds., *This Fine Place So Far from Home: Voices of Academics from the Working Class*; and Tea, Michelle, ed., *Without a Net: The Female Experience of Growing Up Working Class*.
5. See Adair and Dahlberg's collection for essays addressing this topic.
6. The notion that groups have distinct cultural repertoires that are made up of core values was proposed by Michele Lamont and utilized by Jack Metzgar in his work. In addition to responsibility and hard work, the cultural repertoire of the working class includes morality.
7. See Adair and Dahlberg's anthology for essays by African American women, all undergraduate or graduate students, who went on welfare and experienced disapproval from various segments of society.
8. Part of the difficulty with Irene's words is that from a literary point of view, they constitute too much "telling" rather than "showing" and they are reductive. See Petry for a discussion of this story and Walker's other short fiction.
9. In her introduction to a collection of oral histories of impoverished women, Susan Contratto notes that the women in the book do not share the middle-class myth of maternal power; rather, "the women recognize the clear limits of mothering as their mothers practiced it and as they themselves practice it" (9). The harshness of the conditions under which they mother and were mothered likely makes impoverished women more realistic.
10. See Brodkin for a discussion of the assimilation of Jews into American society.
11. Pavletich argues that the "emotionally excessive" immigrant was exoticized and othered.
12. See Allison for a discussion of the belief that some poor people are noble and thus deserving of assistance whereas others are shiftless and irresponsible and thus unworthy of assistance.
13. There are, of course, many working-class texts that represent protagonists' struggle to maintain dignity while being shamed for their socioeconomic status. To name a few: Dorothy Allison's *Bastard Out of Carolina*, Grace Lumpkin's *To Make My Bread*, and John Steinbeck's *The Grapes of Wrath*.
14. Thanks to Inline Francois and Christie Launius for comments on earlier versions of this article.

BIBLIOGRAPHY

Adair, Vivyan C. "Class Absences: Cutting Class in Feminist Studies." *Feminist Studies* 31.3 (Fall 2005): 575–603. Print.
———."Disciplined and Punished: Poor Women, Bodily Inscription, and Resistance through Education." In Adair and Dahlberg 25–52. Print.
———. "U. S. Working-Class/Poverty-Class Divides." *Sociology* 39.5 (Dec. 2005): 817–34. Print.
Adair, Vivyan C., and Sandra L. Dahlberg, eds. *Reclaiming Class: Women, Poverty, and the Promise of Higher Education in America*. Philadelphia: Temple UP, 2003. Print.

Allison, Dorothy. "A Question of Class." *Skin: Talking About Sex, Class, and Literature*. Ithaca: Firebrand, 1994: 13–16. Print.
Bakhtin, M.M. *The Dialogic Imagination: Four Essays*. Ed. Michael Holquist. Ed & Trans. Vadim Liapunov. Trans. Kenneth Brostrom. Austin: U of Texas P., 1982. Print.
Brodkin, Karen. *How Jews Became White Folks and What That Says about Race in America*. New Brunswick: Rutgers UP, 1998. Print.
Coiner, Constance. *Better Red: The Writing and Resistance of Tillie Olsen and Meridel Le Sueur*. New York: Oxford, 1995. Print.
Coles, Nicholas, and Janet Zandy, eds. *American Working-Class Literature: An Anthology*. New York: Oxford UP, 2007. Print.
Cong. Rec. 24 March 1995. "Support Welfare Reform: Don't Feed the Alligators." Proceedings and Debates of the 104th Congress, 1st Session. Web. 21 April 2009.
Contratto, Susan. Introduction. *Dignity: Lower Income Women Tell Their Stories*. By Fran Leeper Buss. Ann Arbor: U of Michigan P, 1985. 1–12. Print.
Dews, C.L. and Carol Leste Law, eds. *This Fine Place So Far from Home: Voices of Academics from the Working Class*. Philadelphia: Temple UP, 1995. Print.
Frye, Joanne S. "I Stand Here Ironing: Motherhood as Experience and Metaphor." In Nelson and Huse 128–33. Print.
Gold, Michael. "Go Left, Young Writers!" In Coles and Zandy 380–83. Print.
Hapke, Laura. *Daughters of the Great Depression: Women, Work, and Fiction in the American 1930s*. Athens: U of Georgia P, 1995. Print.
Lamont, Michele. *The Dignity of Working Men: Morality and the Boundaries of Race, Class, and Immigration*. New York: Russell Sage, 2000.
———. *Money, Morals, and Manners: The Culture of the French and American Upper- Middle Class*. Chicago: U of Chicago P, 1992.
Lubrano, Alfred. *Limbo: Blue-Collar Roots, White-Collar Dreams*. New York: Wiley, 2005. Print.
Metzgar, Jack. "Are 'the Poor' Part of the Working Class or in a Class by Themselves?" *Labor Studies Journal* 35.3 (Fall 2010): 398–416.
Moody, Joycelyn K. "To Be Young, Pregnant, and Black: My Life as a Welfare Coed." In Adair and Dahlberg 85–96. Print.
Nelson, Kay Hoyle, and Nancy Huse, eds. *The Critical Response to Tillie Olsen*. Westport: Greenwood P, 1994. Print.
Olsen, Tillie. "I Stand Here Ironing." In Coles and Zandy 629–33. Print.
Pavletich, Joann. "Anzia Yezierska, Immigrant Authority, and the Uses of Affect." *Tulsa Studies in Women's Literature* 19.1 (Spring 2000): 81–104. Print.
Petry, Alice Hall. "Alice Walker: The Achievement of the Short Fiction." *MLS* 19.1 (Winter 1989): 12–27. Print.
Rubin, Lillian Breslow. *Worlds of Pain: Life in a Working-Class Family*. New York: Basic, 1976. Print.
Sennett, Richard, and Jonathan Cobb. *The Hidden Injuries of Class*. New York: Knopf, 1972.
Tea, Michelle, ed. *Without a Net: The Female Experience of Growing Up Working Class*. Emeryville, Ca.: Avalon Publishing Group, 2004. Print.
Tokarczyk, Michelle M. and Elizabeth A. Fay, eds. *Working-Class Women in the Academy: Laborers in the Knowledge Factory*. Amherst: U of Mass. P, 1993. Print.
Walker, Alice. "Source." In *You Can't Keep a Good Woman Down*. Orlando: Harcourt, 1981: 138–67. Print.
Yezierska, Anzia. "The Free Vacation House." In Coles and Zandy 328–33. Print.
Zweig, Michael. *The Working Class Majority: America's Best Kept Secret*. Ithaca: Cornell UP, 2001. Print.

8 Homeless in Seattle
Class Violence in Sherman Alexie's *Indian Killer*[1]

Michele Fazio

Since its publication in 1996, *Indian Killer*'s critical reception has been controversial to say the least. The second novel of contemporary writer Sherman Alexie (Spokane/Coeur d'Alene), *Indian Killer* recounts the gruesome crimes committed by a serial murderer who scalps and, at times, consumes the eyes and hearts of white male victims. Set in Seattle, the novel's sensationalized plot also features the story of protagonist John Smith, an American Indian adopted at birth and raised by an upper-middle-class white couple. His ensuing struggle to negotiate these two competing worlds illustrates, in part, the sociocultural conflicts American Indians experience in relocating from reservations to urban centers. Together, these distinct narrative threads of physical and psychological violence intersect and create a suspenseful mystery that provocatively raises questions about American race relations and the cost of upward mobility in American society, particularly the challenges these issues pose for indigenous communities. It is this blending of subject matter and, to a larger degree, of genre that makes *Indian Killer* worth exploring as to why many, including the author himself, remain disturbed by the novel's graphic account of racial hatred and rage between whites and American Indians.

Initially, in an interview conducted in 1999, Alexie explained that the novel's storyline on mixed-race adoptions addressed "the ways in which Indians are culturally, psychologically, physically, and emotionally killed. Still" (Blewster 73). This statement makes clear Alexie's politics to address the cultural dislocation of American Indians as a contemporary rather than an historical matter. Yet, some three years later in another interview, Alexie admits his own discomfort about the novel, stating that *Indian Killer* "was the book that was hardest to write, that gave me the most nightmares, that still, to this day, troubles me the most because I can't even get a grasp on it. It's the only one I re-read. I think a book that disturbs me that much is the one I probably care the most about" (Campbell 116). Alexie's change of heart took an even more distinct turn when he announced in 2007 during the keynote address to the Native American Literature Symposium, as Nancy Peterson writes in her introduction to *Conversations with Sherman Alexie*, "his ongoing dissatisfactions with *Indian Killer*, going so far as to call it 'racist'"(xv), and later in the same year referred to it in an interview as "a pile of crap novel" (Weich 173). Alexie's self-reflection—his emphatic rejection of the novel more than ten years after its publication—reveals the extent to which the novel's subject matter haunts him both personally and professionally. Although his disavowal of a work that helped him to achieve literary and commercial success, including the *New York Times* Notable Book of the Year award, is a tempting trajectory to follow, recognizing *Indian Killer's* cultural significance as a working-class text is a more compelling matter in need of exploration.

Indeed, the subject of work is a pervasive feature in the novel as Alexie introduces nearly every character based on their occupation: the young doctor who works on the reservation to meet the obligations of his government education loans; John Smith's adoptive parents (Olivia, who works part time at the Bellevue Art Museum, and Daniel, who works as an architect); the university professor Dr. Clarence Mather, whose approach to teaching American Indian literature is ethically suspect; and conservative radio talk show host Truck Schultz, whose racist rhetoric incites riots soon after the murders begin. Alexie's focus on labor establishes class division between white middle-class professionals who are currently employed and people of color who work in the service industry and hold more physically demanding jobs. Paul and Paul Too, two African Americans who work the late-night shift at a local donut shop John Smith frequents, and Reggie Polatkin, an American Indian who works minimum-wage jobs to support himself, are just two examples of the latter group. The uncertainty of permanent employment is portrayed as well with the minor characters of Sweet Lu (an old Hupa Indian woman who charges nominal fees to search for Bigfoot in the woods on her reservation) and the temporary saleswoman who promotes a local phone company's long distance plan in Occidental Park. Together, these characters contribute to the novel's extensive inventory of contemporary work culture.

With its focus on Seattle's contingent labor force as well as the indeterminate future of the unemployed, *Indian Killer* confronts the impact globalization has on local communities, emphasizing the precarious relationship and unequal power relations between individuals and the capitalist system. The instability of workers' lives and their exploitation, for instance, points to the long-lasting consequences of U.S. neoliberal economics; such a reading of Alexie's representation of class violence offers a different interpretation of the warlike atmosphere depicted in the novel, especially if we contextualize *Indian Killer* within the immense economic insecurities that existed prior to its publication. The decline in industry in the Rust Belt region, the sociocultural impact of deindustrialization and corporate globalization, and the increased focus on global power—of shoring up U.S. domination abroad—all but ensured the growing vulnerability of the nation's workforce since the 1980s. The anxieties, too, about the anticipation of a resurgent labor movement with John Sweeney's election as president of the American Federation of Labor and Congress of Industrial Organizations (AFL-CIO) along with the outcomes of welfare reform and free-trade agreements in the 1990s produced even greater concerns about the division between the rich and the poor.[2]

Since then, concerns about the working class have only become more amplified by the significant loss of jobs and recent economic crises that have shaped the twenty-first century. In a 2003 interview, Alexie recognized how the changing political landscape since 9/11 has altered his portrayal of American Indians in his fiction. He concludes:

> I've become less and less Indian-centric as the years have gone on. After September 11th, I barely talk about it. I talk about poor people; I talk about disadvantaged people, and that sort of covers everything I need to cover. It becomes not about race, region, or country, but about a particular group of people sharing the same circumstances. I talk about the universal condition of the poor, and thinking and talking about it that way helps eliminate the negativity of tribalism. That's been my response; to see people by their power or lack thereof, rather than the color of their skin. (Harris 130)

Alexie's shifting position from his earlier "tribalism" to this more "universal" approach focuses on the condition of the poor, and these words reveal an impulse to distance himself from *Indian Killer* as being too race specific. However, as one of Alexie's earliest forays in exploring the economic battles taking place within contemporary American society and, more specifically, how class defines the experiences of urban Indians, *Indian Killer* deserves another look. Writing against the privatization of corporations, the volatility of financial markets, and high unemployment, Alexie's novel examines the structural, psychological, and cultural effects of class violence on human life. Upward mobility with its potential to improve the quality of life instead contributes to class anger and conflict, and Alexie's cynicism about contemporary American culture serves as a potent reminder to recognize the collective power and shared experiences of the nation's diverse workforce. A consideration of the dilemma *Indian Killer* poses in satisfying genre expectations provides a framework to examine how the subject of class expands an understanding of the struggle between the domestic and political sphere.

(CLASS)IFYING THE LANDSCAPE

While the novel's violence greatly troubled Alexie, he was also bothered by the book's violation of genre and form. To be sure, *Indian Killer* has received both laudatory and excoriating reviews from the *San Francisco Chronicle*'s acclaim of the novel's "extraordinary achievement" (Wiegand) to *Time Magazine*'s criticism of it being "septic with what clearly seems to be [Alexie's] own unappeasable fury" (Skow). The novel's reception by scholars in the fields of Native American and ethnic studies appears equally mixed as well. Although some have explored the novel's depiction of the cultural impact of illness, storytelling, language, and trauma in advancing a greater understanding of contemporary ethnic relations, others have found *Indian Killer* too angry and too exploitative of American Indian culture overall.[3] As Eric Cheyfitz explains in "The (Post)Colonial Construction of Indian Country: U.S. American Indian Literatures and Federal Indian Law," "[t]he absence of some form of nationalist, indigenist, or cosmopolitan foundation makes it difficult to accept the violence of the novel as imaginatively or politically productive" (168).[4] Louis Owens sees *Indian Killer* as "commodified Indian fiction" that "titillate[s] white readers . . . [by] presenting . . . a darkly comical, pathetic, self-destructive 'lost-generation' Indian" in the ironically-named protagonist of John Smith (78). I include these quotations to underscore *Indian Killer*'s style as crime fiction with its use of type characters, gratuitous murder scenes, and antagonistic dialogue to further dramatize the whodunit plot as blurring the boundaries that separate ethnic texts from other kinds of literature.[5] The novel's blending of genres speaks to *Indian Killer*'s multidimensionality in presenting the darker realities of class disparity in the United States.

According to Maureen T. Reddy, crime novels from "[t]he 1990s resemble the 1920s in the high level of public attention to and anxiety about race" (190). But crime fiction also has its origins in class resistance, and embracing the intersections between these two social categories creates alternative ways of interpreting violence in *Indian Killer*. Violence takes on many forms beyond the physical, and Alexie's description of the collapse of community as well as Seattle's economic stability addresses how class division culturally and symbolically contributes to social anxiety. As Woody Haut explains, pulp-culture crime fiction "retained the basic themes of proletariat writing: the corrosive power of money, class antagonism, [and] capitalism's ability to erode the community" (10), which reflect "the prevailing conditions of an era" (7). National insecurity in terms of mass unemployment and cross-cultural conflict defines the 1990s urban culture Alexie depicts in *Indian Killer* whereas the city, in comparison to life in suburbia, becomes a space of contestation and fear, what Haut refers to "as sites of potential danger, inhabited by immigrants and ethnic minorities" (19). Thus, Seattle's "distinct and divided neighborhoods" (Alexie 112) reinforce the dominant national narrative of post-1950s consumerism and mid-1980s urban decay.

Seattle, however, is no stranger to the pursuit of economic and social justice, and the city's rich activist history becomes an important backdrop to consider Alexie's representation of the urban poor in the novel. The labor struggles of Filipino and Japanese workers in the Cannery Workers and Farm Laborers Union (CWFLU-AFL) in the 1930s, the union organizing of

African Americans in the United Construction Workers Association (UCWA) in the 1970s, and the rise of grunge rock bands such as Pearl Jam and Nirvana in the 1990s starkly contrast the wealthy, corporate image of Starbucks whose global operations originated in Seattle.[6] The city's namesake himself also symbolizes the struggle for land rights, and during the late 1960s, Seattle, according to Vine Deloria Jr., served as "the high point of the red power movement" (qtd. in Krupat 105). Although *Indian Killer*'s politics may not be overtly advancing tribal sovereignty, Alexie's continuous referencing of Seattle's skyline suggests that the city's streets function as more than the background setting to the action taking place in the novel; they appear as sites of resistance and struggle for power. Queen Anne Hill, Capitol Hill, and Pioneer Square thus become contemporary battle scenes between angry whites and urban Indians that recall the history of cultural violence the city has endured in the past, demonstrating how class complicates race relations in the present. Carlotta Lott, one of the homeless John Smith encounters, says it best when she claims, "All these white people think I'm homeless. But I ain't homeless. I belong here ... I'm the landlady" (Alexie 251). Alexie's panoramic view of the city juxtaposes the natural landscape of Lake Washington and Mountain Rainier with artificial constructions of American progress—that is, the skyscrapers, bridges, jet planes, and ferries that situate Seattle as an economic epicenter of the modern world. As a colonized space, Seattle's cultural and social boundaries are continually being redrawn by acts of violence and by those defending their rights to "claim" the land.

But viewing *Indian Killer* solely as crime fiction also has it limits, as Alexie has pointed out in a number of interviews that he failed to meet genre expectations. With the identity of the killer remaining unknown and the crimes left unsolved by the novel's end, *Indian Killer* emulates the crime fiction formula but without a satisfying end result. Alexie admits, "'I wrote a genre novel that I didn't complete as a genre novel. If I had, it would be a far superior book ... instead of turning it into some pretentious murder literary piece of shit'" (Weich 174). Critic James Giles, however, sees Alexie's "anti-detective novel" as "turn[ing] the conventions of the [genre] against the reader" (142), which suggests that the text's subversive message about racism and American culture emerges out of its incongruity. Given the homeless status of the novel—a result of being renounced by the author and by some critics in the field of literary studies—I would like to suggest that the novel's lack of genre coherence creates a space to view the text alternatively as working-class literature. The politicized landscape of Seattle and the ever-present homeless in *Indian Killer* introduce readers to the unsettling facts of wage labor as shaping American Indian culture both in the past and present. Such a focus does not divest itself from race, but rather encourages a reading of the varied aspects of working-class life.

To identify *Indian Killer* as working-class literature begins a dialogue about the text's representation of power relationships among classes, and this is an essential step to take in recognizing how American ethnic literature contributes to the vast experiences that encompass U.S. labor history. As Janet Zandy argues, "Working-class writing is not 'White' writing. . . . Many texts ordinarily categorized as ethnic or African American can also be read as working-class texts. This is not a privileging of class over race or gender or sexual identities, but rather an insistence that any analysis of race, gender, sexuality, even disability, cannot be complete if class is excluded" (91). Laura Hapke also advocates for intersectionality, stating that texts not immediately identified as working-class still contribute to the growing body of work that depicts working-class lives in late twentieth century and contemporary American literature, even if "narrative references to marginalized, jobless, or itinerant laboring protagonists as laborers are limited to a passage or a few pages" (13).[7] The approaches offered by Zandy and Hapke do not diminish the integrity of what constitutes working-class literature or ethnic literature for that matter; rather, they show how fundamental class is to the formation of American identities, especially if we are to dispel the myth that American society is largely middle class, or worse, classless.[8]

Work identity is neither static nor singly defined, and in documenting the lived experience of workers, working-class literature illustrates the cultural and sociopolitical markers that shape the struggles of the working class.[9] Although the dominant image of the working class in the United States has traditionally been understood as white and male, immigrant narratives and fiction of industrial labor originating out of the Proletarian movement of the 1930s only tell part of the history of labor struggle. Class cuts across cultural and temporal boundaries, and as Martha C. Knack and Alice Littlefield state in "Native American Labor: Retrieving History, Rethinking Theory," "wage labor forms an intrinsic part of the study of indigenous affairs, both in the historical past and in the contemporary world" (44). From colonial times to the present, American Indians have participated in the U.S. labor market as skilled and unskilled laborers in the industries of agriculture, construction, mining, and fishing (Albers 245); with the rise of industrial labor and urban relocation programs brought about by the labor shortages of World War I and the reform initiatives of the New Deal, men and women entered the workforce alongside immigrant laborers of the early twentieth century (Knack and Littlefield 16, 19, 31).[10] Confronting how class works in Alexie's novel may help not only to end the silence about American Indian wage labor, but also redefine the parameters of what constitutes U.S. labor history and working-class culture.

OUT ON THE STREET

Street life becomes a critical characteristic of working-class culture in *Indian Killer*—one that raises awareness of the effects local and global economies have on individuals seeking employment. Alexie's descriptions of affluent Seattle neighborhoods counter the representation of the lack of agency among the novel's unemployed urban Indians and depict a labor crisis that is difficult to ignore. For example, Alexie emphasizes the class conflict between residents and tourists of the city by including condensed work histories of numerous minor characters who are homeless. Consider the story of Cornelius, "a Makah Indian . . . [and a] deep-sea fisherman" who takes care of Zera, "a Puyallup . . . [and] manic-depressive" (Alexie 212). Ruthlessly attacked by three white college students seeking to avenge the death of David Rogers, a suspected victim of the Indian Killer, this homeless couple illustrates a shared powerlessness to combat the uncertainty of seasonal work and mental illness. Alexie also explains how King, a Flathead Indian, a former college student who majored in education turned fisherman, became destitute after a random car accident: "too injured to work, without access to disability or workers' compensation, King had been homeless for most of the last ten years" (233). Though often eclipsed by the intrigue created by the killings, these accounts reveal the precarious position of urban Indians in obtaining steady work due to inadequate health care and social services; furthermore, they illuminate the invisible injuries of psychological trauma. The minor characters of Cornelius, Zera, and King (and many others like them in the novel) do more than establish sympathy; they give voice to the all-too-familiar tale of the disenfranchised and dispossessed—of how downward mobility leads to individuals and groups becoming orphans within the nation's domestic sphere.

Alexie's homeless, as a result of this class division, occupy an insecure space within the city, belonging nowhere. Yet by providing the names of individual workers, Alexie humanizes them, shifting the focus from personal blame to a lack of structural support. That Alexie also lists the specific tribal identities of each of his characters points to the cultural mixing in cities as a result of urban relocation. With over "two-thirds of the total American Indian population of 2.1 million liv[ing] in urban areas" like Seattle (Fixico ix), the story of American Indian migration and federal termination programs speaks directly to the belief that wage labor would improve their quality of life, enabling American Indians to integrate more fully into American society. According to Knack and Littlefield, "American Indian employment retained many of its earlier characteristics—higher turnover of jobs than was generally true for U.S. workers, more dependence on temporary or seasonal work, greater dependence on public employment, and below average incomes" (15). These realities magnify the isolation and expendability of the working poor and unemployed in Alexie's novel where he draws readers' attention to the crimes of capital than just to the clues of mutilated bodies and owl feathers left behind by the killer.

Alexie's "street people," however, are also characterized as being unproductive laborers and consumers, which adds another dimension to recognizing their vulnerability in society (228). A primary example of this occurs when King calls home to his reservation courtesy of a telephone company's promotional plan. Broke and broken by the system, King cannot afford to open an account of his own, and his attempt to reconnect with his estranged family ultimately fails. On the one hand, this scene tells the personal story of King's short-lived career as one who paid the price in seeking economic advancement. On the other hand, Alexie makes a larger political statement by showing how the homeless as a group are stigmatized in the city and forced by local businesses to relocate from public spaces such as Pike Place Market to the Alaskan Way Viaduct to seek shelter among the city's alleyways. Such policing of the homeless to restore the city's reputation occurs throughout the novel, and their continuous displacement by city ordinances signals another forced removal—a reshifting of boundaries that makes American Indians once again strangers in their own land. The recurring image of the un(der)employed in *Indian Killer* forces a recognition of the public's neglect of this national crisis and raises questions about the ethics of a society that privileges consumerism over humanitarianism.

The character of Marie Polatkin, the American Indian graduate student activist whose subsistence living is scarcely higher than the homeless Indians she serves from her sandwich van, demonstrates the familiar narrative of education as a means of achieving upward mobility. Supported by a full scholarship to attend the University of Washington, Marie is articulate, hardworking, and dismissive of the status quo. Like Cornelius and King, Marie leaves the reservation to escape poverty, but she too struggles to maintain a quality of life above the poverty line and often resorts to eating "cereal for breakfast and dinner every day, and also for lunch on weekends" (85). Marie's volunteer work at the Seattle Open Heart Mission and her activism to organize protests on behalf of American Indian rights are acts of resistance against the dominant culture's propensity to ignore the needs of those who cannot work or who have lost their jobs. As Marie admits, "she believed that homeless people were like an Indian tribe, nomadic and powerless . . ." (146). Marie's logic (and Alexie's shift from general to specific in identifying the poor treatment of the homeless) points to cultural solidarity—of recognizing the collective condition of America's "tribal" underclass, the new global proletariat.

As one interviewer reports, class conflict was an impetus for Alexie writing *Indian Killer*:

> 'If you look at the history of the U.S. and chart what's happening, we are brewing a revolutionary stew,' [Alexie] says, comparing the present disparity among classes and races to France just before the French Revolution. 'There's a tremendous level of anger out there, and the anger in the Indian community has not really been talked about. There's a huge open wound.' (Himmelsbach 33)

One way that Alexie wages a war against class violence—what I'm referring to as the unethical treatment of the poor—is to employ humor and irony to offset the anger about racial injustice. Alexie accomplishes this strategy by revolutionizing his "ragtag bunch of homeless warriors" (374) to take a stand against a common enemy.[11] When John Smith, along with Marie and a group of homeless Indians, ward off a vicious assault by the same group of college students who attacked Cornelius and Zera earlier in the story, Alexie references Custer's epic battle by having King exclaim, "The Indians won again!" (376). Their defensive stance should not be read as resistance to white hegemony only because Alexie shows how work and their unemployed status connects these strangers to one another as well. "The newspaper man, Crazy Robert, who was a reporter for the *Seattle Times* when he was twenty-five and homeless by the time he was thirty-five" or "Annie . . . [who] used to sing standards in a Holiday Inn Lounge in Norman, Oklahoma" are but two examples of capitalism's surplus labor (377). What is perhaps most remarkable about this scene is that it not only breaks the stereotype of "lazy Indians" that Truck Schultz perpetuates in his radio program—the kind of talk that incites racial confrontations such as this scene portrays—but that it also exposes how class further marginalizes the social position of Alexie's urban Indians. The gaps of their life histories and how these individuals became unemployed may not be essential to determining the identity of the killer, but they illustrate the creation of a new group identity. In its representation of collectivity and radical protest through these characters, Alexie's *Indian Killer* espouses an anticapitalist agenda, displaying what Laura Hapke calls an "alternative proletarianism"—a kind of "pervasive postmodern cynicism" (296) that describes the relationship between the self and systems of power. Though Marie's future may be less uncertain than those of the homeless she helps, higher education does not guarantee that she will achieve success. On the contrary, she must continue to negotiate the alienating effects of cultural dislocation and class mobility, undergoing the same intense struggle that ultimately consumes John Smith by the novel's end.

CROSSING THE CLASS DIVIDE

John Smith's upper-middle-class upbringing creates a profound sense of detachment about his cultural background. Throughout the novel, he appears uneasy and disconnected from the people who seek a relationship with him, especially with his adoptive parents, Olivia and Daniel. Emotionally distressed as a result, John constructs a fantasy about his birth mother where he imagines being kidnapped from the reservation Indian Health Service hospital and flown by helicopter to his new, plushly landscaped suburban Seattle home. Through John's myth making, as the chapter title "Mythology" suggests, Alexie makes "public" the cultural genocide of American Indian children, whom he identifies as "'lost birds'" (Highway 28), due to the Indian Adoption Project during the 1950s through the 1970s, which resulted in over

90 percent being placed with non-Indian families (Agtuca 17; White and Martin 297–98).[12] Alexie acknowledges, "The social problems and dysfunctions of these Indians adopted out are tremendous. Their suicide rates . . . [and] their drug and alcohol abuse rates are off the chart" (Highway 28). John's insecurity about being "homeless" intensifies his mental illness—he suffers from schizophrenia—and Alexie's fictional portrayal of John's alienation confronts the ongoing impact domestic colonialism has on families and tribal communities. Equally troubling is John's psychological journey from depression and psychosis to eventual suicide, which portrays a nightmarish inversion of the American Dream in which class mobility and assimilation hinder rather than secure his chance of survival.

Though his interracial adoption has provided him with a private school education, a loving home, and economic stability, John's cultural impoverishment makes him desperate to recover from the loss of his "real" family, and he does so by forgoing college in order to join the local steelworker union.[13] John's inspiration stems from learning in high school about the history of Mohawk Indian steelworkers who constructed New York City's World Trade Center building, and he models his life after this ideal. Although Alexie does not further interrogate this historical fact, the details as to how John enters the world of high-rise construction as opposed to pursuing a professional, white-collar career connect his character to a particular time where, according to anthropologist Patricia Albers, the Bureau of Indian Affairs (BIA) supported "off-reservation employment" (254). John forges both a cultural and social connection with the Mohawk steelworkers from the Caughnawaga Reservation in Quebec, who relocated to Brooklyn during the "building boom" of the 1920s to build numerous skyscrapers and bridges in Manhattan and its surrounding areas such as the Empire State Building, the Daily News Building, and the George Washington Bridge (Mitchell 23).[14] In making this connection, Alexie traverses the nation's coastal borders by linking the skylines of New York and Seattle, emphasizing the importance of regional economies as well as the migrant history of American Indian wage labor.

John's reconnection to his ancestral past—not economic advancement—is the driving force behind his decision to work steel. Similar to the Mohawks, John experiences "cultural continuity" (Albers 257), which leads him to identify with the physicality of his job rather than with work culture created by the trade. When John encounters the iconic sculpture of *The Hammering Man* located outside the Seattle Art Museum, for instance, the landmark not only serves as a reminder of the universal struggles of the working class but also reveals John's empathy with the solitary figure. Like the steel monument, John wants to feel "[i]mportant and powerful" (Alexie 134) and works steadily and quietly throughout the day but his "strange" (24) behavior on the job does not go unnoticed and neither does his unwillingness to become "one of the guys." This point is made clear as John ignores invitations to meet his coworkers for drinks after work. For John, worker solidarity resonates with a past that is recreated in the present; consequently, he is tolerated at work because of his physical strength and work ethic. In writing about working-class life, and in particular, describing at length the skilled work John performs as a steelworker, Alexie rewrites the predominant stereotype that Albers argues against: "that Native Americans do not work and that when they do, their work patterns are irregular and unproductive" (247). This false impression, she claims, has led to "the modern emergence of class formations within Native American communities [to be] ignored" (271). Capitalist labor and indigenous culture are not "incompatible," but as Albers suggests, evidence that American Indians participate in the U.S. labor force and an acknowledgement of their contributions would increase their political power culturally and socially (258, 270).

John's recurring fantasies of killing white men counteract his silence on the job and reveal a keen awareness of class position. Alexie writes, "John hated poor white men, but knew killing them was a waste. They were already dead. They were zombies" (29). This apocalyptic reading of late-twentieth-century capitalism speaks to the oppression of the socially and economically underprivileged. Their torment, according to John, is so palpable that relieving their misery would be futile. In contrast, John speculates:

> If he killed the richest white man in the world, then the second-richest white man would take his place. Nobody would even notice the difference. All the money would be switched from one account to another. All the slaves would stop making toys, move to another factory, and begin making car alarms, director's chairs, or toasters. [He] could kill a thousand rich white men and not change a thing. (28)

As a narrative device meant to implicate John as a potential suspect of the serial murders, Alexie's account of exploitative business practices depicts an endless cycle of greed and profit. John's words make clear that the corrupt values of corporate executives and global capitalism are his target, and his powerlessness to change the production of material goods illustrates a form of structural violence against those who rely on this system to survive.[15]

The gap between the rich and the poor in *Indian Killer* underscores class conflict and depicts a world out of balance. John is attuned to the insecurity such imbalance creates and, therefore, questions the "pointless" construction of Seattle's "last skyscraper" (103):

> Why were they finishing this tall building when most of the skyscrapers in downtown Seattle were already in financial trouble? So many vacant spaces, so many failed businesses. None of the buildings in downtown

Seattle were owned by the people who had originally financed their construction. Nothing was original. (103)

Once again, John articulates class consciousness on a personal and global level. Worried about his future in the diminishing industry of new construction, John also considers the costs of corporate takeovers, urban development, and an impending economic crisis. The building also symbolizes John's own cultural and social displacement; he is not "original"—the natural landscape has been altered, and this metaphor further alludes to John's sense of feeling homeless. Moreover, the Seattle skyline signifies the exchange of real estate as both historic (the appropriation and theft of tribal lands) and contemporary (the selling of property to make a profit), which leaves John feeling stripped of the power created by the production of his own labor.

While social unrest and fear sweep through the city of Seattle, John's attention rarely strays from noting the spiritual decay of contemporary life. Alexie's critique of capitalism, in particular, becomes an inextricable part of John's character as shown by his uneasiness about the past: "[He] knew that every building in Seattle contained the bones of fallen workers. Every building was a tomb" (405). The sacrifices of those who came before him from his birth mother to fellow construction workers trigger a recognition of the immense loss of life and individuality in the name of progress, and John decides retired police officer turned detective fiction writer Jack Wilson should be the one to pay for these crimes. Claiming to be part Shilshomish Indian, Wilson's success as a writer of "authentic" Indian novels—a fact protested by Marie and celebrated by John's mother, Olivia—is the means through which John measures Wilson's guilt for exploiting culture and humanity. Work, once again, becomes a focal point in the narrative as John holds Wilson captive on the roof of the fortieth floor of the skyscraper he helped to build, taking into account "the smaller offices between corner offices" and the presence of "a janitor push[ing] a vacuum back and forth" in a building across the way (396).

In the midst of the novel's climax—the culmination of John's rage, which results in his using a knife to nearly slice Wilson's face in two—Alexie slows down the action by noting the dawn of a new workday in Seattle. Sensory images such as cars leaving the ferry, street sweepers returning to the garage, jets and helicopters flying above, and ringing alarm clocks flood John's mind (404). Yet the sights and sounds of familiar work routines do not comfort John; instead, they incite him to escape this spiritually empty world by falling to his death. Nancy Van Styvendale's interpretation of John's suicide as "the ultimate return to roots, albeit a tragic and paradoxically unfulfilled return, which rehearses the discourse of the 'vanishing Indian'" (211) suggests his death is an act of rebirth to return to his biological mother and Father Duncan, the Indian Jesuit priest who baptized him as a child. But the novel's fatalistic ending also imparts a message about the multifaceted process of achieving selfhood. The final image of John's lifeless body, "in blue jeans, red plaid shirt, [and] brown work boots," represents the typical work clothes of construction workers and leaves a lasting imprint on how to read his long journey of exile and dispossession to recovery (Alexie 412). Like many working-class narratives, assimilation exacts a price on individual and group identity and John constructs a new beginning by reclaiming the past—that is, what he identifies as home—an act that initially begins with his desire to work steel.

NO END IN SIGHT

Alexie's *Indian Killer* begins a critical conversation about the intersections between labor and race relations in unconventional ways. Although the novel may not neatly satisfy genre expectations, it weaves history and myth to tell the story of contemporary American Indian culture, exposing the uncertainty of assimilation and class mobility within an urban context. The subject of class performs a significant role in *Indian Killer* in documenting the impact deindustrialization, mass unemployment, and a rapidly changing workforce has on local communities and, more specifically, class formation among urban American Indians. If we read Alexie's novel as working-class literature, which I think we can, *Indian Killer* performs the ideological work of advocating for economic and social justice both in fiction and in the real world, and this has far-reaching implications in how we identify and teach literature of class struggle. A class-specific reading calls into question earlier interpretations of anger in the novel as related to race only; in this case, viewing anger as a political construct creates possibilities of exploring Alexie's representation of working-class culture.

The intrigue surrounding the serial killings, the escalating fear and anger in the city, and John's spiraling decline have for too long overshadowed a recognition of Alexie's class critique in *Indian Killer*. John's death, for instance, does not signal the end of the murders; on the contrary, the novel's final chapter features the killer performing an empowering ceremony to exact further revenge and restore balance, and this ending suggests the continuation of not only physical violence but of class violence as well. With assimilation failing John and the fragility of the urban poor, including the depiction of an uncertain future for Marie and the wandering homeless, *Indian Killer* generates more questions than answers; pedagogically, this can be a constructive approach to introducing class as an essential component of cultural diversity. The novel captures a multitude of voices and experiences that promote the examination of working-class history and culture in the United States. For example, in an upper-level class I taught on multiethnic literature, students raised the following questions about *Indian Killer*: how can these individuals, who are portrayed as second-class citizens in the novel, achieve a voice in society? What can be done to improve the lives of the poor and unemployed? How do we lessen the disconnect that exists between classes and ethnic groups? These questions attempt to collapse the differences that separate and divide to explore collective power as a possibility in creating a just and equitable world.

Analyzing class in *Indian Killer* thus extends the narrative beyond the murder mystery to consider more carefully the "hidden" history of American Indian wage labor (Albers 245). As Albers rightly claims, we cannot "divorce [American Indians] from the economic system at large" (264). To do so, she argues, would set up "false dichotomies" that ignore the ways in which indigenous communities "have contributed to the accumulation of capital by Europeans and their descendants in North America," as John's character suggests (264). The novel's depiction of the relationship among race, class, and power and its effects on the human condition registers the discontent and hostility between those who make it and those who do not. Moreover, the focus on contemporary labor relations reflects the need to see the production of American Indian culture as critical to understanding the ever-changing dynamics of the global economy. In doing so, *Indian Killer* advances a deeper appreciation for reading class conflict beyond the condition of poverty itself. The stories of the homeless articulate the struggle of class mobility—upward and downward, as both are characteristics of working-class life—and Alexie's representation of these experiences serves as a powerful reminder of the many individuals and groups living on the fringes of society. Much work remains to be done in bridging the fields of ethnic and working-class studies, and *Indian Killer* is but one example of recent American ethnic fiction that illustrates the importance of engaging in intersectional analysis. Simply put, class matters in *Indian Killer*, and Alexie uses this subject as a vehicle to shed light on the invisibility of the underprivileged in contemporary American society.

NOTES

1. I would like to thank Nicholas Coles, Shirley Carrie, Cherie Rankin, Kette Thomas, Christie Launius, and Michelle Tokarczyk for insightful feedback. Special thanks to Eric Lott and fellow participants in his seminar at the 2010 Futures of American Studies Institute at Dartmouth College for suggestions in shaping this essay.
2. *A New Labor Movement for the New Century*, edited by Gregory Mantsios, provides an extensive overview of issues facing the working class from scholars and activists during the early 1990s. See especially the afterword written by John J. Sweeney.
3. For a range of scholarship about *Indian Killer,* see the following: Arnold Krupat's "The 'Rage Stage'": Contextualizing Sherman Alexie's *Indian Killer*"; Stuart Christie's "Blood Legacies: Pathology and Power in Works by Sherman Alexie and A.A. Carr"; James H. Cox's "Muting White Noise: The Popular Culture Invasion in Sherman Alexie's Fiction"; Martha Cutter's "Translation as Revelation: The Task of the Translator in the Fiction of N. Scott Momaday, Leslie Marmon Silko, Susan Power, and Sherman

Alexie"; Daniel Grassian's *"Indian Killer"*; James Giles's "The Return of John Smith: Sherman Alexie's *Indian Killer*"; Nancy Van Styvendale's "The Trans/Historicity of Trauma in Jeannette Armstrong's *Slash* and Sherman Alexie's *Indian Killer*"; Janet Dean's "The Violence of Collection: *Indian Killer's* Archives"; and Patrice Hollrah's "Sherman Alexie's Challenge to the Academy's Teaching of Native American Literature, Non-Native Writers, and Critics."

4. For a critical review of the different positions within Native American studies, see Huhndorf.
5. See Pepper; and Fischer-Hornung and Mueller for a discussion of how race, ethnicity, gender, and class intersect with the elements of crime fiction. Both contain critical analyses of *Indian Killer.*
6. See the University of Washington, "Seattle Civil Rights and Labor History Project" for a fascinating compilation of photographs, film, oral histories, and research pertaining to Seattle's trade unions and labor history from which this information was gathered. My comments also derive from the summary of events leading up to the protests of the World Trade Organization in 1999 provided in Schrager Lang and Tichi.
7. Russo and Linkon argue for exploring the many features of class—one that resists nostalgia and considers carefully the lived experiences of workers across cultures and time periods (10). Such work is already being done in the field of Native American studies. Christopher observes that "[v]ery little has been written about Native Americans and social class and even less about contemporary Native American writers' relationship to social class" (154). Exploring Louis Owens's working-class background and resistance to upward mobility in *Wolfsong* and *I Hear the Train,* Christopher advocates for situating Owens (Chocktaw/Cherokee) as both a Native American writer and working-class writer. Dyck also addresses working-class culture and argues that a reading of class hierarchies and changing economic conditions in Anishinaabe writer Louise Erdrich's *Love Medicine* creates a deeper understanding of the cultural and social forces that shape the novel's characters. Libretti identifies elements of Marxism and class liberation in Leslie Marmon Silko's (Laguna Pueblo) *Almanac of the Dead* and Simon Ortiz's (Acoma Pueblo) *Woven Stone.* These essays advance the study of race and class in U.S. ethnic literature, and as Christopher aptly notes, "[i]t is important to look at writers of color in terms of their representation of class as well as of race, so that not only white working-class writers count as 'classed' (instead of also 'raced') and so that writers of color count as 'classed' (instead of only 'raced')" (157).
8. See Zweig for a discussion of how power shapes the lived experiences of workers and the larger society beyond income and life-style.
9. For a fuller discussion of definitions of working-class literature, see Zandy, esp. 90–93; Tokarczyk; Christopher and Whitson; and Lauter.
10. Littlefield and Knack do the important work of situating American Indian labor within the U.S. economy as integral to the history of economic relations. The case studies of tribes such as the Mi'kmaq and Laguna Pueblo are particularly interesting in exploring the specificities of region and cultural identities within the production of labor.
11. Miller considers how urbanization functions as a movement of "'(re)taking place' . . . from federally designated boundaries historically intended to isolate and contain Native people" (29). This scene defies the notion of the doomed, vanishing Indian and instead posits a compelling image of a population disempowered by this stereotype.
12. See Barsh for a summation of the act's accomplishments and shortcomings, including the power differential between state and tribal governments in

156 *Michele Fazio*

which he argues the "emphasis [remains] on removal and placement, not prevention" (266). See also Nancy Van Styvendale's discussion of Alexie's depiction of the trauma and displacement John Smith's character experiences because of his adoption, particularly 209–10 and 216–17.
13. Throughout the novel, Alexie alternates among the terms ironworker, steelworker, and high-rise construction worker to describe John's occupation.
14. Two projects documenting this extraordinary, often overlooked, chapter of American labor history include the National Museum of the American Indian's online photography and oral history exhibit, *Booming Out: Mohawk Ironworkers Build New York*, and PBS's documentary commemorating the hundredth anniversary of the Quebec Bridge disaster, *To Brooklyn and Back: A Mohawk Journey*. Both resources offer unique perspectives of workers' relationship to labor, community, and memory, and Alexie's inclusion of this experience in *Indian Killer* broadens how U.S. labor has traditionally been defined. As Orvis Diabo (Scotch-Irish/Caughnawaga) states in Mitchell's essay, "[w]hen they talk about the men that built this country, one of the men they mean is me" (28). The recovery of these working-class histories is an essential aspect of what constitutes working-class studies.
15. See Giles's chapter, "The Return of John Smith," in which he examines more fully John's powerlessness to combat the capitalist system, esp. 130–35. Describing John as a "naturalistic victim of external forces," Giles argues that the racism he has endured keeps him from "consider[ing] poor whites, also economic victims, as allies" (133).

BIBLIOGRAPHY

Agtuca, Jacqueline. "Beloved Women: Life Givers, Caretakers, Teachers of Future Generations." *Sharing Our Stories of Survival: Native Women Surviving Violence*. Ed. Sarah Deer, Bonnie Clairmont, Carrie A. Martell, and Maureen L. White Eagle. Lanham: Altamira, 2008. 3–27. Print.
Albers, Patricia C. "From Legend to Land to Labor: Changing Perspectives on Native American Work." *Native Americans and Wage Labor: Ethnohistorical Perspectives*. Ed. Alice Littlefield and Martha C. Knack. Norman: U of Oklahoma P, 1996. 245–73. Print.
Alexie, Sherman. *Indian Killer*. New York: Warner, 1996. Print.
Barsh, Russel Lawrence. "The Indian Child Welfare Act of 1978: A Critical Analysis." *Recent Legal Issues for American Indians, 1968 to the Present*. Ed. John R. Wunder. New York: Garland, 1996. 219–68. Print. Native Americans and the Law: Contemporary and Historical Perspectives on American Indian Rights, Freedoms, and Sovereignty.
Blewster, Kelley. "Tribal Visions." *Conversations with Sherman Alexie*. Ed. Nancy J. Peterson. Jackson: UP of Mississippi, 2009. 71–82. Print.
Campbell, Duncan. "Voice of the New Tribes." *Conversations with Sherman Alexie*. Ed. Nancy J. Peterson. Jackson: UP of Mississippi, 2009. 113–20. Print.
Cheyfitz, Eric. "The (Post)Colonial Construction of Indian Country: U.S. American Indian Literatures and Federal Indian Law." *The Columbia Guide to American Indian Literatures of the United States Since 1945*. Ed. Eric Cheyfitz. New York: Columbia UP, 2006. 1–124. Print.
Christie, Stuart. "Blood Legacies: Pathology and Power in Works by Sherman Alexie and A. A. Carr." *Plural Sovereignties and Contemporary Indigenous Literature*. New York: Palgrave Macmillan, 2009. 39–72. Print.

Christopher, Renny. "Louis Owens's Representations of Working-Class Consciousness." *Louis Owens: Literary Reflections on His Life and Work*. Ed. Jacquelyn Kilpatrick. Norman: U of Oklahoma P, 2004. 154–74. Print.

Christopher, Renny, and Carolyn Whitson. "Toward a Theory of Working Class Literature." *Thought and Action: The National Education Association Higher Education Journal* (1999): 71–81. Web. 28 Mar. 2009.

Cox, James H. "Muting White Noise: The Popular Culture Invasion in Sherman Alexie's Fiction." *Muting White Noise: Native American and European American Novel Traditions*. Norman: U of Oklahoma P, 2006. 145–99. Print.

Cutter, Martha. "Translation as Revelation: The Task of the Translator in the Fiction of N. Scott Momaday, Leslie Marmon Silko, Susan Power, and Sherman Alexie." *Lost and Found in Translation: Contemporary Ethnic American Writing and the Politics of Language Diversity*. Chapel Hill: U of North Carolina P, 2005. 89–136. Print.

Dean, Janet. "The Violence of Collection: *Indian Killer's* Archives." *Studies in American Indian Literatures* 20.3 (2008): 29–51. Print.

Dwight, John. "Booming Out: Mohawk Ironworkers Build New York." Smithsonian National Museum of the American Indian. Web. 16 Feb.2010.

Dyck, Reginald. "When Love Medicine is Not Enough: Class Conflict and Work Culture on and off the Reservation." *American Indian Culture and Research* 30.3 (2006): 23–43. Web. 1 June 2007.

Fischer-Hornung, Dorothea, and Monika Mueller, eds. *Sleuthing Ethnicity: The Detective in Multiethnic Crime Fiction*. Madison: Fairleigh Dickinson UP, 2003. Print.

Fixico, Donald L. Foreword. *American Indians and the Urban Experience*. Ed. Susan Lobo and Kurt Peters. Walnut Creek: Altamira, 2001. ix-x. Print.

Giles, James. "The Return of John Smith: Sherman Alexie's *Indian Killer*." *The Spaces of Violence*. Tuscaloosa: U of Alabama P, 2006. 128–44. Print.

Grassian, Daniel. "*Indian Killer*." *Understanding Sherman Alexie*. Columbia: U of South Carolina P, 2005. 104–26. Print.

Hapke, Laura. *Labor's Text: The Worker in American Fiction*. New Brunswick: Rutgers UP, 2001. Print.

Harris, Timothy. "Seriously Sherman: Seattle's Favorite Pissed Off Poet Talks about Truth, Terror, Tradition, and What's So Great about America Anyway?" *Conversations with Sherman Alexie*. Ed. Nancy J. Peterson. Jackson: UP of Mississippi, 2009. 128–34. Print.

Haut, Woody. *Pulp Culture: Hardboiled Fiction and the Cold War*. New York: Serpent's Tail, 1995. Print.

Highway, Tomson. "Spokane Words: Tomson Highway Raps with Sherman Alexie." *Conversations with Sherman Alexie*. Ed. Nancy J. Peterson. Jackson: UP of Mississippi, 2009. 21–31. Print.

Himmelsbach, Erik. "The Reluctant Spokesman." *Conversations with Sherman Alexie*. Ed. Nancy J. Peterson. Jackson: UP of Mississippi, 2009. 32–35. Print.

Hollrah, Patrice. "Sherman Alexie's Challenge to the Academy's Teaching of Native American Literature, Non-Native Writers, and Critics." *Studies in American Indian Literatures* 13.2–3 (2001): 23–35. Print.

Huhndorf, Shari. "Literature and the Politics of Native American Studies." *PMLA* 120.5 (2005): 1618–27. Print.

Knack, Martha C., and Alice Littlefield. "Native American Labor: Retrieving History, Rethinking Theory." *Native Americans and Wage Labor: Ethnohistorical Perspectives*. Ed. Martha Knack and Alice Littlefield. Norman: U of Oklahoma P, 1996. 3–44. Print.

Krupat, Arnold. *Red Matters: Native American Studies*. Philadelphia: U of Pennsylvania P, 2002. Print.

Lang, Amy Schrager, and Ceceila Tichi. "A New Critical Realism: Introduction." *What Democracy Looks Like: A New Critical Realism for a Post-Seattle World.* Ed. Amy Schrager Lang and Ceceila Tichi. New Brunswick: Rutgers UP, 2006. 3–23. Print.

Lauter, Paul. "Working-Class Women's Literature: An Introduction to Study." *Radical Teacher* 15 (1980): 16–26. Print.

Libretti, Tim. "The Other Proletarians: Native American Literature and Class Struggle." *Modern Fiction Studies* 47.1 (2001): 166–89. Print.

Mantsios, Gregory, ed. *A New Labor Movement for the New Century.* New York: Monthly Review, 1998. Print.

Mitchell, Joseph. "The Mohawks in High Steel." 1949. *Apologies to the Iroquois.* Ed. Edmund Wilson. New York: Vintage, 1959. 3–36. Print.

Miller, Carol. "Telling the Indian Urban: Representations in American Indian Fiction." *American Indians and the Urban Experience.* Ed. Susan Lobo and Kurt Peters. Walnut Creek: Altamira, 2001. 29–45. Print.

Owens, Louis. *Mixedblood Messages: Literature, Film, Family, Place.* Norman: U of Oklahoma P, 1998. Print.

Pepper, Andrew. *The Contemporary American Crime Novel: Race, Ethnicity, Gender, Class.* Chicago: Fitzroy Dearborn, 2000. Print.

Peterson, Nancy J. Introduction. *Conversations with Sherman Alexie.* Ed. Nancy J. Peterson. Jackson: UP of Mississippi, 2009. ix-xviii. Print.

Reddy, Maureen. T. *Traces, Codes, and Clues: Reading Race in Crime Fiction.* New Brunswick: Rutgers UP, 2003. Print.

Russo, John, and Sherry Lee Linkon. "Introduction: What's New about New Working-Class Studies?" *New Working-Class Studies.* Ed. John Russo and Sherry Lee Linkon. Ithaca: Cornell UP 2005. 1–18. Print.

Skow, John. "Lost Heritage." *Time Magazine* 21 Oct. 1996. Web. 5 Mar. 2010.

To Brooklyn and Back: A Mohawk Journey. Dir. Reaghan Tarbell. Vision Maker Video, 2008.

Tokarczyk, Michelle M. *Class Definitions: On the Lives and Writings of Maxine Hong Kingston, Sandra Cisneros, and Dorothy Allison.* Selinsgrove: Susquehanna UP, 2008. Print.

University of Washington. "Seattle Civil Rights and Labor History Project." Web. 1 June 2010.

Weich, Dave. "Revising Sherman Alexie." *Conversations with Sherman Alexie.* Ed. Nancy J. Peterson. Jackson: UP of Mississippi, 2009. 169–79. Print.

White, James G., and Sarah Michèle Martin. "The Indian Child Welfare Act and Violence Against Women." *Sharing Our Stories of Survival: Native Women Surviving Violence.* Ed. Sarah Deer, Bonnie Clairmont, Carrie A. Martell, and Maureen L. White Eagle. Lanham: Altamira, 2008. 297–308. Print.

Wiegand, David. "Somebody's Scalping White Men in Seattle: Gripping Thriller has Profound Things to Say About Prejudice and Identity." *San Francisco Chronicle* 29 Sept. 1996. Web. 5 Mar. 2010.

Van Styvendale, Nancy. "The Trans/Historicity of Trauma in Jeannette Armstrong's *Slash* and Sherman Alexie's *Indian Killer.*" *Studies in the Novel* 40.1–2: 203–23. Print.

Zandy, Janet. *Hands: Physical Labor, Class, and Cultural Work.* New Brunswick: Rutgers UP, 2004. Print.

Zweig, Michael. *The Working Class Majority: America's Best Kept Secret.* Ithaca: Cornell UP, 2000. Print.

9 Cultural Geography and Local Economies
The Lesson from Egypt, Maine

Phoebe S. Jackson

In a 2000 *PMLA* special topic issue on class, Cynthia Ward in her article "From the Suwanee to Egypt, There's No Place like Home" questioned the lack of critical attention to two working-class novels, Zora Neale Hurston's *Seraph on the Suwanee* and Carolyn Chute's *The Beans of Egypt, Maine*. Commenting on the academy's interest in "issues of identity," she asked, "[w]hy has no critical perspective emerged to examine these novels' representations of working-class identity?" (Ward 76).[1] Ward answered her question in part by arguing that their novels "expose and resist commodifying reading practices" (80). Ward effectively demonstrates the novel's resistance to middle-class readers, but the central question she posed in 2000 persists a decade later. Although any list of working-class literature would necessarily include Chute's 1985 novel, her work continues to receive very little critical attention, no doubt because of its refusal to make valuations about the working poor and because of its implicit resistance to middle-class mores.

Academics routinely place Chute's novel in the generic category of working-class literature. However, her characters, the Beans, defy such easy classification. First of all, there is the problem of identifying them as working class. When writing about Chute's novel, scholars seem reluctant to use the term working class to describe the Beans. Unable to firmly and conclusively classify Chute's characters, critics search around for words—all coming up with different ones—to describe the Beans. Renny Christopher, for example, argues that "Chute's characters are not really working-class, they are the working poor." To amplify this distinction, she further explains that "there is a great deal of difference between working-class culture and underclass culture" (Christopher 51). Other academics writing about Chute's text use words like "lower-class experiences," (Adams 6) "lower class situation," (Tapley 9), "working poor class" (Tapley 9) and "working poor" (Adams 7) when speaking of Chute's characters. Their different ways to describe the Beans demonstrate the problematics of naming or of trying to identify who should be part of the working class and/or of the working poor. Although Chute's novel generically falls into the classification of working-class texts, critics are hard pressed to categorically define her characters as working class.

Then there's the problem of reader identification. As Cynthia Ward notes, reviewers very often wrote about the book in terms of a "we-they discourse"; that is, they could see no redeeming characteristics about the Beans because their poverty made them so different from a middle-class audience. Besides an inability to find identification with a middle-class audience, Chute's novel also struggles with finding a receptive working-class one. In her book *Hands: Physical Labor, Class, and Cultural Work*, Janet Zandy lists "observations" that would be apparent in a given working-class text. One such shared characteristic would be "readers who are of the working class have the opportunity to recognize themselves in working-class writing" (91). But Renny Christopher challenges that observation in regards to Chute's novel. Because "they are the working poor," Christopher argues, "some working-class students might find it as hard to deal with *The Beans* as some middle-class students might" (51). Chute's book dramatizes the central problem of trying to define who is working class. Her novel and her characters purposely resist such classification. In this essay, I will argue that the inability to categorically define the Beans tells us a lot about the workings of class and its complexity. Moreover, as will soon become apparent, Chute's novel challenges us to rethink terms such as working class and class in general.

In their introduction to their edited collection *New Working Class Studies*, John Russo and Sherry Lee Linkon observe that "dramatic changes in work raise new and significant questions about class in general and working-class culture specifically" (10). Although they argue that the working class should "take center stage," they also acknowledge that defining the working class is no easy task. As they explain, "In the twenty-first century, perhaps more than ever before, defining who is or is not working class is a slippery, complex task, and class as a concept carries multiple, contradictory, and complementary meanings" (11). Instead of offering narrow, proscriptive terms to define the working class, Russo and Linkon realize "conversations about class must take into account multiple definitions of class as well as changes in social and economic structures at the end of the millennium and the beginning of a new one" (5). "Rather than embracing any single view of class," they argue for the greater consideration of "how class works, as both an analytical tool and a basis for lived experience" (11).

Critics in other fields have championed the idea that working-class studies needs to expand its purview to include an investigation of "class processes and relations" (Roberts 193). According to sociologist Ian Roberts, the field of working-class studies needs to underscore the premise that "the creation and representation of working-class people and communities is a process that involves social dynamics and references to other classes in society" (193). Adding to Roberts's conclusions, Alison Stenning, a cultural geographer, argues that changes to the "nature of work and working lives" necessitate "new ways of studying and representing working class lives, cultures and politics" (9). Like Roberts, Stenning posits that the study of the working class should be viewed "as a dynamic and relational category which is simultaneously economic and cultural" (9–10). For cultural geographers, an understanding of the working class would include "both symbolic processes of representation and the more material processes of everyday life" (Stenning 10). Taken together, the critical understanding and work of academics like Russo and Linkon, Roberts, and Stenning move us beyond considerations of the working class that formerly focused on "objectifying" them (Roberts 193). They argue, instead, for looking at class in relational terms. Moreover, in their work, they advocate the importance of thinking about the working class from an interdisciplinary perspective.

In line with current thinking about working-class studies, Chute's novel intentionally complicates issues of class. With *The Beans of Egypt, Maine*, Carolyn Chute creates the fictional town of Egypt, Maine, mapping onto the town its own societal sedimentation of differing classes. The book demonstrates how late capitalism has of necessity changed the cultural geography of rural communities. Rampant urbanization of exurban areas has acted as a catalyst to displace rural residents. Traditional jobs such as logging and farming are disappearing, and formerly open lands are being replaced by vacation homes. These changes have set the stage for a clash of interests based on differences in social class. Chute's novel examines how the seemingly isolated rural poor interact with people from other social classes and how those interactions help to inform and define class relations for both groups. Mapping a new cultural geography where the rural poor come into contact with an encroaching urbanization, Chute interrogates the complications that arise from such an interaction. In the fictional Egypt, Maine, social class helps to shape and structure the way people experience their lives. While the cross-class encounter between rural poor and urban middle-class wreaks havoc on everyone concerned, Chute also gives the reader a better understanding of how "uneven geographical development" informs all aspects of our lives and might even offer up new possibilities for rethinking social relations.

READING LANDSCAPES, SCALE, AND URBANIZATION

One of the clarion calls of the new working-class studies is its emphasis on what Russo and Linkon call "multidisciplinary as well as interdisciplinary" approaches to "ongoing debates about what class is and how it works" (Russo and Linkon 14). Russo and Linkon cite in their introduction "the influence of geography on the field" of working-class studies, which "offers a model for studying class that links the local with the global" (Russo and Linkon 13). To help understand the workings of class, I will focus my discussion on the field of cultural geography, which "explores how social groups engage with their landscapes, how people construct and make sense of their places and spaces" (Atkinson et al. xv). As my argument will demonstrate, cultural geography has proven to be a productive avenue by which to explore issues of class.

Central to the academic discipline of cultural geography is the examination of landscape as it relates to culture. In brief, for most cultural geographers, the study of landscape as a field begins with Carl Sauer and the Berkeley School in the 1920s. Sauer and his adherents were primarily interested in the way culture affects landscape. However, since the 1980s, influenced in part by work in cultural studies, cultural geographers have shifted their focus. Rather than look at landscape as a product of culture, they see landscape as a process that interacts with culture. In the words of Don Mitchell, "landscape (as form, meaning and representation) actively incorporates the *social relations* that go into its making. The landscape (in all its senses) is both an outcome and the medium of social relations, both the result of and an input to specific relations of production and reproduction" ("Landscape" 49).

A prominent feature of the study of landscape is the issue of scale. When cultural geographers think about scale, they typically have in mind "local, regional, and national" (Newstead, Reid, and Sparke 485). In the past, these categories were considered as fixed properties. However, cultural geographers understand that the lines are no longer fixed between aspects of scale but are under constant negotiation. The importance of scale cannot be underestimated. As Don Mitchell poignantly observes, "understanding how the histories and geographies of particular places and landscapes cannot be understood outside an analysis of processes working at smaller and larger scales, and that scale is a means to see how the violent destruction of landscape (and livelihood) in one place can redound very much to the benefit of landscapes (and people) in other places" ("Cultural Landscapes" 791). Scale, as will soon be made clear in my discussion of urbanization, needs to be kept in mind when discussing landscape.

In an article entitled "Political Landscapes," cultural geographer Karen Till poses yet another way to think about landscape. Influenced by two separate schools of thought, landscape as representative of institutional power and as perpetuator of "unequal social relations," Till advocates marrying both approaches to propose investigating "landscape as everyday practice" (349). Thinking about landscape as everyday practice would, in her words, "examine how individuals and social groups self-consciously construct symbolic and material landscapes, or use the landscape in informal ways, to alter or question existing social and political relationships" (349). Additionally, a focus on everyday practice, Till further explains, "allows for more sophisticated understandings of power relations, politics, and agency" (355). Observing everyday practices of individuals and/or groups can tell us "about who should and should not belong to a particular social group, place, or political community" (355). Moreover, it gives us insight into how one constructs "identity" and how that identity is differentiated in relation to other social groups. Finally, and most important to the discussion of class, using the lens of everyday practice allows for a better understanding of how "multiple positions of identity are performed, enacted, challenged, and negotiated" (358).

Last, an overarching issue related to landscape and everyday practice in Chute's novel is the impact of urbanization. The effect of urbanization on the characters helps to explain and to shape class relations and for that reason is a central issue of the novel. One of the most provocative practitioners in the field of geography is David Harvey, who has directed critical attention to the importance of urbanization as part of the larger discussion of class relations and social justice. In *Justice, Nature and the Geography of Difference* (1996), Harvey argues that "understanding urbanization is integral to understanding political-economic, social, and cultural processes and problems" (419). Undergirding the process of urbanization is capitalism's relationship to geographical landscape, which Harvey contends produces "its own dynamic of accumulation at a particular moment of its history, only to have to destroy and rebuild that geographical landscape to accommodate accumulation at a later date" (412). As a process itself, Harvey explains that urbanization functions to create what he calls "uneven geographical development" (429). In his words, a focus on uneven geographical development helps both to explain the "historical-geographical conditions" that impact the lives of rural and urban people and at the same time how "human activity transforms socio-ecological conditions" (429). But equally important to this reciprocal process is the realization that solving environmental issues related to urbanization will not be easy because "'environment' means totally different things to different people, depending not only on ideological and political allegiances, but also upon situation, positionality, economic and political capacities, and the like" (428).

Using the lens of cultural geography, we can see how Chute's novel challenges the reader to rethink the dynamic between urban and rural living and the impact it has on individual characters. In Chute's account, middle-class readers learn much to their horror that the rural poor no longer live in isolated geographic regions. Instead, fictional Egypt, Maine, appears to be within easy driving distance from Portland, Maine, the southern part of the state where the tourist industry is strongest. In the novel, the presence of the Smiths' house signifies the continual encroachment of the urban landscape. The existence of their house blurs the distinction between rural and urban, suggesting that rural geographical poverty can no longer be isolated or contained in formerly out-of-the-way pockets of America. As a result, with the increasing urbanization of rural Maine comes a demographic change that impacts everyone. Fictional Egypt, Maine, functions as an example of what Harvey calls "uneven geographical development" as we see an area undergoing the process of urbanization. It is a place in transition where different social class groups live in close proximity to one another, at least for the present, each group defining and informing the other's way of living.

LANDSCAPES AND EVERYDAY PRACTICE

In arguing that landscape should be viewed as political, cultural geographer Karen Till locates the "political" in the practices of the everyday. She explains that feminist geographers have demonstrated in their research how everyday practices don't necessarily "conform to socially dominant mores," but they also participate in "creat[ing] and challeng[ing] new social relations" (357). Everyday practices also offer a window into "the particular contexts in which social relations are contextually situated and multiple positions of identity are performed, enacted, challenged, and negotiated" (358). As an example, Till cites the practice of "looking" as an everyday practice. "Looking," as Till argues, is never an impartial practice but one that is overdetermined. As a result, in Till's words, "viewing positions and situated interpretations are always intensely humanized, embodied, and contextual" (358). In Chute's novel, the characters participate actively in "looking" as an everyday practice. But interestingly, the looking involves both real and imagined landscapes.

Although the book is obviously about Maine (as the title suggests), Chute's novel surprisingly opens up with a romanticized vision of the West. The narrator, young Earlene, describes how she and her father, Lou Pomerleau, live in "a ranch house" (3). She informs her audience that "Daddy built it. Daddy says it's called RANCH 'cause it's like houses out West which cowboys sleep in. There's a picture window in all ranch houses and if you're in one of 'em out West, you can look out and see the cattle eatin' grass on the plains and the cowboys ridin' around with lassos and tall hats" (3). Central to Pomerleau's own identity is locating himself in relation to an imagined geographical West.

By building his own ranch house with its picture window, the working-class Lee Pomerleau, who works as a carpenter, has created a mythical vision of Western living. Interpolating himself into a mythical creation of the American West brings the promise of spatial freedom for someone who feels boxed in by his family and by the "lower-class" Beans. In *Landscapes of the New West*, Krista Comer argues that the West historically "has connoted outdoor or wild spaces" to correlate with a sense of masculine spatiality (27). "The most often celebrated feature of western space," she avers, "is its spatial *non*containment, its expansiveness, its vastness, its sheer weighty limitlessness" (Comer 28). Besides evoking a vision of wide-open spaces, "Western discourse answers modern problems by revisiting the past, invoking the masculine competence required of frontier days" (Comer 25). In that sense, Pomerleau harkens back to a different time that no longer exists. As Earlene explains about her self-reliant father, "Not only did Daddy build this house and most of the furniture in it, but he also whittles. He whittles little fishermen, horses, deer, and gulls for Gram to take to the church fairs" (Chute 59). However, people like Lou Pomerleau, according to Comer, although eager to hold on to a Western discourse evoking the past, cannot stop the speeding train of modernity and urbanization. As we see, his artisan skills seem quaint, fit only for "church fairs." Moreover, he does not realize that corporate ranches have long ago swallowed up many of his imagined "cowboy" ranches.

But creating such a vision is a way to distance himself from his own environment that he sees as degraded primarily because he has to live next door to the economically disadvantaged Bean family who live in a "mobile home" (5). Unlike the cowboys in the West whom he sees as natural inhabitants, for Lee Pomerleau, the Beans in their trailer are too close for comfort. When he looks out his picture window, rather than seeing "cattle eatin' grass and "cowboys ridin' around," he sees the Beans, or as he calls them "uncivilized animals. PREDATORS" (3). For him, unlike the cowboys who herd cattle grazing on great expanses of the plains, poor people like the Beans represent a degradation of the environment and a degeneration of humans to animal-like behavior. But as Cynthia Ward notes, the Beans are symbolically "essential" to Lee Pomerleau's view out his picture window. In an astute observation, she remarks that "it is his superior taste that assures him that he has value" (84).

But just as his imagined West is important to his male identity, so the Beans are necessary to the identity of Pomerleau's whole family. Looking at the Beans through the picture window enables the family to position themselves hierarchically in relation to the downtrodden Beans. Moreover, for members of the Pomerleau family, the Beans provide one of their primary forms of entertainment. As Earlene remarks, "we can see a lot through our picture window" (Chute 59). Even Earlene's mother, temporarily on leave from a mental hospital, participates in looking at the Beans for entertainment purposes. The roar of Rubie Bean's logging truck "crash[ing] down onto the right-of-way" propels both Earlene and her mother to the picture window (66). As Earlene narrates, "I get up and look out at him, Rubie Bean. . . . She [Earlene's mother] gets up, carries her soda and cigarette to the window" (66). The residents inside the ranch house—Lou, his wife, and Earlene—can be entranced and horrified by the spectacle of the Beans and by the emotions the family projects onto them. For the Pomerleaus, the Beans and their everyday activities are the equivalent of a "mystery" as they fantasize what the Beans might be doing in their trailer (59).

However, Lou Pomerleau's imagined "value" requires continually rehearsing the perceived attributes of his ranch house to keep them "real." As his daughter Earlene comments, "Daddy has said a million times that his house is a real peach . . . artesian well . . . dry cellar . . . the foundation was poured . . . lots of closet space" (6). And that when he built the house, "he went by the blueprints" (7). All of these characteristics provide a sharp contrast with the Beans' dilapidated trailer. His eagerness to create an imagined class difference between himself and his neighbors, the Beans, suggests how Pomerleau himself is terrified that he might fall in terms of his own unstable economic situation. As a carpenter, Pomerleau's gainful employment relies on building new structures to accommodate the influx of new people. But even that can be uncertain. At one point in the novel, we learn that Pomerleau has been laid off and that "there won't be any presents" at Christmas (58). Construction workers like Pomerleau depend upon the creation of new building projects—like the three new schools being built in the book, which for him "means no layoffs for a year" (151). All of this demonstrates how little class difference exists between Pomerleau and the Beans, no matter how much he repeats the perceived attributes of his ranch house.

Years later, Earlene engages in a different type of "looking" from her new perspective as a Bean. Formerly, the physical existence of the Beans next door and actions like the noise of Rubie Bean's logging truck vibrating through the Pomerleau's house seemed an assault on the family's values. Chute, however, makes it clear that the building of Smiths' new house represents a symbolic violence of a whole different magnitude. Commenting on the construction, Beal's cousin Rosie remarks, "The hammers across the way sound like machine guns" (228). Moving in on Thanksgiving with the aid of the Mayflower moving company, the Smiths are modern-day colonizers, relocating to extend the boundaries of exurbia (236).

In the past, the sheer presence of the Beans enabled Earlene and her family to reinforce their supposed social status. Now married to a Bean, Earlene continues her practice of looking but from another class perspective, focusing her gaze onto a wholly different social group—the wealthy Smiths. Although looking at the Smiths represents a reversal of fortune for her, Earlene seems to be divided in her perception of the Smiths' house. As she remarks to Rosie, "I look over and think what a crazy thing this new house is. Until now, there ain't been neighbors . . . and now we got 'em. I says, 'It's a pretty place'" (230). Although she finds the house subjectively "pretty," Earlene doesn't seem to know what to make of people who don't belong in this landscape but suddenly are there. And as Rosie points out, the arrival of the Smiths offers a point of comparison in economic circumstance, which previously didn't exist. "'Earlene,' Rosie asks, 'what's them classy folks gonna think of *this*?' She leans back on the legs of the chair and picks at the tarpaper wall" (230). But for Earlene, other than offering an opportunity to "look," the Smiths don't mean much to the reality of her everyday life. She knows only too well that she and her family are invisible to the Smiths. Her father, Lou Pomerleau, harbored a "fear of falling" and thus worked tirelessly to affect a social distance between himself and the Beans. But for the Smiths, who have "moocho" money and thus enough economic distance, the Beans aren't a concern. Instead, Earlene understands that "Bonny Loo and Allen [who] go over and set in the tall weeds and watch [the building of the house]" remain invisible to the Smiths (230).

However, as Cynthia Ward points out, "[n]ever appearing as characters, the Smiths nevertheless exert a powerful presence, indexed by the luxurious house they are having built across the road from the tar-paper shack shared by Earlene, Beal, Reuben's wife (Madeline), and four children" (86). Their "powerful presence," I would argue, affects a type of symbolic violence that has real economic repercussions for Beal and his family and the community. The building of the Smiths' house portends radical economic changes in the rural America. As noted previously, geographer Don Mitchell argues it's necessary to consider scale when analyzing changes in geographical landscape. He goes on to assert that an "understanding [of] the histories and geographies of particular places and landscapes cannot be understood outside an analysis of processes working at smaller and larger scales" (791). First of all, the Dunlaps' orchards are sold to make way for the Smiths' house, signifying the loss of agricultural land and the loss of farming as a profession. At the same time, Beal's ability to earn a living through logging is slowly eroded by the importation of cheaper "perfect blond boards" to build the Smiths' house. The traditional economy of logging, which used to afford Beal a subsistence-level income, has to make way for building of palatial homes in exurban areas, a more profitable market for developers than logging. Chute's novel argues that Beal will not be the beneficiary of new capital in the area, creating the demand for a new housing market and extending its borders of urbanization. Instead, uneven geographical development in rural America like Egypt, Maine, portends future problems.

The Smiths' new house mocks Beal's inability to provide for his family. As Cynthia Ward asserts, the "blazing electric lights are direct assault against a man who is unable not only to provide his family with electricity but even to afford flashlight batteries so he can hunt for game when the grocery money runs out" (86). But it's more than that. The presence of the Smiths' house puts into stark relief the uneven geographical development in housing depending on one's socioeconomic class. Not only does Rubie Bean's house lack electricity, but it also does not have running water, requiring Bonny Loo and her friend, Allen, to collect "dozens of empty milk jugs" to fill up (Chute 227). Moreover, the "Necessary Room," the outhouse they use, ironically does not have the other necessary item—toilet paper (228). Finally, besides having a surfeit of electricity, the "million tall windows" of the house also bespeak the Smiths' ability to pay exorbitant heating costs.

While Earlene and Rosie watch the Smiths' house rise in construction, the reader at the same time pays witness to Beal's economic circumstances degenerating downward. Beal and his wife and children are forced to move in with Madeline and her children because he cannot afford to rent his own place. His boss doesn't pay him; he is unable to get proper medical care and loses the sight of his one eye; he gets laid off from his job, and finally he can't even buy food for his family. While Beal loses his eyesight in one eye due to a work-related accident, the Smiths gain a new visibility in the neighborhood through the appearance of their very large house. Signifying increasing urbanization, the Smiths' house also demonstrates the high price exacted on rural residents, whose skills seem out of place in exurban landscapes. The destruction of Beal's livelihood and the retailing of his landscape ultimately work to the benefit of the Smiths. In that respect, like Earlene's mailbox sitting "alongside . . . [the Smiths'] prettiest mailbox [she'd] ever seen" (Chute 236), each social group in fictional Egypt, Maine functions relationally informing the existence of the other.

Thus, it's no great surprise that Beal turns his anger and frustration onto the Smiths' house by shooting out some of its million tall windows. But the police cannot tolerate such violence against private property so Beal is shot and killed. As such, class difference is accentuated; private property is deemed more important; poor people are deemed as expendable (Ward 86). Under Reagan's presidency, working-class people like Beal did not benefit from the financial boom of the '80s as did much of the upper class whose wealth increased exponentially. Instead, their economic situation got worse. Chute's novel argues that the Smiths' new house with its "millions of tall windows" actually depends upon Beal's poverty for its existence—that in the late capitalist economy of the Reagan era there were clear winners and losers.

READING THE BODY: LIVED EXPERIENCE, GENDER, AND LOCAL ECONOMIES

Increasingly important to the field of cultural geography is work on understanding the body in relation to space. To theorize the body, cultural geographers have looked to other fields of enquiry to inform their discussions. Doing so has meant rethinking issues of the body that extend beyond Cartesian notions of the mind/body binary. Informed by poststructuralist thinking, critics argue instead that the body is constituted by culture. To help us understand the connection between the physical body and culture, feminist scholars like Susan Bordo look back to Karl Marx and his role "in reimagining the body as a historical and not merely a biological arena" (33). For Marx, in the words of Bordo, the body is "an arena shaped by the social and economic organization of human life and, often, brutalized by it" (33). Echoing the sentiments of Marx, feminist scholars like Bordo and Elizabeth Grosz place emphasis on a consideration of the body beyond its biology. Both contend "our bodies, no less than anything else that is human, are constituted by culture" (Bordo 142). In thinking of bodies in terms of cultural production, Grosz argues, "[cultural and historical] representations and cultural inscriptions quite literally constitute bodies and help to produce them as such" (x). Therefore, "the body must be regarded as a site of social, political, cultural, and geographical inscriptions, production, or constitution" (Grosz 23).

Building upon the earlier work of feminist critics like Bordo and Grosz, cultural geographers Pamela Moss and Isabel Dyck argue for "a feminist materialist perspective" (67) in theorizing about the body. Important to their discussion is their insistence on "thinking of the body as simultaneously and mutually constituted as corporeal and discursive" (67). Included in their theoretical paradigm is recognition of "the *material* ways in which bodies are constituted, experienced and represented" (60 [emphasis in original]). Finally, they advocate "a focus on lived experience" as a way to "bring abstract subjects/bodies into the materiality of life in specific spaces and locations" (62). Using a theoretical approach like feminist materialism, Moss and Dyck argue, "usefully challenge[s] binary thinking by opening up categories for analyzing embodied subjectivity, a concern that must be central in understanding the constitution of social divisions, their intersections of carving out social experience, and the ways in which powerful discourses frame both subject positions and forms of resistance" (67).

In Chute's novel, the physical body figures prominently in her portrayal of all her characters. But there are gendered differences. In the chapter "Tall Woman Love," everyone, regardless of class, participates in reading Roberta Beal's body. Along with the characters' casual remarks and thoughts about Roberta's physical body, Chute offers a portrayal of Roberta Bean that simultaneously challenges the reader's perception of received notions of social class constructed about poor rural white women.[2] Through Roberta's cross-class encounter with Donald Goodspeed, the "celebrated highway engineer," the reader along with Goodspeed learns how representations of her "abject" body only tell part of the story.

When looking at Roberta, most of the characters in the novel define her by her sheer physicality. But her physical attributes are described in radically different terms, depending on who is looking at her. For Lou Pomerleau, whose working-class identity is dependent upon his ability to compare himself to others, the Beans, including Roberta are "lower class." Thus Pomerleau, who traffics in stereotypes of the poor, sees her in negative terms as defined solely by her nine "illegitimate" pregnancies. In his remarks to Earlene, his daughter, he disparagingly comments, "there should be a law that after you've had nine kids and no husband, you get the knife. They call it tyin' the tubes. Hers. . . . They should cut 'em, then tie 'em in twenty knots" (Chute 153). Whereas Pomerleau views her in pejorative terms related to female fecundity, other men in the novel are more impressed with her physical stature. Her tallness distinguishes her because, as Letourneau observes "with awe," "she is taller than either [him or Beal]" (155). And for them, her tallness speaks for her capability as a woman. For Donald Goodspeed, her size, her poverty, and all of her children make her an overwhelming presence that is larger than life and that can't be contained in an image of a rearview mirror. As the omniscient narrator observes, "the tall woman is so tall she divides Donald's rearview mirror into two clean halves" (109).

Along with her size, the reader learns how class is marked differently on Roberta and Donald. Although "she is so eerily thin" (128) from Goodspeed's perspective, Roberta possesses the physical strength of a man. When he first sees Roberta, Donald notes her "assiduous, straining, bony neck and long, long young arms work the axe" (109) as she chops wood. But the necessity to do physical labor also marks Roberta's body in a different manner. Taking a ride with her, Goodspeed notices her "broad scarred hands grip the vibrating wheel" of her pickup truck (121). By contrast, Roberta observes that Donald's "hands look brand-new, never used" (129), although earlier in the novel he is described as a middle-aged man with gray hair. Because of their differing social and economic situation, they in effect change or swap expected gender roles. Roberta, who is called upon to split wood, hunt rabbits for food, and literally do the work of both a man and a woman, is often described in the novel as wearing male clothing, "dressed in a man's ribbed undershirt and green wool pants" when chopping wood (108). Donald, on the other hand, who performs "clean" labor and who can afford to wear jewelry seems feminized from Roberta's perspective wearing as he does "cuff links shaped like little eagles . . . a wedding band and another ring, a school ring [Roberta] believes is a ruby" (129).

Although people like Lou Pomerleau and initially Donald Goodspeed fixate on all of Roberta's children as the definitive characteristic of her person, the reader and eventually Donald Goodspeed learn to see her in more complex ways that dispel stereotypes about poor rural white women as perpetually barefoot and pregnant. Economic and social circumstances and the necessity to do men's work have also informed Roberta's identity, leading to her refusal to "perform" female.

In one scene, Chute quite comically describes the self-important Goodspeed trying to start his Lincoln, while in the background Roberta Bean is chopping wood. When Roberta walks over to see if she can help him, he summarily dismisses her. Visibly horrified by her physical presence and attendant poverty, he focuses his gaze on one part of her body—her teeth, which to him look "like the far-apart teeth of a Doberman, long, fat, yellow, sharp" (111). For Goodspeed, Roberta's body, marked by poverty, is also coded as predatory, clearly something to fear.

When she goes off for help, Donald assumes she will ask the men hanging out at "Beans' Variety Store," which immediately elicits a feeling of "sweaty dread" in him (112). In this rural landscape, the urban engineer Donald Goodspeed understands only too well that he is the person who is out of place. In his cross-class encounter with the "other," Goodspeed comes to realize that he might be the odd one out for the men of Egypt, Maine, rather than the other way around. Overwhelmed by his nervousness, he sees himself as he imagines they might see him—as some type of specimen to be studied, "the way visitors to hospitals gape through Plexiglas at newborns" (112). Although Goodspeed views Roberta with repulsion, he suddenly understands that the gaze can be turned in the other direction, disrupting his sense of identity.

But much to his surprise, "[Roberta] returns without them" (112). Instead, she appears with her own truck and jumper cables. As she proceeds to open up both the hood to the Lincoln and her truck, he interrupts by stating authoritatively, "I'll do that now" (113). By the time he is ready to take control of the situation, she has already finished jumpstarting the car. Although he would like to define her in terms of rural female domesticity, imagining her "worrying the rubber from a Mason jar of cloudy green beans" (113), Roberta has overturned that stereotype and assumptions about female/male work in a rural landscape. Clearly out of his realm, the celebrated highway engineer has only been able to sit by passively and watch the very capable Roberta execute "a man's job."

Later on, Donald Goodspeed completely misinterprets Roberta's welcome gift "of the best bunny parts," which she leaves in a bag tied to his front door. Unaware of the local economy and local customs, Goodspeed initially sees the bag of rabbit parts as a prank played on him. It's only after yet another attempt at helping him that Goodspeed begins to see Roberta as more than just a poor person. When she sees him stuck in a culvert one night, she offers to give him a ride. He suggests condescendingly that all he needs is a phone because he has "got Triple A" (122). While she gives him a ride to his house to make the phone call, he asks her if she knows anything about the bag of rabbit parts. She explains, "I know you been livin' in the neighborhood almost a year now, but you know how it is, you're still the new fella to us all. Massachoosits an' all" (106). Realizing that the "best bunny parts" are a gift initiates a change in his attitude toward her. Forced to reassess his relationship to her, he no longer defines her by her straitened economic circumstances, but comes to see her as the fully capable and compassionate woman she is.

Ironically, from Roberta's perspective, Donald Goodspeed is the one who needs help. He, after all, is part of what Newitz and Wray call the new "diasporic" economy, which requires workers to move in order to stay employed. As they explain, "[i]f workers wish to stay afloat on the seas of economic change, they must be prepared to follow capitalist wealth from region to region, or country to country" (69). Donald Goodspeed is a case in point. "The celebrated highway engineer" from Massachusetts has moved to Egypt, Maine, to help develop shopping sites in nearby communities (108). In doing so, we learn that Goodspeed has had to leave behind his paraplegic wife in Amesbury, Massachusetts, while he works in Maine, thereby disrupting his family life.

Unlike Donald Goodspeed, who must migrate to another state to follow capital, Roberta Bean embraces a traditional economy that does not make her so beholden to capital. Through her resourcefulness, she grows her own vegetables to use for herself and to sell at a stand. She also raises chickens and hunts for rabbits. As a result, she is able to provide for all of her children and at the very least feed them. Her self-sufficiency enables her to be independent of an economic system that does little to provide for poor people except to stigmatize them for their poverty. By living on her own traditional economy, she eludes a system that exacts a high price from others around her.

Moreover, Roberta recognizes the cost exacted by working at the mill. Early in the novel when Beal is only thirteen, he mentions to Roberta that his Auntie Hoover is "back at the mill." When Roberta asks, "Third shift," Beal responds in the affirmative. Roberta then remarks, "Bet she hates it goin' back . . . I ain't never goin' back" (28). We then learn the reason she won't return to doing millwork: "you can't have no feelin's in that ol' hole . . . They treat you like you was a machine that runs on gas" (28). In her inimitable way, Roberta sees the system of exploited labor for what it is and through her own skills is able to defy it. Six years later when she reappears in the novel, we see that she continues to eke out a living through use of the local economy.

Unlike Goodspeed, she is able to live with her family and stay in her community. However, those people who remain behind in their community, like Roberta Bean, and who are unwilling to follow capital's siren call are blamed for their poverty. As the critic Tracy Campbell comments, "stereotypes [of the poor] serve to deflect critical inquiries into structural economic forces by focusing, instead, on perceived weaknesses with the [people] themselves" (168). But Chute argues against such a classification of poor people. Instead, her novel articulates how the process of urbanization informs and defines cross-class encounters in multiple ways. For Beal, his inability to earn a living logging, caused in part by globalization, has meant his demise. For Roberta, her refusal to participate in an unjust economy that sees poor people like Beal as expendable has proved to be the key to her survival.

Using the lens of cultural geography to interrogate Chute's novel demonstrates how the practices of everyday life inform the identities and social relations of the fictional inhabitants of Egypt, Maine. Through the everyday practice of looking, we learn in what manner characters from different social classes position and define themselves in relation to each other and the role that landscape plays in informing their subjectivity. Moreover, analyzing the body through the lived experiences of individual characters illustrates the way social, economic, and political factors help to determine identity formation. In rethinking issues of class, Chute's novel argues the necessity of considering the vital connection of cultural and economic landscapes to the formation of social class.

NOTES

1. An exception to Ward's statement is Renny Christopher's article written in 1995. Christopher's essay, however, mainly addresses the different ways in which her university students "read" Chute's characters in part dependent upon their class background.

    Some recent works have examined how a focus on identity politics has replaced discussions of class. See Martha E. Gimenez's "Back to Class: Reflections on the Dialectics of Class and Identity" in *More Unequal: Aspects of Class in the United States* edited by Michael D. Yates (NY: Monthly Review Press, 2007); and Walter Benn Michael's *The Trouble with Diversity: How We Learned to Love Identity and Ignore Inequality* (NY: Henry Holt, 2006).
2. See Vivyan C. Adair's "Branded with Infamy: Inscriptions of Poverty and Class in the United States" in *Signs: Journal of Women in Culture and Society* (2001) for a discussion, which focuses on poor urban women and the ways in which their bodies and those of their children are marked by class.

BIBLIOGRAPHY

Adair, Vivyan C. "Branded with Infamy: Inscriptions of Poverty and Class in the United States. *Signs: Journal of Women in Culture and Society* 27.2 (Winter, 2002): 451–471. JSTOR. Web. 17 March 2010.

Adams, Katherine. "Chute Dialogics: A Sidelong Glance from Egypt, Maine." *National Women's Studies Association Journal* 17.1 (Spring 2005): 1–22. Web. 10 July 2007.

Atkinson, David, Peter Jackson, David Sibley, and Neil Washbourne. "Editors' Preface: On Cultural and Critical Geographies." *Cultural Geography: A Critical*

Dictionary of Key Concepts. Ed. David Atkinson, Peter Jackson, David Sibley, and Neil Washbourne. London: I.B. Taurus, 2005. vii-xviii. Print.

Bordo, Susan. *Unbearable Weight: Feminism, Western Culture, and the Body*. Berkeley: U of California P, 2003. Print.

Campbell, Tracy. *The Politics of Despair: Power and Resistance in the Tobacco Wars*. Lexington: UP of Kentucky, 1993. Print.

Christopher, Renny. "Cultural Borders: Working-Class Literature's Challenge to the Canon." *The Canon in the Classroom: The Pedagogical Implications of Canon Revision in American Literature*. Ed. John Alberti. NY: Garland, 1995. 45-55. Print.

Chute, Carolyn. *The Beans of Egypt, Maine*. 1985. San Diego: Harcourt Brace, 1995. Print.

Comer, Krista. *Landscapes of the New West: Gender and Geography in Contemporary Women's Writing*. Chapel Hill: U of North Carolina P, 1999. Print.

Gimenez, Martha E. "Back to Class: Reflections on the Dialectics of Class and Identity." *More Unequal: Aspects of Class in the United States*. Ed. Michael D. Yates. New York: Monthly Review Press, 2007. 107-117. Print.

Grosz, Elizabeth. *Volatile Bodies: Toward A Corporeal Feminism*. Bloomington: Indiana UP, 1994. Print.

Harvey, David. *Justice, Nature and the Geography of Difference*. Malden: Blackwell, 1996. Print.

Michael, Walter Benn. *The Trouble with Diversity: How We Learned to Love Identity and Ignore Inequality*. New York: Henry Holt, 2006. Print.

Mitchell, Don. "Cultural Landscapes: Just Landscapes or Landscapes of Justice?" *Progress in Human Geography* 27.6 (2003): 787-96. Web. 2 June 2010.

———. "Landscape." In Atkinson et al. 49-56. Print.

Moss, Pamela, and Isabel Dyck. "Embodying Social Geography." *Handbook of Cultural Geography*. Ed. Kay Anderson, Mona Domosh, Steve Pile, and Nigel Thrift. London: Sage, 2003. 58-73. Print.

Newstead, Clare, Carolina K. Reid, and Matthew Sparke. "The Cultural Geography of Scale." *Handbook of Cultural Geography*. Ed. Kay Anderson, Mona Domosh, Steve Pile and Nigel Thrift. London: Sage, 2003. 485-97. Print.

Newitz, Annalee, and Matthew Wray. "What is 'White Trash'? Stereotypes and Economic Conditions of Poor Whites in the U.S." *Minnesota Review* 47 (1997): 57-72. Print.

Roberts, Ian. "Working-Class Studies: Ongoing and New Directions." *Sociology Compass* 1.1 (2007): 191-207. Print.

Russo, John, and Sherry Lee Linkon. "What's New about New Working-Class Studies?" *New Working-Class Studies*. Ed. John Russo and Sherry Lee Linkon. Ithaca: Cornell UP, 2005. 1-15. Print.

Stenning, Alison. "For Working Class Geographies." *Antipode* 40.1 (Jan 2008): 9-14. Web. 5 June 2010.

Tapley, Heather. "Conflating Class and Gender: The Dystopic Vision of Carolyn Chute's Fiction." *River Review/La Revue Riviere: A Multidisciplinary Journal of Arts and Ideas* 2 (1996): 9-16. Print.

Till, Karen. "Political Landscapes." *A Companion to Cultural Geography*. Ed. James S. Duncan, Nuala C. Johnson, and Richard H. Schein. Malden: Blackwell, 2004. 347-64. Print.

Ward, Cynthia. "From the Suwanee to Egypt, There's No Place Like Home." *PMLA* 115.1 (Jan. 2000): 75-88. Print.

Zandy, Janet. *Hands: Physical Labor, Class, and Cultural Work*. New Brunswick: Rutgers UP, 2004. Print.

Part IV

Reconsidering Class, Gender, and Nation

Mike Gold's pivotal article "Go Left, Young Writers" has been seen as emblematic of the equation of working-class jobs with masculinity and with the American spirit of expansionism. Class is experienced in relation to national identity as well as other identities. The United States' frontier experience and the manual labor that immigrants performed strengthened the equation between working-class status and masculinity. A new generation of scholars is bringing masculinity studies to working-class studies and making connections between class, gender, and nation, while young feminists build upon the considerable work that has been done on the intersection of female gender and working-class status.

Matthew Brophy examines Jack London's *The Sea-Wolf*, focusing on its classed gender identity, expressed in racialized terms in the "primitive masculinity" of Wolf Larsen. London's novel, Brophy argues, speaks not only to broad cultural anxieties about American masculinity and empire, but also to what Paul Lauter has identified as a persistent anxiety experienced by working-class male writers as to whether writing is a legitimate calling for an American man. Brophy argues that in responding to a national tradition of heroic masculinity rooted in the frontier experience, London constructs an imperialist vision—that of rejuvenating American manhood by reintroducing it to the labor of American empire—which rests on the embodied knowledge of working-class men.

Drama has received little attention among working-class scholars, and Brandt's chapter takes an important step in correcting this omission. Her work interrogates Depression-era drama—specifically Clifford Odets' *Waiting for Lefty* and the Bertolt Brecht-inspired living newspaper plays—as representations of the gender disruptions people experienced as men lost their jobs and women were forced to take more responsibility for supporting their families.

Tim Libretti raises questions about the relationship of national identity and class consciousness in his critique of Henry Roth's reconceptualization of class consciousness from *Call It Sleep* through the *Mercy of a Rude Stream* novels. Libretti argues that Roth's later work confronts national and political difference in new ways, reflecting his embrace of a nationalist Israeli identity after the Six-Day War in 1967. This move was striking in an era in which both literary and cultural studies, informed by Marxist and postcolonial perspectives, viewed the category of nation with suspicion. Roth's evolving political beliefs are reflected in his changing literary techniques, particularly his disavowal of modernism. Ultimately, Libretti notes, Roth embraces nationhood because he believes that the individual must affiliate with an institution; although Roth's allegiance to nation is unusual for a working-class writer, his focus on group rather on individual identity is not. At a time when nationalism is gaining prominence in many parts of the world, Libretti's work suggests how relatively disempowered people may gain a sense of power by affiliating with a nation offers and new insights into the politics of class identification.

Ultimately, the articles in this section illuminate how gender and nationality continually inflect class identification and are inflected by it.

10 A Body of Work
Imperial Labor and the Writing of American Manhood in London's *The Sea-Wolf*

Matthew Brophy

In *Culture and Imperialism*, Edward Said writes that "cultural forms like the novel ... were immensely important in the formation of imperial attitudes, references, and experiences" (xii). Not only does the novel play a role in structuring the subjectivities of those in imperial nations, but the practice of empire reciprocally structures the generic form of the novel: "Without empire, I would go so far as saying, there is no European novel as we know it" (Said 69). The nineteenth-century American novel functioned similarly, but with a slightly different valence. While engendering the "'structures of feeling' that support, elaborate, and consolidate the practice of empire," they also tended to figure empire not as "imperialism," but rather as national expansion and, in fact, the fulfillment of a national destiny (Said 14). Said notes that in American writing there is a "ferocious anti-colonialism, directed at the Old World," which paradoxically "shows a peculiarly acute imperial cast" (63). This paradox became all the more potent—in its potential to unravel a foundational national ethic—when, at the turn-of-the-century, the United States pursued relationships with Puerto Rico, the Philippines, and Hawaii that were quasi-colonial and indisputably imperial. A cultural crisis presented itself: were the structures of attitude and reference toward "the West" and the "frontier" transferable and adaptable overseas, such as in the Pacific? How would national narratives about race, gender, class, and citizenship change as a result of—and as legitimating discourses for—this new imperialism?

In examining how these questions play out in Jack London's 1904 novel *The Sea-Wolf*, issues of class and gender are foregrounded, though racial discourse is also at work. The novel seeks to revitalize a bourgeois cultural form, in the service of empire, by means of an appropriation of proletarian energy.[1] The source of this energy is located in the "primitive masculinity" of Wolf Larsen, an identity that is both classed and gendered, with racialized overtones. By staging this narrative of revitalization, London's novel speaks not only to broad cultural anxieties about American masculinity and empire, but also to what Paul Lauter has identified as a persistent anxiety experienced by working-class writers around the following question:

"is writing a legitimate calling for an American man?" (74). London's novel answers this question by suggesting that writing is work if and only if it emanates from the lived experience of embodied labor. Responding to a national tradition of heroic masculinity situated on the frontier, London constructs an imperialist vision—that of rejuvenating American manhood and the American novel by reintroducing them to the labor of American empire—that rests on the embodied knowledge of working-class men.[2] However, the "primitive" source of working-class masculinity (Wolf Larsen) is ultimately disavowed, whereas the bourgeois protagonist (Humphrey van Leyden) is able to assume the work of writing a national narrative after his successful lessons in manly labor. London's turn, then, to working-class lived experience is momentarily disruptive, eventually conservative, and ultimately riddled with contradiction.[3]

This chapter will frame a discussion of the way class, gender, and empire inflect the generic conventions that structure the body of London's text, and also the bodies represented by that text. I will look at the way London constructs the working-class male body as both a source of knowledge and a vulnerable biological object.[4] Finally, I will examine the contradictions embedded within London's representation of power and authority, which suggest the paradoxes of an emergent culture of U.S. global power that simultaneously valorized and marginalized the experiences of working-class men on the frontiers of empire.

GENDER AND GENRE

Lisa Lowe, in *Immigrant Acts*, writes that the "link between historical narratives of the U.S. nation and novelistic narratives of the individual is mediated by adherence to a realist aesthetic, a fetishized concept of development, and the narration of a single unified subject" (107). Despite the fact that London's realism is severely strained (by which I mean that the plot of his novel is largely implausible), *The Sea-Wolf* exhibits all three of the central features to which Lowe points our attention. In particular, London fetishizes the "development" of his protagonist, Humphrey van Leyden (Hump)—especially the development of his body and his embodied knowledge and affect—and in doing so imbues his novel with the narrative trajectory of a bildungsroman. For Lowe, the form of the bildungsroman "structurally impl[ies] an integration and submission of particularity to a universalized social norm," and for Hump, these social norms seem to focus on the value of work, violence, and heterosexuality in a larger national and imperial rhetoric (45). Because Hump is himself a writer, the stakes seem to be centered on the development of he who will write the nation; put another way, the novel's concern is that the man who represents the nation is himself a representative man. Christopher Gair writes, "*The Sea-Wolf* . . . is . . . centrally concerned with redefining (or justifying) the status of the author within a society deeply suspicious about the value of the aesthetic" (2). This suspicion is largely gendered, and hence we see London's desire to "masculinize the literary" (Gair 2). Building on Gair's observations, I want to add that London's *own* suspicion of "the aesthetic" was, more specifically, a suspicion of a *bourgeois* aesthetic. Consequentially, his effort to "masculinize the literary" was simultaneously an effort to "proletarianize" it—to reconfigure the bildungsroman as a passage not from (bourgeois) boyhood to (bourgeois) manhood, but from bourgeois effeminacy to laboring manhood.

London does not, however, desire this classed masculinization of the novel to be totalizing—he is not, after all, writing *only* for working-class men. By tempering the more "masculine" narrative strain of adventure and violence with the more "feminine" strain of sentimental romance, London's novel achieves a kind of generic androgyny. London also sets out to achieve a readership hybridized along class lines, by designing a novel that exists at the threshold of popular, "low-brow" fiction and serious, "high-brow" literature. Susan Ward points out how London tried "to include more popular fiction elements in the novel," and London himself wrote in a letter, "[t]he superficial reader will get the love story and the adventure; while the deeper reader will get all this, plus the bigger picture" (qtd. in Ward 322–23). Despite the contradictions that emerge from this gesture, London nonetheless tried to democratize the form of the novel across class and gender lines by writing for both masculine and feminine, formally and informally educated readers.[5]

To trace the generic influences of the novel more specifically, I would like to turn to the evolution of the dime novel from 1860 to 1900.[6] The dime novel tradition, as Bill Brown argues, played a significant part in enabling the project of Manifest Destiny: "The dime Western was the medium most responsible for disseminating that image of violence; it was the means of carrying a sensational, violent West with you while you rode on an elevated train in Manhattan" (5). Much as the European novel, as Said argues, structured colonialism as a noble, "civilizing mission," so did the dime novel structure U.S. expansion as a point of national identity and pride. The violence of the project, however, was not repressed as in the European novel, but *aestheticized*, and thus celebrated. It is this aestheticization of violence—and the white, working-class male body that enacts such violence—especially as displayed by the brutal and hypermasculine Wolf Larsen, that London appropriates from the dime novel tradition. In *The Sea-Wolf*, the frontier is transfigured as the seal-hunting *Ghost*, an extralegal, amoral, "primitive" space. Violence rules the day, and order is provided by the sovereign, but amoral, rule of Wolf Larsen. Although heroes of dime novels tended to provide a moral center in an amoral world, this sense of stability was often fleeting or contradictory. The novels were often publicly ridiculed for "contaminating the morals of the working class" due to their excessive violence (Brown 3). Brown notes that the *Atlantic Monthly*, in particular, assumed the role of "cultural authority" in denouncing the immorality of dime novels. Some recurrent dime-novel characters such as Kit Carson often seemed to "cross over" from "defender of civilization" to "perpetrator of savagery," unsettling any easy sense of moral order. Hampton Sides describes the cover art of one particular dime novel as follows: "It showed an image of Carson with his arms draped around the slender waist of a beautiful buxom girl, surrounded by the corpses of countless freshly killed savages from whose clutches he had just rescued her" (392). One can see here that Carson's presence denotes sexuality as much as violence, and in fact his body, like Larsen's, is represented as an erotic spectacle: "Carson's slight stature has [in its fictional representation] swelled to superhuman proportions—he has a 'mighty frame,' 'massive arms,' 'prodigious strength,' and a chest built like 'a fortress'" (Sides 251). Considering that Carson's "superhuman" image appeared in over seventy books in the late nineteenth century, it seems likely that Wolf Larsen echoes Kit Carson in more ways than one.

Whereas Carson, according to Sides, became a "single heroic character who could personify the surge of Manifest Destiny," the broader aesthetic of the dime novel served other ideological functions as well (252). Early dime-novel publishers marketed their products as "National and American Romances," representative of the "Purely American Novel," thus differentiating the form from "the republication of European fiction," and coding the industry as "a patriotic project, responding to the ongoing calls for a national literature" (Brown 21). The nationalist valence of the dime novel was complemented by a masculinist one. Brown notes that "the dime-novel increasingly became an enterprise of men writing for men about men" (32). These nationalist and gendered ideological strains seem to converge around the mythology of the frontier. The myth sustains a sense of gendered national identity in which men identify as American through the fantasy of participation in the act of nation building, a fantasy that is always-already nostalgic. Michael Kimmel writes that for London, "the frontier could simply be transported elsewhere," but it retains its sense of nostalgia, impermanence, and anachronism (152).[7] The fantasy of self-made, authentic manhood, proved on the frontier seems to be continually vanishing as it is compulsively rearticulated and reimagined.

London seems ready and willing to extract the spectacles of sexuality and violence from the dime novel, as well as its emphasis on masculine, national identity and its predominantly nostalgic mood. The dime-novel hero is a "heroic, self-reliant individual—unimpeded by urbanization, industrialization, and mechanization . . . [who] favors anti-intellectual intuition, interrupts a class-coded system of taste in the name of authenticity, and hence protects America from what Theodore Roosevelt called the dangerous ease of 'over-civilized man'" (Brown 30). London injects that dime-novel "authenticity" into the embodied, working-class subjectivity of Wolf Larsen; yet he also seems to deny Larsen that elevated, heroic status which such a character likely would have possessed in an actual dime novel. Wolf is at most a *tragic* hero, but he is perhaps best understood as a *sacred* hero, using Agamben's definition of "sacred" as that which "cannot be sacrificed and yet may be killed" (82). Despite his crucial role as a masculine model of embodied labor, thought, and desire, Wolf's body becomes "bare life" by the novel's end—one whose termination occurs beyond the domain of the Law. I will return to this question—London's ambivalent disavowal of Wolf Larsen—at the end of this chapter, but for now, it is sufficient to say that Larsen, instead of protecting America from the "overcivilized man," ends up protecting the "overcivilized man" from himself and, by playing the part of the *sacred* man, enables the "overcivilized man" to become the *hegemonic* man.

PHYSICAL EDUCATION

Whereas critics such as Christopher Gair and Madonne Miner have analyzed the dynamics of gender and sexuality in *The Sea-Wolf*, including Hump's "education" in masculinity, there has yet to be an analysis that historically situates Hump's "crisis" of masculinity within the contemporaneous public anxiety surrounding ideals of manliness at the turn of the century and the reverberations this anxiety had for popular attitudes about class, race, and national identity. Turning to Gail Bederman's impressive historical study *Manliness and Civilization*, we can begin to chart out the discursive field within which London was working in the first years of the twentieth century. Bederman cites as the primary economic cause of this perceived "crisis" in masculinity the shift in the form of American capitalism away from small businesses and individual entrepreneurship to increasingly corporate structures. She notes that "[b]etween 1870 and 1910, the proportion of middle-class men who were self-employed dropped from 67 to 37 percent" (12). Not only were middle-class men less likely to be self-employed, but in seeking jobs they found themselves competing more often with "New Women," immigrants, and socially mobile working-class men (14). Michael Kimmel has shown how the discourse of social Darwinism responded to these fears of increased competition among men for good jobs, and how many white men—working class and middle class alike—became more zealous in expressing racist, antifeminist, and nativist ideas in order to make claims for the supremacy of white Anglo males (90–93). White men who appeared "unmasculine" suddenly became *scandals*, upsetting the social Darwinist framework: how could men of the most highly evolved race be weak, effeminate, or degenerate? This anxiety prompted the invention of the term "overcivilized" (Rotundo 251). The term implied that white men, having achieved *too much* wealth and comfort by means of their evolved dominance, ran the risk of not needing to struggle for existence, and thus lapsing into a weakened, feminized state. Several proposed solutions to this problem arose, ranging from interventions in the physical education of young boys to increased emphasis on competitive athletics for men, but the most relevant to our study here was the increasingly accepted view that imperial warfare was *healthy* for the development of American manhood. Theodore Roosevelt in particular espoused the turn to empire in order to ensure the sustained vigor of American men (Rotundo 235).

Although *The Sea-Wolf* is not explicitly a novel about imperial conquest, it is indeed a novel set in a space—the Pacific Rim—opened up to American commercial conquest by contemporaneous imperial developments in Hawaii, the Philippines, and Guam. It is also a novel that imagines and values a particular masculine development that is formed as a result of violent struggle in such a space. The novel's protagonist, Hump—an iconic "overcivilized" man—is able to overcome his subordinated masculinity through a homosocial rivalry with a "primitive," working-class man. The key for Hump's development is the attainment of bodily strength on par with a white working-class man and the embodied knowledge associated with it, while at the same time retaining his commitment to civilized morality. Although this bildungsroman values the lived experience and epistemology of physical labor, it is unable to envision a collectivist, working-class *ethos*. The reason for this, I will argue, lies in the fetishization of the white, laboring-male body as a symbol of national (and imperial) power, and a reliance on bourgeois gender ideology.

Hump's initial overcivilized status is marked by symptoms of the physiological "disease" neurasthenia, which was commonly diagnosed at the turn of the century (Bederman 84–88). These symptoms, such as overall bodily weakness and impotence, are the corporeal obstacles—presumably caused by his privileged life as a gentleman—that Hump must overcome on the *Ghost* through homosocial rivalry with working-class male bodies. To understand the stakes of this struggle, one must consider the social significance of neurasthenia as it was constructed at this time: "Neurasthenia ... expressed the *cultural* weakness of civilized, manly self-restraint in *medical terms*. ... In short, neurasthenia posed a paradox. Only white male bodies had the capacity to be truly civilized. Yet, at the same time, civilization destroyed white male bodies" (Bederman 88). For white men to function as agents of civilized progress, their bodies must overcome the specter of overcivilized decadence. London presents the working-class male body as the key to this solution: white enough to be civilized, but industrious enough to be immune from a "leisure-class" disease.

Hump's bildungsroman charts his development from an overcivilized, potentially neurasthenic man to the embodiment of hegemonic masculinity via his engagement with a "primitive" working-class masculinity. Two questions arise, before we follow this trajectory: why is working-class masculinity figured as "primitive"? And why does primitive masculinity appear as an antidote to neurasthenia? To answer the first question, I would like to quote Anne McClintock, who has noted the discursive overlap at the turn of the century in articulations of racialized, gendered, and classed *primitivism*: "colonized people—like women and the working class in the metropolis—do not inhabit history proper but exist in a permanently anterior time within the geographic space of the modern empire as anachronistic humans, atavistic, irrational, bereft of human agency—the living embodiment of the archaic 'primitive'" (30). Although it is not likely that London saw working-class *white* men as "irrational" or "bereft of human agency," his thinking does seem to be at least partially structured by this colonial epistemology. The *white* primitivism of Larsen is linked to, though distinct from, the *savage* primitivism that London would construct for a racialized character such as Oofty-Oofty. Although it was common for white middle-class writers of empire at this time to use the language of primitivism to express *class* difference, *class* confrontation, and *class* anxiety in racialized terms, London instead insists on the whiteness of working-class primitivism, locating it in the idealized essence of an "ennobling heroic Anglo-Saxon Warrior" that is imagined to be contained within white male bodies and released once those bodies are engaged in physical struggle (Kaplan, "Nation" 264).

To answer the second question, let us turn to Bederman's analysis of the work of psychologist G. Stanley Hall, a contemporary of London's. Bederman writes that Hall "believed it was his responsibility to make sure American boys received a virile education that avoided overcivilized effeminacy" (77). The way to do this was "to turn America's sons into savages," by which he meant that "boys should be seen as racially primitive" and indulged in their natural instincts toward aggression (78). Hall's ideas were based on quasi-Darwinian theory that emphasized the need for "primitive struggle" to ensure the fitness of both a species and an individual. His solution to neurasthenia, known as "recapitulation theory," suggested that a boy needed to relive the evolutionary history of his race (from savage boyhood to civilized manhood) in order to achieve optimal health. To "skip" the savagery of boyhood brought on the danger of an overcivilized, effeminate adulthood (Bederman 92–94).

Hall's "recapitulation theory" is in a sense its own bildungsroman, and mapping it onto Hump's development is fairly straightforward. Raised a gentleman, Hump was "robbed" of his savage boyhood and thus developed as a neurasthenic man. Although he cannot return to his childhood to relive it, he can in adulthood seek out savagery, struggle with it, and master it. Working-class men presumably had rougher, wilder boyhoods, and thus developed into more vigorous men with lessened chances of neurasthenia. Working-class men who worked in imperial spaces—apart from domestic, civilized life—potentially retained all the savagery of boyhood into adulthood. This savagery is represented by Wolf Larsen himself, whose strength is described as that which "we are wont to associate with things primitive, with wild animals, and the creatures we imagine our tree-dwelling prototypes to have been" (London 16).[8] Hump's "tutelage" under Wolf—his study in a working-class "primitivism"—enables his ultimate assertion of dominance. The sign of this achievement is Hump's acquisition of a new body—one capable both of "manly" *work* and *violence*. As William Dow has argued, the body was of primary importance to London in his conception of social power, organization, and knowledge: "In order to construct social order . . . the cure begins with the body" (94). Dow insists that, for London, "the body becomes a way to index class, gender, and race in order to create hierarchies of power that support the economic, cultural, and moral state of a nation" (91). Hence, London imagines the transcendence of class difference through the homosocial rivalry of male bodies: as Hump is able to remake his body in Wolf's image, he acquires the embodied knowledge of the imperial worker, making him, in London's view, manlier, more American, and less bourgeois. The body is not *everything* for London—as we shall see, it is not enough to save Wolf himself—but a revolution of the body is a precondition for social and cultural change. A nation of bodies strengthened by work and violent struggle, London implies, is a nation that can be self-sufficient, egalitarian, and sovereign.[9]

After Hump is rescued, Wolf interrogates him, asking him what he does for a living. Hump replies that he is "a gentleman," receives a "swift sneer" in reply, and insists (unconvincingly) that he, too, is a man of labor: "I have worked, I do work." Wolf, unimpressed, asks an emasculating question: "Who feeds you?" (London 22). The message here is clear: a man who does not earn his own livelihood through his labor is not a man, but a creature both feminized and infantilized. Wolf refuses to put Hump on a vessel returning to San Francisco, insisting that he work as a member of the crew. Wolf claims he is doing this not to exploit Hump's labor, but for Hump's *own good*. Wolf says, "It will be the making of you. You might learn in time to stand on your own legs and perhaps to toddle along a bit" (23). This challenge to Hump—to develop new legs—initiates the narrative of bodily transformation routed through imperial labor, all with the implicit goal of achieving an independent, sovereign, and *national* manhood.

At the onset, Hump's body is painfully unprepared for the work that awaits him. He admits that he "had never done any hard manual labor" in his entire life (37). The lack of this, which is not compensated for with exercise, results in a feminized and subordinated body:

> I was not strong. The doctors had always said that I had a remarkable constitution, but I had never developed it or my body through exercise. My muscles were small and soft like a woman's, or so the doctors had said time and again in the course of their attempts to persuade me to go in for physical-culture fads. But I had preferred to use my head, rather than my body. . . (37–38)

Hump's sedentary life of the mind has produced a transgendered effect on his body. Despite the advice of his doctors, Hump will only "exercise" his intellect. Yet this privileging of the mind's development over the body's is one that London rejects. The disembodied intellect which Hump has cultivated has imperiled him in a fog of abstractions: he is alienated from the materiality of his physical being, from homosocial rivalry, and from heterosexual desire.[10] This is seen as a real waste, as Hump was endowed with a "remarkable constitution" by nature—most likely, in keeping with London's racial ideology, from his northern European heritage.

On the opposite extreme of Hump, with his all-mind/no-body development, are the crew's seal hunters, who seem to have developed their bodies quite fully but their minds not at all. Although presumably they are all white men, except for the overtly racialized Oofty-Oofty, they are all likened to "savages," with childlike minds and manly bodies (36–37). Wolf appears as the only *exceptional* man, who has developed both his mind and his body. His physical strength, previously noted, is combined with his extensive personal library, which includes works by Shakespeare, Tennyson, Poe, and Darwin (43). Wolf's worldview seems shaped as much by his extensive reading as by his experience laboring in imperial spaces. His is a philosophy marked by an amoral materialism, an often contradictory blend of Marxian, Darwinian, and Nietzschean ideas.[11] Hump realizes that Wolf is not only a physical rival but also an intellectual one and that he must compete with him on two fronts. While Hump remains deficient in his body, however, he can never win an intellectual argument. The body remains the *basis* of homosocial power, and without it, intellectual skills are irrelevant. This is best demonstrated in the scene where Wolf and Hump are debating the relative importance of a man's instinct for life versus his instinct for immortality. Wolf, the materialist, demonstrates the predominance of the instinct for life by *strangling* Hump, as he simultaneously lectures him until he loses consciousness. Coming to, Hump concedes the point, saying, "Your arguments are too—er—forcible" (99). Without a body that can defend its right to speak, Hump will never be able to combat the materialism of Wolf's thinking.

To be fair, though, the force of materialist thinking—and not just the material force of Wolf's body—also has its effect on Hump. Wolf is not *simply* a bully, forcing his thinking upon Hump; his ideas have their own rhetorical force and challenge some of Hump's basic assumptions. Hump notes how disarmed he is by Wolf's thinking, how he "lacked expression" when engaged with Wolf in debate (61). Wolf's materialism is not an academic materialism, which Hump may have been better prepared to resist, but a materialism based on the lived experience of violence and labor. Not only is he able to make reference to his life at sea—clubbing seals whose skins were to be sold to bourgeois women—to support his viewpoint, but he also cites the "poor people in the slums of cities" who cannot find work and are plagued by "famine and pestilence" (62). The experiences of such people have likely never been seriously considered by Hump, who has never had to work in order to feed himself. Although Hump will never share the cynical conclusion that Wolf extracts from this material evidence—that the sacredness of life is a myth—Wolf has nevertheless opened Hump's eyes to the importance, or even the primacy, of materiality and the embodied lives of the working class. He is aware, from this point forward, that philosophical truths cannot be determined solely through idealized conjecture or abstract deduction, but must be grounded in reference to the physicality of social life.

Hence, Hump receives both an education of the body, through an introduction to manual labor, and an education of the mind, through an introduction to a materialist and socialist viewpoint rooted in lived experience. Both educational processes prove to be initially discomforting, but ultimately rejuvenating. Hump describes his grappling with Wolf's amoral materialism as a pioneer experience: "I was exploring virgin territory. A strange, a terribly strange, region was unrolling itself before my eyes" (73). Although Wolf's mode of thinking and seeing the world at first stuns Hump, leaving him overwhelmed and speechless, he is able to eventually understand, incorporate, and critique Wolf's positions with confidence and authority. Hump acknowledges a certain epistemological debt to Wolf for this education: "He had opened up for me the world of the real, of which I had known practically nothing and from which I had always shrunk" (141). Yet, he will not go so far as to take the Nietzschean step and reject what Wolf calls "conventional morality" (274). Instead, he takes what he has learned from Wolf, but differentiates himself from Wolf's thinking on the point of morality. Hump states this nicely when he says to Wolf, "I may have learned to stand on my own legs. . . . But I have yet to stamp upon others with them" (173). That he states this moral distinction in terms of the body—the development of his legs—reinforces the interconnectedness of intellectual and bodily development in the novel. (This is not to say that the body and the mind always develop in tandem, but rather that such a balanced development is idealized.) Hump would never have been able to presume, in any effective way, a position of moral authority over Wolf were it not for his education of the body—his development, through working with the crew as a mate, of his own legs and the "secret pride" that went along with this development (133). Hump becomes aware of a "toughening or hardening" of himself, which seems to apply both to his character and to his body. He will no longer be referred to as "Sissy" van Weyden. Even Wolf, who continues to address Hump as a subordinate, nevertheless admires the progress of Hump's body since coming aboard: "True, he is not what you would term muscular, but still he has muscles, which is more than he had when he came aboard. Also, he has legs to stand on" (173). Hump may still not be "muscular" compared to Wolf, but he has muscles enough to carry an embodied sense of confidence and autonomy.

AFFECTIVE EDUCATION

In addition to the development of Hump's body and the embodied knowledge of "the real" that he gains through engaging his muscles in physical labor and his mind in philosophical debate with Wolf's materialism, Hump must also develop (i.e., masculinize) his affect. This involves cultivating a heterosexual desire that has its basis not in relations *between* the sexes, but, once again, in homosocial male relations. Male heterosexuality is represented more as the development of a certain kind of masculine embodiment and less as the pursuit of sexualized female bodies. It is a profoundly *homosocial* heterosexuality that we encounter here. Although it is from Wolf that Hump learns this complex mode of desire, which serves as the basis of his masculine affect, Hump must also develop feelings that go beyond the "primitive" heterosexual impulse for rivalry and conquest. Just as Hump's social idealism allows him to transcend the amorality of Wolf's materialism, his sense of *chivalry* allows him to transcend Wolf's rapacious sexuality. Both of these "triumphs," however, are only made possible by their initial appropriations of what is imagined to be "primitively" masculine. An idealism with no basis in materiality is meaningless for London, just as chivalry without heterosexual desire would be either impotent or perverted.

This threat of "perversion" in *The Sea-Wolf* is coded in Hump's possible homosexual relations with Charley Furuseth, vaguely hinted at in the beginning of the novel. To put this "threat" in historical context, consider that "[a]fter the 1880s, medical experts ceased to see homosexuality as a punishable act, and began to see it as an aberrant and deficient male identity, a case of the male body gone wrong through disease or congenital deformity" (Bederman 15). Thus, historically, the fact that London imagines a "cure" for homosexuality through the homosocial desire for a more "healthy" male body makes sense, though it may seem ironic to modern readers. We can see Hump's homosocial desire directed at Wolf clearly in the text, especially in his description of Wolf's eyes, from which I will quote at length:

> The eyes—and it was my destiny to know them well—were large and handsome, wide apart as the true artist's are wide, sheltering under a heavy brow and arched over by thick black eyebrows. The eyes themselves were of that baffling protean gray which is never twice the same; which runs through many shades and colorings like intershot silk in sunshine; which is gray, dark and light, and greenish gray, and sometimes of the clear azure of the deep sea. They were eyes that masked the soul with a thousand guises, and that sometimes opened, at rare moments, and allowed it to rush up as though it were about to fare forth nakedly into the world on some wonderful adventure,—eyes that could brook with the hopeless sombreness of leaden skies; that could snap and crackle points of fire like those which sparkle from a whirling sword; that could grow chill as an arctic landscape, and yet again, that could warm and soften and be all a-dance with love-lights, intense and masculine, luring and compelling, which at the same time fascinate and dominate women till they surrender in a gladness of joy and of relief and sacrifice. (21)

In some aspects this passage evokes Cooper's description of Uncas in *The Last of the Mohicans,* and for good reason: Wolf Larsen functions as a kind of "exotic other" for Hump. The end of the passage heightens the sense of "taboo" underlying this desire by attempting to resituate Hump's longing in heterosexual terms (Wolf's eyes "fascinate and dominate women"). Yet, of course, it is *Hump* who is fascinated by these eyes, and this transference to hypothetical women fails to mask his own desire—a desire to be, perhaps masochistically, dominated by (the sadistic) Wolf, to have his ineffectual bourgeois body broken, blown, and burned into a body of *work.* London suggests that the "first step" of homosexual reformation is a self-abnegating, homoerotic desire for a markedly heterosexual man.

Hump must ultimately convert Wolf from a love object to a model of working-class, heterosexual masculinity. Scott Derrick characterizes this trajectory as a "will to heterosexuality" within the text (and within several of London's works), which "produces a remaindered homoeroticism visible only as a text repressed" (127). London attempts to represent this heterosexuality as "natural" rather than compulsory by constructing "nature" as a force in the narrative that pushes characters toward traditional, patriarchal sex/gender roles. Christopher Gair makes this argument, pointing out how key "accidents" in the novel are necessary for Hump to arrive at his ultimate heterosexual coupling with Maud. These "accidents," Gair suggests, are better understood as acts of nature—such as the fog that prevents Hump's visit to his intimate male friend Charley Furuseth and the improbable appearance of Maud Brewster in the middle of the ocean. This is a nature that is "an active agent within a patriarchy striving to impose old ideals . . . on the male as well as the female world" (8). In other words, the metaphysical force Derrick refers to as the "will to heterosexuality" appears in the text as a *physical* (as well as natural and inevitable) force, attempting to effect the naturalization of compulsory heterosexuality, while at the same time leaving traces and slippages of repressed homoerotic desire.

One can see this strained attempt to convert Hump's homoeroticism into a homosocial heterosexuality in two key paragraphs that appear later in the novel. Whereas the gaze into the eyes may have suggested a desire for intimacy with Wolf's soul (or his embodied knowledge), the following passage reflects more a desire for intimacy with Wolf's body and coincides with the development of Hump's own body into a "body with muscles":

> But Wolf Larsen was the man-type, the masculine, and almost a god in his perfectness. As he moved about or raised his arms the great muscles leapt and moved under the satiny skin. I had forgotten to say that the bronze ended with his face. His body, thanks to his Scandinavian stock, was fair as the fairest woman's. I remember his putting his hand up to feel of the wound on his head, and my watching the biceps move like a living thing under its white sheath. It was the biceps that had

nearly crushed out my life once, that I had seen strike so many killing blows. I could not take my eyes from him. . . .
He noticed me, and I became conscious that I was staring at him.
"God made you well," I said. (129)

Although Hump clearly still sees Wolf as an aesthetic object and an object of desire in this passage, two key maneuvers attempt to shift the homoeroticism toward a homosocial, yet heterosexual, male gaze upon a male body. First, there is the momentary feminization of Wolf, as Hump notes that his body "was fair as the fairest woman's." The attempt is to feminize what is aesthetic about Wolf while (and this is the second key maneuver) appreciating the power of the body in its capacity for violent, and thus masculine, action. The latter attempt seeks to convert male homoeroticism into a homosocial deification of heterosexual male power—the power of conquest. Hump and Wolf debate whether or not this power is a result of metaphysical "purpose" (Hump's interpretation) or evolved, physical "utility" (Wolf's). Hump's language tends back toward the aesthetic—linking the power of the body as part of a divine art or design, whereas Wolf's language emphasizes the power of the body to destroy other life in order for self-preservation, a thing Hump acknowledges "is not beautiful" (130). When Hump is invited to *feel* Wolf's musculature, his description of the body shifts away from aestheticizing its form and toward a veneration of its substance and function. Although this tactile examination is not without an element of homoeroticism, the language evokes more of a sense of fear and awe rather than desire. Wolf appears both as a weapon, "hard as iron," and as a predatory animal, with "hands . . . like talons." He poses not only to exhibit himself as a spectacle, but with a "watchfulness . . . of battle" (130). The "remaindered homoeroticism" is still clearly present, but Hump's deep respect for Wolf's primitive potency is nevertheless meant as a move away from homosexuality and toward a homosocial heterosexuality. This development prepares Hump to see Wolf as a *rival* in pursuit of Maud's love (rather than Maud as a rival for Wolf's love) and, at the same time, links a naturalized male sexuality of conquest with the imperial setting and *mission* of the narrative. Working on the front lines of empire and cultivating heterosexual desire are represented as continuous extensions of the healthy, empowered white male body—a body that, through labor, maintains a readiness for action and, when the opportunity presents itself, seizes what nature "naturally" yields to it.

Hence, it is through watching Wolf—the object of Hump's homoerotic gaze—that Hump "learns" heterosexuality. For London, as Miner points out, "[t]o be a man means, at least in part, experiencing the desires of a man; Wolf Larsen models these desires for Hump" (112). Even after Maud enters the narrative, Hump's heterosexual development remains structured by his homosocial connection to Wolf. For example, after seeing Maud "straining and struggling and crushed in the embrace of Wolf Larsen's arms," Hump's "primitive" aggression ignites, and he attacks Wolf (227). A few pages later, Hump reflects that he "had failed till now in grasping much of the physical characteristics of love." Prior to this moment, Hump's sexuality had been a "sublimated something," and the "bonds of the flesh" had not entered into his understanding of love. It is only after fighting with Wolf over Maud that Hump finds himself "learning the sweet lesson . . . that the soul transmuted itself, expressed itself, through the flesh." This is an admission that, for Hump, heterosexual desire is something that *must be learned*. The passage unwittingly seems to denaturalize the very desire the narrative attempts to privilege as natural and inevitable. Moreover, Hump avoids any detailed description of the "flesh" that ignited such desire—all he alludes to is "the sight and sense and touch of the loved one's hair" (235). Never does Maud's body become a spectacle of desire anywhere comparable to Wolf's body. In terms of narrative emphasis, Maud is a second-rate sexual object. Or, to put it another way, it is not the femaleness of the love object that is rendered as the most important element of heterosexual identity; the most crucial element is the physical embodiment of the subject, the willingness to *fight* for sexual advantage with another aggressive, masculine body. For London, Hump's becoming heterosexual is much more about becoming a certain kind of man (through an inter-classed homosociality) than about learning to love a woman.

Despite the fact that Hump's relation to Maud is not as central as one might expect in the development of his sexuality, the relationship is far from unimportant. Maud is responsible for Hump's further affective development—the cultivation of his sense of chivalry, which signifies not only his capacity to provide for and defend *her* but also, symbolically, his capacity to serve the "civilization" she represents—the social space of the American metropole. Anne McClintock, who has given theoretical scrutiny to the ways in which nationalisms are gendered, notes that "[w]omen are typically constructed as the symbolic bearers of the nation, but are denied any direct relation to national agency" (354). When Maud first enters the narrative, she seems to take on this symbolic role. In the primitive, anachronistic space that is the *Ghost*, she represents the return of the civil and moral ideals of the nation. Hump sets Maud up in a binary relationship to Wolf: "I likened them to the extreme ends of the human ladder of evolution—the one the culmination of all savagery, the other the finished product of the finest civilization" (London 191). Maud's appearance in the novel coincides with Hump's readiness to "evolve" beyond the primitivism of Wolf. Having developed, through physical labor, a new body and embodied knowledge, he is poised to apply his new power for social purposes. The capacity to go beyond Wolf's amoral individualism and self-interested aggression—to fight and work *for another* and not solely *for the self*—marks the final step in Hump's masculine development. He has, at this point, progressed from impotent, overcivilized man to potent, civilized man by virtue of a temporary regression to, and recapitulation of, an imagined state of primitive manhood.

Maud's presence is thus necessary to prevent Hump from remaining "trapped" in the regressive state—from becoming too "Wolfish" and losing the *feeling* of a civilized man. This threat—that the return to primitive masculinity might prove to be degenerative rather than rejuvenating—is most visible in Hump's affective responses to the homosocial environment on the *Ghost*. For example, early in the novel, Hump articulates his antagonism for Mugridge, the ship's Cockney cook, in terms of passionate hatred: "how I hated him! And how my hatred for him grew and grew, during that fearful time, to cyclopean dimensions. For the first time in my life I experienced the desire to murder" (59). He then goes on to wonder if this novel sensation of rage is the result of his being "tainted by the brutality" of his "environment." Whereas homosociality in an imperial space has the potential to reinvigorate men—to help them develop physical strength through manly labor and competitive struggle—it also has the potential to overdevelop certain brutal impulses.[12] Later, Hump will directly connect this "brutality" to the absence of women on the *Ghost*. He reflects, "Where are the mothers of these twenty and odd men. . . ? It strikes me as unnatural and unhealthful that men should be totally separated from women and herd through the world by themselves" (116). Whereas Hump is recovering from his *overcivilized* state, he sees that these men are suffering from an *undercivilized* state, which is coded as unnaturally hypermasculine. "There is no balance in their lives," he concludes. "Their masculinity, which in itself is of the brute, has been overdeveloped. The other and spiritual side of their natures has been dwarfed—atrophied, in fact" (117). Although that "brutish" masculinity is elsewhere privileged as a necessary basis for male power, here we see that without a complementary "spiritual" (and presumably feminine) refinement, that masculinity actually *dehumanizes* its practitioners. These men-without-women are "a half-brute, half-human species, a race apart, wherein there is no such thing as sex" (117). Without women, London implies, men fail to develop the impulse to act ethically; men need women to learn the necessary social affective capacities for "softness, and tenderness, and sympathy" (116).

Once Maud enters the narrative, interposed between Wolf and Hump, we see Hump begin to enact London's ideal of a "balanced manhood," one that is capable of violent exertion, but is simultaneously tempered by a feminine, civilized, and ethical principle.[13] A good illustration of this is the scene in which Hump spies Wolf attempting to force himself upon Maud. Hump responds with the affect of "primitive" masculinity—an "overmastering rage"—and attacks Wolf, stabbing him with a knife in the shoulder (227). When Hump prepares to stab Wolf again, in a "more vital part," Maud cries out for him to stop and successfully restrains him (228). Maud's agency here is interestingly contradictory—as a sexual object, she inspires Hump's "primitive" affective response, his murderous rage to kill the man who is taking what he believes rightfully belongs to him; as a voice of ethical restraint, however, she checks the very impulse she inspires. Maud is both an object of exchange, generating homosocial violence, and an ethical counterforce, structuring the expression of that violence so that it does not become "excessive." Keeping in mind Maud's symbolic status, representing "civilization" or the "nation," we are reminded that gendered national symbols both provide motivation for violence and signify the "ethical" principles that rationalize such violence. Maud gives Hump both a *reason* for conquest and the means for imagining that conquest as ethical.

Once Hump has secured Maud as a possession through this "ethical conquest," he must provide for her and protect her. He has evolved from a man who could not provide for himself to a man who can provide for another: "I had stood on my father's legs. . . . I had had no responsibilities at all. Then, on the *Ghost* I had learned to be responsible for myself. And now, for the first time in my life, I found myself responsible for someone else" (256). He has, at this culminating moment of his development, both the primitive power to fight and work for his own survival and the civilized ethics to fight and work for another. We see this fusion of primitive and civilized manhood when Hump hunts for Maud on their Crusoe-like island: "I shall never forget, in that moment, how instantly conscious I became of my manhood. The primitive deeps of my nature stirred. I felt myself masculine, the protector of the weak, the fighting male. And, best of all, I felt myself the protector of my loved one" (263). The instinct to kill is properly tempered by the ethic to protect. He goes on to give credit to Wolf for this realization of his potential as a man: "I had much for which to thank Wolf Larsen," he acknowledges, certain that his previous self would not have been man enough for Maud.[14]

Yet, Hump is only able to thank Wolf by overseeing his painful and pathetic decline from a once-godlike force of pure masculine strength to a tortured, disembodied consciousness. The fact that Hump's arrival at hegemonic masculinity—his successful achievement of an idealized, balanced manhood—coincides with the abjection of the very homosocial connection which enabled his development signifies a turning away from the narrative's earlier privileging of the social value of working-class identities. The reason for this abjection, I would argue, lies in London's internalization of bourgeois gender ideology, which is visible in the narrative not only in its obsession with masculine development but also in the primitivization of the working-class male body, the absence of the working-class woman, and the idealization of an isolated heterosexual union as the basic unit of society. Although London's novel does not represent the working class as homogenous—they range from the contemptible Mugridge to the noble Johnson to the amoral Wolf—they are nevertheless *all male* and brutally fragmented. They comprise both a homosocial and antisocial group. Their shared labor in this imperial space does not provide them with a sense of fraternity, nor a connection with working men or women in the metropole.[15] This is sharply contrasted with the ethical and functional cohabitation of Maud and Hump, who emerge as a rejuvenated, heterosexual, bourgeois dyad.

They become a microcosm for a vital civilization; the *Ghost* becomes a microcosm for a savage, anarchical past. Because London's romanticization of American manhood is so rooted in an ideology of imperialist conquest and the bourgeois family, he is able to see embodied working-class subjectivity only as male and only as a fetishized source of masculine power—not as a source of knowledge that could provide alternative, more egalitarian, social models.

PRIMITIVE MAN, WOLF-MAN, SACRED MAN

Whereas Hump is able to exercise and develop his manhood by performing imperial labor, other members of the *Ghost's* crew, such as Oofty-Oofty and Wolf Larsen, are afforded no such redemption. Their masculinities remain subordinated and/or marginalized, despite their laboring bodies. These men, both regarded as "primitive" (though in starkly divergent ways), are excluded from civilized social spaces, despite their economic service to those who live in such spaces. Thus, while their laboring bodies are *included* in a national economy, their social/political bodies are *excluded* from the national citizenry. In the final section of this chapter, I will use Agamben's theory of *homines sacri*, or "sacred men," to characterize this inclusive exclusion of these two "primitive" men. This will, I hope, explain London's ultimate ambivalence toward Wolf Larsen's primitivism in terms of a fundamentally racial anxiety. London's "politics of the body," to use William Dow's phrase, rested on a social Darwinist assumption that the colonization and oppression of nonwhite races were effects of the biological superiority of Anglo-Saxon bodies (85). Yet, this same premise threatened to "naturalize" the oppression of working-class white bodies—a contradiction that London, as a socialist, struggled to suppress. The figure of the "white primitive" thus occupied a crucial tipping point between London's socialism and his social Darwinism—between his ideological investments in class equality and Anglo-Saxon supremacy. Unable to resolve these contradictions, London makes Wolf both a *super* man and a *sacred* man—a man who is paradoxically both invincible and condemned.

Although the major criticism on *The Sea-Wolf* has largely ignored Oofty-Oofty as a marginal character, to examine him enables us to offer what Said calls a "contrapuntal reading" and to "give emphasis and voice to what is silent or marginally present or ideologically represented" (66). Oofty-Oofty is described as a "Kanaka," a word used at that time to refer to a native from the South Sea Islands, usually someone who labors on British sugar plantations (London 125). The word itself is Hawaiian, and its usage as a signifier for such a diverse number of indigenous peoples (from Canada, Hawaii, Fiji, Queensland, New Zealand, etc.) reveals its Orientalizing effect in imperial discourse (Kanaka, n.). If Oofty-Oofty is a Hawaiian, then it seems significant to note that his presence in London's novel coincides with the historical conquest of Hawaii by the United States. In 1893, European and American capitalists overthrew the Hawaiian monarchy, usurping Hawaiian sovereignty, and in 1898—six years prior to the publication of *The Sea-Wolf*—Hawaii became a territory of the United States. This, along with the "annexation" of Puerto Rico, the Philippine Islands, and Guam (all in 1898) signaled a concerted national effort to make "new frontiers" via imperial expansion (Kimmel 111). Unlike the imperial expansion of "Manifest Destiny," this new imperialism was colonial as opposed to incorporative. As Amy Kaplan has argued, these spaces disrupted the "foreign/domestic" binary of nationhood and became transnational formations.[16] Additionally, this new "imperial strategy" was represented in public discourse as a strategy for masculinizing the nation; cultural anxieties about gender were exploited for militaristic purposes. As one journalist wrote, in 1898, "a nation needs a war from time to time to prevent it from becoming effeminate, to shake it up from demoralizing materialism, and to elevate the popular heart by awakening heroic emotions and the spirit of patriotic self-sacrifice" (qtd. in Kimmel 112).

Empire thus became a way for American men to prove their racial superiority over the Oofty-Ooftys of the Pacific and other spaces beyond the nation. London's ambivalence toward Oofty-Oofty is apparent in the contradictory ways he is represented. His manliness is apparent in his competence as a "splendid seaman," yet he is also very effeminate (121). Hump describes him as "a beautiful creature, almost feminine in the pleasing lines of his figure, and there was a softness and dreaminess in his large eyes which seemed to contradict his well-earned reputation for strife and action" (126). Later in the novel, as Hump gazes at Oofty-Oofty, momentarily lost in his "velvety and luminous eyes," he must force himself to remember that "the barbaric devil . . . lurked in his breast and belied all the softness and tenderness, almost womanly, of his face and form" (219–20). It is particularly striking how far the representation of Oofty-Oofty's gender is from the "primitive" masculinity of Wolf Larsen. London represents Oofty-Oofty's "savagery" as always lurking, but never manifest. It is always concealed behind his feminine, delicate veneer. One might expect to see Oofty-Oofty—as a representative of a cultural group that, according to colonial discourse, was indeed *primitive*—portrayed as a hypermasculine, savage, ruthless, and aggressively sexual. Yet the only character to match such a description is the Scandinavian Wolf Larsen. The implication seems to be that various racial types possess competing primitive energies, and Oofty-Oofty's subordinated, effeminate savagery marks his primitive energy as racially deficient. He is "out-savaged" by Wolf Larsen's northern European savagery. This discursive maneuver in London's novel reinforces an imperial, racial ideology that designates the inferiority of the Kanaka as a biological, evolutionary fact.

The marginalization and subordination of Oofty-Oofty, and their ideological coincidence with U.S. imperial expansion into the Pacific, are perhaps more easily explained than the narrative's ultimate disavowal of Wolf Larsen and his "primitive" vitality. The difficulty arises because of the amount of hero worship directed at Wolf during the first half of the narrative. He is a proponent of a Darwinian worldview, which London himself espoused, and he offers a Marxist critique of bourgeois privilege, which London, as a socialist, also endorsed. Moreover, despite being Danish, Wolf is portrayed as a profoundly American icon. His "soul" is referred to as "virgin territory," as if he were the spirit of the frontier incarnate (73). He also seems to evoke a simple, direct rhetorical style, which stands in opposition to Hump's more ornate, European style of speech: "He drove so directly to the core of the matter, divesting a question always of all superfluous details, and with such an air of finality, that I seemed to find myself struggling in deep water with no footing under me" (61). It is in Wolf's embodiment of a kind of hyperindividualism that we begin to see him fall into authorial disfavor. Although one might consider this individualism as distinctly American, London renders it as antisocial: "he is certainly an individualist of the most pronounced type. Not only that, but he is very lonely. There is no congeniality between him and the rest of the men aboard ship. His tremendous virility and mental strength wall him apart" (68). While Wolf's manliness is valorized as a model of strength, authenticity, and self-sufficiency, it is also inseparable from his antisocial brutality in his dealings with the crew. His masculinity is ultimately marked by an unprincipled lust for power and domination.

For London, Wolf is insufficiently socially evolved; his individualism is too excessive for civilization, especially for the kind of socialist democracy for which London hoped.[17] Wolf, thus, occupies an ambiguous and ambivalent relationship to the nation: he simultaneously strikes the reader as iconically American and fundamentally antidemocratic. Perhaps what is most notably "un-American" about Wolf is his commitment to a materialist ontology, a position that profoundly challenges the narrative of American exceptionalism; Hump describes Wolf's chronic "sadness" as "the penalty which the materialist ever pays for his materialism" (203). This points to an intriguing contradiction within London himself—a socialist writer trying to divorce Marxism from historical materialism (or, alternatively, a profoundly anti-Marxist socialist). By reinscribing Hump's bourgeois idealism, however, Wolf's socialist sentiments—however valorized early in the novel—are ultimately undercut. Miner articulates this very point:

> [A]lthough the novel strives to forget this insight, it suggests to us that the realization of one individual's opportunity . . . is often built upon the denial of similar opportunities to others. In other words, one man may purchase middle-class, heterosexual manhood at the expense of other men; the novel reveals, somewhat reluctantly, that the superstructure of civilization depends upon a substructure of bestiality. (113)

This is done precisely by figuring imperial spaces such as the *Ghost* as anachronistic, and thus outside of history. The "primitive" subjugations that occur in the primordial space-time of empire are rendered as necessary struggles in the service of progress to a more socially idealized civilization.

The violence of Wolf Larsen cannot, however, be ultimately disavowed. Like Oofty-Oofty, whose presence reminds us of the appropriation of indigenous laborers and the rejection of indigenous rights to sovereignty in the spaces of American empire, Wolf similarly haunts the narrative despite his demise, by revealing the essential connection between the development of hegemonic American manhood and the brutality of America's imperial conquests. Wolf, like Oofty-Oofty, is not only a "sacred man," reduced to "bare life" and abandoned by the nation he serves—but he is, as his name suggests, a "wolf-man" in precisely the sense that Agamben theorizes:

> What had to remain in the collective unconscious as a monstrous hybrid of human and animal, divided between the forest and the city—the werewolf—is, therefore, in its origin the figure of the man who has been banned from the city. That such a man is defined as a wolf-man and not simply as a wolf . . . is decisive here. The life of the bandit, like that of the sacred man, is not a piece of animal nature without any relation to law and the city. It is, rather, a threshold of indistinction and of passage between animal and man, *physis* and *nomos*, exclusion and inclusion. (105)

By drawing this parallel to Agamben, we may read Wolf Larsen as both an idealization of U.S. sovereign power and a disavowal of its extra-legal brutality. Wolf is simultaneously a metonym for the nation and abjected from the nation—an icon of masculinity that is constructed as distinctly American, yet has no place in America. As McClintock writes, "the abject returns to haunt modernity as its constitutive, inner repudiation: the rejected from which one does not part" (72). Wolf represents the spirit of U.S. expansion somehow divorced from the ideals of the nation. On board the *Ghost*, Wolf represents sovereign power while all other crew members and passengers are denied any rights as citizens (or basic human rights). Wolf's deterioration marks the disavowal of his relationship to the nation, and it reads as a denial of the excesses of an imperial American masculinity—a male identity that has become individualistic to the point of being undemocratic, and dominant to the point of being savage and brutal. However, Hump's indebtedness to Wolf for his own transformation—his appropriation of primitive masculinity—as well as Hump's projected return to the United States as an empowered, elite man, reveals the traces of Wolf that are included in and valorized by the nation. London unconvincingly attempts to resolve his ambivalence toward Wolf by having it both ways—by disavowing the very source from which national revitalization is imagined.

Agamben writes that the wolf-man, or *homo sacer*, dwells in a "state of nature" that is not antithetical to, but constitutive of, the juridical order of civilization: "Far from being a prejuridical condition that is indifferent to the law of the city, the Hobbesian state of nature is the exception and the threshold that constitutes and dwells within it" (106). It is this fact that disallows Wolf's radical exclusion from the nation. David Heckerl's reading of the novel makes a similar point, suggesting that "Larsen's behavior restores to view ... market society's origin in the state of nature, that nasty and brutish condition of egoistic warfare upon which the liberal economic order supervenes" (213). Not only does Larsen reveal the origins of modern capitalism in the brutal state of nature/state of exception, but he also reveals its tendency to *compulsively return* to such a state: "Larsen's actions occasion the *devolution* of the market society toward its origins in the bloody conflict of 'each against all'" (214). Hence, we are forced to confront the fact that Wolf Larsen is, in fact, not an anachronistic primitive man but a man *produced by* imperialist capitalism. He is the product of an imperialist/capitalist ideology that silently insinuates that one "*ought to act immorally in order to act rationally,*" while paradoxically proclaiming that domination is proof not only of physical but moral superiority (Heckerl 208).

Amy Kaplan has observed how London's primitivism "takes two opposing narrative trajectories of degeneration and regeneration. The same process of shedding the veneer of modern civilization can reveal the debased criminal within ... or can reawaken the ennobling heroic Anglo-Saxon warrior" ("Nation" 264). These two trajectories—Hump's ascendancy and Wolf's decline—are also figured as the development of one male body *through work* and the degeneration of another male body *by disease*, as if punished for an inherent moral failing. That Wolf imagines his disease to be the result of a brain tumor, which leaves him paralyzed and disembodied, suggests that London is punishing him for his materialism—for his belief in the primacy of the body over the soul and his rejection of moral responsibility. It is Hump, and not Wolf, who is entrusted with the task of articulating London's vision of American manhood. The labor that empowers Hump to be man enough for this task is the same labor that Wolf spent his life doing—the imperial labor that alienated him from the nation. At least implicitly, then, London's text speaks to an ambivalence about such labor: although it has the potential to reform atrophied male bodies, it also has the potential to create long-lasting, isolated, homosocial spaces divorced from women, morality, and civil society. London does not envision such spaces as rife with fraternal communities, but rather as filled with cutthroat, competitive, and brutally antagonistic individuals. These reservations about the effects of imperial labor on male bodies, however, are not sufficient for London to stage a broader critique of American empire or transnational economic practices. As William Dow has observed, London held to a "fervent nationalism" as part of his complex and often contradictory ideological commitments, which also included his adherence to "international socialism, ... class equality, and Anglo-Saxon supremacy" (92). In *The Sea-Wolf*, nationalism takes priority over socialism. Despite the power ascribed to the working-class male body, both in its physicality and epistemology, it is nevertheless constructed as merely instrumental in the development of a *national* male body that transcends its class position.

That this transcendent, national manhood is both indebted to and *superior to* the working-class, "primitive" masculinity that it appropriates signifies a complicity with the capitalist hierarchical structures of the nation, as does the idealization of the heterosexual bourgeois marriage at the novel's end. Hump emerges as a patriarch, empowered by his work—not a working man, connected with other workers.

By some criteria, then, such as Janet Zandy's, *The Sea-Wolf* only partially succeeds at doing what a "working-class text" is "supposed" to do. Although the narrative "invites, cajoles, even insists, that the reader step into the skin of a worker" (Zandy, *Hands* 87) just as Hump is coerced into the very labor that is his making, it nevertheless fails to establish a "heightened consciousness of the multiple 'we' inside the writer's 'I.'" (*Hands* 86) The only "we" that endures to the end of the novel is that of Hump and Maud, but the latter, subordinated by her gender role (however momentarily empowered), functions primarily to further elevate Hump's hegemonic authority. He is *the man*, and she is his "mate-woman." But what about his other mates? What about the mate who made him find his own legs? Zandy writes: "[w]orking-class writing recognizes and resists the transformation of the human I/we into an it—a thing, a commodity, a working unit, a disembodied hand" (*Hands* 87). London's text does just this to the very source of its protagonist's vitality.

I would argue, however, that such a shortcoming provides insufficient grounds to exclude the novel from a canon of working-class American literature. To mandate that any text must be committed to a recognizably collectivist politics in order to be authentically "working class" elides a long history of working-class Americans (especially men) who have subscribed to a national mythology of heroic, artisanal individualism. London's work, which presents such a multitude of discursive contradictions, illuminates many of the ideological obstacles toward forming a more collectivist working-class identity brought on by a simultaneous desire to identify as white, masculine, and American. The fetishization of the male body, the idealization of marriage as the basic social unit, and the abjection of "primitive" men are a few such obstacles. To identify these, along with each working-class "we" that London represses, is to make audible key anxieties that troubled American working-class culture at the turn of the century. It is to use these social anxieties, and the political limitations they produce, not to disqualify a text's achievement, but to understand the mechanisms by which some working-class voices were marginalized by men whose stated goal was precisely to dignify the physical and epistemological value of work. It is precisely the failures of such working-class texts that make critical analyses of them potentially so instructive.

NOTES

1. London's ambition is an early example of an attempt to prove what Renny Christopher has asserted, that "the novel need not be bourgeois," despite

the fact that "it might have arisen as *the* bourgeois art form" (47). Christopher argues that the novel "can be wrested from its origins and profoundly reconfigured" (47). London's success at this maneuver is mixed, as he is able to center the lived experience of working-class men while simultaneously reproducing certain oppressive racial and gender ideologies in his celebration of masculinity at work in the service of empire.
2. London's foregrounding of the lived experience of those working aboard the *Ghost*, the importance of such labor in forming both class and gender identities, and the structures of power that emanate from such relations all make *The Sea-Wolf* a rich text to investigate in the field of new working-class studies. This field, as articulated by John Russo and Sherry Lee Linkon, "begins with some combination of the power relations associated with work, political struggle, and lived experience, grounding the study of how class works in the lives, words, and perspectives of working-class people, and using these as the foundation and location for analyses of systems of power, oppression, and exploitation" ("What's New" 11).
3. This analysis is in accordance with the kind of critical investigation outlined by Constance Coiner, in which she urges readers "to decipher the cultural work done by working-class texts and the ways in which readers are invited to participate in that cultural work" (230). Coiner defines "cultural work" as "the work any text does, implicitly or explicitly, to support or subvert the dominant culture" (229). My argument here suggests that London's novel both supports *and* subverts the dominant culture. His subversion is effected by his critique of American cultural forms that are divorced from the lived experiences of the working class, whereas his complicity is visible in his reproduction of bourgeois gender ideology and his commitment to national/imperial narratives.
4. I see London's construction of the working-class male body as a source of knowledge in line with Janet Zandy's theorization of "laboring bodies" as sites of "an epistemology, a way of knowing and understanding the world that comes out of the physicality of work" (*Hands* 3). By contrast, the reduction of the working-class male body to a biological object, which I see happening at the novel's end, is an example of the production of what Giorgio Agamben calls "bare life," meaning life that is excluded from the political order (9).
5. By mentioning London's inclusion of an "informally educated" reader in his imagined audience, I mean someone of the working-class whose education, not unlike Wolf Larsen's, was founded on self-selected readings and the epistemology of laboring bodies rather than formal schooling.
6. Zandy and other scholars of working-class literature have tended to disregard genres such as the dime novel, arguing that it is more important to investigate texts that reflect the lived experience of working-class people rather than texts produced for consumption by working-class readers (*Hands* 85). Yet, understanding the aesthetic and ideological patterns of such mass-produced texts seems crucial for understanding the cultural values of working-class readers. This is not to say that the values of any class of people are wholly determined by the mass culture they consume, but surely we can assume that popular cultural forms were popular for a reason, and some degree of interpellation was inevitable.
7. James Papa Jr. reveals this point by arguing that Death Larsen, Wolf's brother, "in his mechanical steamship on the horizon, is the new twentieth-century man. He is more brutal in his mechanistic approach to life than Wolf, in his animalism, can ever be. There is no room, and no need, for philosophy or poetry in Death Larsen's world" (277).

8. Anthony Rotundo has noted the surge in "primitive" masculine icons in American culture at the turn of the century, as well as the cultural practice of middle-class white men identifying with men of so-called "primitive" races, especially in the ritualistic practices of male fraternal lodges (227). My own research suggests that Rotundo may have overstated this "identification," considering the racial anxieties that surely problematized such cultural appropriations. Additionally, he seems to unduly restrict the importance of this phenomenon to this particular historical moment, rather than fully acknowledging the long tradition, dating back to frontier fiction, of white male protagonists adopting a quasi-"savage" manhood en route to heroic status in American literature.

9. Of course, any social revolution based on a fetishized notion of the white male body could never be truly egalitarian. London's push for class equality extended only to the Anglo-Saxon men he deemed biologically capable of developing such embodied strength.

    It should also be noted here the extent to which London's ideological construction of a *nationalized* white male body, acting as a metonym for a virile, aggressive, militant state, had in common with Theodore Roosevelt's "equating [of] individual manliness with national strength and individual power" (Kimmel 183). Roosevelt (much like Hump) was subordinated as an effeminate man early in his career. Several daily newspapers made fun of him, using emasculating nicknames, while he served as a state assemblyman in Albany, New York. Realizing he would have to transform his image in order to achieve his ambitions for political power, he drew on the *mythos* of the frontier, reinventing himself as the "Cowboy of the Dakotas." In his famous historical narrative, *The Winning of the West*, "manhood and national worth were proven by their ability to stamp out competing, savage races" (Bederman 178). Later, in famous speeches such as "The Strenuous Life" and "The Pioneer Spirit and American Problems" (both delivered less than five years prior to the publication of *The Sea-Wolf*), Roosevelt insinuated that men who were not ready to take up the "responsibilities" of American imperialism in Hawaii, Cuba, Puerto Rico, and the Philippines were either not *real* men, or not *real American* men (Kimmel 182–83).

    London's elaboration in his fiction of such a gendered, nationalist, imperial narrative necessarily troubles his ability to envision a socialist revolution, or even accurately articulate working-class experience. By focusing so much on the male body and the nation, London pays little heed to actual communities formed by working people, either at the local or global level. Instead of envisioning a transformation of the communal life of the *Ghost*'s working crew, we see only the transformation of Hump's individual body. At the novel's most idyllic moment, there is no social space for a community of working men and women, but only a space for an isolated bourgeois dyad, composed of a hegemonic man and his subordinated helpmate of a woman. In the end, London's elevation of working-class experience serves not to promote working-class solidarity, but instead constructs that experience as *instrumental* in maintaining a masculinized image of the nation. The commitment to projecting both individual and state power trumps any commitment to class equality.

10. This "fog of abstractions" that has surrounded Hump's cerebral existence is literalized in the opening sequence of the novel, in which Hump boards a ferry immersed in deep fog and finds himself "alone in the moist obscurity" (1). He places complete trust for his life in the labor and knowledge of working men, and when an accident occurs, he is unable even to swim for his life. All he is able to do is to shriek for help, "as the women had shrieked" (8).

11. See Heckerl for a discussion of the presence of Darwinian, social Darwinian (Spencerian), and Nietzschean thought in the novel. See also Mitchell; and

Naso for further analysis of the connection between London's thinking and Spencerian social Darwinism. Finally, see Ward for a discussion of London's rejection of the Nietzschean philosophy of the "superman."

12. This function of the space of the *Ghost* as a "double-edged sword"—a space that can both reinvigorate manhood or degenerate it—is reminiscent of Don Mitchell's observation that mobility, in the global labor marketplace, can be both beneficial and destructive for working-class people. Although the men on the *Ghost* are able to pursue work where they find it, and thus make a living that is not contingent on a local economy, they are also alienated from larger communities of working people and unable to improve their working conditions. As Mitchell writes, "[m]obility—or really control over the *conditions* of mobility—is thus an aspect of class power and struggle" (85). Hump demonstrates this in his ability to take what he needs from the *Ghost*—his initial rescue and his training in manhood—but also escape when he needs to do so. His class power is signified by his capacity to walk away (or float away) from the labor that traps other male bodies.

13. Madonne Miner also points out London's idealization of Hump's balanced manhood, calling him the novel's only "complete man," opposed both to Wolf's animalized brutality and the effeminacy of Hump's prior self (111). Anthony Naso makes a similar claim, suggesting that Hump "achieves the proper balance between the instinctive and spiritual sides of human nature" according to the Spencerian theory guiding London's narration (24).

    London's idealizing of a manhood that is not "pure masculinity" but rather contains within it a "spiritual" side, implicitly coded as feminine, has prompted critic Sam Baskett to call the gendering in the novel "androgynous" (97). Although this may be a bit of an overstatement, Baskett's observation is in line with Christopher Gair's comment, which strikes me as fairly accurate, that there exists "a tension within *The Sea-Wolf* between the desire to establish the fundamental difference between men and women and the simultaneous desire to blur the distinction" (5).

14. Although the majority of this final section of the novel emphasizes Hump's ability to provide for and protect Maud, the dynamic is momentarily reversed. When Wolf makes one last effort to attack Hump, Maud strikes Wolf with a seal club. Hump sees in her at this moment a fleeting glimpse of "primitive" womanhood: "she was my woman, my mate-woman, fighting with me and for me as the mate of a caveman would have fought, all the primitive in her aroused" (307–08). The Tarzan-Jane moment is swiftly undercut, however, as Maud falls into Hump's arms, crying. He remarks, "After all, she was only a woman" (308). London displays his belief that the male body, more than the female, is capable of withstanding the return to a primitive state. He is eager to give Maud agency in one moment, but anxious to keep that agency contained within existing patriarchal norms in the next.

15. Janet Zandy, in her introduction to *What We Hold in Common*, emphasizes the importance of a "collective sensibility" in working-class cultural studies (xiv). It is this sense of the collective that is lost at the end of *The Sea-Wolf* by the narrative's abandonment of the *Ghost*'s crew and the demise of Wolf Larsen, both of which enable the elevation of Hump and Maud as a triumphantly romantic, bourgeois couple.

16. See Kaplan, *Anarchy of Empire*.

17. Susan Ward has explained London's disavowal of Wolf as a rejection of the Nietszchean philosophy of the "superman," and Anthony Naso has explained it from the point of view of London's adoption of Spencerian philosophy (Ward 326). Naso writes, "Larsen is not a good leader or even a benevolent dictator exercising his authority for the good of the state and people as a

whole. He is, in fact, a beast, a Wolf in the strictest sense of the word. He is a malevolent utilitarian using everything and everyone for his advantage" (23). In Specerian terms, life on the *Ghost* is "anachronistic"—between the primitive and altruistic stages of social development.

BIBLIOGRAPHY

Agamben, Giorgio. *Homo Sacer: Sovereign Power and Bare Life*. Trans. Daniel Heller-Roazen. Stanford: Stanford UP, 1998. Print.
Baskett, Sam S. "Sea Change in *The Sea-Wolf*." In Cassuto and Reesman 92–109. Print.
Bederman, Gail. *Manliness and Civilization*. Chicago: U of Chicago P, 1995. Print.
Brown, Bill. "Reading the West: Cultural and Historical Background." *Reading the West: An Anthology of Dime Westerns*. Ed. Bill Brown. Boston: Bedford, 1997. 1–40. Print.
Cassuto, Leonard, and Jeanne Campbell Reesman, eds. *Rereading Jack London*. Stanford: Stanford UP, 1996. Print.
Christopher, Renny. "Cultural Borders: Working-Class Literature's Challenge to the Canon." *The Canon in the Classroom*. Ed. John Alberti. New York: Garland, 1995. 45–55. Print.
Derrick, Scott. "Making a Heterosexual Man: Gender, Sexuality, and Narrative in the Fiction of Jack London." In Cassuto and Reesman 110–29. Print.
Dow, William. *Narrating Class in American Fiction*. New York: Palgrave MacMillan, 2009. Print.
Gair, Christopher. "Gender and Genre: Nature, Naturalism, and Authority in *The Sea-Wolf*." *Studies in American Fiction* 22.2 (1994): 131–47. Web. 2 Feb. 2008.
Heckerl, David K. "'Violent Movements of Business': The Moral Nihilist as Economic Man in Jack London's *The Sea-Wolf*." *Twisted From the Ordinary: Essays on American Literary Naturalism*. Ed. Mary E. Papke. Knoxville: U of Tennessee P, 2003. 202–16. Print.
"kanaka, n." *OED Online*. Nov. 2010. Oxford UP. Web. 16 Feb. 2011
Kaplan, Amy. *The Anarchy of Empire in the Making of U.S. Culture*. Cambridge: Harvard UP, 2002. Print.
———. "Nation, Region, and Empire." *The Columbia History of the American Novel*. Ed. Emory Elliott. New York: Columbia UP, 1991. 240–66. Print.
Kimmel, Michael. *Manhood in America*. New York: Free Press, 1997. Print.
Lauter, Paul. "Under Construction: Working-Class Writing." In Russo and Linkon, *New Working-Class Studies* 63–77. Print.
London, Jack. *The Sea-Wolf*. 1904. Oxford: Oxford UP, 2000. Print.
Lowe, Lisa. *Immigrant Acts*. Durham: Duke UP, 1996. Print.
McClintock, Anne. *Imperial Leather*. New York: Routledge, 1995. Print.
Miner, Madonne. "'It Will Be the (Un)Making of You': Manhood Besieged in Jack London's *The Sea-Wolf*." *Jack London Newsletter* 21 (1988): 106–16. Print.
Mitchell, Don. "Working-Class Geographies: Capital, Space, and Place." In Russo and Linkon, *New Working-Class Studies* 78–97. Print.
Mitchell, Lee Clark. "'And Rescue Us from Ourselves': Becoming Someone in Jack London's *The Sea-Wolf*." *American Literature* 70.2 (June 1998): 317–35. Print.
Naso, Anthony J. "Jack London and Herbert Spencer." *Jack London Newsletter* 14 (1981): 13–34. Print.

Papa, James A., Jr. "Canvas and Steam: Historical Conflict in Jack London's *Sea-Wolf.*" *Midwest Quarterly* 40 (1999): 274–84. Print.
Rotundo, Anthony. *American Manhood.* New York: Basic, 1993. Print.
Russo, John, and Sherry Lee Linkon, eds. *New Working-Class Studies.* Ithaca: Cornell UP, 2005. Print.
———. "What's New about New Working-Class Studies?" In Russo and Linkon, *New Working-Class Studies* 1–15. Print.
Said, Edward. *Culture and Imperialism.* New York: Vintage, 1994. Print.
Sides, Hampton. *Blood and Thunder: An Epic of the American West.* New York: Doubleday, 2006. Print.
Ward, Susan. "Social Philosophy as Best-Seller: Jack London's *The Sea-Wolf.*" *Western American Literature* 17.4 (1983): 321–32. Print.
Zandy, Janet. *Hands: Physical Labor, Class, and Cultural Work.* New Brunswick: Rutgers UP, 2004. Print.
———. Introduction. *What We Hold in Common: An Introduction to Working-Class Studies.* Ed. Janet Zandy. New York: Feminist at CUNY, 2001. xii-xv. Print.

11 "The Man in the Family"
Staging Gender in *Waiting for Lefty* and American Social Protest Theatre

Maria F. Brandt

One of the more ambiguous images to emerge from social protest literature during the 1930s is that of Rose of Sharon offering her breast to a starved man at the end of John Steinbeck's novel *The Grapes of Wrath*. This image emerges an affirmative symbol for women experiencing the deprivation of the Great Depression in its celebration of Rose's female body as a life-giving force; it also emerges dangerous in its call for women to solder themselves to the female-specific parts of their bodies.

It is this tension between the simultaneous empowerment and disempowerment of women characters when confronted with the poverty of the 1930s that interests me, and in this chapter I will examine representations of this tension as seen on the American stage. Unlike Rose of Sharon, however, the women characters I will examine experience this tension not by embracing their feminine potential but by taking on roles prescribed for men, roles male characters are unable to fulfill due to rampant unemployment. As such, these women characters become recognizable symbols to audience members of the topsy-turvy times, times that allow women to be the "man in the family," as Edna complains in Clifford Odets's play *Waiting for Lefty*. My first impulse in analyzing and even in teaching this trope is to complain of its antifeminist impulse, its implicit assertion that for things to be "right," women must be restored to their proper domestic positions. However, upon closer study, I wonder to what extent the theatricality of these characters in particular allows for a more subversive reading, and it is this potential I will explore in these pages.

It is no surprise that hostility toward working women intensified during the Great Depression. As Sara Evans explains in *Born for Liberty*, "[a]nger and frustration at the loss of jobs made women easy scapegoats" (201). In particular, this hostility was leveraged against married women, whose employment represented what Evans calls a "psychic shock" for families invested in the idea that the husband should function as primary breadwinner while the wife works at home (198–99). Indeed, fewer than one-fifth of respondents to a 1936 Gallup poll "approved" of married women working full time (qtd. in Kleinberg 219). However, as cultural historian Nancy Cott points out, although more married women got work during the Depression than before the Depression, most of these jobs continued to be domestic or personal (210). As such, although women seeking employment may have challenged traditional gender roles, these roles were simultaneously being reinforced, leading many working women to justify their employment in terms not of self-fulfillment but of how this employment met specific domestic, or household, economic needs (248).

In addition, working wives often balanced their employment outside the home with extra efforts toward domesticity within the home. But insofar as these women retained responsibility for household chores while working long hours elsewhere, "[t]he Great Depression [further] reinforced female domesticity, even as it [further] weakened women's ability to conform to the domestic ideal" (Kleinberg 246, 241). Moreover, this burden was exacerbated in that economic wretchedness strengthened the idea of the family unit as refuge, so that "the cultural perception of woman as wife and mother assumed renewed force and frequency," as Evans points out (200). Again, the economic crisis of the Great Depression caused severe disruption to traditional gender roles within the family even as it demanded these gender roles be upheld with renewed stringency.

Invoking this historical context is useful when studying Clifford Odets's 1935 episodic play *Waiting for Lefty* in that the play accrues much of its polemical power in its reflection of the idea that an unhealthy economic system destroys families and, by extension, gender roles within families. When Joe faces Edna in an empty playing space and asks, "Where's all the furniture, honey?" (7), Odets's 1935 working-class audience would have recognized the horror of losing the material things of day-to-day life and would have understood the implications of this loss for Joe and Edna's family. When Edna complains, "Everything was gonna be so ducky! A cottage by the waterfall, roses in Picardy" (9), Odets's audience would have recognized how quickly idealized images of future family happiness dissipate when the current family begins to lose its economic foothold. Both instances align Odets's audience with his characters and reaffirm what both already know: poverty erases the familiar world as suddenly and completely as the bare stage upon which Joe and Edna stand.

Not surprisingly, accompanying this erasure of the familiar—even emerging a symbol of it—is a distortion of gender roles otherwise upheld. Edna does not work outside of the home, but both she and Joe are represented as struggling to maintain their gender-specific personas. When the audience first meets Joe, he alludes to his failure to perform a masculine function by saying to the other cab drivers in his union, "There's us comin' home every night. . . . 'God,' the wife says, 'eighty cents ain't money—don't buy beans almost . . . ,' she says to me, 'Joe! you ain't workin' for me or the family no more!" (7). More significant, in Joe and Edna's scene, when Joe asks Edna what he should do, she responds, "Who's the man in the family, you or me?" (9). This question is loaded with implication. Joe's apparent inability both to support his family and to stand up to his employer recognizably strips him of his manhood, while Edna is forced into the role of the family's decision maker and metaphoric backbone. Furthermore, Edna's distress clarifies that this role reversal would have been represented as a problematic signifier to Odets's audience of difficult times, times of such economic stress that women—not men—were forced to wear the proverbial pants in the family.

However, as tempting as it is to interpret this moment as antifeminist in its implicit assertion that in order for family stability to be restored, women must be restored to their "proper" roles, this moment also challenged such an interpretation for at least two reasons.[1] First, by the end of the scene, Edna's gumption emerges a positive force in the play. Edna calls Joe a "gutless piece of boloney," but she also pushes him out of the house, exclaiming, "Sweep out those racketeers like a pile of dirt!" (12), using her temporary assumption of masculinity to restore a semblance of masculinity to her husband, encouraging Joe to take a stand, to work with his fellow cab drivers and strike against the capitalist forces that are keeping them down. Indeed, it is not a stretch to assume that in constructing her as a catalyst for Joe's conversion, Odets was asking his contemporary audience members to *identify* with Edna as they too demanded Joe to change. That is, even as audience members may have recognized "something wrong" with Edna, they also would have cheered her on—often literally standing on their feet and participating in the action, as attested to by audience accounts of actual performances.[2]

Second, and more subversive, is the degree to which Edna's momentary assumption of a masculine role would have exposed the constructivity of this role at its core. Despite the above-mentioned reverence for traditional gender roles during the 1930s, cultural historian Gail Bederman argues that the beginning of the twentieth century in the United States also brought with it an "evolutionary collapse" of these roles. Grounding her argument in the hegemonic assertion that "gender . . . was an essential component of civilization [and] one could identify advanced civilizations by the degree of their sexual differentiation," Bederman points to a direct correlation in the United States between clearly defined and distinct gender roles and a perceived nationalist identity, and she posits that the simultaneity of struggling socioeconomic groups with an increasing number of women acting like men often triggered a cause-and-effect analysis, or a popular sense that gender bending and the collapse of a recognizable middle class were intrinsically linked (25).

Indeed, as the American middle class visibly shrunk in the 1930s with more families struggling to pay their bills, traditional gender roles were at the very least implicated. In *Engendering Culture: Manhood and Womanhood in New Deal Public Art and Theater*, Barbara Melosh argues that despite widespread images of men and women in their "proper" roles, the 1930s showed Americans that any return to these roles was only a nostalgic fiction—that fundamental changes to the economy and therefore culture were demanding a new way of conceiving gender. Accordingly, both

Bederman and Melosh point to a powerful cultural desire for a character like Edna to be the "woman" and a character like Joe to be the "man"—whether to preserve the perceived evolutionary superiority of a wavering middle class or to provide a vehicle for imagining economic stability for the working class—but both also point to a larger and deeper awareness that "woman" and "man," as such, are always already constructs. Edna's subversive weight, therefore, would have existed in that audience members would have been forced to reconcile their admiration of her with their recognition of her fundamental ability to exhibit masculine traits, ultimately exposing these traits as up for grabs.

In fact, gender and gendered traits are up for grabs throughout Odets's play, suggesting the play as an important mode of resistance to other efforts at reifying discrete gendered behavior in the 1930s. For example, at a time when money was tight, working women frequently were lured to stores to buy products that could reestablish their femininity: "Ads encouraged consumption of household products," Evans suggests, "by playing on women's anxiety about not doing enough for their families" (201). Yet, in Odets's play, when Joe tries to embrace Edna, she says, "Do it in the movies, Joe—they pay Clark Gable big money for it" (8). Later in the play, when another cab driver, Miller, enters his former boss's office, he says, "I've never seen an office like this outside the movies." His former boss responds, "Yes, I often wonder if interior decorators and bathroom fixture people don't get all their ideas from Hollywood. . . . Soap, cosmetics, electric refrigerators—just let Mrs. Consumer know they're used by the Crawfords and Garbos—" And Miller interrupts, "I'm afraid it isn't that easy" (13). These examples expose, first, the man who sweeps his woman off her feet and, second, the woman who buys beautiful things for her home as dangerous myths challenged by the reality of having no disposable income. In the process, they critique the marketing of gendered behavior as the work of a capitalist system that has learned to exploit, in part, the artificial big screens of Hollywood. And, the gender roles behind these myths also are exposed as the ace-in-the-hole illusion for a capitalist economy that requires faith in illusions to thrive, especially in a time of economic distress.

This notion of a collusion between capitalism and Hollywood entertainment to reify illusions actually emerges as a theme in Odets's play. In a romantic moment between the lovers Sid and Florrie, for example, Florrie tells Sid that he looks tired and he responds, "Naw, I just need a shave." The two then role-play an elaborate scene, "like in the movies," during which she draws his chair to the fire and rings for brandy and soda while wearing her Paris gown, and he brings her "fifty or sixty dozen" roses, "the kind with long, long stems." Then, after she "poses grandly" and he takes a pretend photograph of her, the stage directions announce, "Suddenly she falls out of the posture and swiftly goes to him, to embrace him, to kiss him with love." At first, this moment is not as clear in its critique insofar as

Hollywood provides Sid and Florrie an important and even lovely moment of escape. But, Sid's next line is "You look tired, Florrie," and Florrie's next line is "Naw, I just need a shave" (19). Now, even the use of illusion to create a moment of lovely escape becomes dangerous in that—and this is underlined by the repetition of the lines—this illusion changes nothing in the real world, and therefore is not only an innocent escape but also a distraction from actions that, perhaps, could offer a viable alternative. As such, this moment emerges a call to its audience for investment in alternative forms of escape: not the money-driven, illusion-perpetuating world of Hollywood, but perhaps the revolutionary forms of social protest theatre nurtured by Odets and the Group Theatre company.

Furthermore, underlining this revolution is the exceptional gender bending that has occurred almost imperceptibly during the same scene's enactment. That is, by mimicking Sid's exact words, "Naw, I just need a shave," Florrie in fact "performs" a masculine role; but unlike Edna whose masculinity is addressed and even presented as a problem, Florrie's threat is less visible in that she remains a highly feminized character who holds onto her lover and weeps when he leaves at the scene's end. Indeed, it is precisely this invisibility that makes Florrie's performance so significant. In *Bodies that Matter*, Judith Butler writes, "[p]erformativity is . . . not a singular 'act,' for it is always a reiteration of a norm or set of norms, and to the extent that it acquires an act-like status in the present, it conceals or dissimulates the conventions of which it is a repetition (12)." Butler is not talking about stage performance, per se, but she does address the apparent "theatricality" of a performance like Florrie's: "its apparent theatricality is produced to the extent that its historicity remains dissimulated" (12). In other words, Butler's argument suggests, although an audience may dismiss Florrie's act as "performance," the existence of her act belies its function not as a singular occurrence but as a repetition of a series of occurrences that audience members have incorporated on multiple, even subconscious levels, occurrences that in fact have been normalized through historically situated (and therefore concealed) events. As such, Florrie's apparently innocuous ability to slip into and out of masculine roles again indicates that these roles are inherently "stageable," suggesting on an almost invisible level not only that gender roles are not as static but also that performances such as Florrie's are not as unusual as audience members might have liked to believe.

Moreover, the apparent naturalness with which all of these characters would have been played, a naturalness that underlines the work of Clifford Odets and the Group Theatre to which he belonged, would have further normalized their actions. Self-consciously adapting the Russian Constantin Stanislavsky's theories of method acting to the 1930s American stage, Odets argued that he would "reveal America to itself by revealing myself to myself." Similarly, Group Theatre director Harold Clurman argued that "our interest in the life of our times must lead us to the discovery of those methods that would most truly convey this life through theatre" (qtd. in

Chinoy 479). This "depth and sureness of acting technique that sometimes startled audiences with its realistic detail and range," as theatre scholars Mel Gordon and Laurie Lassiter describe the Group Theatre's work, was deliberately incorporated into—indeed, tested through—the 1935 production of *Waiting for Lefty* (6). And the test was a success. Actress Ruth Nelson, who played Edna, remembers: "We were all lined up . . . and when they couldn't applaud any more, they stomped their feet." Critic Henry Senber wrote, "I had witnessed an event of historical importance in what is academically referred to as the drama of the contemporary American scene" (qtd. in Seward and Barbour 40). Clurman recalls that "[t]he first scene of *Lefty* had not played two minutes when a shock of delighted recognition struck the audience like a tidal wave" (147–48).

These responses demonstrate both the Group Theatre's self-conscious attempt to perform naturalistically and the degree to which this attempt reached its 1935 audience, suggesting that whereas "traditional" gender roles could be critiqued as Hollywood illusions on Odets's stage, any gender bending performed by the women characters within Odets's play was not only rendered as realistic, but also celebrated. Accordingly, the "crisis of masculinity" commonly experienced in the 1930s and represented in *Waiting for Lefty* is blamed not on the "psychic shock" of women who might act like men but squarely, polemically on a money-hungry, war-driven capitalist economy.

Importantly, this phenomenon of gender bending in plays that challenged capitalist principles was not limited to *Waiting for Lefty* but spread across American working-class theatre in the 1930s. Perhaps most notable were the epic living-newspaper plays, which like *Waiting for Lefty* had widespread popular appeal with working-class audiences. As theatre historian Stuart Cosgrove attests in his introduction to a collection of living-newspaper plays, "[t]o the audiences of the depression, their own immediate economic and environmental problems provided the material for a campaigning theatre of social reform" (ix).[3] However, unlike *Waiting for Lefty*, the living-newspaper plays employed antinaturalistic acting techniques more in line with Bertolt Brecht's theories of alienation, techniques that involved hyperperformativity or the hyperpresence of the actor's body on stage so that audience members would be invited not so much to enter the world of the play as to critique the play's subjects from a place of intellectual distance. Studying living-newspaper plays alongside *Lefty*, therefore, is relevant for at least two reasons. First, it affirms that the gender bending in Odets's play was broadly present on a number of American stages around the country. Second, it allows for closer examination of the stage itself—in its use of real bodies "performing" their roles—as a medium exceptionally conducive for this kind of fluidity.

Central to Brecht's impact is his call for an epic theatre that appeals to the audience's intellect, not empathy. As he writes, "[t]he essential point of the epic theatre is perhaps that it appeals less to the feelings than to the spectator's reason. Instead of sharing an experience the spectator must come to grips with things" ("Epic" 23). In its experimental staging, *Waiting for Lefty* certainly would have encouraged audience members to talk about the ideas in the play, but the primary goal of the Group Theatre's naturalistic acting style aimed more to reach an audience's emotions, even empathy, than intellect, encouraging audience members to recognize themselves in the characters and to weep or cheer accordingly. In contrast, in his "Short Description of a New Technique of Acting which Produces an Alienation Effect," Brecht calls for an acting style that makes "the spectator adopt an attitude of inquiry and criticism in his approach to the incident." He continues, "[i]t is well known that contact between audience and stage is normally made on the basis of empathy. . . . [The] technique which produces an A-effect is the exact opposite of that which aims at empathy" (136–37). As Brecht explains:

> Because he doesn't identify himself with [his character,] [the actor] can pick a definite attitude to adopt towards the character whom he portrays, can show what he thinks of him and invite the spectator . . . to criticize the character portrayed. The attitude he adopts is a socially critical one. In his exposition of the incidents and in his characterization of the person he tries to bring out those features which come within society's sphere. In this way his performance becomes a discussion (about social conditions) with the audience he is addressing. ("Short" 139)

As such, the actor pursues techniques that tend to heighten the theatricality of his or her performance, using gesture, for example, to "pretend" he or she is inhabiting the character's body but ensuring the audience always is aware that in fact it is the actor's body they are watching on stage.

Part of what Brecht's alienation effect achieves, then, is a re-envisioning or making-strange of reality for audience members. According to Brecht, "characters and incidents from ordinary life, from our immediate surroundings, being familiar, strike us as more or less natural. Alienating them helps to make them seem remarkable to us" ("Short" 140). Fredric Jameson focuses on this phenomenon in *Brecht and Method*: "To make something look strange, to make us look at it with new eyes, implies the antecedence of a general familiarity, of a habit which prevents us from really looking at things, a kind of perceptual numbness. . . . Brecht . . . inventoried the techniques whereby things could in fact be 'estranged'" (39). Here, Jameson points to Brecht's artistic methods as a means of exposing to an audience the constructivity—or historicity, as Jameson calls it—of day-to-day realities the audience might otherwise accept as somehow natural or universal. This has tremendous political implication. According to Jameson, the estrangement of the familiar or habitual "shows the object to be instead 'historical,' to which may be added, as a political corollary, made or constructed by human beings, and thus able to be changed by them as well" (40). Indeed, as Brecht's theories spread across the ocean to the United States in the 1930s, this ability of theatre to reveal to an audience its own role in historical activity was perhaps their most appealing addition to contemporary dramaturgy.

And, perhaps more than any other theatre genre, the living-newspaper plays of the 1930s reflected Brechtian dramaturgy.[4] *The Concise Oxford Companion to the Theatre* describes a living-newspaper play as a "a form of stage production which employed documentary sources to present subjects of current social importance, usually in a sequence of short scenes with individualized dialogue alongside more abstract, often didactic, presentation." Cosgrove writes, "[b]y the time the Living Newspaper came to the Federal Theatre Project, its more dynamic form of dramatic expression and theatrical modes of presentation were already well developed.... As a form of drama, it irrefutably belongs to a materialist tradition within modern drama, which like the work of Bertolt Brecht, Erwin Piscator, and Vsevolod Meyerhold was committed to using new and political forms of stagecraft" (ix-x). In 1990, Gerry Cobb connects the form even more clearly to the experimental forms of political theatre theorized by Brecht: "Central to [the Living Newspaper plays] is the question of anti-naturalistic practice.... [The] use of symbol rather than fleshed-out characterization serves ... to subvert the audience's tendency for empathetic identification.... [Instead,] the makers of agit-prop theatre invited their spectators to receive their political message through a process of rational and objective analysis, to position themselves in the processes of history and to perceive their own role in it" (281).

More to my argument, living-newspaper plays frequently featured an array of women characters in masculine roles, similar to *Waiting for Lefty*, but the antinaturalistic hyperperformativity of these roles—even more than in *Lefty*—would have emphasized the femaleness not only of the character, but also of the actor. In *Unmaking Mimesis*, Elin Diamond argues that Brechtian historicization enables exactly this phenomenon:

> Brechtian historicization insists that [the] body is not a fixed essence but a site of struggle and change. If feminist theory is concerned with the multiple and complex signs of a woman's life—her desires and politics, her class, ethnicity, or race—what I want to call her *historicity*, Brechtian theory gives us a way to put that historicity in view—in the theatre.... [The] performer's body is ... loaded with its own history and that of the character, and these histories roughen the smooth edges of the image, of representation. (52)

When looking at living-newspaper plays, Diamond's argument suggests, it therefore becomes important to remember that these plays' Brechtian dramaturgy in particular would have made more visible the bodies of female actors as well as characters and to imagine the effect this might have had on their contemporary audiences.

The living-newspaper pageant play *1935* employs gesture, for example, a familiar Brechtian acting technique, to highlight the similarities rather than differences between working male and female bodies in an economically exploitive system. At the end of scene 4, a factory girl stands up to her boss: "Well, we're not going back to work. What the hell do you think this is? We're going to strike. Girls, how about it?" At this point, a group of at least ten other factory girls echo, "Strike! Strike!" and then one girl steps toward the boss and exclaims, "Come on, girls. We demand our rights" (24–25). In scene 14 of the same play, this memorable gesture is nearly repeated but with male characters. Now, a male character exclaims, "Strike!"; another male character demands, "Restore the wage cuts"; and as in the previous scene the workers take a single step forward, toward their boss (50). Both scenes forcefully demonstrate to their audience the power of multiple bodies—women's bodies as well as men's bodies—in seeking equity within a capitalist framework. More significant, the staging of the scenes would have heightened this power by downplaying the psychological realism of each moment and emphasizing instead its material reality, encouraging audience members to see and think about the literal, physical connection between male and female bodies, especially when these bodies are demanding rights from a more privileged sector of the economy.

This movement toward sex equality would have been even more evident in the 1936 living-newspaper play *Injunction Granted*. Similar to the above scenes from *1935*, scene 28 in *Injunction Granted* features a group of female laundry workers arguing for a law to protect their rights and then features a group of male steelworkers arguing for a similar law. These two groups use almost the same language—"I tell you, what we need is a law!" and "What we need is a law" (136–37)—and the response to this language is almost the same as well: a voice over the loudspeaker announces the implementation of the requested law, but then a judge follows this announcement by declaring the requested law unconstitutional. Furthermore, as the scene continues an unidentified worker enters the playing space and asks the female laundry workers, "Can you get a living wage without collective bargaining?"; one laundry worker responds, "No!"; the unidentified worker asks the male steel workers, "Will the courts help you?"; the steelworkers respond, "No!"; and the unidentified worker concludes, "Then the answer is in ourselves. In you . . . in me. All workers must be brought into unions" (138). As in *1935*, this moment highlights the radical connection between male and female workers, a connection clearly informed by an equalizing communist ideology, but now this connection is established within a single scene, self-consciously underscoring the inclusiveness of the phrase "all workers" and demanding that audience members recognize and think harder about the fluidity of gender roles.

In fact, these more overt representations of sex equality—especially given other efforts in the 1930s to emphasize sex distinction—are not surprising given the communist overtones of most living-newspaper plays. As Sara Evans writes, "[t]he Communist party in the 1930s was at the center of a radical ferment encompassing a wide range of socialist and anarchist groups" (213), including the integration of sexes in reform movements.

However, although women were readily accepted into the Communist Party and encouraged to organize, advocacy of women-centered issues often was relegated to the sidelines. Evans explains, "[w]ithin such radical circles there was discussion of 'the woman question,' but feminism was considered a bourgeois reform in the context of the socialist revolution" (213). More surprisingly, Evans argues, "for the most part, unions continued to share the view that women belonged in the home, not in the factory. . . . Organizers rarely operated with a sensitivity to the specific problems of women workers" (215). And, to a degree, this antagonism between advocating for women's involvement in issues of social justice and dismissing the need for reform specific to women's interests is highlighted in living-newspaper plays such as *1935* and *Injunction Granted* in their radical movement toward equalizing the concerns of working-class Americans, whether male or female. This movement marks these plays as significant sites for exposing contemporary tensions between validating women's voices in labor reform and making it more difficult to imagine the validity of concerns that might implicitly single out women workers as different.

These tensions are complicated further in the 1939 living-newspaper play *Medicine Show*, which launches a wide critique on America's health care industry. Toward the beginning of the play, Mr. Busby showcases what the play appears to uphold as an "ideal hospital," what Mr. Busby calls "a complete picture of all the facilities of modern medicine that social organization and science could make available" (182). In the process of demonstrating the benefits of this more socialized vision of health care to First Citizen, who functions as a conduit for the play's actual audience, Mr. Busby learns that First Citizen is married. Immediately and significantly, he directs First Citizen, "Then you'd be interested in the maternity ward" (178). Here and elsewhere in this staged version of an "ideal" health system, as Mr. Busby calls it, the relationship between women's bodies and maternity is represented not as fluid, or constructed, but as natural—suggesting the play as propaganda for the idea that the creation of an economically ideal world in part means restoration of "natural," biologically encoded gender roles.

Furthermore, as the scene shifts from Mr. Busby's tour of an idealized situation to one of economic deprivation, childbirth is no longer something to be shown off in a special maternity ward, suggesting a connection between the *un*naturalness of poverty and the *un*naturalness of a woman who doesn't want to have babies. When asked if she has children, the "cheaply dressed" Mary responds, "Please don't make me talk about that. Do I have to answer?" (192). And when she is told by her diagnostician that she is going to have another child, Mary responds, "No. ... No!" and then "begins to cry quietly" (228). The dichotomy here between the ideal, represented through the celebration of a maternity ward, and the real, represented through the fears of an impoverished expectant mother, is brutally exposed to audience members, who may begin to wonder (as with *Waiting for Lefty*) if the contemporary separation of women from their traditional gender roles could in part be a result of poverty—and by extension, if returning women to their traditional gender roles could impossibly provoke a return to economic equity.

However, this provocation of a nostalgic desire for traditional, distinct gender roles in response to the harsh realities of poverty is importantly challenged elsewhere in the play. Indeed, *Medicine Show* emerges an especially potent case study for Brecht's insistence on what Marvin Carlson calls the "Hegelian dialectic [as] a stimulating tool for dramaturgical exploration" (383). On a smaller scale, after four chairs are placed on stage for "the ladies," who had been on their feet all day, the stage directions indicate, "[t]hree of the chairs are occupied by the three women, the fourth is taken by Ben C." (195). These directions are not accompanied by any explanation, are not presented as a joke or as having any hidden significance. Instead, the most legitimate explanation simply is that Ben C. also had been on his feet all day, and that any need to justify or apologize for the body of a working man having biological needs similar to the body of a working woman isn't that reasonable in times of economic distress.

More significant for being lifted outside a context of economic distress are the female characters who, like characters in other living-newspaper plays, are positioned in masculine roles but who, unlike these other characters, demonstrate that women can play these roles above the poverty line as well as below. For example, a female character from the Sacramento Health Department explains, "Smears from lungs of the patient show gram negative hi-polar straining bacilli—diagnosis confirmed!" (175). This female character's technical language and knowledge indicate her position of power, which is explosive for a 1930s audience in its suggestion that gender bending is not by necessity limited to a matrix of economic deprivation. And, the female actor playing this role would have emphasized this suggestion by heightening the theatricality of the moment and encouraging audience members to notice and think about details of the scene represented on the stage. Again, the living newspapers of the 1930s strove for intellectual engagement. According to Carlson, the goal of Brecht's theatre was educative, "to expose the hidden contradictions within ... society" (384). Accordingly, as much as *Medicine Show* offers a link between economic stability and healthy maternity, it also represents options other than motherhood for its more economically stable women characters, prodding audience members toward the realization that traditional gender roles and economic equity might not be a "natural" pairing after all.

Indeed, it is arguable that social protest theatre in the 1930s provided its audience options for reconsidering gendered norms that weren't always available in mainstream culture or even in more radical cultural networks. As Sarah Evans laments, "[t]he absence of a movement which articulated women's specific concerns and interests, even as women attained new positions of power, deprived many activists outside the New Deal of the supportive networks of other women as well as a feminist perspective with which to interpret the sexism pervading their lives" (210–11). The plays these activists saw as audience members at the very least provided perspective and insight into the complex intersections of economic and sex discrimination that touched the lives of working-class Americans during the 1930s.

In his 1935 *New York Times* review of *Waiting for Lefty*, critic Brooks Atkinson wrote, "the progress of the revolutionary drama in New York City during the last two seasons is the most obvious recent development in our theatre." Atkinson recognized the revolutionary potential of the plays that were emerging around him. And, whereas much of this potential existed in the degree to which these plays used new dramaturgical techniques—whether rooted in Stanislavsky or in Brecht—to call for an economic equity informed by political ideology, part of it lay in the extent to which the economically overturned world represented in these plays was related to the ability of women characters to escape identification tropes a more stable world might demand. Then and now, this relationship has the extraordinary power to lead audience members to a spectrum of difficult questions: is economic stability imaginatively or even materially linked to the preservation of traditional gender roles? If so, to what extent does watching women's bodies perform the roles of men invoke nostalgia in economically distressed audience members for discrete gender identification? And to what extent does watching women's bodies perform the roles of men instead pave the way for gender fluidity and perhaps equity above as well as below the poverty line in America?

NOTES

1. Almost no recent critical interpretations of *Waiting for Lefty* exist, despite the play's tremendous popularity in the 1930s and its continued anthologizing today. Alan File's 1999 article engages with the more political aspects of Odets's play by analyzing the history of the play's textual changes; Russell DiNapoli's 2001 article uses *Waiting for Lefty* as a case study for the broader idea that dramatic texts can teach students how to think more dialogically; and Lawrence Raw et al. write about staging a revival of *Waiting for Lefty* in Ankara, Turkey, in 2004. Lee Papa's 1995 dissertation looks a bit at the relationship between gender and the labor drama of the American 1930s, including *Waiting for Lefty*, but largely insofar as this drama "became an educational and organizational tool [for reflecting an] expanding female presence" in the labor movement at large (Papa, "Staging Communities").

2. The first *New York Times* review of the performance described the play as "warmly received" ("Group Theatre's Benefit"). Harold Clurman writes about the play's opening performance: "Deep laughter, hot assent, a kind of joyous fervor seemed to sweep the audience toward the stage. The actors no longer performed; they were being carried along as if by an exultancy of communication such as I had never witnessed in the theatre before. Audience and actors had become one. Line after line brought applause, whistles, bravos, and heartfelt shouts of kinship" (148). Lori Seward and David Barbour write about the same performance, "[n]o one was prepared for the overwhelming audience reaction to the play. The cast took approximately 28 curtain calls. 'The audience was absolutely transported.' Ruth Nelson [the actress who played Edna] remembers it this way" (39). Furthermore, as the play continued its run, its popularity rose, in particular with working-class audiences. According to Seward and Barbour, "despite the publicity accorded the Broadway production, *Waiting for Lefty*'s greatest fame came from the many productions by unions, schools, and amateur groups across the country throughout the 1930s. It is no longer revived as frequently as other Odets plays, but it nonetheless exerted an extraordinary power over 1930s audiences" (48).
3. There are very few primary resources for scholars of the living newspaper on the American stage. One is the Library of Congress, in particular files pertaining to the New Deal and more specifically to the Federal Theatre Project. Some of these files can be accessed online through the Library of Congress's homepage. Others are in the *New York Times*, in particular reviews by Brooks Atkinson published during the 1930s; and Hallie Flanagan's memoir *Arena*, which details the living newspaper's history as part of the Federal Theatre Project. Other out-of-print resources are the Federal Theatre Playscript Publication published by the Federal Theatre Project's Play Bureau in 1937; two collections (*Federal Theatre Plays: Triple-A Plowed Under, Power, Spirochete* and *Federal Theatre Plays: Prologue to Glory, One-Third of a Nation, Haiti*) both introduced by Hallie Flanagan and published by Random House in 1938; and *Liberty Deferred*, introduced by Stuart Cosgrove and used in this chapter. The first American living newspaper, *Ethiopia*, is introduced by Dan Isaac and reprinted in *Educational Theatre Journal* in 1968. Finally, in his introduction to *Staged Action*, Lee Papa voices his intent to publish "in the future" a much-needed collection of plays from the Federal Theatre Project (xii).
4. It is worth noting that the antecedents of the living newspaper in America are contested. Living newspaper actor Norman Lloyd writes, "[m]y first knowledge of [the living newspaper] comes from Piscator, who was a European director and who worked with Brecht. They had what they called Epic theatre, a theatre that was antinaturalistic and more expressionistic. You use film and you use projections. It was quite stylized. Its purpose was a learning kind of theatre, so to speak" (28). Conversely, theatre scholar Ilka Saal claims, "[w]hen Bertolt Brecht attempted to transfer his concept of political theatre to the United States in 1935, he was faced with two dilemmas: his American colleagues had no idea what epic theatre was, and even more importantly, they had no interest in it" (101). *The Cassell Companion to Theatre* defines the living newspaper as "a form of didactic documentary theatre that arose in America in the 1930s"; *The Cambridge Guide to Theatre* alternatively claims that "antecedents can be identified"; *The Oxford Companion to the Theatre* claims further that "many antecedents have been claimed for the Living Newspaper technique, from Russia, Germany, China, and particularly from Vienna, whose Spontaneity Theatre, founded

by J. L. Moreno in 1921, brought psychodrama to New York in 1925"; and *The Oxford Encyclopedia of Theatre and Performance* posits that the living newspaper is a "species of documentary theatre pioneered by the Blue Blouses and others in the Soviet Union and by Piscator in Berlin in the 1920s ... [and] adapted in the 1930s by the Unity Theatre and Theatre of Action in Britain and the Federal Theatre Project in the United States." Part of the problem is that so few critical interpretations of the living newspaper exist. Lynn Mally's important 2003 article discusses the Soviet roots of the living newspaper (*zhivaia gazeta*); Douglas McDermott's older article discusses the living newspaper's Russian as well as German roots; John W. Casson's 2000 article distinguishes the living newspaper plays from Moreno's spontaneity theatre, arguing that "the Living Newspaper movement, which from 1919 to 1940 was a global, creative, revolutionary theatre, owed nothing to Moreno" (121); and John E. Vacha's 1986 article studies the development and political/aesthetic history of the living newspaper in America.

BIBLIOGRAPHY

1935. Liberty Deferred and Other Living Newspapers of the 1930s. 1936. Fairfax: George Mason UP, 1989. Print.
Atkinson, Brooks. "*Waiting for Lefty*." Rev. of *Waiting for Lefty*, by Clifford Odets. *New York Times* 11 Feb. 1935. Web. 8 Aug. 2009.
Bederman, Gail. *Manliness and Civilization: A Cultural History of Gender and Race in the United States, 1880–1917*. Chicago: U of Chicago P, 1995. Print.
Brecht, Bertolt. "The Epic Theatre and its Difficulties." *Brecht on Theatre: The Development of an Aesthetic*. Trans. John Willett. 1927. New York: Hill and Wang, 1964. Print.
———. "Short Description of a New Technique of Acting which Produces an Alienation Effect." *Brecht on Theatre: The Development of an Aesthetic*. 1941. Trans. John Willett. New York: Hill and Wang, 1964. Print.
Butler, Judith. *Bodies that Matter: On the Discursive Limits of "Sex."* New York: Routledge, 1993. Print.
Carlson, Marvin. *Theories of the Theatre: A Historical and Critical Survey, from the Greeks to the Present*. 1984. Ithaca: Cornell UP, 1993. Print.
Casson, John W. "Living Newspaper: Theatre and Therapy." *Drama Review* 44.2 (2000): 107–22. *MLA Database*. Web. 20 Jan. 2010.
Chinoy, Helen Krich. "The Poetics of Politics: Some Notes on Style and Craft in the Theatre of the Thirties." *Theatre Journal* 35.4 (1983): 475–98. *MLA Database*. Web. 8 Aug. 2009.
Clurman, Harold. *The Fervent Years: The Group Theatre and the Thirties*. New York: Da Capo, 1983. Print.
Cobb, Gerry. "*Injunction Granted* in its Times: A Living Newspaper Reappraised." *New Theatre Quarterly* 6.23 (1990): 279–96. *MLA Database*. Web. 8 Aug. 2009.
Cosgrove, Stuart. Introduction. *Liberty Deferred and Other Living Newspapers of the 1930s*. Fairfax: George Mason UP, 1989. Print.
Cott, Nancy F. *The Grounding of Modern Feminism*. New Haven: Yale UP, 1987. Print.
Diamond, Elin. *Unmaking Mimesis: Essays on Feminism and Theater*. New York: Routledge, 1997. Print.
DiNapoli, Russell. "The Logical Status of Dramatic Activity When Teaching American Literature." *Teaching American Literature in Spanish Universities*. Ed. Carme Manuel. U de Valencia, 2001. *MLA Database*. Web. 20 Jan. 2010.

Evans, Sara M. *Born for Liberty: A History of Women in America*. 1989. New York: Simon and Schuster, 1997. Print.

Filewood, Alan. "A Qualified Workers Theatre Art: *Waiting for Lefty* and the (Re) Formation of Popular Front Theatres." *Essays in Theatre/Etudes Theatrales* 17.2 (1999): 111–28. MLA Database. Web. 20 Jan. 2010.

Flanagan, Hallie. *Arena*. New York: Duell, Sloan and Pearce, 1940. Print.

Gordon, Mel, and Laurie Lassiter. "Acting Experiments in the Group." *Drama Review* 28.4 (1984): 6–12. MLA Database. Web. 8 Aug. 2009.

"Group Theatre's Benefit." *New York Times* 28 Jan. 1935. ProQuest Historical Newspapers. Web. 29 Nov. 2009.

Injunction Granted. Liberty Deferred and Other Living Newspapers of the 1930s. 1936. Fairfax: George Mason UP, 1989. Print.

Jameson, Fredric. *Brecht and Method*. New York: Verso, 1998. Print.

Kleinberg, S. J. *Women in the United States, 1830–1945*. New Brunswick: Rutgers UP, 1999. Print.

"Living Newspaper." *The Cambridge Guide to Theatre*. Ed. Martin Banham. New York: Cambridge UP, 1995. Print.

———. *Cassell Companion to Theatre*. Ed. Jonathan Law et al. 1994. Aylesbury: Market House, 1997. Print.

———. *The Concise Oxford Companion to the Theatre*. Web. 12 Nov. 2009.

———. *The Oxford Companion to the Theatre*. Ed. Phyllis Hartnoll. 4th ed. New York: Oxford UP, 1983. Print.

———. *The Oxford Encyclopedia of Theatre and Performance*. Ed. Dennis Kennedy. New York: Oxford UP, 2003. Print.

Lloyd, Norman. "The Living Newspaper." *Voices from the Federal Theatre*. Ed. Bonnie Nelson Schwartz and the Educational Film Center. Madison: U of Wisconsin P, 2003. Print.

Mally, Lynn. "Exporting Soviet Culture: The Case of Agitprop Theater." *Slavic Review* 62.2 (2003): 324–42. MLA Database. Web. 20 Jan. 2010.

McDermott, Douglas. "The Living Newspaper as a Dramatic Form." *Modern Drama* 8 (1965): 82–94. MLA Database. Web. 20 Jan. 2010.

Medicine Show. Liberty Deferred and Other Living Newspapers of the 1930s. 1939. Fairfax: George Mason UP, 1989. Print.

Melosh, Barbara. *Engendering Culture: Manhood and Womanhood in New Deal Public Art and Theater*. Washington, DC: Smithsonian Institute P., 1991. Print.

Odets, Clifford. *Waiting for Lefty. Waiting for Lefty and Other Plays*. 1935. New York: Grove, 1979. Print.

Papa, Lee. Introduction. *Staged Action: Six Plays from the American Workers' Theatre*. Ithaca: Cornell UP, 2009. Print.

———. "Staging Communities in Early Twentieth-Century American Labor Drama." Diss. U of Tennessee-Knoxville, 1995. ProQuest. Web. 20 Jan. 2010.

Raw, Lawrence, et al. "Staging *Waiting for Lefty*: Or, Agit-Prop in Ankara." *Journal of American Studies of Turkey* 19 (2004): 117–25. MLA Database. Web. 20 Jan. 2010.

Saal, Ilka. "Vernacularizing Brecht: The Political Theatre of the New Deal." *Interrogating America through Theatre and Performance*. Ed. William W. Demastes and Iris Smith Fischer. New York: Palgrave Macmillan, 2007. Print.

Seward, Lori, and David Barbour. "Waiting for Lefty." *Drama Review* 28.4 (1984): 38–48. 1995. MLA Database. Web. 8 Aug. 2009.

Vacha, John E. "The Federal Theatre's Living Newspapers: New York's Docudramas of the Thirties." *New York History* 67.1 (1986): 67–88. MLA Database. Web. 20 Jan. 2010.

12 Henry Roth's Reimagination of Class Consciousness from *Call it Sleep* to the *Mercy of a Rude Stream* Novels

Class Consciousness, Nationalist Politics, and Working-Class Studies in the Age of Cosmopolitanism

Tim Libretti

Writing in 1985 about the Six-Day War between Arab and Israeli forces in 1967, famed author of *Call It Sleep* Henry Roth recalls:

> When the '67 War broke out it acted upon me like a second vector, to borrow a term from mathematics, a second impulse acting in the same direction as the first, and reinforcing it. The Jewish identity came to the fore, asserting itself in consciousness. Not only that, but something else was being catalyzed, a changed personality, at last, an individual with an increasingly firm point of view, an ideology, however spotty, but durable, tenable, a new bond with tradition, a new reunion with folk. (*Shifting* 173)

Specifically, what he discovers is not just his Jewish ethnic identity but, as he puts it, importantly, he rediscovers his "nation." He relates becoming conscious of his "latent conviction that the individual *per se* disintegrates unless he associates himself with an institution of some sort, with a larger entity. I could not find that kind of bond in religion, and I do not think Israelis do either. I found it in the existence of a nation" (175). Interesting here is Roth's comprehension of his Jewish identity in not simply ethnic terms but in national terms, an identification that would evolve and strengthen until his death in the mid-1990s, during a time when in literary and cultural studies the category or political subject of the nation was being largely maligned—as it still is—as an agent of historical change, understood in rather one-sided terms by the then-ascendant and still current postcolonial and cosmopolitical theory as a largely regressive agency and politics, favoring instead a cosmopolitanism over what it tends to view as the narrowness of nationalism.

Similarly, the Marxist Left, in its most traditional articulations of working-class internationalism, has a strong, though admittedly not univocal, hostility to nationalist politics, especially Zionism, tending to see nationalist politics as not rooted in a materialist understanding of global political economic relationships, but rather as an irrational political exuberance and psychological outbreak resulting from a reactionary cultural politics divorced from history and objective material relationships. Yet Roth, who arguably remained a Left-identified writer and Marxist sympathizer to the end, recounts in 1997 his struggles in "trying to think what the hell do I feel about Communism, what do I feel about Israel, what do I feel about Judaism, and why" (*Shifting* 173), suggesting that he did not so much see the politics of each as necessarily incompatible with each other but rather as a web of relationships constituting an ideological puzzle of sorts to be worked out as a way of comprehending not only class politics on a global scale but his own working-class identity. Indeed, to take his analogy most literally, his Zionist attachment sparked by the Six-Day War did not alter or in any way redirect his political thinking or consciousness but was a "second vector . . . a second impulse acting in the same direction as the first, and reinforcing it," indicating that this emergent political sensibility elaborated and deepened, even strengthened, his Marxist understanding of class politics and working-class identity. As Roth tended to work through these issues in deeply personal ways in the thinly veiled autobiographical narratives that are his novels, from *Call It Sleep* to the later *Mercy of a Rude Stream* series, these narratives provide fertile empirical ground for exploring the vexed and historically controversial place of nationalist politics and identity in formulations of radical working-class politics, culture, and consciousness.

His struggles to reconcile Marxism and Judaism spurred by the Six-Day War finally achieve fruition in the *Mercy of a Rude Stream* series precisely through his rejection of the high modernism of Joyce, whose "severance from the folk," Roth writes, "had provided no exchange . . . from a specific people to a universal one, from the parochial to the cosmopolitan" (*From Bondage* 68). Whereas in *Call It Sleep* Roth's narrative works to resolve, even dissolve or erase, potentially conflictive ethnic and racial identities into a unified multiethnic or polyglot working-class identity and solidarity, these later novels constitute a recognition that these identities—particularly as they constitute *national* identities—cannot merely be swept under the rug by the universalizing wish-fulfillment of high modernist representational forms but that there must be a dialectical process, "an exchange," that addresses and negotiates, if only to move through, national and ethnic identities in order to adequately resolve questions of cultural, ethnic, and racial difference, and—most important for the purposes of this chapter—national identity within the class question.[1]

Roth, in finally coming to terms with his Jewish identity and Israeli national identification, can be read as both diagnosing and advancing working-class or proletarian literary forms of the 1930s and as providing a complex rethinking of the relationship between the categories of working class and nation. Just as *Call It Sleep* motivated a rethinking of proletarian literature in the 1930s because of its deployment of modernist form and its profoundly psychologistic approach to representing working-class experience, the later *Mercy of a Rude Stream* novels, as they effectively reread and rewrite the working-class experiences—and extended experiences—of *Call It Sleep* through the lens of a Jewish national identification, in both political and literary terms, also invite us to reevaluate and broaden the boundaries of our understanding of working-class literary practice and politics. They invite this reevaluation of cultural practice precisely because they represent working-class identity in at once broader and more specific ways; that is, in these novels, Roth presents a broadened sense of working-class identity by focusing on the "parochial" or "specific" Jewish national components of his working-class identity in order to facilitate the "exchange" to a revised and more complex "universal" or "cosmopolitan" working-class identity and politics that is comprehensive of the internal differences of its various constituencies.

In this chapter, focusing on Roth's literary career, I will argue for the necessity of a critical approach to working-class literature that focuses on the internally colonized nations of the U.S. working class, comprehending their literary production as often constituting working-class literatures and exploring the way their representations of working-class experience correct impoverished nondialectical understandings of class and class consciousness that preclude the comprehension that classes are composed not only of peoples of different genders, diverse races, and sexual orientations but also of different nations within the United States. I follow, among others, Robin D. G. Kelley, who underscores theories of intersectionality, emphasizing that "[t]here is no universal class identity, just as there is no universal racial or sexual identity," offering a critique of Left ideologues who take "for granted that movements focused on race, gender, or sexuality necessarily undermine class unity and, by definition, cannot be emancipatory for the whole" (86–87). Kelley's point challenges simple dichotomies between so-called Marxist politics and identity politics, underscoring how Marxist constructions of the proletariat as the agent of revolutionary transformation also constitute an identity politics. Moreover, any construction of the proletariat, of working-class identity, implicitly contains a racial, gender, sexual, and indeed, a *national* political dimension, just as constructions of sexual, racial, gender, or national identities contain a class politics, whether explicitly acknowledged or not.

Kelley's critique of a universal class identity provides an impetus to my explorations into the identity politics underlying our understandings of working-class literature and culture. I want to extend his analysis to consider the category of nation. Just as Kelley reminds us that any construction of working-class identity has a sexual, racial, and gender political dimension, so Vladimir Medem reminds us that any working-class culture must, of necessity, have a national component, its pretensions to internationalism notwithstanding, stressing that "internationalist culture is not anational" and that an "anational culture" is "an absurdity"(qtd. in Traverso 7). In this chapter I want to draw out the often invisible national dimensions of working-class identity, and Roth provides the perfect study given that the national component of his working-class identity was hidden from himself, repressed, for so long.

As I chart through Roth's literary career the evolution of a U.S. "third world" radical working-class consciousness, I will bring to bear the developmental models of national culture theorized by Frantz Fanon on U.S. working-class literature to comprehend the literary practice of U.S. third-world, or internally colonized, working-class writers in the production of class consciousness. In part 1, I explore Roth's relationship between his ethnic/national and working-class components of his identity in political and literary terms in the context of his development as a writer in the 1930s and in relation to American working-class writers of color on the Left, such as Richard Wright, who did in fact comprehend their racial identity in nationalist terms. In connecting Roth—via the belated return of his repressed national consciousness in the 1960s—to the 1930s working-class writers who reconciled nationalist and internationalist politics and to debates on the Marxist left in that era over whether to understand people of color as racial minorities or oppressed nations, I hope to provide a radical working-class literary and political tradition in which to rethink the contours of an American working-class literary tradition and class consciousness. In part 2, I assess the significance of Roth's later writings in the context of the shared antinationalist discourse of versions of working-class internationalist politics and contemporary postcolonial theory that threaten to disarm more supple and vitally necessary comprehensions of class and formulations of class consciousness.

I. NATIONALISM AND '30S WORKING-CLASS LITERARY AND POLITICAL RADICALISM

In his famous defense of Bigger Thomas in Richard Wright's 1940 novel *Native Son*, Boris Max articulates an understanding of the racial oppression African Americans endure in the U.S. as a form of colonial or national oppression, as he argues to the jury, "Taken collectively, [African Americans] are not simply twelve million people; in reality they constitute a separate nation, stunted, stripped, and held captive *within* this nation, devoid of political, social, economic, and property rights" (Wright 463). Max's closing statement here echoes a variation of the Communist Party's Black Belt thesis of the era, which understood African Americans as an oppressed or colonized nation within the U.S. nation and entitled to their own territory to practice self-determination.

Wright was not alone in representing this political perspective on the class situation of African Americans and other racialized populations. Among Left writers and intellectuals of color in the 1930s, the perspective that the experience of racial oppression and exploitation in the United States was one of colonization, or internal colonization, and necessitated a nationalist political response, understood not as separate from working-class struggle but as an integral part of it, held considerable currency. Eugene Gordon argued at the American Writers' Congress in 1935 that the social problems facing African Americans grew out of their "peculiar economic position in the United States" that developed "in the Black Belt of the United States, from a heterogeneous hodge-podge of antagonistic tribes and races, representing different levels of economic growth, into a homogeneous people representing all the characteristics of a nation" (145). In *Black Bolshevik*, Harry Haywood recounts arguing at the Sixth Congress of the Comintern in 1928 that African Americans' struggle for self-determination as a nation be understood "as a struggle attacking the very foundation of American imperialism, an integral part of the struggle of the American working class as a whole" (264). Similar debates on the Left regarding whether racialized peoples be understood as racial minorities, whose political mission was to fight for full social equality, or as oppressed nations, whose liberation would be achieved most effectively by struggling for self-determination, took place with regard to people of Mexican descent living in the American Southwest. Américo Paredes's 1930s novel *George Washington Gómez*, for example, implicitly enters this debate, advocating a nationalist anticolonial politics for Mexicans and Mexican Americans enduring racial labor exploitation in the Southwest, whereas the Communist Party argued that Mexicans in the Southwest constituted a racial minority that needed to ally with the Anglo working class to fight for liberation.[2]

Thus, within the radical working-class and Left literary tradition, we see writers committed to a Marxist internationalist revolutionary politics who also comprehend the experience of the racial group with whom they affiliate in national terms. These writers grapple with issues of national identity and the place of nationalist politics within a larger political narrative of working-class struggle, at times with ambivalence but often with a sense of historical inevitability. The case of Carlos Bulosan provides an interesting analogue and context for studying Roth's relationship with his national identity. In March 1946, in the wake of World War II, as the rhetoric and repression of the cold war heightened and U.S. imperialism picked up in the Philippines where the Japanese left off, Filipino American proletarian writer Bulosan writes to a compatriot in exile, "[t]here are things for us to do in America in the name of our country, of course, though the word 'country' has become obsolete" (119). The national consciousness that Bulosan here simultaneously expresses and negates he describes as a "feeling" which "is just the last residue of a nationalistic philosophy which we have acquired from our ancestors ... but now the fight is for certain democratic principles, certain universal principles that belong to all mankind" (119). Writing within a Marxist discourse of socialist liberation, Bulosan's statements register the ambivalence of a U.S. Left discourse at once animated by the concept of imperialism but also informed by the haunting prophecy of Marx and Engels of the imminent decline of nationalism and the nation-state. Bulosan wants to transcend nationalism, even in the face of the U.S. colonization of the Philippines and internal colonization of Filipinos in the United States, while at the same time he cannot avoid the language of nation and the concept of nation as a political agency, suggesting that the word "country" and the concept of "nation" still have a useful and unavoidably necessary currency in his political vocabulary and this hopeful universalism is premature.

The tension here in Bulosan's attempt to formulate an effective political praxis for internally colonized Filipinos in the United States with respect to their homeland reflects the dual and contradictory impulses informing the internationally oriented socialist consciousness of the third-world or nationally oppressed author: the fantasy of a postcolonial wish-fulfillment counterbalanced by the reality of the colonial and internal colonial situations facing third-world writers that not only inevitably informs their cultural and material praxis, but also shapes their consciousness in ways that refuse repression, demanding address just as history does. Bulosan's predicament is symptomatic of internally colonized writers in the United States who finally deconstruct the illusion of a "post"-colonialism in their negotiations between Marx and Engels's recognition that "united action, of the leading civilized countries at least, is one of the first conditions of the emancipation of the proletariat" but that "the struggle of the proletariat with the bourgeoisie is at first a national struggle" (102, 93). Authors like Bulosan—and Roth, I will argue—in encountering the national dimensions of their historical identities and situations, finally arrive at a firmer, a surer, and an indubitably more effective comprehension of working-class identity and consciousness, providing a more promising basis for an internationalist politics that also more perspicuously grasps the meaning of Marx and Engels. If we look beyond their oft-invoked statement that "the working men have no country" and read on, we find them clarifying:

> We cannot take from them what they have not got. Since the proletariat must first of all acquire political supremacy, must rise to be the leading class of the nation, must constitute itself *the* nation, it is, so far, itself national, though not in the bourgeois sense of the word. (102)

Although the working class in its state of dispossession might not have a nation, what the language of Marx and Engels suggests is that the working class effectively needs to decolonize the nation and *become* the nation, that is, give the national subject a working-class political content. This passage argues against a facile internationalism that ignores the national dimensions of working-class experience, suggesting that fostering a national consciousness in working-class terms is a necessary process in the narrative of working-class cultural and political struggle.

Part of the importance of rereading this passage is to rectify the common argument, exemplified by Barbara Foley's work *Spectres of 1919: Class and Nation in the Making of the New Negro*, that nationalist politics have historically been the bane of the Left, undermining class struggle. Foley rejects the distinction made by such writers as Richard Wright between radical and bourgeois nationalisms, arguing "that *all* nationalisms have proven to be essentialist and class collaborationist, insofar as they assume that one or another kind of nonclass-based unity—articulated as identification with a 'people,' a 'folk,' or a 'nation'—is necessary, even if only temporarily, to the emancipation of the producing masses" (80). The passage from *The Communist Manifesto*, however, suggests that all nationalisms are not necessarily class collaborationist, but that the nation can and needs to become the working-class political subject of class struggle, which helps explain why so many radical writers gravitated toward nationalism in working out problems of class and working-class identity.

In the careers of writers such as Bulosan, Wright, and Roth we see that like Dubois' color line, the borders of the nation, whether imagined in cultural form or mapped in legalistic terms, cannot be leapt over in the class struggle, as these writers at certain moments in their literary and political lives find themselves squarely confronting and unable to avoid, despite their best efforts, the concrete historical realities of the national contours of their consciousness and identity within and as part of their working-class identities. The colonized author has historically stumbled into a recognition of the national dimensions of his or her working-class identity.

Many radical Jewish writers and intellectuals, however, eschewed ethnic and national political identifications in the 1930s in ways that Roth's political and literary development suggest were finally damaging, even arresting, to the formulation of a politically effective and materially comprehensive working-class consciousness. Roth is interesting as a Jewish writer on the Left in that, like many radical Jews, he sought to escape his ethnic or national identity by dissolving it into a revolutionary internationalism. In an interview, Roth comments on this mistake, speculating that joining the Communist Party may have been motivated by a desire to replace the communal sense he felt as a child in a Jewish neighborhood on the East Side of New York City. Identifying himself with a much larger cultural trend, Roth says, "I think that's the reason why so many of us—especially so many Jews—in the '30s headed that way—because we lacked the larger thing with which to identify. We were all seeking for a re-entry into the people as a whole. And for a while we thought we could do it irrespective of Judaism. It was a much larger reintegration—a wonderful idea—but it doesn't work that way" (qtd. in Lyons 163). This larger movement to which Roth refers very much resonates with what Alan Wald identifies with the term revolutionary internationalism. "For the revolutionary internationalist," Wald writes, "the responsibility of the intellectual became to advance the interest of the working class, and, hence, the search for the place of Jewish culture in modern society lost its special significance." In the '30s, according to Wald, "a strong anti-Semitism in the U.S. coupled with a larger Jewish working class made revolutionary internationalism attractive to many Jewish intellectuals who saw their cultural and religious heritage as being of little use to a forward, socialist development" (44–45). Additionally, the power of anti-Semitism served as a negative catalyst that Michael Lerner suggests motivated socialist-minded Jewish intellectuals to evade the ethnic or national components of the power dynamics of the class system and to seek refuge in the hope that "the Jewish question could be solved by ending capitalism, and that no special attention need to be given to anti-Semitism or to the possibility that anti-Semitism might persist after the socialist revolution, or within the Communist Party itself" (Lerner 33). What Roth's literary and political odyssey suggests, however, is that this evasion, this escape into an abstract working-class identity, results in a regressive class politics and an arrested sociopolitical and basic human development.

If working-class literary studies involves, in part, analyzing how the class experience is represented in cultural terms, which is how E. P. Thompson defines class consciousness; and if the objectives of working-class literary studies include identifying and analyzing literary and cultural narratives that provide paths to create a liberated world in which people develop to their full creative abilities and have their basic needs met, the lesson of Roth's later novels, as he writes to come to terms with the diverse historical elements of his working-class identity, is a crucial one for working out a fully historical materialist understanding of class and for formulating a class consciousness accurately aligned with and comprehensive of history. The lesson of Roth's odyssey is akin to that which Richard Wright offers in his "Blueprint for Negro Writing" to African American writers: that they "must accept the nationalist implications of their lives, not in order to encourage them, but in order to transcend them. They must accept the concept of nationalism because, in order to transcend it, they must *possess* and *understand* it" (41–42). Working-class literary studies must address the colonial relations *within* the working class in order to understand working-class identity and the dynamics of the class system, domestically and globally. In this regard, a key moment in *A Star Shines Over Mt. Morris Park* occurs when Ira struggles to understand—even struggles against understanding—his class position in the world, which he does by identifying with the colonized Indian subject living under British domination:

> What made him think about H. S. M. Hutcheson's book, *The Happy Warrior*, which he had finished reading only a few days before. Why did the passage come back to tease his mind: about a hero begin a gentleman on a modest income of fifty pounds a year from a legacy

consisting of shares in an Indian textile mill. How did that faraway mill by itself make him a gentleman? Those funny, swarthy people he had seen in geography books, barefooted, in crazy white diapers. How could that make an Englishman a gentleman? They didn't count, that was why. So what did that have to do with him, with the Dreyfus Uncle Louie was talking about, with the West Point that didn't like Jews? If only he had Uncle Louie to explain it. . . .

Why did he have to think about those Indians in their big diapers when no one else did? Out of a whole book, a long book, why should that have come back to him? He wasn't an Indian. No, it was that he didn't count. So he noticed what he wasn't supposed to about what didn't count. So they didn't want him at West Point. . . . No, just because he thought about things that didn't count didn't mean *he* didn't count. Just because he thought about Indians in white diapers in spinning mills that made the hero a gentleman of leisure—and Ira himself was the son of a waiter, and they lived in a Harlem dump, too—didn't mean he wasn't a different kind of "high degree," as the fairy tales put it. (172)

Here Ira begins to link the conditions of labor exploitation colonized Indian subjects endure in the spinning mills in India with the discrimination, exclusion, labor exploitation, and poor living conditions working-class Jews experience in the United States. Ira's developing class consciousness, his understanding of class dynamics here in which the exploitation of one group produces the wealth and distinction of another, is decidedly contextualized here in the dynamics of colonial exploitation. The implicit recognition in the novel for Roth at this point, as he captures a moment in the young Ira's maturation to class consciousness, is that the oppression and exploitation Jews endure distinguish their working-class experience as one of internal colonization, just as Wright, Gordon, and Bulosan above represent the experiences of African Americans and Filipinos, respectively, in terms of colonization. For this reason, I argue that we gain much insight into Roth's representation of working-class identity if we understand him in terms of the Left radical working-class nationalist literary tradition composed of writers like Richard Wright, Carlos, Bulosan, Jesus Colon, and others.[3]

Indeed, I have discussed Roth as an internally colonized author whose literary career very much shares the cultural dynamics of Left writers of color. The perspective might seem an odd one, but it helps us uncover otherwise invisible divisions or colonial relations within working-class identity. As Sven Lindqvist has argued, a global unwillingness to understand the Jewish condition in the world as one of colonization abides, based in a denial to understand that the Holocaust was a repetition of the mass violence and genocide Europe had been perpetrating in Africa. "Auschwitz," he writes, "was the modern industrial application of a policy of extermination on which European domination had long since rested" (160); but he continues, "when what had been in the heart of darkness was repeated in the heart of Europe, no one recognized it. No one wished to admit what everyone knew" (172). Likewise, Jewish radical writers such as Roth often had difficulty comprehending themselves and their class condition as one of colonization in ways other internally colonized writers of the 1930s did. For this reason, Roth's literary career is of special importance to working-class literary studies precisely because his narrative struggles provide insight into how to work out the dynamics among the many nations *within* the U.S. working class. Why Roth's national consciousness was not triggered by the Holocaust is not entirely clear, although it makes sense that his national consciousness would emerge in the 1960s amidst the third world national movements of African Americans, Asian Americans, Chicanos, and Native Americans. His later encounter with his national identity, however, attended by a rethinking of his cultural attachments and of his previous conception of the socialist ends of working-class struggle, bears all the marks of the cultural dynamics of the decolonizing author, as I will elaborate below and in the concluding section.

In his later works, Roth, through his character Ira Stigman, analyzes his own evasion, indeed flight, from his Jewish culture and identity into a kind of socialist universalism as motivated by an internalized self-loathing and anti-Semitism, representing this gesture as finally personally, sociopolitically, and culturally repressive rather than liberatory for him. "Socialism," Roth writes of Ira in *From Bondage*, "addressed his self-contempt; socialism fluoresced against the pall over him," inspiring hope that "maybe *he*, Ira, could stop being himself, through socialism" (35). In literary terms, Roth's attraction to the elite modernist poetics of Eliot, intensely ideologically informed by nativism and anti-Semitism, constitutes the cultural correlative of his political evasion of Jewish identity. Interestingly, he represents the cultural persuasion of Eliot's modernism for him as a result of the fact that he had already been alienated from a Jewish collective identity, from the folk, when his family moved from the East Side to Harlem in his childhood, leaving him vulnerable to this kind of cultural colonization. He writes of Ira's fascination with Eliot:

> He was all too conscious of the poet's anti-Jew bias, but he accepted it, shared it, even approved of these thoughts—since leaving the East Side and becoming conscious of himself, not as a member of a homogeneous folk, but as an individual Jew, distinct from his milieu, nullified, demeaned, experiencing the entire spectrum from sufferance through malevolence to violence. And with relatives all sordidly straining for success, and home life what it was. . . . eventually, Ira became averse to Jews and repelled by Jews. Eliot's clever aspersions and disdainful caricatures seemed no more than just. Deft and diverting and oh so apt, their contemptuous attributions didn't apply to him, for the simple reason that Ira *appreciated* them. (*From Bondage* 138)

Both Ira's conversion to socialism and his appreciation of Eliot, which he believes marks him as a member of an elite distinguished from the mass of Jews, signal for Roth the extent to which Ira's subjectivity has been colonized and to which he has been alienated from central historical and cultural dimensions of his identity. We can begin to see in these passages that the older, retrospective Roth, in comprehending his assumption into socialist politics and elite modernist culture as a means of repressing his Jewish identity, does not understand his connection to the Israeli nation as a newly formed aspect of his identity born out of radically new historical developments but rather as the return of a repressed part of himself that was triggered by the Six-Day War and that his flight into the refuge of a premature internationalism had prevented him from fully comprehending in formulating a working-class consciousness and culture.

Indeed, what needs to be emphasized is that in reuniting with his Jewish identity and culture in national terms in the 1960s, Roth is not abandoning socialist or working-class politics. Rather, as he represents the process, he is exercising a more genuine Marxist method in understanding the historical materialist underpinnings of his identity to ground working-class politics in a fuller, more comprehensive consciousness of the U.S. working class in all its diverse constituencies. As Ira in *A Star Shines Over Mt. Morris Park* reflects on the lost literary riches his experiences growing up in Harlem constituted for him and how he thinks about those experiences in the present, Roth writes, "[p]erhaps because his view of it had changed: he couldn't accept *only* a surface perception of it anymore. Was that the effect of Marxism? Of the Party's influence? He had to consider, to recognize, somehow to indicate implicitly in his writing the cruel social relations beneath, the cruel class relations, the havoc inflicted by deprivation concealed under the overtly ludicrous" (73). In short, Roth has not abandoned Marxism but rather employs its historical materialist method to comprehend his working-class identity in a more deeply historical and dialectical way.

In *A Star Shines Over Mt. Morris Park*, Roth in fact represents his Jewish identity as a crucial aspect of himself he had not adequately addressed or come to terms with, which creatively hobbled him. He recalls in this work, again through his alter-ego Ira Stigman, going with his friend Farley to see a film titled *The Golem*, and recounting the role of the sorcerer-rabbi who brings to life the clay figure of the golem and then just as quickly snatches "from the newly animate figure the little plug in his bosom, where life resided, snatched it not a moment too soon against the ponderous defense of the lumpish, sentient giant, who toppled backward to the ground" (238). Roth then takes this moment and creates an allegory of his own identity:

> The plug became symbolic over the years, but of what, Ira was never sure: essence, crystal of life's principle, a vestige of 1920, of himself and Farley, hurrying full of anticipation out of the subway kiosk into Broadway's crowded sunshine and then toward the movie theater. No, there was something else: his Jewishness, wasn't it? That he had to deal with afterward, in a serious vein, not as humorous counters, something, the

little he knew, the essential plug he had retained of his Jewishness, of Jewish tradition. Odd. And when he tried to pluck it out ... creative inanition followed. (238)

Here the rejection of his foundational Jewish identity, which he would later understand as a national political identity, Roth represents as creatively and personally stifling, just as he would represent it elsewhere in his writings as politically disarming. We can see here the importance of Roth's writing to radical working-class literary studies and to Marxist thought generally, as he underscores the importance from a Marxist perspective of grappling with the historical components, including ethnic and national ones, of working-class identity. For Marx, the objective of class struggle is to create a society that eliminates or minimizes the condition of alienation, unleashing people's creative powers in the service of the social good, birthing a world in which "the free and full development of each is the precondition for the free and full development of all" (Marx and Engels 79). Roth here represents the repression of his national identity and culture as cutting him off from his creative energies and abilities, as, in effect, enforcing a condition of alienation. Thus, while Foley, for example, has argued that the Left's support of nationalism, against a stricter and purer internationalism, early in the twentieth century "would end up hobbling the ability of the Left to oppose racism and organize and effective postwar 'reconstruction'" (104) and asserts that "nationalism may well turn out to have been the Achilles heel of twentieth-century mass movements for liberation" (viii), I would argue, however, that what we see in Roth's writing, through the arc of his career, is that what has been most damaging to a radical Left working-class politics is the refusal or inability of the Left to grapple with the national components of working-class identity and to formulate a working-class politics that comprehends the dialectical relationship between nationalism and internationalism, as writers such as Bulosan, Wright, and finally, Roth do.

What we come to see, however, is that while fundamentally the struggle is between classes, that there are also important differentiations—national differentiations—within the U.S. working class that need to be understood and worked out with a more sophisticated theorization of the relationship between race, nation, and class. In the concluding section, I will explore in more detail the significance of Roth's encounter with national consciousness and underscore the stakes and importance of this encounter in the context of contemporary postcolonial theory and traditional revolutionary internationalisms.

II DE-COLONIZING ROTH IN THE COSMOPOLITICAL MOMENT

I have thus far resituated Roth, no doubt oddly for some audiences, among proletarian writers of color from the 1930s and 1940s who wrote from the perspective of the internally colonized, understood the national dimensions of their working-class experience, and saw nationalist and internationalist politics not as antagonistic but as necessarily complementary. In this section, I will explore in more detail the significance of Roth's engagement with his national identity in his later writings, published during a time when in literary and cultural studies the category of nation was being largely maligned as an historical agent of change, understood in rather one-sided terms by the ascendant postcolonial theory as a largely regressive agency, linked with "ethnic cleansing," "ethnic absolutism," and zealous chauvinism, as opposed to decolonization or liberation. Indeed, postcolonialist Kwame Anthony Appiah rejects both "the Western *imperium* and also the nationalist project" in favor of "an ethical universal" that "appeal[s] to a certain simple respect for human suffering" (66).

Roth, conversely, was in the process of rejecting any universalism as premature and asserting a national identification with Israel. But when he writes about adopting his "ex post facto native land," he writes, "[w]hat seemed important was that I identified with Israel without being a Zionist and without having the least curiosity about Israel as a practical, political entity" (*Shifting* 174). So is the nation just a postcolonial imaginary for Roth? Is it just, as Marxist Tom Nairn has argued, an irrational response to global frustration or, in Benedict Anderson's terms, just an imagined community?[4] The critical army of contemporary postcolonial theory would be tempted to see Roth's national identity as a purely imaginary, discursive, psychological construction composed of what Ernest Gellner calls "the contingent and arbitrary signs and symbols that signify the affective life of the national culture," of "the cultural shreds and patches used by nationalism" which "are often arbitrary historical inventions" (qtd. in Bhabha 292–93). To the contrary, writing in the age of postcolonial theory, Roth's writings reassert both the persistence of colonial relationships and of the necessity of anticolonial struggle, rescuing the category of nation from the merely contingent discursive and imaginary or psychological status to which postcolonial theory has consigned it, a status that evacuates the category of an objective significance and reality by divorcing it from material historical contexts. Moreover, in doing so, Roth writes to reassert progressive Zionist possibilities not only against postcolonial theory but also against simplistic Marxist internationalist narratives that similarly deride nationalism and that have historically stridently demonized Zionism.

His embrace of Zionism is significant to Roth in profoundly psychotherapeutic terms in the Fanonian sense; he undergoes a psychotherapeutic process of disalienation and decolonization through a confrontation with rather than evasion of history, articulating, like Fanon, the development of national consciousness as a necessary moment in the achievement of genuinely universalizing values, of a genuine internationalism. His stated lack of concern for Israel as "a practical political entity" indicates not that he imagines the nation in ahistorical psychologistic terms but rather that he does not understand the contemporary manifestation of Israel as the only possible expression of the Zionist project; rather, he seems to see the Zionist nation as a necessary historical form that can be invested with a radical content (as socialist Zionists such as Ber Borokov, Nahman Syrkin, and Moses Hess believed);[5] as he says in 1979, "I now see that Israeli society has some serious problems within, not only the Arabs but also a class problem. It's badly stratified" (*Shifting* 179).

In his later novels, he rejects the high modernism of his "quondam idol" James Joyce. His evaluation and dismissal of Joyce as an adequate model is largely, perhaps even solely, based on the inability of Joyce's modernist method to comprehend the nation, what for Roth constitutes an evasion of history: "*Ulysses* had become to him," he writes, "an evasion of history; its author resolved to perceive nothing of the continuing evolution of Ireland. . . . History may have been a nightmare, but the ones who could have awakened him were the very ones he eschewed: his folk" (*From Bondage* 67). He continues:

> The book was the work of a man who sought to fossilize his country, its land, its people, to rob them of their future, arrest their ebullient, coursing life, their traditions and aspirations . . . for him to have transformed his contempt for 'the sow that ate her young' into sympathy for the desperate strivings of his people to free themselves from abysmal want, from their [bondage] under British economic and social domination, would have required a complete overhaul of the haughty psyche that derided the very source of its identity, the Irish folk . . . (67–68)

Roth returns to the analytical concept of colonialism in thinking about the national liberation of the Irish as he forges his own connections with Israel, imagining this connection as a reattachment to himself, a disalienation, that is part and parcel of a larger historical process, the "exchange" he imagines that will move "a specific people to a universal one"—a step Roth accuses Joyce of skipping, with dangerous, arresting consequence, very much echoing Frantz Fanon in his valorization of the development of national culture when he writes: "The consciousness of self is not the closing of the door to communication. Philosophic thought teaches us, on the contrary, that it is its guarantee" (247). For Fanon, "the mistake, which may have very serious consequences, lies in wishing to skip the national period," as he asserts that the "building of a nation is of necessity accompanied by the discovery and encouragement of universalizing values. Far from keeping aloof from other nations, therefore, it is national liberation which leads the nation to play its part on the stage of history. It is at the heart of national consciousness that international consciousness lives and grows" (247–48).

We certainly see Roth imagining the national/international dialectic in similar ways when, in a letter dated 1 February 1976, Henry Roth writes to the imprisoned radical black nationalist Eldridge Cleaver, thanking him for his "excellent statement on racism appearing in the overseas *Jerusalem Post* of January 20, 1976" (*Shifting* 184). In this statement, Cleaver condemns the U.N. resolution of 10 November 1975 that defined Zionism as "a form of racism and racial discrimination." He tells Cleaver, "Your statement on racism coming so close to the announcement of Paul Robeson's death brought to mind the vast and hazy notion I once entertained about a better world created by a Black-Jewish-Labor-Intellectual coalition, to all of which Paul Robeson's song gave incomparable resonance" (185). Prior to writing this letter, Roth had already undergone the transformation in his thinking, allying with Israel and the nationalist project in direct contradiction to the Communist Party line. "Quite contrary to party discipline, party program, party line," he recounts in 1977, "I felt myself turning away from party directives and turning toward Israel. . . . According to the party line, the Arabs were anti-imperialists and they were only fighting for their own freedom from imperialists. As a good Communist Party member, it was manifest duty to support them, but on the contrary, it was for Israel that I felt a tremendous sense of concern" (*Shifting* 175–76). Contrary to party line, Roth's response to the Six-Day War of 1967 instinctively comprehends Zionism far more dialectically than the Communist Party, and the Left generally, which has never properly worked out "the Jewish question"; that is, Roth understands Zionism, its current concretization in the state of Israel notwithstanding, as a struggle for survival against a history of global genocidal practice and, in the contemporary situation in which he writes, as a national working-class struggle against imperialism. Indeed, I would contend that the alliance Roth here imagines between black and Jewish labor and radicalized intellectuals is essentially imagined as an alliance of oppressed nations against imperialism and its regime of labor exploitation. Recall that in his 1968 essay "The Land Question and Black Liberation," Cleaver asserts what he deems a "fascinating" parallel "between the situation of the Jews at the time of the coming of Theodore Herzl and the present situation of black people in America" (67). Cleaver likewise sees both Zionism and black nationalism as struggles against colonialism and its genocidal mission. My point here in highlighting Roth's coalition-building imagination is that he begins to think about his Jewish identity in national terms and specifically in terms of a nation oppressed and exploited as labor within an imperial context. Roth implicitly identifies with the other Third World movements in the U.S. (Chicano, Native American, Asian American) and links the Zionist struggle with them, a somewhat rare gesture but one performed by Cleaver as well. For Roth, then, Zionism is primarily a decolonization movement, importantly, both inside the United States (and for all Diasporic Jews in their respective nations) and for Israeli Jews resisting Syrian efforts to drive them into the sea.

Additionally, what Roth is working out here in his disenchantment with—but never abandonment or disavowal of—the Left is a more complex Marxist theorization of class that understands the category of nation as the conceptual mediation of race and class and that challenges rigid and simplistic conceptions of "internationalism" on the Left that see nationalism, and particularly Zionism, as politically regressive and potentially if not inevitably imperialist. His invocation of Robeson certainly underscores his continuing identification with a Left cultural and political legacy. Again, the national project for Roth is not exclusionary but rather, as we see in this communication with Cleaver, opens the door to genuine communication, to a genuine internationalism.

Stretching over sixty years, Roth's career of literary production affords those of us involved in working-class literary studies with the wisdom gained through his constant—and constantly painful—revision of his working-class identity, exploring it with ever-increasing sophistication and honesty in ways that challenge us to rethink class and interrogate the doctrinaire politics that at times characterize the Left, discrediting the beauty and humanism of the Marxist tradition, curtailing our understanding of our own humanity, and inhibiting our ability to imagine and chart the course toward full liberation.

NOTES

1. For extended readings of *Call It Sleep* that elaborate the interpretations I am offering in brief, see my chapter "'What a Dirty Way of Getting Clean': The Grotesque in Proletarian Literature" in *Literature and the Grotesque*, ed. Michael Meyer. Amsterdam: Rodopi, 1994, 171–93 and the chapter on Roth in my forthcoming book *The Making of American Working-Class Literature and Consciousness*, University of Mississippi Press.
2. For a discussion of Paredes's novel and the Mexican nationalist question, see Libretti, "'We can starve too.'"
3. For a discussion of Jesús Colón's nationalism, see Libretti, "Looking Backward."
4. For a discussion of Marxist rejections of nationalism as merely an irrational psychological reaction to world events, see Berberoglu.
5. For a view of socialist Zionist thought that departs from Herzl's brand of Zionism, see Hertzberg.

BIBLIOGRAPHY

Anderson, Benedict. *Imagined Communities: Reflections on the Origin and Spread of Nationalism*. London: Verso, 1983. Print.

Appiah, Kwame Anthony. "Is the Post- in Postmodernism the Post- in Postcolonial?" *Contemporary Postcolonial Theory*. Ed. Padmini Mongia. London: Arnold, 1996. 55–71. Print.

Berberoglu, Berch. *Nationalism and Ethnic Conflict: Class, State, and Nation in the Age of Globalization*. Lanham: Rowman and Littlefield, 2004. Print.

Bhabha, Homi. "DissemiNation: Time, Narrative, and the Margins of the Modern Nation." *Nation and Narration*. Ed. Homi Bhabha. New York: Routledge, 1990. 292–311. Print.

Bulosan, Carlos. *Sound of Falling Light: Letters in Exile.* Ed. Dolores Feria. Quezon City: U of Philippines P, 1960. Print.
Cleaver, Eldridge. *Post-Prison Writings and Speeches.* New York: Random House, 1968. Print.
Fanon, Frantz. *The Wretched of the Earth.* Trans. Constance Farrington. New York: Grove, 1963. Print.
Foley, Barbara. *Spectres of 1919: Class and Nation in the Making of the New Negro.* Urbana: U of Illinois P, 2003. Print.
Freeman, Joseph. *An American Testament: A Narrative of Rebels and Romantics.* London: Victor Gollancz, 1938. Print.
Gordon, Eugene. "Social and Political Problems of the Negro Writer." *The American Writers Congress.* Ed. Henry Hart. New York: International, 1935. 35–39. Print.
Haywood, Harry. *Black Bolshevik: Autobiography of an Afro-American Communist.* Chicago: Liberator P, 1978. Print.
Hertzberg, Arthur. *The Zionist Idea.* Philadelphia: Jewish Publication Society, 1997. Print.
Kelley, Robin D. G. "Identity Politics and Class Struggle." *New Politics* 6 (1997): 84–97. Print.
Lerner, Michael. *A Socialism of Fools: Anti-Semitism on the Left.* New York: Institute for Labor and Mental Health, 1992. Print.
Libretti, Tim. "Looking Backward, Looking Forward: Jesús Colóm's Left Literary Legacy and the Adumbration of a Third World Writing." *Recovering the U.S. Hispanic Literary Heritage.* Ed. María Herrera-Sobek and Virginia Sánchez Korrol. Vol. 3. Houston: Arte Público, 2000. 351–70. Print.
———. "'We can starve too': Américo Paredes' *George Washingto Gómez* and the Proletarian Corrido." *Recovering the U.S. Hispanic Literary Heritage.* Ed. Erlinda Gonzales-Berry and Chuck Tatum. Vol. 11. Houston: Arte Público, 1996. 118–30. Print.
Lindqvist, Sven. *"Exterminate All the Brutes."* New York: New Press, 1992. Print.
Lyons, Bonnie. *Henry Roth: The Man and His Work.* New York: Cooper Square, 1976. Print.
Marx, Karl, and Friedrich Engels. *The Communist Manifesto.* New York: Viking, 1967. Print.
McClintock, Anne. "The Angels of Progress: Pitfalls of the Term 'Post-Colonialism.'" *Social Text* 31/32 (1992): 84–98. Print.
Roth, Henry. *Call It Sleep.* New York: Avon, 1964. Print.
———. *From Bondage.* New York: St. Martin's, 1996. Print.
———. *Shifting Landscape.* Ed. Mario Materassi. New York: Jewish Publication Society, 1987. Print.
———. *A Star Shines Over Mt. Morris Park.* New York: Picador, 1994.
Traverso, Enzo. *The Marxists and the Jewish Question: The History of a Debate, 1843- 1943.* New Jersey: Humanities, 1994. Print.
Wald, Alan M. *The New York Intellectuals.* Chapel Hill: U of North Carolina P, 1987. Print.
Wright, Richard. "Blueprint for Negro Writing." *Richard Wright Reader.* Ed. Michel Fabre. New York: Harper and Row, 1978. 36–50. Print.
Wright, Richard. *Native Son.* New York: Harper Collins, 1996. Print.

Notes on Contributors

Maria F. Brandt is assistant professor of English at Monroe Community College in Rochester, New York. At MCC, Dr. Brandt directs the award-winning interdisciplinary drama initiative "The Sixth Act" and has won the NISOD Excellence in Teaching Award. She published "'For His Own Satisfaction': Eliminating the New Woman Figure in *McTeague*" in *American Transcendental Quarterly* (2004) and has delivered numerous conference presentations.

Matthew Brophy is a visiting professor of English in the Division of Communications, Arts, and Humanities at Delaware County Community College in the greater Philadelphia area. He received his PhD from Binghamton University, State University of New York, in 2010.

Renny Christopher is associate provost and professor of English at California State University, Channel Islands. *A Carpenter's Daughter: A Working-Class Woman in Higher Education* addresses her experiences as the first in her family to attend college. Her previous book, *The Viet Nam War/The American War: Images and Representations in Euro-American and Vietnamese Exile Narratives* was named Outstanding Book on Human Rights by the Gustavas Myers Center for the Study of Human Rights in North America. She has also published three works of poetry: *My Name is Medea*, *Longing Fervently for Revolution*, and *Viet Nam and California*.

Nicholas Coles is associate professor of English at the University of Pittsburgh. With Peter Oresick, he edited the anthology *Working Classics: Poems of Industrial Life* and a companion volume, *For a Living: The Poetry of Work*. *American Working-Class Literature: An Anthology*, coedited with Janet Zandy, was published by Oxford University Press in 2007. Active in the Working-Class Studies Association, Coles also serves as a field director of the National Writing Project.

Sylvia J. Cook is professor of English at the University of Missouri-St. Louis. She is the author of *From Tobacco Road to Route 66: The Southern*

Poor White in Fiction and *Erskine Caldwell and the Fiction of Poverty*. Her most recent book is *Working Women, Literary Ladies: The Industrial Revolution and Female Aspiration*. Her current project is "Clothed in Meaning: Literary Dress and Working-Class Americans."

Michele Fazio is assistant professor in the Department of English and Theatre at the University of North Carolina, Pembroke. Her work has appeared in *MELUS: The Society for the Study of Multi-Ethnic Literature of the United States* and *Voices in Italian Americana: A Literary Journal and Cultural Review*. She is currently working on a book project examining the representation of labor and class conflict in multiethnic literature of the United States.

Phoebe S. Jackson is associate professor of English at William Paterson University, where she is graduate program director. With Emily Isaacs, she is coeditor of *Public Works: Student Writing as Public Text*. She is currently working on a book project entitled "Cultural Dislocations and Geographical Migrations: Cross-Class Encounters in 20th Century American Women's Fiction."

Karen Kovacik, professor of English, directs the creative writing program at Indiana University-Purdue University Indianapolis. She's the author of three collections of poetry: *Metropolis Burning*, *Beyond the Velvet Curtain*, and *Nixon and I*. Her articles on working-class women poets have appeared in *NWSA Journal* and *Women's Studies Quarterly*, and her translation of contemporary Polish poets can be found in *American Poetry Review*, *Boston Review*, *Crazyhorse*, *Southern Review*, and *West Branch*.

Tim Libretti is professor of English, women's studies, and Latino and Latin American studies at Northeastern Illinois University. He has published articles and book chapters on U.S. racial and ethnic literatures, U.S. working-class literature and culture, Marxism and cultural studies, as well as on film and popular culture. His book *The Making of U.S. Working-Class Literature and Consciousness: The Nations, Genders, and Sexualities of U.S. Proletarian Literature from the 1930s to the Present* is forthcoming from University of Mississippi Press, and his edited volume *Exterminating Narratives of Genocide: Identifying and Resisting the Cultural Logics of Genocide* is forthcoming from Lexington Books.

David McCracken is associate professor of English at Coker College in Hartsville, South Carolina. He has published work on contemporary literature and on teaching composition. His research interests are F. Scott Fitzgerald, working-class literature, contemporary fiction, and American popular culture.

Paula Rabinowitz, professor of American literature, cultural studies, and moving image studies at the University of Minnesota, is the author of *Labor and Desire: Women's Revolutionary Fiction in Depression America*; *They Must Be Represented: The Politics of Documentary*; and *Black and White and Noir: America's Pulp Modernism*. She is coeditor (with Charlotte Nekola) of *Writing Red: An Anthology of Women's Writings, 1930–1940* and is currently coediting with Cristina Giorcelli a four-volume series on clothing, dress, fashion, and identity entitled *Habits of Being*. In 2011, Dr. Rabinowitz held the Fulbright Distinguished Lectureship in American studies at East China Normal University in Shanghai. She is working on a study of paperback culture, *American Pulp: A Biography* for Princeton University Press.

Michelle M. Tokarczyk is professor of English at Goucher College. She has published *Class Definitions: On the Lives and Writings of Maxine Hong Kingston, Sandra Cisneros, and Dorothy Allison*; *E. L. Doctorow's Skeptical Commitment*; and *The House I'm Running From: Poems*. She is coeditor with Irene Papoulis of *Teaching Composition/Teaching Literature: Crossing Great Divides* and with Elizabeth A. Fay of *Working-Class Women in the Academy*. Dr. Tokarczyk is currently working on representations of working-class solidarity across racial and ethnic differences.

Index

12 Million Black Voices (Wright), 19
49th Parallel (Dos Passos), 19, 25

A

accidents. *See* injury; death
"Acknowledgments" (Tokarczyk), 79
activism, 77–78
Adair, Vivyan, 7–8, 125–26, 132, 134, 138
Agamben, Giorgio, 181, 196–97, 199n4; *homo sacer*, 196–97
Agee, James, 29; *Let Us Now Praise Famous Men*, 19
agency, 123, 128, 131–138
Albers, Patricia, 150–151, 154
Alcarón, Norma, 75
Alexie, Sherman, 7, 123–24; *Indian Killer*, 7, 123–24, 141–154
Alger, Horatio, 31n8
Allison, Dorothy, 3, 137
All I Asking for Is My Body (Murayama), 45–46
Althusser, Louis, 29
American Exodus: A Record of Human Erosion (Lange and Taylor), 19
American Working-Class Literature (Zandy and Coles), 3, 9, 103–20
Anderson, Benedict, 231
Anthology, 103–120
"Another Abraham: for my Father-in-Law, John, Who Worked in the Mill" (Bryner), 44
Appiah, Kwame Anthony, 231
assimilation, 72, 91; academic 82; poetry of, 83, 153
Atkinson, Brooks, 215

B

Baca, Jimmy Santiago, 41–42
Baird, Irene: *Waste Heritage*, 25
Bakhtin, Mikhail, 133
Beans of Egypt, Maine, The (Chute), 7, 8, 124, 159–172
Beatty, Jan: "A Waitress's Instructions on Tipping," 108–9
Bederman, Gail: *Manliness and Civilization*, 181, 206
Becher, Bernd and Hilla: *Industrial Facades*, 27
Beck, Glenn, 87
Benjamin, Walter, 28
Berkeley School, 162
Better Red: The Writing of Resistance of Tillie Olsen and Meridel Le Sueur (Coiner), 2
Bishop, Elizabeth, 29
Black Bolshevik (Haywood), 223
Black Feminist Thought (Collins), 3
Blair, Peter: *Last Heat*, 43
Blanchard, I.G.: "Eight Hours," 108–9
Blind Horse (Bryner), 42–43
"Blonde White Women" (Smith), 77
Blood Dazzler (Smith), 76
"Blueprint for Negro Writing" (Wright), 226
bodies, 81–82, 204; incorporated into building material, 41–42, 152; masculine, 177–198; power of multiple, 212; space and, 168–69
Bodies that Matter (Butler), 208
"Book of the Dead" (Rukeyser), 27–28
Bordo, Susan, 168
Born for Liberty (Evans), 204, 215
Bourdieu, Pierre, 106
Bourke-White, Margaret: *You Have Seen Their Faces*, 19
"Boy Died in My Alley, The" (Brooks), 79

Brandt, Maria, 9–10, 175
Bread Givers, The (Yezierska), 22, 89, 97
Brecht and Method (Jameson), 210–11
Brecht, Bertolt, 209–12, 215
Brooks, Gwendolyn: "The Boy Died in My Alley," 79
Brophy, Matthew, 10, 175
Brown, Bill, 179–80
Bryner, Jeanne: "Another Abraham: for my Father-in-Law, John, Who Worked in the Mill," 44; *Blind Horse*, 42–43; "Our Fathers," 42–43
Bulosan, Carlos, 223–24
Bureau of Indian Affairs, 150
Bureau of Labor Statistics, 45
Bushman, Richard, 61
Butler, Judith: *Bodies that Matter*, 208

C

Caldwell, Erskine: *You Have Seen Their Faces*, 19
Call it Sleep (Roth), 10, 22, 176, 219–21
Calling Home: An Anthology of Working-Class Women's Writing (Zandy), 1–4
Campbell, Tracy, 171–72
canon, 104–108, 198
Carlson, Marvin, 214
Castillo, Ana, 73, 74–75; *My Father Was a Toltec*, 74–75
Center for Working-Class Studies, 3
charity, 134–38
Charlip, Julie: "A Real Class Act," 97
Chasin, Barbara: *Inequality and Violence in the United States*, 37
Cheyfitz, Eric: "The (Post)Colonial Construction of Indian Country: U.S. American Indian Literatures and Federal Indian Law," 144
Children's Defense Fund, 76
Christ in Concrete (di Donato), 2, 7, 15, 19, 22, 38–39, 48
Christopher, Renny, 5, 11, 15, 159–60, 198n1: "Toward a Theory of Working Class Literature," 5, 88
Chute, Carolyn: *The Beans of Egypt, Maine*, 7, 8, 124, 159–172
Cisneros, Sandra, 3, 5
Citizens (Levin), 25
class: assimilation, 72; conflict, 87, 143, 147, 151–52; consciousness, 71, 73, 152, 221–22, 224–29; differences, 93; divisions, 138n1, 144, 147; gender and, 75–76; identity, 8, 71, 83, 107, 159, 172, 176, 192, 219–34; inequity, 15, 144; mobility, 71–72, 82, 83–84, 88, 90–91, 135; national identity and, 10, 175, 219–34; poverty and, 123; race and, 8, 16, 52–53, 57, 65, 153, 234; slavery and, 52–52, 65; social aspects, 88; transition, 87, 99; violence, 142–43
Class Definitions (Tokarczyk), 3
Cleaver, Eldridge, 232–34
Clurman, Harold, 208–9
Coal Mountain Elementary (Nowak), 28–29
Cobb, Gerry, 211
Cobb, Jonathan: *The Hidden Injuries of Class*, 72–73, 126–27
Coiner, Contance, 133, 199n3; *Better Red: The Writing of Resistance of Tillie Olsen and Meridel Le Sueur*, 2
Coles, Nicholas, 1, 38–39, 70; *American Working-Class Literature*, 3, 9, 103–120
Collapse (Diamond), 22
collapse: and The Great Depression, 19; location of, 17, 18, 21, 24, 26, zones of, 26
Collins, Particia Hill: *Black Feminist Thought*, 3
Comer, Krista: *Landscapes of the New West*, 164
Communist Manifesto (Marx and Engels), 225
Conversations with Sherman Alexie (Peterson), 141–42
Cook, Sylvia, 6, 16
Cooper, James Fenimore: *The Last of the Mohicans*, 188
Cosgrove, Stuart, 209, 211
Cott, Nancy, 204–205
Cultural Capital: The Problem of Literary Canon Formation (Guillory), 106–7
cultural geography, 124, 159–172
Crisis (NAACP), 77

D

Daniels, Jim, 2; "Digger Gets a Checkup," 48–49; *Digger's*

Blues, 48–49; *Punching Out*, 44; "Small Catch," 44
Daughter of Earth (Smedley), 2
Dead Reckoning (Fearing), 17–20
death: and occupational illness, 37; at work, 15; blame and, 49; of Geremio, 38–39; of mills, 43; rate 35–37
depression: and madness, 23, 29; early usage of, 18–19; diagnosis of, 30n4; in the landscape, 29; spatial arrangement of, 22; spatialized narratives of, 25; victims of, 26
Deloria, Vine, Jr., 145
Denning, Michael, 18
Derrick, Scott, 188
Detroit, 28
Dews, C. L. Barney: *This Fine Place So Far From Home: Voices of Academics from the Working Class*, 97
Diamond, Elin: *Unmaking Mimesis*, 211
Diamond, Jared: *Collapse*, 23
Dickens, Charles, 31n8
di Donato, Pietro: *Christ in Concrete*, 2, 7, 15, 19, 22, 38–39, 48
"Digger Gets a Checkup" (Daniels), 48–49
Digger's Blues (Daniels), 48–49
dignity, 127, 137
"Disabled List" (Watson), 40–41
Dobler, Patricia, 72, 73–74
Douglass, Frederick, 58
Doro, Sue, 2
Dos Passos, John, 24–27; *49th Parallel*, 19, 25
Dow, William, 184, 193, 197
Down in the Dumps (Scandura), 17
Dred, A Tale of the Great Dismal Swamp (Stowe), 54–5
Dreiser, Theodore: *Sister Carrie*, 100
dump, 20–22, 27, 30
Dyck, Isabel, 168–69

E
Eagleton, Terry, 2
Edelman, Marian Wright, 76
Ernest, Jerry: "Scottie," 42
Edmunds, Susan, 21
education, 69–70, 71–84; affective, 186–93; alienation and, 8–9; campus life, 87; cultural, 95; economic security and, 69, 89; higher, 8–9; in masculinity, 181; physical, 181–86; slavery and, 62–63; unequal, 29
"Eight Hours," (Blanchard), 108–9
Eliot, George, 31n8, 228
Engels, Friedrich: *Communist Manifesto*, 225
Engendering Culture (Melosh), 206–7
Evan, Walker: *Let Us Now Praise Famous Men*, 19
Evans, Sara: *Born for Liberty*, 204, 215

F
Fanon, Frantz, 222, 231–32
Farrell, James: *Young Lonnigan*, 22
Fay, Elizabeth: and Fredric Jameson, 4; and Henry Giroux, 4; *Working-Class Women in the Academy: Labors in the Knowledge Factory*, 2, 7
Fazio, Michele, 7, 123–24
Fearing, Kenneth: *Dead Reckoning*, 17–20
feminism, 4, 71, 169
Fildes, Samuel Luke, 18
Foley, Barbara: *Radical Representations*, 2; *Spectres of 1919*, 225
Foucault, Michel, 135
"Free Vacation House, The" (Yezierska), 128, 133–136, 136–138
freedom, 127, 164
From Bondage (Roth), 228–29, 232
"From the Suwanee to Egypt, There's No Place like Home" (Ward), 159–60, 165–67
Fussell, Paul: *The Great War and Modern Memory*, 37–39

G
Gaffney, Karen, 3
Gair, Christopher, 178–79, 181, 188
Gaskell, Jane, 73
Gellner, Ernest, 231
gender, 204–215 masculinity and, 175, 177–198, 206–211; nationalism and, 180, 193–98, 200n9; poverty and, 126
Giles, James, 145
Gilfillan, Lauren: *I Went to Pit College*, 23
Girl, The (Le Sueur), 2
Giroux, Henry, 4
globalization, 142

244 Index

George Washington Gómez (Paredes), 223
"Go Left, Young Writers!" (Gold) 127, 175
Gold, Michael, 10, 18, 22, 24; "Go Left, Young Writers!," 127, 175
Gordon, Eugene, 223
Gordon, Mel, 209
Grapes of Wrath (Steinbeck), 26, 204
Great Depression, 6, 15, 204–5; as a collapse, 19; as spatial and metaphorical convention, 22; naming of the, 19
Great Recession, 6, 15, 17, 29, 112
Great War and Modern Memory, The (Fussell), 37–38
Grosz, Elizabeth, 168
Grotesque Relations (Edmunds), 21
Group Theatre, 208–10
Guillory, John: *Cultural Capital: The Problem of Literary Canon Formation*, 106–7
Gutierrez, Joe: "Missing at Work," 41

H

Hall, G. Stanley, 183–84
Hands (Zandy), 4–5, 160, 198
Hapke, Laura, 11, 146, 149
Harvey, David: *Justice, Nature and the Geography of Difference*, 163
Haut, Woody, 144
Haywood, Harry: *Black Bolshevik*, 223
Heat: Steelworkers Lives and Legends, The (Institute for Career Development), 41–42
Heath Anthology of American Literature, The (Lauter), 2
Heckerl, David, 197
Herkomer, Hubert von, 18
Hidden Injuries of Class, The (Sennett and Cobb), 72–73, 126–27
Hogan, David, 83
Holl, Francis Montague, 18
homo sacer (Agamben), 196–97
hooks, bell: *Where We Stand: Class Matters*, 97–98
Hoovervilles, 15, 26
Hurston, Zora: *Their Eyes Were Watching God*, 22

I

I Am Charlotte Simmons (Wolfe), 8, 69–70, 87–100
"I Stand Here Ironing" (Olsen) 128, 131–133, 136–138
I Went to Pit College (Gilfillan), 23
Immigrant Acts (Lowe), 178
Incidents in the Life of a Slave Girl (Jacobs), 6, 16, 52–65
Indian Killer (Alexie), 7, 123–24, 141–154
Industrial Facades (Becher), 27
Industrial Valley (McKinney), 25
Inequality and Violence in the United States (Chasin), 37
Injunction Granted (Living Newspaper), 212–13
Injury: agricultural, 45–49; blame and, 49; in war and work, 36–37; work related, 15, 35–49
Institute for Career Development: *The Heat: Steelworkers Lives and Legends*, 41–42
Irr, Caren, 25–26; *The Suburb of Dissent*, 17

J

Jackson, Phoebe, 8, 124
Jacobs, Harriet: *Incidents in the Life of a Slave Girl*, 6, 16, 52–65
Jameson, Fredric, 4; *Brecht and Method*, 210–11
jargon, in theory and criticism, 5–6
Jews without Money (Gold), 22
Johnson, Josephine: *Jordanstown*, 25; *Now in November*, 25
Jordanstown (Johnson), 25
Joyce, James, 220, 232
Justice, Nature and the Geography of Difference (Harvey), 163

K

Kaplan, Amy, 194, 197
Karen, David, 72
Kelly, Robin D. G., 221
Kimmel, Michael, 180, 181
Kingston, Maxine Hong, 3
Kirn, Walter, 17
Knack, Martha: "Native American Labor: Retrieving History, Rethinking Theory," 146–47
Kolodny, Annette: *The Lay of the Land*, 10
Kovacik, Karen, 8, 69
Kozol, Jonathan, 76; *Shame of the Nation*, 76

L

Labor and Desire (Rabinowitz), 2
Landscapes of the New West (Comer), 164
Lange, Dorothea: *American Exodus: A Record of Human Erosion*, 19; "Slums of San Francisco, California," 18; *White Angel Bread Line*, 19
Lassiter, Laurie, 209
Last Heat (Blair), 43
Last of the Mohicans, The (Cooper), 188
Lauter, Paul, 175, 177–78: and Raymond Williams, 4; *The Heath Anthology of American Literature*, 2; "Working-Class Women's Literature: An Introduction to Study," 2, 88
Laux, Dorianne, 72, 75–76, 83; "What My Father Told Me," 75–76
Law, Carolyn Leste: *This Fine Place So Far From Home: Voices of Academics from the Working Class*, 97
Lay of the Land, The (Kolodny), 10
Le Sueur, Meridel: *The Girl*, 2
Lerner, Michael, 226
Let Us Now Praise Famous Men (Agee and Evans), 19
Levin, Meyer: *Citizens*, 25
Liberty City, Miami, 76–79
Libretti, Tim, 10, 176
Lillie C. Evans School, 76–79
Linkon, Sherry Lee, 199n2: Center for Working-Class Studies and, 2; *New Working-Class Studies*, 1, 71, 160–61; *Radical Revisions: Rereading 1930's Culture*, 2
Littlefield, Alice: "Native American Labor: Retrieving History, Rethinking Theory," 146–47
Lindqvist, Sven, 227–28
Living Newspaper, 212–214, 216n3, 216–17n4; *Injunction Granted*, 212–13; *Medicine Show*, 213–14
London, Jack, 10; *The Sea-Wolf*, 175, 177–198
Lorde, Audre: "The Master's Tools Will Never Dismantle the Master's House," 5
Lowe, Lisa: *Immigrant Acts*, 178
Lowney, John, 24
Lubrano, Alfred, 130
Lumpkin, Grace: *To Make My Bread*, 2

M

Manliness and Civilization (Bederman), 181, 206
Marx, Karl, 168, 224–25; *Communist Manifesto*, 225
Marxist Scholars: as distinct from working-class scholars, 3
Marya, A Life (Oates), 89–90, 97
"Master's Tools Will Never Dismantle the Master's House, The" (Lorde), 5
Mazurek, Raymond: "Work and Class in the Box Store University: Autobiographies of Working-Class Academics," 97
McClintock, Anne, 182–83, 190, 196
McCracken, David, 8, 69–70
McKinney, Ruth: *Industrial Valley*, 25
Medicine Show (Living Newspaper), 213–14
Melosh, Barbara: *Engendering Culture*, 206–7
Metzgar, Jack, 125–126, 128, 137
memory, 15
Medem, Vladimir, 221–22
Mercy of a Rude Stream (Roth), 10, 176, 219–21
Miner, Madonne, 181
Mitchell, Don, 8, 162, 166–67, 201n12
"Missing at Work" (Gutierrez) 41
Moody, Jocelyn: "To Be Young, Pregnant, and Black," 135
Moss, Pamela, 168–69
Moynihan, Patrick, 59
Mullen, Bill: *Radical Revisions: Rereading 1930's Culture*, 2
Murayama, Milton: *All I Asking for Is My Body*, 45–46
My Father Was a Toltec (Castillo), 74–75

N

NAACP: *Crisis*, 77
Nairn, Tom, 231
Napolitano, Louise, 39
national identity. *See* class
National Safety Council, 36–37
"Native American Labor: Retrieving History, Rethinking Theory" (Knack and Littlefield), 146–47
Native Son (Wright), 222
Nelson, Ruth, 209

New Working-Class Studies (Russo and Linkon), 1, 71, 160–61
New York, 30, 150; Lower East Side, 18, 24
New Yorker, 83
Now in November (Johnson), 25
"Now It Is Broccoli" (Tagami), 48
Nowak, Mark: *Coal Mountain Elementary*, 28–29; *Shut Up Shut Down*, 27–30

O

Oates, Joyce Carol: *Marya, A Life*, 89–90, 97
Odets, Clifford: *Waiting for Lefty*, 9–10, 175, 204–215
Olsen, Tillie, 2; "I Stand Here Ironing," 128, 131–133, 136–138; *Yonnondio*, 6, 20–24, 29
Omaha, 21, 29–30
Orvell, Miles, 19–20
"Our Fathers" (Bryner), 42–43
Owen, Wilfred: "The Parable of the Old Man and the Young," 44–45
Owens, Louis, 144

P

"Parable of the Old Man and the Young, The" (Owen), 44–45
Paredes, Américo: *George Washington Gómez*, 223
Pavletich, Joann, 134
pedagogy, 103–120; anthology and, 104–108; anthology project, 112–13; classroom strategies, 108–13; family work history, 110–11; group theatre project, 111–12; online discussion, 108–109
Peterson, Nancy: *Conversations with Sherman Alexie*, 141–42
Pfister, Joel, 65
"Political Landscapes" (Till), 162, 163–64
"(Post)Colonial Construction of Indian Country: U.S. American Indian Literatures and Federal Indian Law, The" (Cheyfitz), 144
poverty: class, 7, 90, 125, 127–28, 131; gender and, 126, 204–215; physical places of, 15; structural conditions of, 125; women and, 125–138; working class and, 123, 125–128
"Promises to Keep: Working Class Students and Higher Education" (Tokarczyk), 90–91
Punching Out (Daniels), 44

R

Rabinowitz, Paula, 6, 15; *Labor and Desire*, 2
race, and class, 52–53, 57, 65, 129, 136, 141, 153, 234
Radical Representations (Foley), 2
Radical Revisions: Rereading 1930s Culture (Mullen and Linkon), 2
"Real Class Act, A" (Charlip), 97
refuse, as refuge, 21
Reagan, Ronald, 28, 168
representations of working-class experiences, 6–7, 15–16, 70
resentment, 126
Rich, Adrienne, 73
Rich, Frank, 17, 29
Riis, Jacob, 18
Rivera, Tomás: *Y no se lo tragó la tierra/And the Earth Did Not Devour Him*, 46–48
Roberts, Ian, 160–61
Robinson, Lillian: rereading of Virginia Woolf, 4; *Sex, Class and Culture*, 2
Rodgers, Carolyn, 79
Room of One's Own, A (Woolf), 4, 21
Roosevelt, Eleanor, 26
Roosevelt, Franklin Delano, 26
Roosevelt, Theodore, 180, 182, 200n9
Roth, Henry, 219–234; *Call it Sleep*, 10, 22, 176, 219–21; *From Bondage*, 228–29, 232; *Mercy of a Rude Stream*, 10, 176, 219–21; *A Star Shines Over Mt. Morris Park*, 226–27, 229
Rukeyser, Muriel: "Book of the Dead," 27–28
Russo, John, 199n2; Center for Working-Class Studies and, 2; *New Working-Class Studies*, 1, 71, 160–61

S

Said, Edward: *Culture and Imperialism*, 177, 179
Sauer, Carl, 162
The Sea-Wolf (London), 175, 177–198
Seattle, 141, 144–153
Sex, Class and Culture (Robinson), 2

Scandura, Jani, 24; *Down in the Dumps*, 17
Scott, James, 24
Scott, William, 111–12; *Troublemakers: Power, Representation, and the Fiction of the Mass Worker*, 111
"Scottie" (Ernest), 42
Senber, Henry, 209
Sennett, Richard: *The Hidden Injuries of Class*, 72–73, 126–27
Showalter, Elaine, 92, 101n2
Shut Up Shut Down (Nowak), 27–30
Sides, Hampton, 180
Sister Carrie (Dreiser), 100
slave: agency, 60–61; as member of the proletariat, 61, 65; as working class, 6, 16, 53, emancipation and underclass, 59; moral conduct and, 59–60, 61–65
"Slums of San Francisco, California" (Lange), 18
"Small Catch" (Daniels), 44
Smedley, Agnes: *Daughter of Earth*, 2
Smith, Betty: *A Tree Grows in Brooklyn*, 22
Smith, Patricia, 72, 76–79; "Blonde White Women," 77; *Blood Dazzler*, 76; "Building Nicole's Mama," 76–79
social services, 80–81, 127–28, 131–138
"Source" (Walker), 128–131, 136
space, 30, 144–45; as marginal area, 17, 20; body and, 168–69; concept of, 6; depressed narratives of, 25; Depression-era literature and, 17–34; high-modernist state and, 24; of alterity, 21; of economic collapse, 6; order and, 17;
Spectres of 1919 (Foley), 225
Stanislavsky, Constantin, 208, 215
Star Shines Over Mt. Morris Park, A (Roth), 226–27, 229
Steedman, Carolyn, 24
steel, 40–45, 150–151
Steinbeck, John: *Grapes of Wrath*, 26, 204
Stenning, Alison, 160–61
Stewart, Kathleen, 17
Stowe, Harriet Beecher: binary oppositions in, 55; *Dred, A Tale of the Great Dismal Swamp*, 54–55; *Uncle Tom's Cabin*, 6, 16, 52–65

Suburb of Dissent, The (Irr), 17

T
Tagami, Jeff: "Now It Is Broccoli," 48
Tatum, Beverly Daniel, 76
Taylor, Paul: *American Exodus: A Record of Human Erosion*, 19
Teh, Ian, 29
Their Eyes Were Watching God (Hurston), 22
This Fine Place So Far From Home: Voices of Academics from the Working Class (Dews and Law), 97
Thompson, E.P., 83, 226
Those Winter Sundays: Female Academics and Their Working-Class Parents (Welsch), 110
Till, Karen: "Political Landscapes," 162, 163–64
"To Be Young, Pregnant, and Black," (Moody), 135
To Make My Bread (Lumpkin), 2
Tokarczyk, Michelle, 7–8, 72, 79–82, 123; "Acknowledgments," 79; and Fredric Jameson, 4; and Henry Giroux, 4; *Class Definitions*, 3; "Promises to Keep: Working Class Students and Higher Education," 90–91; *Working-Class Women in the Academy: Labors in the Knowledge Factory*, 2, 7, 79
"Toward a Theory of Working Class Literature" (Christopher and Whitson), 5, 88
Tree Grows in Brooklyn, A (Smith), 22
Troublemakers: Power, Representation, and the Fiction of the Mass Worker (Scott), 111

U
Uncle Tom's Cabin (Stowe), 6, 16, 52–65
Underclass, 54, 57–59, 65, 137
Unmaking Mimesis (Diamond), 211

V
values: middle-class, 52, 57–58, 61–65, 73; representation of, 107; working-class, 88, 92–96, 129
van Gogh, Vincent, 18
Van Styvendale, Nancy, 152
Vietnam Veterans Memorial, 37

Violas, Paul, 73
visual culture, 15

W

Waiting for Lefty (Odets), 9, 175, 204–215
"Waitress's Instructions on Tipping, A" (Beatty), 108–9
Wald, Alan, 24, 225–26
Walker, Alice: "Source," 128–131, 136
Ward, Cynthia: "From the Suwanee to Egypt, There's No Place like Home," 159–60, 165–67
Ward, Susan, 179
Waste Heritage (Baird), 25
Watson, Will: "Disabled List," 40–41; "Wire, Wireman, Stripper, Splice," 41
Welsch, Kathleen, 110–11; *Those Winter Sundays: Female Academics and Their Working-Class Parents*, 110
West, The American, 164–65, 177, 179
What's Class Got to Do With It? (Zweig), 71
"What My Father Told Me" (Laux), 75–76
Where We Stand: Class Matters (hooks), 97–98
Whitson, Carolyn: "Toward a Theory of Working Class Literature," 5, 88
Who's Afraid of Virginia Woolf? (Robinson), 4
Williams, Raymond, 2, 4
"Wire, Wireman, Stripper, Splice" (Watson), 41
Wolfe, Tom, 95–96; *I Am Charlotte Simmons*, 8, 69–70, 87–100
Woolf, Virginia, 4; *A Room of One's Own*, 21; "Who's Afraid of Virginia Woolf?," 4
work: agricultural, 45–49; as living death, 46; ethic, 82, 83, 151; industrial, 37–45; war and 36–37, 45
"Work and Class in the Box Store University: Autobiographies of Working-Class Academics" (Mazurek), 97
workers, as tools, 39
working class: difficulty in defining, 160; diversity, 126; image of, 146; poverty and, 123, 125–128
working-class culture, 83, 88, 91, 107, 114, 126, 146, 153
working-class literature, 88, 159; anthologies of, 1, 103–20; as literature of the 1930s, 2; as similar to the war novel, 35; as white male literature, 2; critical approaches to, 4–11; double character of, 104; ethnicity and, 3–4, 145–146; masculinity and, 10; MLA search of, 1; poverty and, 123; working-class studies and, 1–2; workplace casualties and, 38
Working-Class Majority, The (Zweig), 7
working-class men, 177–198
working-class scholars: as literary critics, 3–4; in contrast to Marxist scholars, 3; on poverty, 123–24
working-class students, 69–70, 73–79, 91; college experience 69, 96–98, 113–117
working-class studies, 1–2, 4, 71, 123, 125–28, 154, 160–61, 219, 226–30, 234
Working-Class Studies Association, 3, 69
working-class women, 8, 71–84, 79–82, 89–90, 125–138, 169–72
Working-Class Women in the Academy: Labors in the Knowledge Factory (Tokarczyk and Fay), 2, 7
"Working-Class Women's Literature: An Introduction to Study," (Lauter), 2, 88
workplace casualties, 35–49; representations of, 37–39; and working-class literature, 38
Wright, Richard, 222–23, 226; *12 Million Black Voices*, 19; "Blueprint for Negro Writing," 226; *Native Son*, 222

Y

Y no se lo tragó la tierra/And the Earth Did Not Devour Him (Rivera), 46–48
Yellin, Jean Fagan, 60–61
Yezierska, Anzia: *The Bread Givers*, 22, 89, 97; "The Free Vacation House," 128, 133–136, 136–138
Yonnondio (Olsen), 6, 20–24; and family crisis, 10
You Have Seen Their Faces (Caldwell and Bourke-White), 19

Young Lonigan (Farrell), 22

Z

Zandy, Janet, 1, 72, 198, 199n4; *American Working-Class Literature*, 3, 9, 103–20; and Raymond Williams, 4; as editor of *Women's Studies Quarterly*, 4; *Calling Home: An Anthology of Working-Class Women's Writing*, 1–4; *Hands* 4–5, 160, 198

Zweig, Michael, 110, 125–26, 138n1; *The Working-Class Majority*, 7; *What's Class Got to Do With It?*, 71

For Product Safety Concerns and Information please contact our EU
representative GPSR@taylorandfrancis.com
Taylor & Francis Verlag GmbH, Kaufingerstraße 24, 80331 München, Germany

www.ingramcontent.com/pod-product-compliance
Lightning Source LLC
Chambersburg PA
CBHW070558300426
44113CB00010B/1303